SERIES ENDORSEMENTS

"There are so many fine commentaries available today, but it's great to have a reliable author you can turn to for solid Reformed reflection on Scripture. In this case, there are sixteen of them—friends and fellow shepherds who have given me great insight into God's Word over the years. I'm looking forward eagerly to Fesko's Galatians commentary—and to each one after that!"

Michael S. Horton

J. Gresham Machen Professor of
Apologetics and Systematic Theology at
Westminster Seminary California

Host of the *White Horse Inn* Talk Show

Editor-in-Chief of *Modern Reformation* magazine

"Those of us who have promoted and practiced *lectio continua* expository preaching through the years eagerly await the volumes Tolle Lege Press has announced in its *Lectio Continua Expository Commentary on the New Testament*. We are equally eager to read such a series written by pastors who have practiced the method in their churches. The international and interdenominational character of the series will only add to the richness of its insights."

T. David Gordon

Professor of Religion and Greek at Grove City College

Author of *Why Johnny Can't Preach* (P&R, 2009)

SERIES ENDORSEMENTS

"As the history of preaching is unfolded, it becomes clear how important the orderly, systematic preaching through the Scriptures has been, and why it has been a favorite homiletic approach over the centuries. One is surprised to discover how many of history's great preachers made a regular practice of preaching through one book of the Bible after another. Origen, the first Christian preacher from whom we have any sizable collection of sermons, preached most of his sermons on the *lectio continua*. We find the same with John Chrysostom who is usually referred to as the greatest Christian preacher. We find the same true of Augustine as well. At the time of the Protestant Reformation, Zwingli, Calvin, Bucer, and Knox followed this system regularly, and they passed it on to the Puritans. Today, we see a real revival of *lectio continua* preaching. *The Lectio Continua Expository Commentary on the New Testament* represents a wonderful opportunity for the Church to recover a truly expository pulpit."

Hughes Oliphant Old

John H. Leith Professor of Reformed Theology and Worship at Erskine Theological Seminary

Author of *The Reading and Preaching of the Scriptures in the Worship of the Christian Church* (7 vols., Eerdmans, 2007)

"The concept behind this series is a fascinating one and, given the list of authors, I am confident that the final product will not disappoint. This promises to be a great resource for churches seeking to know the Word of God more fully."

Carl R. Trueman

Professor of Church History at
Westminster Theological Seminary in Philadelphia, PA

THE LECTIO CONTINUA
EXPOSITORY COMMENTARY ON THE NEW TESTAMENT

First Corinthians

Kim Riddlebarger

Series Editor
Jon D. Payne

TOLLE LEGE PRESS
POWDER SPRINGS, GEORGIA

The Lectio Continua Expository Commentary Series

First Corinthians
by Kim Riddlebarger
Series Editor: Jon D. Payne

© 2013 Tolle Lege Press. All rights reserved. No part of this publication may be reproduced, stored in a retrieval system or transmitted in any form or by any means, electronic, mechanical, photocopy, recording or otherwise, without the prior permission of the publisher, except as provided by the copyright laws of the United States of America.

Produced and Distributed by:

Tolle Lege Press
3150-A Florence Road
Powder Springs, GA 30127

www.TolleLegePress.com
800-651-0211

This publication contains The Holy Bible, English Standard Version®, copyright © 2001 by Crossway, a publishing ministry of Good News Publishers. The ESV® text appearing in this publication is reproduced and published by cooperation between Good News Publishers and Tolle Lege Press and by permission of Good News Publishers. Unauthorized reproduction of this publication is prohibited.

The Holy Bible, English Standard Version (ESV) is adapted from the Revised Standard Version of the Bible, copyright Division of Christian Education of the National Council of the Churches of Christ in the U.S.A. All rights reserved.

English Standard Version®, ESV® and the ESV® logo are trademarks of Good News Publishers located in Wheaton, Illinois. Used by permission.

Jacket design by Jennifer Tyson

Typeset by Luis Lovelace

Photograph of St. Pierre Cathedral by Seth Zenz

ISBN: 978-1-938139-00-0

Printed in the United States of America.

Consulting Editors

Dr. Joel R. Beeke (Ph.D. Westminster Seminary)
Professor of Systematic Theology and Homiletics and President of Puritan Reformed Theological Seminary
Pastor of the Heritage Netherlands Reformed Congregation
Editorial Director of Reformation Heritage Books,
Grand Rapids, Michigan

Dr. T. David Gordon (Ph.D. Union Theological Seminary)
Professor of Religion and Greek at Grove City College, Pennsylvania
Former Associate Professor of New Testament at
Gordon-Conwell Theological Seminary, Boston, Massachusetts

Dr. David W. Hall (Ph.D. Whitefield Seminary)
Pastor of Midway Presbyterian Church (PCA) in
Powder Springs, Georgia
General Editor of and contributor to *The Calvin 500 Series* (P&R)

Rev. Eric Landry (M.Div. Westminster Seminary California)
Pastor of Christ Presbyterian Church in Murrieta, California
Executive Editor of *Modern Reformation* magazine

Dr. Malcolm Maclean (D.Min. Highland Theological College)
Pastor of Greyfriars Free Church of Scotland in Inverness
Editor of Christian Focus Publication's Mentor imprint

Dr. William M. Schweitzer (Ph.D. University of Edinburgh)
Pastor of Gateshead Presbyterian Church (EPCEW) in
Newcastle/Gateshead, England

Dr. Guy P. Waters (Ph.D. Duke University)
Professor of New Testament at Reformed Theological Seminary
Former Assistant Professor of Biblical Studies at
Belhaven College, Jackson, Mississippi

Dedicated to
Dave and Mark
from their proud father

Contents

SERIES INTRODUCTION		xv
PREFACE		xxi
INTRODUCTION		xxiii

1	Greetings from Paul	*1:1–3*	1
2	Be United	*1:4–17*	11
3	The Wisdom of God	*1:18–31*	25
4	Jesus Christ and Him Crucified	*2:1–5*	43
5	For the Spirit Searches Everything	*2:6–16*	61
6	The Foundation	*3:1–15*	77
7	You Are God's Temple	*3:16–23*	91
8	For the Kingdom of God Does not Consist in Talk but in Power	*4:1–21*	105
9	God Judges Those Outside	*5:1–13*	119
10	And Such Were Some of You	*6:1–11*	135
11	You Were Bought With a Price	*6:12–20*	151
12	Each Has His Own Gift from God	*7:1–16*	165
13	Do Not Become Bondservants to Men	*7:17–40*	181
14	There Is One God	*8:1–13*	197
15	For the Sake of the Gospel	*9:1–27*	211

Contents

16	The Rock Was Christ	*10:1–13*	227
17	Do All to the Glory of God	*10:14–33*	243
18	The Image and Glory of God	*11:1–16*	257
19	Until He Comes	*11:17–26*	273
20	Let a Person Examine Himself	*11:27–34*	287
21	Jesus is Lord	*12:1–3*	303
22	The Common Good	*12:4–11*	315
23	One Body, Many Members	*12:12–26*	329
24	Earnestly Desire the Higher Gifts	*12:27–31*	343
25	The Greatest of These is Love	*13:1–13*	357
26	Strive to Excel in Building Up the Church	*14:1–19*	373
27	Decently and In Order	*14:20–40*	387
28	The Gospel	*15:1–11*	401
29	Christ Has Been Raised!	*15:12–34*	417
30	He Must Reign	*15:20–28*	433
31	In the Twinkling of an Eye	*15:35–38*	447
32	Be Watchful	*16:1–24*	463

Abbreviations used in the Lectio Continua Series

*	Author's translation
ca.	Circa
CNTC	Calvin's New Testament Commentaries
CTS	Calvin Translation Society
ESV	English Standard Version
KJV	King James Version
LXX	Septuagint
Macc.	Maccabees—Apocryphal Book
NICNT	New International Commentary on the New Testament
NICOT	New International Commentary on the Old Testament
NIV	New International Version
NKJ	New King James
NRSV	New Revised Standard Version
NSBT	New Studies in Biblical Theology
WCF	Westminster Confession of Faith
WSC	Westminster Shorter Catechism
ZECNT	Zondervan Exegetical Commentary on the New Testament

Books of the Bible

Genesis	**Gen.**	2 Chronicles	**2 Chron.**	Daniel	**Dan.**
Exodus	**Exod.**	Ezra	**Ezra**	Hosea	**Hos.**
Leviticus	**Lev.**	Nehemiah	**Neh.**	Joel	**Joel**
Numbers	**Num.**	Esther	**Esth.**	Amos	**Amos**
Deuteronomy	**Deut.**	Job	**Job**	Obadiah	**Obad.**
Joshua	**Josh.**	Psalms	**Ps.**	Jonah	**Jonah**
Judges	**Judg.**	Proverbs	**Prov.**	Micah	**Mic.**
Ruth	**Ruth**	Ecclesiastes	**Eccl.**	Nahum	**Nah.**
1 Samuel	**1 Sam.**	Song of Solomon	**Song**	Habakkuk	**Hab.**
2 Samuel	**2 Sam.**	Isaiah	**Isa.**	Zephaniah	**Zeph.**
1 Kings	**1 Kings**	Jeremiah	**Jer.**	Haggai	**Hag.**
2 Kings	**2 Kings**	Lamentations	**Lam.**	Zechariah	**Zech.**
1 Chronicles	**1 Chron.**	Ezekiel	**Ezek.**	Malachi	**Mal.**

Matthew	**Matt.**	Ephesians	**Eph.**	Hebrews	**Heb.**
Mark	**Mark**	Philippians	**Phil.**	James	**James**
Luke	**Luke**	Colossians	**Col.**	1 Peter	**1 Pet.**
John	**John**	1 Thessalonians	**1 Thess.**	2 Peter	**2 Pet.**
Acts	**Acts**	2 Thessalonians	**2 Thess.**	1 John	**1 John**
Romans	**Rom.**	1 Timothy	**1 Tim.**	2 John	**2 John**
1 Corinthians	**1 Cor.**	2 Timothy	**2 Tim.**	3 John	**3 John**
2 Corinthians	**2 Cor.**	Titus	**Titus**	Jude	**Jude**
Galatians	**Gal.**	Philemon	**Philem.**	Revelation	**Rev.**

St. Pierre Cathedral in Geneva, Switzerland where John Calvin preached

Series Introduction

The greatest need of the church today is the recovery of sound biblical preaching that faithfully explains and applies the text, courageously confronts sin, and boldly trumpets forth the sovereign majesty, law, and promises of God. This type of powerful preaching has vanished in many quarters of the evangelical church only to be replaced by that which is anemic and man-centered. Instead of doctrinally rich exposition which strengthens faith and fosters Christian maturity, the standard fare has become informal, chatty, anecdote-laden messages, leaving unbelievers confused, and believers in a state of chronic spiritual adolescence.[1]

There is indeed a dire need for the recovery of solid biblical preaching. Not only does reformation of this sort lead Christ's sheep back to the verdant pastures of His soul-nourishing Word, it also provides a good example to future generations of ministers. For this reason, I am pleased to introduce *The Lectio Continua Expository Commentary on the New Testament* (LCECNT), a new series of expository commentaries authored by an array of seasoned pastor-scholars from various Reformed denominations on both sides of the Atlantic.

---

1. A stinging, yet constructive critique of modern-day preaching is found in T. David Gordon's *Why Johnny Can't Preach: The Media Have Shaped the Messengers* (Phillipsburg, NJ: P&R, 2009). "I have come to recognize that many, many individuals today have never been under a steady diet of competent preaching.... As starving children in Manila sift through the landfill for food, Christians in many churches today have never experienced genuine soul-nourishing preaching, and so they just pick away at what is available to them, trying to find a morsel of spiritual sustenance or helpful counsel here or there" (Gordon, *Why Johnny Can't Preach*, 17).

First Corinthians

What is the *lectio continua* method of preaching? It is simply the uninterrupted, systematic, expository proclamation of God's Word—verse by verse, chapter by chapter, book by book. It is a system, unlike topical or thematic preaching, that endeavors to deliver the whole counsel of God (Acts 20:26–27). Christian discipleship is impoverished when large portions of Scripture are ignored. Carried out faithfully, the *lectio continua* method ensures that every passage is mined for its riches (even those verses which are obscure, controversial, or hard to swallow). Paul states that "all Scripture is breathed out by God and profitable for teaching, for reproof, for correction, and for training in righteousness, that the man of God may be competent, equipped for every good work" (2 Tim. 3:16–17).

Lectio continua preaching has a splendid heritage. It finds its roots in the early church and patristic eras. Its use, however, was revived and greatly expanded during the sixteenth-century Protestant Reformation. When Huldrych Zwingli (d. 1531) arrived at the Zurich Grossmünster in 1519, it was his desire to dispense with the standard lectionary and introduce *lectio continua* preaching to his congregation by moving systematically through the Gospel of Matthew. At first, some members of his church council were suspicious. They were uncomfortable replacing the lectionary with this seemingly new approach. But Zwingli explained that the *lectio continua* method of preaching was not new at all. On the contrary, important figures such as Augustine (d. 430), Chrysostom (d. 407) and Bernard of Clairvaux (d. 1153) all employed this homiletical strategy. Zwingli is quoted by his successor Heinrich Bullinger (d. 1575) as saying that "no friend of evangelical truth could have any reason to complain" about such a method.[2]

---

2. It is interesting to note that, the year before Zwingli began preaching sequentially through books of the Bible, he had received a new edition of Chrysostom's *lectio continua* sermons on Matthew's Gospel. See Hughes Oliphant Old, *The Patristic Roots of Reformed Worship* (Black Mountain, NC: Worship

Series Introduction

Zwingli rightly believed that the quickest way to restore biblical Christianity to the church was to preach the whole counsel of God verse by verse, chapter by chapter, book by book, Lord's Day after Lord's Day, year after year. Other reformers agreed and followed his pattern. In the city of Strasbourg, just ninety miles north of Zurich, men such as Martin Bucer (d. 1551), Wolfgang Capito (d. 1570), and Kaspar Hedio (d. 1552) practiced *lectio continua* preaching. Johannes Oecolampadius (d. 1531) boldly preached the *lectio continua* in Basel. And let us not forget John Calvin (d. 1564); between 1549 and 1564, the Genevan reformer preached sequentially through no fewer than twenty-five books of the Bible (over 2,000 sermons).[3]

The example of these reformers has been emulated by preachers throughout the centuries, from the Post-Reformation age down to the present. In the last half of the twentieth century, Martyn Lloyd-Jones (d. 1981), William Still (d. 1997), James Montgomery Boice (d. 2000), and John MacArthur all boldly marched straight through books of the Bible from their pulpits. But why? Surely we have acquired better, more contemporary methods of preaching? Is the *lectio continua* relevant in our twenty-first century context? In a day when biblical preaching is being increasingly undermined and marginalized by media/story/therapy/personality-driven sermons, even among the avowedly Reformed, these are important questions to consider.

Shortly before the Apostle Paul was martyred in Rome by Emperor Nero, he penned a second epistle to Timothy. In what proved to be some of his final words to his young disciple, he

---

Press, 2004), 195. Cf. Old's *The Reading and Preaching of the Scriptures in the Worship of the Christian Church*, vol. 4: *The Age of the Reformation* (Grand Rapids, MI: Eerdmans, 2002), and Timothy George, *Reading Scripture with the Reformers* (Downers Grove, IL: IVP Academic, 2011), 228–253. Elements of this introduction are adapted from Jon D. Payne, "The Roaring of Christ through *Lectio Continua* Preaching," *Modern Reformation* (Nov./Dec. 2010; Vol. 19, No. 6): 23–24, and are used by permission of the publisher.

3. T. H. L. Parker, *Calvin's Preaching* (Edinburgh: T&T Clark, 1992), 159.

wrote, "I charge you in the presence of God and of Christ Jesus ... *preach the word*; be ready in season and out of season; reprove, rebuke, and exhort, with complete patience and teaching" (2 Tim. 4:1–2). This directive was not meant for only Timothy. No, it is the primary duty of every Christian minister (and church) to carefully heed and obey these timeless words; according to God's divine blueprint for ministry, it is chiefly through the faithful proclamation of the Word that Christ saves, sanctifies, and comforts the beloved Church for which He died.[4] In other words, the preaching of the Gospel and the right administration of the sacraments are the divinely sanctioned and efficacious means by which Christ and all His benefits of redemption are communicated to the elect. For this reason alone the *lectio continua* method of preaching should be the predominant, regular practice of our churches, providing a steady diet of Law and Gospel from the entirety of God's Word.

Some may ask, "Why another expository commentary series?" First, because in every generation it is highly valuable to provide fresh, doctrinally sound, and reliable expositions of God's Word. Every age possesses its own set of theological, ecclesiastical, and cultural challenges. In addition, it is beneficial for both current and rising ministers in every generation to have trustworthy contemporary models of biblical preaching. Second, the LCECNT uniquely features the expositions of an array of pastors from a variety of Reformed and confessional traditions. Consequently, this series brings a wealth of exegetical, confessional, cultural, and practical insight, and furnishes the reader with an instructive and stimulating selection of *lectio continua* sermons.

This series is not meant to be an academic or highly technical commentary. There are many helpful exegetical commentaries

---

4. See Matthew 28:18–20; Romans 10:14–17; 1 Corinthians 1:18–21; 1 Peter 1:22–25, 2:2–3; Westminster Shorter Catechism Q. 89.

Series Introduction

written for that purpose. Rather, the aim is to provide *lectio continua* sermons, originally delivered to Reformed congregations, which clearly and faithfully communicate the context, meaning, gravity, and application of God's inerrant Word. Each volume of expositions aspires to be redemptive-historical, covenantal, Reformed and confessional, trinitarian, person-and-work-of-Christ-centered, and teeming with practical application. Therefore, the series will be a profound blessing to every Christian believer who longs to "grow in the grace and knowledge of our Lord and Savior Jesus Christ" (2 Pet. 3:18).

A project of this magnitude does not happen without the significant contributions of many people. First, I want to thank Raymond, Brandon, and Jared Vallorani of Tolle Lege Press. Their willingness to publish this voluminous set of commentaries is less about their desire to blossom as a Reformed publishing house and more about their sincere love for Christ and the faithful proclamation of the Bible. Also, many thanks to my fellow preachers who graciously agreed to participate in this series. It is a privilege to labor with you for the sake of the Gospel, the health and extension of the church, and the recovery of *lectio continua* preaching. Thanks to the editorial staff of Tolle Lege Press, especially Eric Rauch, Vice President of Publishing and Michael Minkoff, Director of Publishing. Thanks are also due to Brian Cosby for his detailed editorial contributions.

Thanks also must be given to the elders and congregation of Grace Presbyterian Church, Douglasville, Georgia, for warmly encouraging their minister to work on this time-consuming, yet beneficial, undertaking. Furthermore, I would like to express the deepest gratitude to my dear wife, Marla, and our two precious children, Mary Hannah and Hans. The peace and joy in our home, nurtured by delightful Lord's Days, regular family worship, and a loving, patient wife, makes editing a series like this one possible.

First Corinthians

Finally, and most importantly, sincere thanks and praise must be given to our blessed triune God, the eternal fountain of all grace and truth. By his sovereign love and mercy, through faith in the crucified, resurrected, and ascended Christ, we have been "born again, not of perishable seed but of imperishable, through the living and abiding word of God; for 'All flesh is like grass and all its glory like the flower of grass. The grass withers and the flower falls, but the word of the Lord remains forever.' And this word is the good news *that was preached to you*" (1 Pet. 1:23–25).

Jon D. Payne
Series Editor

Preface

It is an honor and a privilege to contribute this volume on 1 Corinthians for the *Lectio Continua* series. My contribution is based upon a series of Bible studies from 2004 and sermons preached on 1 Corinthians in 2010–2011 to the saints at Christ Reformed Church in Anaheim, California (URCNA), where I am currently senior pastor.

The goal of *Lectio Continua* is "simply the uninterrupted, systematic, expository proclamation of God's Word—verse by verse, chapter by chapter, book by book. It is a system, unlike topical or thematic preaching, that endeavors to deliver the whole counsel of God (Acts 20:26–27)."[1] It is a great joy to preach on the Lord's Day to a congregation which both expects and desires the exposition of God's word such as that just described. Would that all pastors be as blessed in this regard as I am.

I should point out that I am not an original thinker, but I am not afraid of departing from the received tradition in those few instances where I think a better explanation for Paul's line of thinking arises from the biblical text, or from the historical circumstances under which Paul originally composed this epistle. My few points of departure from the consensus will become apparent as I go along.

During my years studying this epistle, I have found several commentaries to be very helpful and feel duty-bound to acknowledge these authors at those points where I have appropriated their thoughts and incorporated their arguments

---

1. See Payne's "Series Introduction," p. xvi.

into my exposition. You will see in my footnotes throughout this volume names you may recognize: Leon Morris, Charles Hodge, and John Calvin. But I have also found several commentaries outside the Reformed tradition to be quite helpful as well. The names of C. K. Barrett, Richard Hays, and Gordon Fee will surface often. While I do not always agree with the latter group, they are quite helpful at points and their views are well-known and need to be addressed by anyone who seeks to preach through 1 Corinthians with its many controversies, and difficult points of application.

First Corinthians is a demanding letter because it addresses so many controversial doctrines and practices in the daily life of the church (such as church discipline and speaking in tongues). These issues were as difficult for the Corinthian church to grasp in Paul's day, as they are to apply in our own. So, we must plow ahead and preach the whole counsel of God, and at the same time trust that the same blessed Holy Spirit who breathed forth this letter when Paul initially composed it, will give us the grace to interpret it correctly, as well as the courage to proclaim it in all its power.

It is my prayer that you will find this effort helpful in helping you understand Paul's remarkable epistle. To that end I recall the anecdote once told me by one of my seminary professors. Seems that a famous New Testament scholar had finally completed the manuscript of his massive commentary on the Gospel of John. Seeking to share the benefits of his labors and get a bit of preliminary feedback about his work, the scholar asked one of the cleaning crew to take a mimeographed copy, read through it, and tell him what he thought. The scholar encountered the man a week or two later. The man looked sheepishly at the scholar and said, "Well, I tried to read through it and didn't get very far. Sorry, but I didn't understand very much of it. So, I decided to read through the Gospel of John, and after I

Preface

did your book made a lot more sense." If I have succeeded in any small way, then you will understand 1 Corinthians a bit better after reading this exposition than you did before.

Kim Riddlebarger
January, 2013
Anaheim, California

Introduction

It has been said that the city of Corinth was the New York, Las Vegas, and Los Angeles of the Apostle Paul's day, all rolled into one.[1] The parallels between the culture and life of this ancient Greek city and modern America are so striking and obvious that a number of theologians have seen fit to make the comparison independently from one another. The church Paul helped to found in Corinth was largely Gentile in ethnicity, yet with a significant Jewish minority. The Gentiles in the Corinthian church were recent converts from Greco-Roman paganism. These new Christians found themselves struggling to learn the doctrines of the Christian faith and then live out their new faith in a city and culture well-known for its rampant sexual immorality and idolatry. To be a Christian in first-century Corinth was much like being a Christian in twenty-first century America. The similarities between the Corinth of Paul's day and America of ours is an important indication that there is much for us to learn from Paul's remarkable letter to the church in Corinth, known to us as 1 Corinthians.

Although Reformed Christians often pride themselves in being students of Paul—devoting themselves to the study of Paul's letters such as Romans, Galatians, and Ephesians—1 Corinthians is often overlooked despite the fact that many of the issues Paul addresses in this epistle are absolutely vital to the health of Christ's church.[2] In fact, many of the issues prompt-

---

1. Gordon Fee, *The First Epistle to the Corinthians*, NICNT (Grand Rapids: William B. Eerdmans, 1987), 3.

2. Indeed, there are very few "Reformed" commentaries on First Corinthians. There is Calvin's commentary, of course, and a solid (but now dated) ef-

ing Paul to write to the Corinthians are facing the church again today. The importance of 1 Corinthians becomes especially clear once we make the connection between the Greco-Roman paganism of first century Corinth and the religious climate of contemporary America.

Paul's two Corinthian letters are often overlooked in Reformed circles presumably because of Paul's discussion of the gifts of the Holy Spirit, tongues being one of them. But this is a letter we should not ignore—in our current historical context. In 1 Corinthians we find a number of important issues addressed by Paul:

- There is a fascinating discussion of the collision between Christianity and Greco-Roman paganism (specifically how Christians are to deal with idolatry).
- There are a number of ethical issues addressed (such as Christians suing each other in secular courts, and questions regarding pagan sexual mores and sexual immorality).
- Paul discusses at length the person and work of the Holy Spirit (in regeneration and the role of spiritual gifts).
- Paul describes Christian worship (in this letter we have a description of the way the Lord's Supper is administered, as well as a call for proper order in worship).
- Paul also discusses the doctrine of the church (the church as the body of Christ and temple of the Holy Spirit, the dangers of division within the church, and the need to exercise church discipline).

---

fort from Charles Hodge. Leon Morris's volume in the Tyndale series is very solid and represents the best of evangelical Anglicanism. But First Corinthians is an epistle Reformed commentators have not often addressed.

Introduction

- Paul's epistle ends with the most important discussion of the resurrection found anywhere in the New Testament.

As you can see, there is much here that is important to the life and health of our churches. Therefore, 1 Corinthians is supremely worthy of our time and attention.

Before we turn to the opening verses of this letter, I will strive to accomplish several things. First, we need to consider the history and background of the city of Corinth. Second, we will consider Paul's connection to the Corinthian church, and then address his reasons for composing this letter to those he knew so well, but who were struggling so mightily against the spirit of the age.

The Corinth of Paul's Day

The city of Corinth was a prosperous commercial crossroad located on the Isthmus of Corinth (a narrow peninsula). The city stood on the main trading road between the two nearby port cites of Cenchreae (to the east) and Lechaeum (to the west), located on the Aegean and Ionian seas, respectively. Given the difficult nature of sailing along the southern coast of the Peloponnesian peninsula (especially during the winter months), much of the commerce between Italy and Asia went through Corinth, transiting across the isthmus on a paved road known as the *diolkos*. Ships would dock at either port, the cargo (or even the ship itself) would be carried across the peninsula to the other port. The ancient geographer Strabo pointed out that Corinth's strategic location made it the master of two harbors. The city dominated virtually all trade between Asia and Italy.

By Paul's time, Corinth was probably like other large commercial seaports of that era, filled with merchants, slaves, and laborers.[3] This trade generated great wealth, and made Corinth

---

3. C. K. Barrett, *The First Epistle to the Corinthians* (San Francisco: Harper and Row Publishers, 1968), 1ff.

into a cultural and ethnic melting pot much like any large American urban area today. Given the content of Paul's two Corinthian letters, and the names mentioned in the chapters of Acts which deal with this period in the apostolic church's development, it appears that the majority of those in the church there were Gentiles. Most of the names are Latin and Greek, indicative of the fact that the area was under Roman law and ethos, although the city's Greek past was certainly still an inescapable portion of the cultural fabric of daily life.

Corinth was home to the Isthmian Games, an athletic event second only to the Olympics in importance, and dominated by celebrity athletes. Held every two years—even during the years the city sat in ruins—the Isthmian Games attracted huge crowds. In fact, the most important political office in the city was that of the sponsor of the games—a position much like that of commissioner of the International Olympic Committee today. The presence of the games made Corinth something of a popular "tourist destination." As we will see, what happened in Corinth did not stay in Corinth.

Much of the city was destroyed by Roman armies in 146 BC, and many of its residents were killed or taken into slavery. Despite the city's strategic importance, the area lay in ruins until 44 BC, when Julius Caesar ordered a Roman colony built on the site. Many of the people living in Corinth when Paul established the church there were descendants of former slaves, Roman freedmen, laborers, or retired soldiers who remained in the area because of the thriving economy. Corinth was filled with "upwardly mobile" people, establishing another of the parallels between Corinth and the modern world.[4] The city was prosperous and self-sufficient, and Paul was there during a time of a great economic boom. This was an important and strategic

---

4. Richard B. Hays, *First Corinthians: Interpretation Bible Commentary* (Louisville: John Knox Press, 1997), 2ff.

Introduction

place for Paul to plant a church, because it was an ideal location from which to evangelize the local population, as well as those many souls who passed through the area heading west to Italy or east into Asia.[5]

In pre-Roman days, Corinth had a notorious reputation for being a center of sexual promiscuity—much like Copenhagen, Amsterdam, and Bangkok have today. One Athenian playwright (Aristophanes) used the phrase *korinthiazesthai* as a synonym for fornication. To call a young lady a "Corinthian girl" was to imply she was promiscuous. The city was filled with prostitutes (many associated with temple worship), with perhaps as many as one thousand prostitutes associated with the temple of Aphrodite alone. Although this was the case before Corinth was destroyed by the Romans, the city had a long history of immorality which in Paul's time was often most evident in the local guild hall (especially among the tradesmen). Because the trade guilds devoted themselves to various "gods" or "goddesses," Corinth was dotted with pagan temples and statues dedicated to these "gods and goddesses." A statue of Athena still dominated the marketplace when Paul was there. The connection between pagan religion and sexual immorality cannot be overlooked. Wherever paganism dominates, sexual immorality is openly accepted. This too is very much like modern America.

All of this is to say that those who were converted to Christianity came from this pagan background, and therefore required much instruction (catechesis) in the Christian faith. Christians in Corinth faced the difficult struggle to give up long-held pagan practices and traditions. As is evident throughout Paul's letter, this was not an easy place to be a Christian.

---

5. Anthony. C. Thiselton, *The First Epistle to the Corinthians* NIGTC (Grand Rapids: William B. Eerdmans, 2000), 1ff.

First Corinthians

Date and General Contents

Paul's strong personal ties to the city figure prominently in this letter. According to Acts 18:1ff., Paul visited Corinth during his second missionary journey. By the time Paul arrived in Corinth, he was badly in need of a break. He had encountered fierce opposition from the Jews in nearby Philippi, and then again in Thessalonica and Berea. Paul also had a difficult time in Athens. So it is no wonder that early on in this letter Paul recalls that he first arrived in Corinth in weakness, fear, and trembling (1 Cor. 2:3). Because of the lack of persecution he experienced in Corinth (Acts 18:10), Paul was able to stay for some eighteen months (Acts 18:11). We also know from the Book of Acts that the Lord told Paul in a vision that he had many people in this city yet to come to faith (Acts 18:10). It is noteworthy that the doctrine of election became the basis for Paul's efforts to evangelize the city.

We can date Paul's stay in Corinth about AD 50–51. Paul probably left the city in the fall of AD 51, and upon the conclusion of his second missionary journey, returned again to Asia during his third journey in the fall of AD 52. According to Acts 19:10 and 20:31, Paul remained in Ephesus for nearly three years, from the fall of AD 52 until the spring of AD 55. It was while Paul was in Ephesus that he likely first wrote to the Corinthians (in response to questions they had put to him), since Paul speaks of the Corinthians misunderstanding a previous (and unknown) letter he had sent to them earlier (1 Cor. 5:9). Paul writes to clear up any misunderstandings, as well as address other issues which had come to his attention.

According to Leon Morris,

> The immediate occasion of the Epistle was the letter Paul had received from the Corinthian church, for which a reply was necessary. But what mattered much more to Paul was clearly the news that had come to him independently of the letter [from

Introduction

Chloe's family who were traveling through Ephesus]. There were disquieting irregularities in the conduct of the believers at Corinth. Paul was troubled by the "tendency on the part of some believers to make the break with pagan society as indefinite as possible . . . . The Church was in the world, as it had to be, but the world was in the Church, as it ought not to be." So much did this matter to Paul that he spends six chapters dealing with it before he so much as touched on the matters about which they had written him.[6]

As just noted, Paul mentions a letter he had written previously to the Corinth church which was badly misunderstood by the Corinthians (1 Cor. 5:9). In that letter he told them not to associate with immoral persons. The Corinthians mistakenly took this to mean *all* immoral persons, while Paul only meant immoral professing believers who behaved in a way that was inconsistent with their profession of faith in Jesus Christ (1 Cor. 5:10–13). This misunderstanding needed to be cleared up—which Paul does in chapter 5.

Furthermore, while Paul was in Ephesus, he received disturbing news from certain members of Chloe's house—a family that Paul probably knew from his time in Corinth. Presumably, the report included other problems such as divisions and factions within the church (1:11), negative attitudes toward the apostles throughout the church (4:1–21), incestuous behavior (5:1–5), and lawsuits between Christians (6:1–11). Paul's response to these matters take up the first six chapters of this letter. Then in chapter 7, Paul writes "now concerning the matters about which you wrote," indicating that in the balance of this letter Paul was also responding to issues raised by the Corinthians in correspondence they had sent to the apostle. Apparently

---

6. Leon Morris, *1 Corinthians*, TNTC (Grand Rapids: William B. Eerdmans, 2000), 25–26.

a delegation of believers including Stephanas, Fortunatas, and Achaicus (16:17), came to Paul in Ephesus with these questions in the form of a letter asking the apostle for a response.

While the first six chapters address the issues raised with Paul in Ephesus by Chloe's family, in chapters 7–15, Paul responds to the specific questions which had come to him in writing through the delegation just mentioned. The questions asked of Paul by the Corinthians in their letter deal, in part, with marriage and the status of those who are unmarried or widowed (7:1–40). Paul is also asked about eating food which had been used in idol sacrifices, and while warning the Corinthians about the incompatibility of Greco-Roman idolatry with their new-found faith in Jesus Christ, the apostle is forced to defend his apostolic authority (8:1–10:33). In 1 Corinthians 11:1–16, Paul takes up the matter of appropriate behavior and decorum during worship, before addressing the improper manner in which the Corinthians were celebrating the Lord's Supper (11:17–34).

The next series of questions put to Paul by the Corinthian believers concerns spiritual things, including spiritual gifts and the way the Holy Spirit distributes these gifts among the Corinthians (12:1–31). Paul points out that these gifts are given for the common good, and especially so that they might love one another (13:1–13). At this point, Paul reminds the Corinthians of the importance of building up one another and conducting worship decently and in good order and at this point addresses one of the most pressing matters of controversy raised by the Corinthians—speaking in tongues and how that particular spiritual gift is to be practiced in the churches (14:1–14).

In answering their final question to him, Paul addresses the resurrection of Jesus Christ, as well as the bodily resurrection of believers at the end of age (15:1–58). The final chapter (16:1–24) contains information about Paul's future plans and he offers several bits of instruction as well as concluding exhortations. It

Introduction

has been said, correctly so, that "no part of the Pauline corpus more clearly illustrates the character of Paul the man, Paul the Christian, Paul the pastor, and Paul the apostle" than does this epistle. In fact, Paul leaves us an "invitation to imitate him, and thereby imitate Christ (1 Cor. 11:1)."[7]

So, with this historical background in mind, we now turn to the opening section (verses 1–3) of this remarkable letter which we now know simply as "First Corinthians."

---

7. D. A. Carson, Douglas J. Moo and Leon Morris, *An Introduction to the New Testament* (Grand Rapids: Zondervan Publishing House, 1992), 285

First Corinthians

1

Greetings from Paul

1 CORINTHIANS 1:1–3

Paul, called by the will of God to be an apostle of Christ Jesus, and our brother Sosthenes, To the church of God that is in Corinth, to those sanctified in Christ Jesus, called to be saints together with all those who in every place call upon the name of our Lord Jesus Christ, both their Lord and ours: Grace to you and peace from God our Father and the Lord Jesus Christ.

Those who know the letters of Paul find a familiar introduction to 1 Corinthians. "Paul, called by the will of God to be an apostle of Christ Jesus, and our brother Sosthenes." Paul's opening greeting is typical of a first-century epistle and includes the name of the sender (Paul), and his co-sender, Sosthenes, who may be the synagogue ruler mentioned in Acts 18:17, who was beaten by a mob.[1] After introducing himself to his readers—many of whom already knew Paul personally because he had been in their midst for eighteen months—he adds the important qualification that he was called to be an apostle by the will of God. We know from Paul's comments in Galatians 1:16 ("God was pleased to reveal his Son to me, in order that I

---

1. Hans Conzelmann, *1 Corinthians*, Hermenia (Minneapolis: Fortress Press, 1976), 19; Barrett, *The First Epistle to the Corinthians*, 30.

might preach him among the Gentiles"), that his particular calling took the form of his office as apostle to the Gentiles. Corinth was a Gentile city with a significant Jewish presence, so Paul's role in Corinth fits naturally with his office, background, and abilities.[2]

Paul introduces himself to the Corinthians as an apostle, because in this epistle he will be speaking with the full apostolic authority of his office in order to both rebuke and instruct the Corinthian congregation in those areas in which they are struggling. The man writing is not just Paul, their friend and acquaintance. The man writing is also Paul the apostle, who addresses them with the full divine authority associated with his office. Paul was not an apostle by his own choice—"I think I'll become an apostle." As recounted in Acts 9:1–31, Paul's apostolic office is one to which he has been called by the will of God and the direct intervention of the Lord of the church, Jesus Christ. The risen Christ appeared to Paul as the young Pharisee was making his way to Damascus to hunt down and arrest Christians in that city. It was Jesus who personally commissioned Paul for his apostolic office.

One of the reasons Paul gives for composing and sending this epistle is to correct the misunderstanding in this church of what the office of apostle actually involves (1 Cor. 4:1–21; 1 Cor. 9:1–23). Since Paul writes with the authority of an apostle, he speaks directly to those who have no such authority, who have impressed the Corinthians with their charm and gifts, but who have not been called by God in any sense to their self-appointed "ministries."[3] Paul has the apostolic pedigree these other teachers do not have. He has seen the risen Christ. Even though Paul

---

2. Philo mentions that Corinth was home to a substantial Jewish settlement (Philonis Alexandrini, *Legatio ad Gaium*, paras. 281–282), and Paul will list Jews among the categories he uses to enumerate members of the church (cf. 1 Cor. 12:13).

3. Barrett, *The First Epistle to the Corinthians*, 31.

Greetings from Paul

originally came to Corinth in fear and trembling, without personal charisma or eloquent speech, the Corinthians must listen to him. Why? Jesus Christ, the Lord of the church says the Corinthians must listen to him. Paul is an apostle. He speaks with the authority of Jesus Christ.

The Church in Corinth

This letter is addressed to the church (*ekklesia*) of Corinth. "To the church of God that is in Corinth, to those sanctified in Christ Jesus" (v. 2). Paul uses the term *ekklesia* twenty-two times in this letter. The word refers to the "assembly" (which not only means "called out from the nations" as often understood), but especially emphasizes that group of Christian believers who assemble together for public worship, presumably to hear Paul's letter read aloud.[4] The word *ekklesia* can be used of any large secular assembly, such as that described in Acts 19:32, 41, during the rioting in Ephesus when a mob assembled bent on doing harm to the apostle Paul. But the term as used throughout the New Testament has acquired a distinctly Christian meaning. Christians were careful not to take over secular words used to refer to guilds or religious groups. They took the term *ekklesia* because it was the term used throughout the Septuagint (the Greek translation of the Old Testament) for the people of Israel. These early Christians saw the church as the New Israel. They were no ordinary public assembly. The church is the *ekklesia* of God.[5] It is this particular assembly of people of whom Paul says are "those sanctified in Christ Jesus."

---

4. Cf. Barrett, *The First Epistle to the Corinthians*, 32. See the discussion of this in: Louis Berkhof, *Systematic Theology* (Grand Rapids: William B. Eerdmans, 1986), 555ff.

5. Morris, *1 Corinthians*, 35. According to Morris, "Christians bypassed the regular [Greek] words for religious brotherhoods, and made [ekklesia] their usual self-designation. They were probably influenced by the fact that it is used in the LXX of the people of Israel. This usage reflects their deep conviction that the church is not merely one religious group among many. It is

In fact, Paul speaks of his hearers as those "called to be saints together with all those who in every place call upon the name of our Lord Jesus Christ, both their Lord and ours" (v. 3). Why is it that Paul emphasizes sanctification and the fact that believers in this church are called unto holiness, rather than emphasize justification as in his epistles to the churches in Galatia or Rome? The term used here (sanctified), is a perfect passive participle, which means that every believer is already reckoned as sanctified, even though many of those in this church were still engaging in sinful and unacceptable behavior typical of paganism. John Calvin contends that Paul is pointing out that because God has begun his work in the Corinthians, he then brings it to completion by degrees.[6] Because the merits of Jesus Christ have been reckoned to God's people through faith (cf. Rom 5:12–18; Phil. 3:7–9), God sees the righteousness of his son, and not the imperfections of the Corinthians. Yet, the grace of God motivates the Corinthians on to obedience.

Called to Be Holy

All believers are called to be "holy" (or saints). In one sense, a complete and "definitive" sanctification occurs by virtue of every believer's union with Christ through faith. All those in Christ are "sanctified" and "holy" by virtue of the fact that Christ's righteousness has already been imputed to them through faith. This latter term, "holy" (*hagioi*), does not apply to certain holy individuals who attain a higher level of personal holiness than others. Instead, it applies to all the members of this church who are set apart by God for his service, just as Israel's priests and vessels had been set aside or "sanctified" for the service of God in the temple.[7] Paul

---

unique. Ordinary religious words will not do. And it is not any 'assembly': it is the ekklesia of God."

6. John Calvin, *The First Epistle of Paul to the Corinthians*, CTNC, trans. John W. Frasor (Grand Rapids: William B. Eerdmans, 1979), 19.

7. Hays, *First Corinthians*, 16.

Greetings from Paul

speaks of all believers as "holy" in this sense. He will also speak of believers as being set apart and endowed with spiritual gifts for service in the true temple, which is the mystical body of Jesus Christ in which all believers are living stones.

What does such holiness actually entail in light of the fact that all those called by God were sinners when they were called (cf. 1 Cor. 6:11)? As Paul reminds them, the Corinthian Christians had been called by God through the preaching of the gospel, and then responded to that gospel in faith. Therefore, they are set apart by God for God's own purposes. God's calling has a goal or a *telos*—holiness. Because the Corinthians have been called by God through the preaching of the gospel to faith in Jesus Christ, their lives should manifest this holiness which flows out of their faith in Christ. The Corinthians cannot live like godless Gentiles any longer. Definitive sanctification (and justification) will manifest itself in "progressive sanctification." Those set apart by God (in definitive sanctification), will demonstrate growth in holiness (progressive sanctification), and in the grace and knowledge of the Lord Jesus. As Michael Horton puts it, "We *are* holy (definitive sanctification), therefore, we are *to be* holy (progressive sanctification). Although we are not saved *by works*, we are saved *for works*."[8]

The reason Paul emphasizes these particular points in his opening greeting probably has to do with the specific issues facing this congregation. The Corinthians have been called out from paganism and are set apart by God. Their calling is unto holiness. Elsewhere Paul explains that God's Son "gave himself for us to redeem us from all lawlessness and *to purify for himself a people* for his own possession who are zealous for good works" (Titus 2:14; emphasis added). But the Corinthian church's conduct as reported to Paul by Chloe's family indicates that their behavior

---

8. Michael Horton, *The Christian Faith: A Systematic Theology for Pilgrims on the Way* (Grand Rapids: Zondervan, 2011), 653.

is anything but "holy." So, Paul begins by reminding his hearers of what they should know to be true. Their calling in Christ is unto holiness, not the kind of sinful behavior which had been reported to Paul. Justification must manifest itself in sanctification. All those who trust in Christ and are reckoned as righteous are also to live in holiness.

When Paul speaks of this congregation as those "called to be saints together with all those who in every place call upon the name of our Lord Jesus Christ, both their Lord and ours" (v. 3b), he is reminding us that the calling together of the assembly at Corinth is not unique. All Christians who call upon the name of Jesus Christ are united to their living head through faith, and are also sanctified in Christ and called to be holy. In this we see the church as the New Israel. In the Book of Deuteronomy (e.g., Deut. 12:8–21) the Israelites were to collectively call upon God's name from one particular place (Jerusalem). With the coming of Jesus Christ and the spread of his kingdom to the ends of the earth, no longer must the people of God go to a certain "holy" place to call upon the Lord. Christians are to call upon the Lord wherever they happen to be, even if that is in a prominently pagan place such as Corinth.[9]

Paul is not in any sense holding the Corinthians to a different or unfair standard. Nor can the conduct in the Corinthian church be seen in total isolation from the other churches. Some of this conduct was so offensive that it came to Paul by word of mouth. If Christians of the first century are like Christians today (and there is no reason to assume otherwise), then we can assume that other Christians in other cities knew all about the things going on in Corinth. If the Corinthians are not living up to their calling in Christ, they will suffer not only the temporal consequences of their actions, they risk the direct judgment

---

9. G. K. Beale, *Commentary on the New Testament Use of the Old Testament* (Grand Rapids: Baker Academic, 2007), 696.

of God. Given the organic nature of the church as the body of Christ, if the Corinthians suffer, all the churches will suffer.

The Marks of the Church

One other point which ought to be raised here has to do with the concept of the "marks" of a true church as stated in the Reformed confessions. The three marks of a true church include the pure preaching of the gospel, the proper administration of the sacraments, and church discipline.[10] Based upon what we know was going on in Corinth, the Corinthian congregation was undisciplined and struggling with the proper administration of the sacraments. And yet, Paul still refers to this congregation as "the church." Some have deduced from this that the church in Corinth was still a true church, but would cease to be one if there was no repentance after Paul's instructions arrive in the form of his two Corinthian letters. Others have concluded that if such a congregation was still considered a church by the apostle, then discipline cannot be a mark of the *essence* of a true church, even though church discipline is necessary for the well-being of the church.[11] In either case, church discipline was lacking, and Paul writes, in part, to correct this serious problem.

Grace and Peace

In verse 3, we find the familiar apostolic greeting: "Grace to you and peace from God our Father and the Lord Jesus Christ." While we quickly read over these greetings without giving them much consideration, it is important to reflect upon the contents we find in them. Grace (*charis*) is a reference to God's free gift to us of our salvation in Christ. As Charles Hodge puts it, "Grace is favor and peace its fruits."[12] While peace comes from the He-

---

10. Cf. *Belgic Confession*, Art. 29.
11. See, for example: Berkhof, *Systematic Theology*, 576–578.
12. Charles Hodge, *I & II Corinthians*, reprint ed., (Carlisle, PA: Banner of

brew greeting *shalom*, it not only refers to the peace the believer has with God through the cross of Jesus Christ (i.e., the war between God and the sinner is over), but also includes the blessing of spiritual prosperity. When these words are pronounced in Christian worship, God is greeting us, extending to us his grace in Jesus Christ, as well as declaring all of the covenantal blessings of his *shalom*. Christians have used these words to open worship since the apostolic age.

In many ways, the religious and cultural climate of America and the Western world is very much like that of first century Corinth. As with the church there, God has called many of our contemporaries to faith in Christ from the pagan culture in which we live, and all of us find ourselves living in a time and place dominated by pagan ways of thinking and doing, along with all the things that go with such a perspective. From our highly sexualized pop culture, to our culture's increasing openness to all forms of paganism (things like interest in paranormal activity, vampires and witchcraft, eastern religions, and the corresponding emphasis upon spirituality, meditation, etc.), to the skepticism of the age (no one dare make a public truth claim about religion, since religion is just a matter of faith and utterly subjective), it is all too apparent that the intellectual climate of the modern world is just like that of ancient Corinth. This is why knowing the contents of this letter, reading it often, and studying it carefully, is so important to the health of Christ's church.

As the people of Israel were to assemble together in Jerusalem to call upon the name of YHWH, so too the people of God in the new covenant era assemble together on the Lord's Day wherever they happen to be. A group of new Christians assembled together in Corinth in the first century, and despite all their sins and troubles, they were still God's people, sanctified and set apart for God's purposes—just as Christians are today. Because

---

Truth Trust, 1988), 5.

Greetings from Paul

of the organic nature of the church as the body of Christ (the so-called "communion of the saints"), we join those in every place and across the ages, as "those who in every place call upon the name of our Lord Jesus Christ, both their Lord and ours." In a church like that in Corinth struggling with division and schism, calling upon the Lord together was not only a wonderful cure in such a situation, but Paul's exhortation should remind each of us that we are part of a universal church with boundaries set far beyond our own congregations and denominations. There are brothers and sisters around the world who join us on the Lord's Day in calling upon our Lord. It is a joy, comfort, and an encouragement to think of unseen and unknown brothers and sisters across the globe who join with us as we worship in our local congregations on Sunday. They too are calling upon our Lord Jesus.

2

Be United

1 CORINTHIANS 1:4–17

I appeal to you, brothers, by the name of our Lord Jesus Christ, that all of you agree, and that there be no divisions among you, but that you be united in the same mind and the same judgment.

There is nothing so tragic and gut-wrenching as a church split. If you have ever been through one, you know that almost nothing good comes from them. This is true even in the case of a "Scottish revival"—the facetious term for the departure of a group of disaffected trouble-makers who cause the problems they are complaining about. Division in the church is still division. Christ's body is torn apart by our sinful behavior. While church splits are probably the worst case scenario, there is another more subtle form of division which is found in Christ's church (and often within Reformed churches). This is the case of factions. "I follow the teaching of so and so." The inevitable response to such an assertion is, "Oh yeah, well I follow the teaching of so and so." It had come to Paul's attention that several factions had formed in the Corinthian church. Paul regards the formation of factions as such a serious matter that this is the very first issue Paul takes up in this letter.

First Corinthians

Why does Paul speak to this congregation as an apostle, and not as a friend who has lived for a time among them? Paul speaks with Christ's authority because he must rebuke and instruct this congregation. Paul's authority is unlike many teachers who had come to Corinth forming their own "ministries" in the church without the sanction of the Lord of the church. Paul had first arrived in Corinth in fear and trembling, without eloquence of speech or personal charisma. A number of self-appointed teachers took advantage of Paul's personal unimpressiveness, and sought to undercut his office and authority. Yet, Paul's authority trumps that of all others. He is an apostle, set apart by the risen Christ to minister to the churches. First Corinthians does not contain mere advice, but amounts to a stern rebuke from an apostle, which is but another way of saying this rebuke is from Christ himself.

It is this undisciplined body of believers in Corinth whom Paul describes as "those sanctified in Christ Jesus, called to be saints" (v. 2). To call the Corinthian church to account, Paul must remind them of their calling unto holiness. Unlike the churches of Galatia (or even of Rome) where there was confusion about the gospel (which is why Paul focuses upon justification in those letters), in Corinth the issues Paul must address center around the behavior of Gentile converts to Christianity who are struggling to give up their pagan ways of thinking and doing now that they are Christians. The Corinthians understand the gospel. Apparently, there was little controversy in this congregation about how someone was made right with God through faith in the person and finished work of Christ.

But the Corinthians were struggling to give up their pagan past. How do they follow Christ in a culture which is dominated by pagan rituals and practices in virtually every area of life? How are they to deal with a pagan sexuality graphically present in every guild hall and public bath in the city? The Corinthians do not know how to behave, so Paul begins by reminding them of what they are in Christ—"holy." Having been set apart as "holy," the Corinthians need to act like those who are sanctified. By God's enabling grace they need to become who they already are in Christ.

Paul Gives Thanks

Having made his introductory remarks, Paul gives thanks before addressing the matter of division within the church. Given the stern rebuke he is about to extend to the Corinthians, we might be surprised that Paul includes a thanksgiving in the opening lines of this letter. We should not be. Paul does not give thanks for the Corinthians' horrible conduct. Instead, he gives thanks for what God has graciously done in their midst, despite their conduct. As he states in verse 4, "I give thanks to my God always for you because of the grace of God that was given you in Christ Jesus." In this word of thanksgiving, Paul introduces some of the theological themes which follow, including discussions of God's grace in Christ, spiritual gifts, as well as eschatological matters (the work of the Spirit and the return of Jesus Christ), and finally the doctrine of the church and the fellowship (*koinonia*) which all believers share in Christ. This is Paul's foundation from which to deal with the problems within the congregation.[1]

That all good things extend from God's grace can be seen in verse 5 when Paul affirms "that in every way you were enriched in him in all speech and all knowledge." It is clear from these comments that Paul's understanding of grace is centered in our union with Christ. God's grace is extended to the Corinthians not in the abstract, but specifically "in him" (i.e., "in Christ"). Because the believers in Corinth are "in Christ," they are "enriched in every way," extending to "all speech and all knowledge." Paul is referring to matters he will discuss later in the epistle. Speech

---

1. Hays, *First Corinthians*, 17.

First Corinthians

refers to Spirit-inspired speech (Christian speech in general and speaking in tongues in particular). Knowledge (*gnosis* in contrast to *sophia*—wisdom) refers to a correct understanding of Christian truth, in contrast to pagan philosophy.[2]

As in his letter to the Galatians when Paul mentions on two occasions that it was the preaching of Christ crucified which established the church (Gal. 3:1–5; 6:14), so now Paul reminds the Corinthians of this truth in verse 6: "Even as the testimony about Christ was confirmed among you." Christian preaching is centered in the "testimony about Christ," (i.e., the preaching of the death of Jesus on behalf of sinners). Through the preaching of Christ crucified, God was pleased to confirm his work among the Corinthians. The verb used by Paul translated "to confirm" (*ebebaiōthē*) means something like "a legal guarantee."[3] The effects of the preaching (i.e., the testimony about Christ) includes such things as people coming to faith, the growth of the church, a demonstrable change in people's lives, and so on. These things are the guarantee of the truth of the gospel. These are effects which everyone can see, and so they point back to their cause, Paul's testimony about Christ's death for sinners.

It is because of the grace of God in Jesus Christ that the Corinthians "are not lacking in any spiritual gift." The word translated "spiritual gift" is *charisma*. Although most people associate the *charisma* with the *charismata* (the so-called "sign gifts" which include the speaking in tongues, miracles, and healing), the word "*charisma*" means "spiritual gift," and is used in three ways by Paul. First, the word can be used of salvation, as in Romans 5:15, where Paul contrasts the gift of God ("salvation" from God's wrath on the day of judgment) with the trespass of Adam. Second, the word can be used in a broader sense of God's good gifts in general (i.e., Rom. 11:29, where Paul mentions that

---

2. Barrett, *The First Epistle to the Corinthians*, 37.
3. Morris, *1 Corinthians*, 37.

Be United

God's gifts and his call are irrevocable). Third, the word can be used for special endowments of the Holy Spirit, as in 1 Corinthians 12:4ff.[4] Because of their union with Christ (the effect of the preaching of the gospel), the Corinthians are not lacking in any spiritual gifts from God. The practical consequences of this statement are obvious. There is no excuse for the Corinthians' current behavior. They lack no gifts from God, because he has been gracious to them. God has given the Corinthians all they need to leave pagan ways of thinking and doing behind. God has done the same for us.

While some are surprised by Paul's sudden introduction of the second advent of Jesus Christ, when he states "as you wait for the revealing of our Lord Jesus Christ" (v. 6), this too should not come as a surprise. Throughout Paul's writings, the Holy Spirit is said to be the herald (or announcer) of the age to come and is often associated with the end of the age.[5] In Romans 8:23, Paul speaks of the first fruits of the Holy Spirit while we await our Lord's return and the redemption of our bodies. Likewise in Ephesians 1:13–14, Paul speaks of the believer's present possession of the Holy Spirit as a pledge or down payment of the redemption of our bodies. To be indwelt by the Holy Spirit is the guarantee that we will participate in the age to come and receive all of Christ's promised blessings, including the resurrection of our bodies.

The reason for the Christian's hope (the second coming of Christ) is explained in verses 8–9. "[God] will sustain you to the end, guiltless in the day of our Lord Jesus Christ. God is faithful, by whom you were called into the fellowship of his Son, Jesus Christ our Lord." In verse 8, Paul makes a direct connection between God "sustaining us" and God confirming his testimony in

---

4. Morris, *1 Corinthians*, 37–38.

5. Geerhardus Vos, *Redemptive History and Biblical Interpretation*, trans., Richard B. Gaffin (Phillipsburg: Presbyterian and Reformed, 1980), 91ff.

us in verse 6. The same verb is used in both places (*bebaioō*). God has confirmed his testimony, and will also confirm all believers until the time of the end. Because God has given the Corinthians his grace in Jesus Christ, he has enriched them in every way (including giving them spiritual gifts) so that they lack nothing. Having done this, God will ensure that the Corinthian believers are blameless on the day of Jesus Christ (i.e., his second advent), when Jesus returns to judge the world, raise the dead, and make all things new. Since believers will be blameless on that day, the second advent of Christ is an event for which Christians should eagerly await because it is for us the day of redemption, not the day of judgment. If we are in Christ, and trust in him to save us, we are to be confident that, when he comes again, he will give us everything he has promised. God confirms this promise in us because he gives his people his grace and his gifts.

Believers can be confident, therefore, because the God who called them to faith in Jesus Christ is faithful. Just as Paul has been called to the office of apostle, so all believers have been called through the testimony of the gospel into mutual fellowship in Jesus Christ (our union with Christ), so that we might have fellowship in this age with the same Savior who will declare us to be blameless at the end of the age. God's grace and the gifts the Corinthians presently possess, point ahead to the day of Christ Jesus when the present blessings of the Holy Spirit lead to final glorification (and the resurrection of our bodies). What God begins in us, he will confirm in us until the end. The knowledge of this fact should give us hope in the face of life's calamities and uncertainties.

There Must Be No Divisions In Christ's Church

In verse 10, Paul sets out what amounts to the central theme of the entire letter. "I appeal to you, brothers, by the name of our Lord Jesus Christ, that all of you agree, and that there be no

Be United

divisions among you, but that you be united in the same mind and the same judgment." In fact, most everything which follows until 4:21 grows out of Paul's appeal here: that there may be no divisions in the church, and that the Corinthians be united in Christ.[6] The divisions within the church stand in sharp contrast to the ideal set forth in the previous verse. "God is faithful, by whom you were called into the fellowship of his Son, Jesus Christ our Lord" (v. 9). Sadly, the Corinthians are not characterized by their fellowship because of the current divisions within their ranks. When Paul had left them earlier, they were united around a common fellowship with the Risen Savior. Now they are divided into various factions formed around identification with their favorite teacher.

Paul does not use as harsh a rebuke or express great amazement as he does in his letter to the Galatians (cf. Gal. 1:6). Rather, he appeals to the members of this church as his brothers (*adelphoi*), a term of endearment which he will use thirty-nine times in this epistle.[7] Paul knows these people personally. They have been called into fellowship with Christ through the gospel Paul had proclaimed to them. Paul makes an appeal to them with Christ's authority with which he, as the apostle to the Gentiles, now speaks.

Paul's appeal is that "all of you agree" (literally, "speak the same thing"). This is a classical way of saying "be united."[8] The problem is that various divisions have formed within the church, threatening to destroy the unity of the congregation. The word Paul uses here, "schism" (*scismata*), should probably be understood in this particular context in the sense of "factions" or "cliques," which had informally emerged in the church as people

---

[6]. Hays, *First Corinthians*, 21. Thiselton, *The First Epistle to the Corinthians*, 107.

[7]. Morris, *1 Corinthians*, 39.

[8]. Morris, *1 Corinthians*, 39.

began following a favorite teacher (as we will see in v. 12). Instead of being divided along such superficial and trivial lines, Paul exhorts the Corinthians to "be united in the same mind and the same judgment," using a verb which means restoring something to its proper condition (*katērtismenoithe*). The same verb is used in Matthew 4:21 in reference to repairing fishing nets. The Corinthians are to repair their fractured unity by restoring their thinking and focusing upon the doctrine of Christ, not the personalities of those teaching them.

News from Chloe's Family: A Number of Cliques Have Formed

As we learn in verse 11, the report of division (contention) within the church has come to Paul from the household of a church member named Chloe. "For it has been reported to me by Chloe's people that there is quarreling among you, my brothers." Unnamed members of Chloe's family somehow got word to Paul regarding some of the disturbing things going on within the Corinthian congregation. We do not know whether Chloe lived in Ephesus (Paul's location when he wrote this letter) or in Corinth. But we do know that people in her household had been in Corinth, were likely members of the church there, had witnessed what was going on, and reported it directly to Paul while he was staying in Ephesus about two years after he had left Corinth.[9]

In verse 12, Paul speaks to the specific cause for the division and factions within the church. "What I mean is that each one of you says, 'I follow Paul,' or 'I follow Apollos,' or 'I follow Cephas,' or 'I follow Christ.'" Each faction was apparently following their favorite teachers. There is no mention of their doctrine, so the faction probably formed around the teacher's style and personality, and more than likely, *without* that particular teacher's

---

9. Fee, *The First Epistle to the Corinthians*, 54.

Be United

permission or encouragement. Individuals joined a particular clique based upon their preference for a particular teacher. These factions were like a rapidly-growing cancer which could quickly kill the body.

Since Paul has a personal history with this congregation, the mention of his name should come as no surprise. At least one clique had formed claiming to be followers of Paul! Others cliques, apparently, were actually challenging Paul's apostolic authority. There was a clique devoted to Apollos (who is mentioned later by Paul, as someone whom Paul felt was important to send to the Corinthians in his own absence, cf. 1 Cor. 16:22). Luke describes Apollos as a learned Jew from Alexandria (cf. Acts 18:24–28).[10] Whatever differences existed between the teaching of Paul and Apollos remain unknown to us, although, from Luke's account, it is easy to see why people would have identified with a skilled teacher like Apollos and with his teaching. From what we know, Paul thought very highly of him.

The inclusion of Peter ("Cephas" being the Aramaic form) in this list is a bit more problematic. What is clear is that some of the Corinthians identified themselves as followers of Peter. We know that Peter was a Christian much longer than Paul, he had been the leader of the twelve, and according to Paul's account in Galatians, Peter remained closer to Jewish piety than did Paul (cf. Gal. 2:11–14). The precise nature of Peter's distinctive influence in the Corinthian congregation remains a mystery.[11] It is likely from the reference to him in 1 Corinthians 9:5 that Peter had been in Corinth with his wife.

Another puzzling question has to do with Paul's statement, "I follow Christ." Is Paul saying, "As an apostle, I am not a member of any such faction, I follow Christ," or is Paul saying there was a faction within the church saying, "We follow no man, in-

---

10. See Hays' discussion of this in *First Corinthians*, 22.
11. Morris, *1 Corinthians*, 40.

stead we follow Christ." The latter seems the most natural and fits with the rhetorical question which begins the next verse ("Is Christ divided?"). One way to understand this matter would be as follows. Some in the church were offended by the factionalism and reacting against it affirm, "We follow no man, we follow only Christ," in effect, forming another faction based upon not joining in the other factions! If true, this is merely another form of boasting. It also means that Christ has been reduced from the head of the church to simply the leader of another faction.[12]

The very thought of such a thing leads Paul to ask three rhetorical questions in verse 13, all of which expose the foolishness of such thinking. "Is Christ divided? Was Paul crucified for you? Or were you baptized in the name of Paul?" The first question, "Is Christ divided?" gets to the logical consequence of what results from this division. Ironically, the body of Christ is torn apart by those who claim to be followers of Christ, not men. In terms of his second question, the very thought of Paul being the Savior serves as a *reductio ad absurdum*. The very thought is patently absurd.

It is the last of these questions ("Were you baptized in the name of Paul?") to which the answer is obviously "no," which leads Paul to conclude in verses 14–16, "I thank God that I baptized none of you except Crispus and Gaius, so that no one may say that you were baptized in my name. (I did baptize also the household of Stephanas. Beyond that, I do not know whether I baptized anyone else.)" Apparently, it was apostolic practice, following the example of Christ, to delegate baptism, which was done in the name of Christ, to the officers of the church to avoid the very problem Paul is dealing with here—"I was baptized by so and so, hence am a follower of so and so." The factions in Corinth may have been based, in part, upon the fact that the individuals were baptized by the people just mentioned (Christ

---

12. Hays, *First Corinthians*, 23.

excepted, of course). This may have led to the unfortunate situation in which the baptized individuals formed an illegitimate connection to the person who baptized them. This is why Paul is thankful that he baptized so few of them, so that people could not claim to be baptized into his name.

Proclaiming the Cross of Christ

So, Paul asserts in verse 17, "For Christ did not send me to baptize but to preach the gospel, and not with words of eloquent wisdom, lest the cross of Christ be emptied of its power." The apostle understands that his divinely-appointed mission is to preach the gospel. Paul's emphasis upon the centrality of preaching contains loud echoes[13] from Isaiah 40:9, 52:7 and 61:1, which speak of the messianic age as one in which the Messiah would establish the preaching of good news.[14] The office of apostle is centered in the responsibility of preaching in an evangelistic context (establishing churches), with the day to day responsibility for church life being assigned to the successors of the apostles—ministers of word and sacrament, elders, and deacons (cf. Acts 14:23; 20:17, 28; 1 Tim. 3:1–11, Titus 1:5).

Notice too that Paul is concerned that the Corinthians realize that the preaching of the cross (the death of Jesus) does not center in "words of eloquent wisdom" (literally "cleverness in speech"). This comment may be added by Paul because people often like the preacher more than his message, or because the Corinthians were preoccupied with "wisdom," which, in Hellenistic Greek culture, was a reference to a skilled rhetorician and logician (story-teller) who could keep an audience in rapt at-

---

13. An "echo" is an allusion to another biblical text without citing it directly (as in a "quotation"). See Richard Hays's discussion of this in *Echoes of Scripture in the Letters of Paul* (New Haven: Yale University Press, 1989), 1–33.

14. G. K. Beale and D. A. Carson, eds., *Commentary on the New Testament Use of the Old Testament* (Grand Rapids: Baker Academic, 2007), 697.

tention. There is a big difference between preaching Christ and impressing people with your "wisdom."[15]

To a Greek audience, the cross of Christ was a very unpopular message of shame and degradation centering in a crucified God ("*skandalon*"). Yet the cross is the only divinely appointed means by which God saves sinners. Preaching which softens, weakens, or "spices up" the cross (as one writer puts it), nullifies the power of the cross by drawing people to the preacher, not to the Savior.[16] As Paul sees it, Christian preaching centers in a particular message—the doing and dying of Jesus—however scandalous that message may be to a Greek. The gospel is not grounded in the eloquence and rhetorical skills of the preacher.

In fact, it was the attraction to the personal styles and technical abilities of various preachers which was the root of the problem in Corinth. People liked other teachers and preachers more than they liked Paul. The members of the church broke into factions without considering the content of what was preached. So the Corinthians ended-up dividing into factions based on the creed, "I follow so and so." Paul says this kind of behavior must stop. Those who are members of this church need to be united. As Paul will remind them later, they are members of the body of Christ (cf. 1 Cor. 12:12ff.).

Paul's warning to the Corinthians about the ease in which destructive factions form in churches needs to be heeded. It is here where we see the wisdom of being a "confessional church." Reformed Christians are not able to say "we follow John Calvin" because the ministers and elders of any given church do not subscribe to Calvin's personal views, or his theology. Instead, we subscribe to a series of "confessional" documents produced and agreed upon by the churches, known collectively as "The Three Forms of Unity" (the *Belgic Confession*, the *Heidelberg*

---

15. Barrett, *The First Epistle to the Corinthians*, 49.
16. Morris, *1 Corinthians*, 42–43.

Be United

Catechism, and the *Canons of Dort*), or to the *Westminster Standards* which include the *Confession of Faith*, and the *Larger* and *Shorter* catechisms. By confessing a common faith, spelled out in some detail in the Reformed confessions, we have a built-in bulwark against factionalism. We confess a common faith. We believe the same doctrines. We do not (or at least should not) follow individual teachers.

In this we also see the wisdom of Presbyterian (and Reformed) church government. Churches are not ruled by a single charismatic pastor, but governed by a group of elders elected by the congregation. This too should be a great safeguard against factionalism.

That said, we too are as sinful as the Corinthians and just as prone to factions and division. We too need to be careful about identifying too closely with a influential teacher or writer. Instead, we should direct our allegiance to that doctrine regarding the person and work of Christ found in those confessional documents which spell out the content of our faith, and to which we agree. When we say we are "Reformed," we are confessing (along with our brothers and sisters) a common faith, defined in the *Three Forms of Unity* or the *Westminster Standards*, which we believe summarizes the Bible's teaching about Christ, his gospel, and his church. Our common doctrine unites us. Or at least, it should.

If we are to heed Paul's warning, we need always to keep before our eyes the glories of the gospel. Jesus died to redeem us as individuals whom he includes in his church which is his spiritual body. Seeking to divide that body which Christ died to create is a serious thing and a great sin. It is because Christ died for us (as individuals and as a church) that Paul can say "I appeal to you, brothers, by the name of our Lord Jesus Christ, that all of you agree, and that there be no divisions among you, but that you be united in the same mind and the same judgment" (v. 10).

First Corinthians

Because we are all self-centered sinners, the only way we can be truly united is to keep our eyes on the death and resurrection of Jesus Christ. Jesus died for our sins and was raised for our justification, so that he might save his people (not only "me," but his "people" collectively) to be members of his body, which is his church. Because Jesus came to save his people, we need to agree and be united in mind by confessing a common faith, and we avoid division by seeking that which is best for his body, even if that means putting our personal issues or agendas aside.

In Jesus Christ we are one, and we are members of his church, which is his body. He has united us together when he redeemed us from the guilt and power of sin, and then called us to faith. Such unity is a precious gift from God, and reflected in the words of Psalm 132:1–3:

> Behold, how good and pleasant it is when brothers dwell in unity! It is like the precious oil on the head, running down on the beard, on the beard of Aaron, running down on the collar of his robes! It is like the dew of Hermon, which falls on the mountains of Zion! For there the Lord has commanded the blessing, life forevermore.

This is why we must strive mightily to "be united." Unity is one of the wonderful blessings which are ours in Jesus Christ. It is also one of the easiest blessings to overlook.

3

The Wisdom of God

1 CORINTHIANS 1:18–31

Where is the one who is wise? Where is the scribe? Where is the debater of this age? Has not God made foolish the wisdom of the world? For since, in the wisdom of God, the world did not know God through wisdom, it pleased God through the folly of what we preach to save those who believe. For Jews demand signs and Greeks seek wisdom, but we preach Christ crucified, a stumbling block to Jews and folly to Gentiles, but to those who are called, both Jews and Greeks, Christ the power of God and the wisdom of God. For the foolishness of God is wiser than men, and the weakness of God is stronger than men.

When someone claims to be an evangelical Christian, and then states that understanding the cross as a sacrifice for sin is a twisted form of cosmic child abuse, we are shocked.[1]

Yet, while the sentiment is shocking, we should not be surprised that people think like this. It is the inspired Apostle Paul who explains in 1 Corinthians 1:18 that the cross is folly to those who are perishing. The message of Christ crucified was foolishness to ancient Greeks, and a stumbling block to Jews.

---

1. Steve Chalke & Alan Mann, *The Lost Message of Jesus* (Grand Rapids: Zondervan, 2003), 182.

The cross is probably both to modern people. While sinful men and women mock the cross because they claim to be wise, God, in turn, mocks them, because from God's perspective, human wisdom is nothing but sinful folly. If you have ever wondered why Christianity is so difficult for non-Christians to understand and accept, here God's Word provides the answer.

God's Wisdom and Human Folly

We now take up the subject of God's wisdom and human folly, or as non-Christians see it, our folly and their wisdom. We also learn that the divisions within the Corinthian congregation reveal a much deeper intellectual problem than people overzealously identifying with the person who baptized them. The divisions within the Corinthian church stem from the fact that people were placing far too much confidence in human wisdom (*sophia*) instead of the gospel, which is centered upon the preaching of the cross of Christ.[2] From a Christian perspective, over-reliance on human wisdom was a serious problem throughout the Hellenistic (Greek-influenced) world. Paul's response to this problem is to remind the Corinthians that the wisdom of God is revealed in the message of Christ crucified. This revelation of God's wisdom stands in complete opposition to the so-called "wisdom" of the Greek philosophical tradition which regarded the preaching of the cross as utter foolishness.

In many ways, this is the same issue we face as Christians today—self-centered, prosperous, and technologically advanced Westerners are very much like the Hellenized citizens of first century Corinth. Both find the preaching of the cross either irrelevant or offensive. Because of the blinding effects of human sin and pride, many of our contemporaries regard the sacrificial death of Jesus as an affront to modern sensibilities.

---

2. Barrett, *The First Epistle to the Corinthians*, 51.

The Wisdom of God

In verse 18, Paul identifies the key issue which explains virtually all of the problems facing the Corinthian church. "For the word of the cross is folly to those who are perishing, but to us who are being saved it is the power of God." The word of the cross is folly (foolishness) to those who rely on human wisdom to understand the things of God (as Paul pointed out in verse 17). The word (*logos*) of the cross is but another way of speaking of the preaching of the gospel.[3] The cross of Jesus Christ not only lies at the heart of God's redemptive work in Jesus Christ, the cross is the heart of that message God commissioned his apostles to preach. In Galatians 3:1, Paul speaks of his preaching as publicly placarding Christ. In 2 Corinthians 2:15, Paul speaks of the cross as a sweet fragrance which is the aroma of life to a believer. The apostle himself indicates that Christ and him crucified *is* the content of his preaching (cf. 1 Cor. 1:23).

Yet the proclamation of a crucified Messiah is not a message non-Christians want to hear, or something to which they will be attracted. When viewed through the intellectual categories of a first-century city like Corinth, the very idea of God incarnate being crucified as a payment for sin was beyond comprehension. The seriousness of Paul's point about the gospel being folly is easily lost upon us until we realize that crucifixion was that form of capital punishment reserved for the lowest dregs of society (e.g., fugitive slaves, or prisoners of war) and the most heinous of criminals (murderers, insurrections, terrorists, etc.). Pain and suffering aside, to die by crucifixion was to die in shame. Preaching a crucified Savior was absolutely scandalous in Greek culture.

In our age, the cross is a well-known and established Christian symbol. However, to speak to a first century Greek of a "crucified God" is to talk nonsense. Crucifixion was a form of punishment used by the Romans to make an example of crimi-

---

3. Barrett, *The First Epistle to the Corinthians*, 51.

nals so that others would think twice about doing what the crucified victim had done. A public display of horrific punishment, crucifixion was the symbol of Roman power. The cross declared to Roman subjects, "Do not mess with us." Yet Paul is now proclaiming that through the cross of Christ, God triumphs over human sin and the powers that be—including Rome. As Richard Hays points out, "Rather than proving the sovereignty of Roman political order, [the cross] shatters the world's systems of authority. Rather than confirming what the wisest heads already know, [the cross] shatters the world's systems of knowledge.[4] That the cross was an offense to Greco-Roman sympathies can be seen in the fact that there is a first century graffiti found in Rome which depicts a crucified body of a man with the head of a mule, with the sarcastic inscription, "Alexamenos worships his god."[5] No doubt, this was indicative of how many non-Christians of Paul's day regarded the message of the cross. God incarnate was difficult enough to grasp. God incarnate and subsequently crucified was just too much.

At this point, Paul divides the human race into two categories, strongly implying a doctrine of particular redemption (i.e., that the death of Jesus is designed to actually save God's elect for whom his death is effectual, rather than to make the entire human race "savable" if only people meet certain conditions acceptable to God). Paul divides the human race into two groups—those who are being saved, and those who are perishing. Those who are being saved are those for whom Christ's power is effectual. Those who see the cross as foolishness are not included among those "being saved." In making this point, Paul indirectly raises the matter of divine election. Do people perish because they reject the gospel? Or, are people perishing because the

---

4. Hays, *First Corinthians*, 31.
5. Morris, *1 Corinthians*, 43.

gospel is foolishness to them?[6] Although the answer to both questions is "yes," here Paul emphasizes the latter. Apart from God's life-giving, illuminating grace, people cannot understand the message of the cross for what it is, the power of God.

According to Paul, the unbelieving world does not think properly about God. What passes for wisdom among unbelievers is from God's perspective only so much foolishness. In fact, Paul associates worldliness not so much with immoral conduct (as taught in much of American fundamentalism), but with the non-Christian way of thinking, which, in turn, leads to immoral conduct. The antithesis between Christian and non-Christian thinking can be seen in the fact that Christians understand the meaning of the cross, while non-Christians do not.

This antithesis between Christian thinking and non-Christian thinking has serious implications for Christian apologetics, reminding us of the intellectual prejudice non-Christians have towards the things of God (i.e., the noetic effects of sin on human thinking). There are also important implications for ethics and culture as well. This is why Reformed approaches to apologetics regard all non-Christian thinking as darkened by human sin (cf. Eph. 4:18–19). This explains why a supernatural act of illumination by the Holy Spirit is required to overturn the prejudicial effects of sin on human thinking and to remove the innate hatred people have toward the things of God.

God's Wisdom and Power

The manner in which God saves sinners manifests his wisdom and his power. Only God's elect can see the cross for what it is—the power of God unto salvation. In his suffering on the cross, Jesus Christ dies for sinners (1 Pet. 2:24), turning away God's wrath (Rom. 5:9), reconciling them to an angry God (Rom. 5:10), redeeming and purchasing them (Gal. 3:13), and dying

---

6. Barrett, *The First Epistle to the Corinthians*, 52.

in their place (Eph. 5:2). In the crucifixion of Jesus, God demonstrates his supreme love for a lost and fallen world, without in any sense sacrificing his justice (1 John 4:10). But this can only be fully understood (in a saving sense) through the eyes of faith. Barring a work of divine grace, non-Christians do not understand this and never will. For them, the cross is typified by Alexamenos worshiping his God.

To bolster his point, in verse 19 Paul cites Isaiah 29:14: "For it is written, 'I will destroy the wisdom of the wise, and the discernment of the discerning I will thwart.'" According to Isaiah, in their natural sinful condition mankind will never figure out nor understand the ways of God, especially when it comes to the redemption of sinners. In Isaiah's prophecy, the prophet warns God's people not to go against his will by seeking protection through an alliance with Egypt. Israel must trust in God to protect them and not make alliances with pagan nations. In Isaiah 29:13, we read that the people draw near to God with their lips, but their hearts are far from him. The application to the Corinthians is simply that talk of human wisdom is cheap. Human wisdom jumps from the lips of a people whose hearts are actually far from God.[7]

The cross of Christ demonstrates the huge gap between God's ways of dealing with his creatures, and the way sinners think things ought to be done. The cross frustrates non-Christian wisdom and intelligence. God's ways are not our ways. His thoughts are not our thoughts (cf. Isa. 55:8). When we try to be wiser than God, God will expose human wisdom for what it is—foolishness. All the wisdom of the ancient philosophers (great as that wisdom was in worldly matters) cannot make sense of Christ's cross. Indeed, the cross remains intellectual and philosophical foolishness to non-Christians, in addition to being scandalous. Human wisdom (great as it may be) cannot

---

7. Hays, *First Corinthians*, 29.

The Wisdom of God

comprehend the gravity of human sin, the complete helplessness of the human condition, and what is required for God to deal with our sin without sacrificing his love for his justice. This is not a matter of human wisdom or intelligence. Rather, God must reveal this to us in the person of his Son.

In verse 20, Paul reminds the Corinthians that God actually mocks the sage, the philosopher, and all those who think themselves wise. "Where is the one who is wise? Where is the scribe? Where is the debater of this age? Has not God made foolish the wisdom of the world?" Can the sage truly understand God's dealings with his creatures? Can the scholar? Can the philosopher? Despite the eloquence and rhetorical skill of such men—prized in Greco-Roman culture—Paul's rhetorical questions demand only one answer. "No." The sage, the scholar, the philosopher, can only comprehend the wisdom of "this age." God's wisdom confounds them all. His wisdom is not the wisdom of this age, or of this world. His wisdom is of the age to come.

That God's wisdom confounds the world is clear from verse 21. "For since, in the wisdom of God, the world did not know God through wisdom, it pleased God through the folly of what we preach to save those who believe." Given the context—God's wisdom revealed in the cross in contrast to human wisdom revealed in the sage, the scholar and the philosopher—when Paul speaks of God's wisdom here, he is not speaking of natural revelation (and the moral law written upon every human heart, cf. Rom. 2:14–15). Rather, since God chose to reveal his wisdom in the cross (specifically through preaching—*kerygma*), the world (with its wisdom firmly anchored in this age) did not know God, nor understand the nature of the salvation that the cross secures for us. God was pleased to save people who believe a message which the world regards as foolishness. Paul is drawing our attention to the fact that God was pleased to do things in a particular way. It was never God's intention to save sinners through the discoveries of human wisdom, nor through the means of human merit. It was his intention to save them through the death of a crucified Savior.

Jews, Greeks, and the Cross

This also means that the gospel is not part of natural revelation. The gospel is not found in the sunrise, nor in the grandeur of Yosemite. Nor is the gospel a message which will make sense to people using the categories of worldly wisdom. It is the wisdom of the world which makes specious claims such as "good people go to heaven" and that "only very bad people go to hell." The content of the gospel is not something which can be discovered by human wisdom. It is a message which must be revealed by God's Spirit, and which must be believed after it is heard. We are not saved through the means of human wisdom (and the things associated with it), but through the means of believing a particular message, a message which the world regards as foolishness. This says a great deal about all those attempts (however well-intentioned they may be) to tinker with the message for the sake of reaching greater numbers of people. To tinker with the message is to rob it of its truth and power. It is to substitute the wisdom of men (which is foolishness) for the wisdom and power of God.

We still witness this sad tendency to tinker with the message of the gospel—which was rampant in the Greco-Roman world of Paul—all around us today. When contrasting the preaching of Billy Graham and Joel Osteen, Ross Douthat (a Roman Catholic columnist for the *New York Times*), points out that in Joel Osteen's "gospel" message, "God gives without demanding, forgives without threatening to judge, and hands out His rewards in this life rather than in the next." Douthat notes that while Billy Graham (who represented the evangelicalism of a previ-

The Wisdom of God

ous generation) saw eternity as hanging in the balance and after the sermon announced that the time had come for the sinner to make a choice for or against Jesus Christ, "Osteen's message is considerably more upbeat" and amounts to a marriage between God and Mammon.[8]

As we see in verses 22–23, Paul's comments are especially germane to two distinct ethnic groups in the Corinthian church. "For Jews demand signs and Greeks seek wisdom, but we preach Christ crucified, a stumbling block to Jews and folly to Gentiles." The Jews of Corinth were not at all interested in the kind of speculative wisdom that the Greeks were famous for. Jews believed that God had acted in redemptive history, made his covenant with them (by grace), and then gave them the law as a means of blessing and curse, with circumcision being the badge of covenant membership. Throughout the gospels, the Jews kept demanding miraculous signs from Jesus because these signs would demonstrate that he was Israel's Messiah (cf. John 4:48). The countless miracles Jesus did do were not enough to convince the Jews that he was the one promised throughout the Old Testament. It was the fact that Jesus must suffer and die for sins which became an intolerable stumbling block (*skandelon*) to the Jews. As Leon Morris so aptly puts it, to a Jew "a crucified Messiah was a contradiction in terms."[9] The Jews expected the coming Messiah to be a conquering king who would deliver them from the stifling oppression of Roman rule. They did not consider the fact that Messiah would also be a suffering servant (cf. Isa. 52:13–53:12)

To the Greeks, on the other hand, the solutions to life's problems were to be discovered through the means of human wisdom. Greeks came to regard sages, scholars, and philoso-

---

8. Ross Douthat, *Bad Religion: How We Became a Nation of Heretics* (New York: Fress Press, 2012), 183.

9. Morris, *1 Corinthians*, 45.

phers as the center of political, cultural, and even religious life. These were the men who provided the answers to life's questions and discovered solutions to life's problems. The Greeks regarded those who did not exalt such ideals as barbarians who were unable to understand true wisdom. Given this set of categories, who needs a revelation from God when we have such a deep well of human wisdom? What use is a crucified God, when the sages, scholars, and philosophers have discovered the keys to living a successful and rewarding life? We are no different with our gurus, prosperity preachers, and life coaches. In such an environment, it is no wonder that Joel Osteen's "gospel lite" attracts large numbers of followers who pack out his church in Houston, and who buy his books and attend his rallies.

However, as Paul reminds his hearers, the critical difference between Christianity and Judaism, and between Christianity and Greek wisdom, is a crucified Savior. Paul reminds the Corinthians that this is precisely the message he had preached to them, and this explains why Jews stumble before the cross, while the Greeks dismiss it as unsophisticated nonsense. And yet, there is more to the story than just the fate of the Jews and Greeks. Paul goes on to say in verse 24–25, "But to those who are called, both Jews and Greeks, Christ the power of God and the wisdom of God. For the foolishness of God is wiser than men, and the weakness of God is stronger than men."

While the cross may be an intolerable stumbling block to the Jew and foolishness to the Greek, the message of the cross is the only means by which God calls elect Jews and Greeks to faith in Jesus Christ. The message of the cross is that "good news" wherein the power of God (to redeem sinners and to call them to faith) and the wisdom of God (both his love and justice) is fully displayed (cf. Rom. 3:21–28). Though foolishness to most, and a stumbling block to others, it is in this message of the cross (and only in this message) that God supremely demonstrates his wisdom and power. This divine wisdom completely transcends the wisdom and power of men.

Consider Your Calling

It is in light of this point that Paul exhorts his readers, "Consider your calling, brothers: not many of you were wise according to worldly standards, not many were powerful, not many were of noble birth." Paul asks the Corinthians to consider their social and economic standing before they came to faith in Christ. The Corinthian church was filled with people of low social standing, and with people who lived lives which went virtually unnoticed outside their immediate circles. Not many of the members of the Corinthian church were wise by human standards. Apparently, few were present in this church who had formal training in philosophy, logic, or rhetoric. There was no one in this church who "discovered" the secret wisdom of God, and then came to faith in Christ. There may have been a philosopher or two in their midst, but they came to faith like everyone else—they were called through the preaching of the gospel. The Corinthian Christians did not come to faith because they were wiser than others. They came to faith because God called them!

The same thing holds true for influential people or people of noble birth. There may have been a leading light or a blue blood or two from the leading families of Corinth in the congregation, but they were not called because of their high-standing or reputation. By and large, the Corinthian church was made up of ordinary people from the various stages and stations of life. It is interesting to note that one of the earliest attacks upon Christianity coming from the pagan philosopher Celsus is the fact that so few intellectuals became Christians, a charge easily refuted.[10] This lack of worldly-wise intellectuals, people of high-social standing, and noble birth is not by accident. This is

---

10. Origen responded to this charge in *Contra Celsum*, III.48.

exactly what we find throughout the gospels when we read that the kingdom of God cannot be entered because of good works or social status. Rather, entrance into God's kingdom must be bestowed upon us (cf. Mark 10:15; Luke 8:10; 18:24). It is God's purpose that the Corinthian church is filled with people who are in no way worthy of the kingdom, nor held in high esteem by the world.

The reason for this is spelled out in verses 27–28. "But God chose what is foolish in the world to shame the wise; God chose what is weak in the world to shame the strong; God chose what is low and despised in the world, even things that are not, to bring to nothing the things that are." Again, Paul emphasizes the sovereign purposes of God in his choice of specific undeserving individuals who will be called, and who will believe the gospel when it is preached to them. God chose a foolish message (the cross) to call those individuals whom the world truly regards as foolish (those not wise by worldly standards, those not of high-standing, or noble birth) so as to shame the wise (those who are truly worldly wise, and of high-standing). God chooses weak and foolish things because his power and wisdom are magnified by the salvation of weak and foolish men and women. Anyone who is of the elect and chosen by God in Jesus Christ to be delivered from his wrath, cannot boast in any sense about being worthy of God's choice. Our only boast, in fact, is Christ crucified for sinners.

To confound the wisdom of the world, God chooses to save many of lowly birth and those whom the world despises, so as to bring to nothing the "things that are."[11] The reason God does this is stated in verse 29: "So that no human being might boast in the presence of God." At the end of the day, we have nothing

---

11. The phrase "things that are" is used 27 times in the NT and translated 17 different ways.

The Wisdom of God

whatsoever about which to boast. The gospel is about the power of God, not our goodness.

Turning from the negative (that God's wisdom flies in the face of worldly wisdom) to the positive (God's method of saving), Paul speaks to the fundamental fact that God saves sinners (weak and foolish) so as to magnify his power and wisdom. In verse 30 we read: "And because of him you are in Christ Jesus, who became to us wisdom from God, righteousness and sanctification and redemption." According to Paul, true wisdom consists in those things now enumerated as benefits of our union with Christ: "righteousness, holiness and redemption."[12]

Jesus Christ: Wisdom from God

Union with Christ is a major theme in Paul's letters.[13] To be united to Jesus Christ (who is the wisdom of God) through faith is to receive all of Christ's saving benefits, including righteousness, sanctification, and redemption. As Michael Horton describes this union, "It is a way of speaking about the way in which believers share in Christ in eternity (by election), in past history (by redemption), in the present (by effectual calling, justification, and sanctification), and in the future (by glorification)."[14]

Furthermore, union with Christ has a corporate dimension which has an important bearing upon Paul's understanding of the organic nature of the body of Christ. One thinks of the vine and the fruit metaphor used by Jesus in John 15:1–17. To be in union with Christ is to be united to all others who are in Christ

---

12. According to Calvin, there are four distinct titles ascribed to Christ by Paul (wisdom being one along with righteousness, holiness, and redemption), and these sum up our Lord's perfections, as well as the benefits we receive from our Savior. Cf. Calvin, *The First Epistle of Paul to the Corinthians*, 45.

13. For an insightful treatment of the development of this concept in the Reformed tradition, see J.V. Fesko, *Beyond Calvin: Union with Christ and Justification in the Early Modern Reformed Theology, 1517–1700* (Göttingen: Vanderhoeck & Ruprecht, 2012).

14. Horton, *The Christian Faith*, 587.

and who are members of his body (which is his church). This is especially important to consider at this point in our discussion of the opening chapters of 1 Corinthians, given the fact that Paul is dealing with the tragedy of schism and division.

When Paul speaks of Christ as "wisdom" from God he is making the point that Jesus is that one whom the Jews had expected, thereby allowing Paul to set forth Christ as true wisdom (personified), over against the so-called wisdom of men. This may serve as a point of contact with the Jews in Corinth, and it certainly is offered as a challenge to the so-called "wisdom" of the Hellenistic world. To speak of Christ as "wisdom from God," is a loud echo from Proverbs 8:22–32, where wisdom is personified. But it may also come from first century Jewish thinking, where Wisdom (personified) was understood to play a major role in the creation of all things, as well as serving as mediator between God and man in terms of the communication to man of the divine will about God's salvation of his people.[15] Paul makes the critical point that it is because of God (*ex autou*) that believers are in Christ Jesus. For all those united to Jesus Christ through faith, Christ is not just the source of all true wisdom, he is true Wisdom. Jesus Christ stands over against all forms of Greek and Roman religion.

Righteousness (*diakiosune*) refers to the right standing given to us by God in Jesus Christ (our justification). The word comes directly from the law courts of Paul's day and is used repeatedly by Paul to indicate that God's just verdict of "not guilty" is rendered of Christ, not us.[16] Because we are "in Christ" through faith, Christ is now said to be our righteousness. Our sins are forgiven because of Jesus Christ's death upon the cross (which paid for these sins and turned aside the wrath of God) and that we are

---

15. Barrett, *First Epistle to the Corinthians*, 60.

16. W. Bauer, W. F. Arndt, F. W. Gingrich, and F. W. Danker, *A Greek-English Lexicon of the New Testament and Other Early Christian Literature*, 2nd ed (Chicago: University of Chicago Press, 1979), 196–197.

regarded (reckoned) to be as righteous as Jesus Christ himself was righteous.[17] By virtue of our union with Christ, our guilt is reckoned to him and his righteousness is reckoned (imputed) as though it were ours. Paul has already spoken of believers as "sanctified in Christ" in 1:2, and will go on to unpack this a bit further in 2 Corinthians 5:21, when he puts it this way: "For our sake he made him to be sin who knew no sin, so that in him we might become the righteousness of God."

Sanctification (*hagiasmos*), refers to Christ's ethical purity (his perfect obedience), which is not only a reference to Christ's active obedience (his obedience to the covenant of works and the Law of Moses), but is also connected to the sanctification (mortification and vivification) that Christ works in all those united to him through faith. According to Hebrews 12:24, without holiness, no man will see God. Yet Jesus Christ is our holiness by virtue of our union with him. Because Jesus is truly without sin, he will not only mortify sin in us (by progressively subduing and weakening sin's hold upon us), but, because we are holy in Christ, we will see God as the ultimate fruit of our glorification. As Paul has stated earlier, those sanctified (reckoned as "holy" because Christ is their righteousness) are also called to be holy (that is to demonstrate through their conduct

---

17. N. T. Wright objects to this interpretation on the ground that "if we are to claim [imputed righteousness] as such, we must be prepared to talk of the imputed wisdom of Christ; the imputed sanctification of Christ; the imputed redemption of Christ, and that, though no doubt they are all true in some overall general sense, will certainly make nonsense of the very specialized and technical senses so frequently given to the phrase 'the righteousness of Christ' in the history of theology." See N. T. Wright, *What Saint Paul Really Said: Was Paul of Tarsus the Real Founder of Christianity?* (Grand Rapids: William B. Eerdmans Publishing Company, 1997), 123. Yet as Beale points out, "Believers' identification and union with Christ means that 'in him' they are considered to have the (perfect) wisdom, righteousness, holiness and redemption that Christ had. . . .The 'for us' (hēmin) in the verse refers to their position 'in Christ Jesus' and identification with his attributes being on their behalf or for their benefit." See G. K. Beale, *A New Testament Biblical Theology: The Unfolding of the Old Testament in the New* (Grand Rapids: Baker Academic, 2011), 473–474.

that they are sanctified and in union with Christ). Paul is reinforcing the idea that all those who are justified will also be in the process of sanctification. Paul will tolerate neither Jewish legalism nor Gentile antinomianism.

The third term Paul uses here, redemption (*apolytrōsis*), points forward to future deliverance from God's eschatological wrath on the day of judgment, and to the resurrection of the body (Eph. 1:3–14). The term also conveys the idea of liberation from that which holds us captive.[18] Because we are in union with him through faith, Jesus Christ is our righteousness, holiness, and redemption. In Christ (who is true Wisdom) we have the divine revelation of what is truly wise, holy, and good. Nothing in either Jewish or Greek thinking can compare. Although the pagans think they are wise, God mocks them as foolish, and the pagans in their foolishness return the favor. Paul is saying to the Corinthians, "You want wisdom? All right, here is the wisdom that God has provided. It is found in Jesus Christ and in him crucified!"[19]

Because Christ is our righteousness, the conclusion stated in verse 31 (a quotation from Jer. 9:24) is now obvious. "Let the one who boasts, boast in the Lord." Instead of boasting in our wisdom, our high standing and our nobility, let all Christians boast in the Lord, who has done all of this for us in Christ. This is very similar to Paul's declaration in Galatians 6:14: "But far be it from me to boast except in the cross of our Lord Jesus Christ, by which the world has been crucified to me, and I to the world." Christian preaching must challenge the boasting of those who are confident in their own righteousness, their own wisdom, their own high-standing in the community, or their nobility. In effect, God mocks these things when the cross is

---

18. Barrett, *First Epistle to the Corinthians*, 61.
19. Hays, *First Corinthians*, 33.

The Wisdom of God

preached because God exposes this pagan wisdom for what it truly is—foolishness.

If you have ever wondered why it is that when you make the best presentation of the gospel you possibly can, and then all you get is a blank stare, or if you have ever felt the sting of having people think you are a fool because you are a Christian, Paul has given you an explanation. The cross is the revelation of both the wisdom and power of God. Yet, to non-Christians the message of Christ crucified is either a stumbling block or foolishness, perhaps both. This will always be the case unless and until God changes a person's heart (the theme of 1 Corinthians chapter 2) through the power of the Holy Spirit so they can now understand that what they thought was foolishness is in reality the wisdom and power of God.

Although pagans think themselves wise, God confounds them by saving sinners through the message of a crucified Savior, something they simply cannot comprehend. Yet, it is only in the message of Christ and him crucified that we find righteousness, holiness, and redemption, which are the fruit of the wisdom and power of God. As John Owen once put it, "Many poor creatures are sensible of their wants, but know not where their remedy lies. Indeed, whether it be light or life, power of joy, all is wrapped up in him."[20]

These are the very things pagans claim to be seeking, but cannot find. The wisdom and power of God are found only in the message of the cross—a message which remains foolishness to Greeks, a stumbling block to Jews, but for us who are being saved, is that message where we find the greatest of all treasures. It is in the cross of Jesus Christ that God reveals to us both his wisdom in dealing with sinners and his power to do what is necessary to truly save us from the guilt and power of sin. All he

---

20. John Owen, *Communion with the Triune God*, ed., Kelly M. Kapic and Justin Taylor (Wheaton, IL: Crossway, 2007), 149.

demands of us is that we reject human wisdom and righteousness, and through the empty hands of faith, humbly receive the glorious treasure God is so willing to give us. But this is the very thing to which human wisdom blinds us.

4

Jesus Christ and Him Crucified

1 CORINTHIANS 2:1–5

And I, when I came to you, brothers, did not come proclaiming to you the testimony of God with lofty speech or wisdom. For I decided to know nothing among you except Jesus Christ and him crucified. And I was with you in weakness and in fear and much trembling, and my speech and my message were not in plausible words of wisdom, but in demonstration of the Spirit and of power, so that your faith might not rest in the wisdom of men but in the power of God.

Greeks (like those living in first century Corinth) loved wisdom. They thought Paul's gospel of a crucified Messiah was nothing but so much foolishness. Yet those Jews living in Corinth could not understand how God's Messiah must suffer and die for our sins. According to Jewish expectations, the Messiah was expected to be an all-conquering king who would lead Israel back to its national greatness. Therefore, for Jews, Paul's gospel of a crucified Messiah was a stumbling block. Yet, according to Paul, the cross of Jesus Christ is the revelation of both the wisdom and power of God. It is through the preaching of the cross that God is pleased to call elect Greeks and Jews to faith in Jesus, while at the same time the cross exposes human wisdom for what it is—human wisdom. It is the cross which stumbles a Jew, confounds a Greek, and yet is the only message through which God saves sinners.

In the first two chapters of this epistle Paul explains *why* the Corinthian church has been plagued with division. The Corinthians are still thinking like pagans, and therefore acting like pagans. The members of this church, apparently, understood the gospel Paul was preaching. They seem to have understood that God saves sinners by grace alone, through faith alone, on account of Christ alone, apart from good works. Although false apostles will soon disrupt this church (a matter Paul will address in chapter 11), at this point in their history, there was no organized group of false teachers distorting the gospel, as the Judaizers had done in the churches of Galatia.

The church in Corinth was relatively new, and this was problematic. Paul first preached the message of Christ crucified to the Corinthians several years earlier. Many in Corinth had responded to Paul's preaching of the cross with faith, were baptized, and now participating in the life of the church. But as new Christians in a new church with so much Christian doctrine still being new to them, the Corinthians were still thinking and acting like the Greek pagans they had been until quite recently. Although saved by the wisdom and power of God as revealed in the cross of Jesus Christ, the Corinthians still loved Greek wisdom. In many ways, they still thought like Greeks, and therefore still acted like those dependent upon human wisdom apart from God's Word.

Because the Greeks loved wisdom (or as we might call it "worldly" or "human" wisdom), they devoted themselves to various teachers within the church (including Paul, Peter, Apollos, and even Jesus) causing factions to form. "I follow Paul." "I fol-

Jesus Christ and Him Crucified

low Peter." "I follow Apollos." There was even a faction contending that "we don't belong to any faction, we follow Jesus." Greeks loved the wise old sage, the clever spinner of tales, as well as the philosopher who apparently had all the answers to the questions of life. Just as the Corinthians were devoted to their favorite local philosopher or rhetorician (who was known for eloquence in public speech), apparently they became devoted to that Christian teacher (or leader) who had baptized them, even though that teacher would have certainly frowned on this kind of devotion.

Paul attributes this tendency in the church to divide into factions to the Corinthians' love of worldly wisdom. Paul responds to this problem in two ways: first, describing the problem, and then, identifying its source. In verse 10 of chapter one Paul exhorts the Corinthians, "I appeal to you, brothers, by the name of our Lord Jesus Christ, that all of you agree, and that there be no divisions among you, but that you be united in the same mind and the same judgment." The Corinthians are divided and should not be. They must confess a common faith, striving to be united in mind and purpose.

The Foolishness of Preaching

In verse 18 of the same chapter, Paul reminds them, "For the word of the cross is folly to those who are perishing, but to us who are being saved it is the power of God." The same gospel which had saved members of this church was folly to their Greek compatriots who had not yet been enabled to believe the gospel by the power of God—specifically through the work of the Holy Spirit. It is human sin which blinds people to the truth of the gospel. It is because of human sinfulness that prejudice toward the things of God arises. Paul's point is that those who love worldly wisdom hate the things of God, because the very notion that God is holy and that he will punish all human sin flies in the face of human wisdom.

First Corinthians

It should strike us that although Greeks saw the cross as a word of folly, nevertheless, a growing (if struggling) church now existed in Corinth in the very heart of Greco-Roman paganism. Why is that? The cross may indeed be foolishness to a Greek, it may indeed be a stumbling block to a Jew, but to those who have been called by God to faith in Jesus Christ, the cross is the very power of God. Paul has identified the problem—human sin blinds people to truth, so that they turn to human wisdom for solutions to their problems. Paul also explains that the message of the cross is God's chosen method to summon God's people to faith, yet in the balance of the chapter (vv. 6–16), Paul reminds us that only through the work of the Holy Spirit can Jews and Greeks come to see the cross for what it is—a demonstration of the wisdom and power of God.

In the closing words of chapter one, Paul had pointed out the irony of the fact that although Greeks see the cross as foolishness, God sees the so-called wisdom of the Greeks as nothing more than human foolishness. The Greeks claim to love wisdom. According to such wisdom, the cross is folly. Yet God says the so-called wisdom of the Greeks is the real folly. Mocking those who love such wisdom, and who take great pride in discovering the keys to a successful and happy life through the various pagan religions of Greco-Roman world, God was pleased to create a church through the proclamation of a message which worldly-wise Greeks could not grasp. The very existence of a growing church in Corinth proves Paul's point. The cross is the demonstration of the wisdom and power of God. But that wisdom is the very thing that human or worldly wisdom refuses to acknowledge.

To make this same point from yet another perspective, Paul reminds the Corinthians in verses 26–29 of chapter one:

> For consider your calling, brothers: not many of you were wise according to worldly standards, not many

were powerful, not many were of noble birth. But God chose what is foolish in the world to shame the wise; God chose what is weak in the world to shame the strong; God chose what is low and despised in the world, even things that are not, to bring to nothing things that are, so that no human being might boast in the presence of God.

Again mocking those who think themselves wise, God reveals his wisdom (the greatest of all treasures) to the very people whom the worldly-wise Corinthians regarded as crude, rude, and contemptible. The gospel cannot be discovered by the philosopher, debater, or the lover of wisdom no matter how wise about worldly things they may be. God must reveal true wisdom through what is preached—the account of a crucified and risen Messiah. To the chagrin of the worldly-wise, God reveals his wisdom to the very people the worldly-wise despise—those not wise, not noble, not powerful. In fact, God has chosen to save such people to shame the wise.

While Paul is reminding the Corinthians that God mocks those who love worldly wisdom, his main point is that if God calls the foolish and the weak so as to shame the wise, then the Corinthians need to begin to act in a spirit of humility. How can they form into factions around their favorite teachers if the whole idea of having a favorite teacher reflects the Greek love of wisdom and devotion to particular celebrities? In this, the Corinthians were just like us. Greeks loved the articulate and dynamic speaker. The Corinthians judged public figures by how they looked, and by how well they kept the audience entertained. Because these things are all a matter of personal preference, soon the Corinthians were divided and fighting among themselves over matters of opinion. This, of course, is where worldly wisdom takes us. One human opinion is as good as another.

First Corinthians

Human Wisdom as a Standard of Evaluation

That said, we need to understand that wisdom is not necessarily a bad thing *if* we are referring to that wisdom revealed by God—even when such wisdom is found in the natural order. What Paul is condemning is human wisdom when it is used as a technique to capture someone's attention so as to convince them of something which is not true. While rhetoric (and the ability to debate or communicate well) is not an evil in itself, the Greeks tended to substitute what they regarded as wisdom, for the wisdom God reveals in his word. But many of them sensed this worldly-wisdom could only take them so far. Plato had even written in the *Phaedo* that he longed for "a raft" of revelation—"some word of God."[1] Paul also knew that the Greek fascination with the skill and eloquence of the speaker was misguided. Instead of seeking truth, or seeking to understand the problem of human sinfulness and God's solution to it, the Greeks of Paul's day substituted their own wisdom for God's revelation. Then, based on that worldly wisdom, Greeks laughed at the cross because they thought it foolish. This is the kind of wisdom which Paul now condemns, and which God mocks.

The Greek did not ask whether Paul's message could be true, and then evaluate the evidence and the truth of what the apostle proclaimed. Rather, Paul's message didn't make any sense, so the Greeks mocked it. Paul was a poor speaker and from one account a rather plain looking rabbi. He did not fit their expectations and cultural norms regarding who was wise and who was not. Paul did not look like a philosopher. He did not speak like a skilled rhetorician. In fact, one ancient source (written about AD 160) recounts Paul's appearance as follows: "A man small in stature, bald-headed, crooked in legs, healthy, with eyebrows joining, nose rather long."[2] In other words, Paul was not some-

---

1. Plato, *Phaedo*, para. 85d.
2. From "The Acts of Paul," cited in Daniel J. Theron, *The Evidence of Tradi-*

Jesus Christ and Him Crucified

one likely to impress a sophisticated pagan audience used to spell-binding oratory from a seasoned rhetorician.

Add to this the fact that Paul's message—the holy God had offered his own Son as a sacrifice for sin—was an offence to those who were perfectly capable of offering sacrifices to the gods in any of the countless pagan temples in town. To argue that there was one true God, that he took to himself a human nature (cf. John 1:1–14), and allowed himself to be crucified by the Romans, made little sense. Paul's preaching was strange and different. Paul was strange and different. None of this fit with Greco-Roman expectations, therefore it was regarded as foolishness.[3] Yet all the while God is mocking paganism by saving Greeks and Romans through Paul's preaching, demonstrating yet again, that God's wisdom shames the wise.

The Source of True Wisdom

Those Corinthians who had listened to Paul, and were converted by the power of the Holy Spirit, were now enabled to see the cross for what it was—God reconciling the world to himself in Christ (cf. 2 Cor. 5:17). This was a message which created faith in the very person whom Paul was proclaiming (Jesus), while at the same time calling all who embraced Christ through faith to leave behind their pagan ways of thinking and doing. The Corinthians grasped the former (the gospel), but were struggling with the latter (giving up pagan ways).

The irony is that Paul was offering the Greeks and the Romans the very thing they claimed to love—true wisdom. Whenever the cross was preached and the wisdom of God in dealing with human sin was revealed (which is the fundamental problem in all of human life), the Greeks did not want to hear Paul's gospel. His message did not meet their needs (or so they

---

tion (Grand Rapids: Baker, 1980), 35.

3. Barrett, *The First Epistle to the Corinthians*, 68.

thought). It was not to their liking. In this regard, the ancient Corinthians are exactly like people in our own day. They may claim to love wisdom. Yet through that message, God exposes the fact that the Greek quest for wisdom was nothing more than a clever excuse to reject that one truth people do not want to face—that we are guilty before a holy God.

Paul recounts his own personal history with the Corinthian church in verses 1–2 of chapter two. Paul writes, "And I, when I came to you, brothers, did not come proclaiming to you the testimony of God with lofty speech or wisdom. For I decided to know nothing among you except Jesus Christ, and him crucified." In the Greek text, the emphatic "and I" (*kago*) indicates that Paul does not make an exception for himself. He did not come to the Corinthians as an eloquent orator, or as a wise sage, nor as a professional philosopher, dazzling the Corinthians with his compelling preaching, his wise advice, or with great abilities to answer the riddles of life. No, Paul came as the apostle to the Gentiles. He proclaimed the testimony about what God had done in Jesus Christ to save sinners from both the guilt and the power of sin. Although the preaching of Christ crucified perplexed (if not offended) the Greeks, and caused Jews to stumble, Paul preached the message of the cross regardless.

Why would the apostle preach a message which he knows is going to offend those to whom he is preaching? Paul knows that it is only through the gospel that God calls his people to faith. As Calvin points out, "It is as if [Paul] said 'the disgrace of the Cross will not prevent me from looking up to him who is the source of salvation, or make me ashamed of finding all my wisdom summed up in Him—Him, I say, whom proud men treat with disdain, and reject on account of the reproach of the cross.'"[4] Paul preached the message of the cross and the empty tomb despite knowing the offense it would cause. The apos-

---

4. Calvin, *The First Epistle of Paul to the Corinthians*, 49.

Jesus Christ and Him Crucified

tle preached that Jesus died in the sinner's place, bearing the wrath of God in his own body, and then God raised Jesus from the dead as proof of his victory over sin and its consequences. Paul's preaching amounted to recounting the facts of the gospel as Christ had commanded him to do, because this is the message through which the Holy Spirit demonstrates the wisdom and power of God, made manifest in the conversion of sinners.

In fact, in 1 Corinthians 15:3–8, Paul defines the gospel as follows:

> For I delivered to you as of first importance what I also received: that Christ died for our sins in accordance with the Scriptures, that he was buried, that he was raised on the third day in accordance with the Scriptures, and that he appeared to Cephas, then to the twelve. Then he appeared to more than five hundred brothers at one time, most of whom are still alive, though some have fallen asleep. Then he appeared to James, then to all the apostles. Last of all, as to one untimely born, he appeared also to me.

To preach the gospel (or to share Christ with our neighbor) is to tell people that they are sinners (which is the purpose of the law—cf. Rom. 3:20), and then to lay out the historical facts surrounding the life, death, and resurrection of Jesus as recounted in the four gospels. Through that simple message, God was pleased to call wise Greeks to faith in what they had previously regarded as folly. God is pleased to do the same today!

Christ and Him Crucified

Paul did not focus upon the cultural expectations of his audience. Paul did not find the hot topic of the day, and then tell jokes and use stories or anecdotes to keep the Corinthians in rapt attention. Paul did not wear the distinctive attire (or trendy clothing) or use the mannerisms of the philosopher or sage. But

First Corinthians

Paul is emphatic that he made it his single-minded purpose to concentrate all of his preaching on a particular message, "Jesus Christ and him crucified." This is why the centrality of the cross in Christian preaching is as vital to maintain in our own day and age as it was in Paul's. Like the Corinthians, modern mankind loves to be entertained and informed. We want our preachers to be clever and witty, hip and up to date, on top of latest cultural trends and technology—the same thing the Corinthians expected. As proud people, we do not like to be confronted with our own sins, and then told we can do nothing to save ourselves, and that instead, we must trust in someone else (Jesus Christ) to do for us what we cannot do for ourselves.

Because of our sinful prejudices against such a message, we must learn to avoid evaluating the sermon we heard the last Lord's Day by the kinds of categories favored by the Corinthians, such as whether we were amused, entertained, or merely found something helpful about how we live our lives. As Paul sets forth this section of 1 Corinthians, the biblical question we must learn to ask is this: "Were the riches and treasures of Jesus Christ on display, and was his death and resurrection proclaimed as the ultimate means of dealing with the human condition?" This is where Paul directs us to find the wisdom and power of God—the cross of Jesus Christ.

The term "crucified" (*estaurōmenon*) is a perfect passive participle, which describes something done in the past which has effects that continue on into the present.[5] What God had done with his Son Jesus Christ, crucified on a Roman cross on a particular Friday afternoon just outside the city walls of Jerusalem about twenty years before Paul wrote this Corinthian letter, will continue to impact everyone who hears Paul's message. Then, as now, the preaching of Christ crucified summons all who hear it to faith, stirring them to renounce their own righ-

---

5. Hays, *First Corinthians*, 35.

Jesus Christ and Him Crucified

teousness, acknowledge their sin (as revealed to them through knowledge of the law), and then humbly accept Christ's payment for our sins as the only means of entering heaven. When we hear this message, are we willing to acknowledge our sins, and admit our need for a Savior? This is the goal and primary purpose of Christian preaching, then and now. In fact, as Paul tells us elsewhere, he cared little about a preacher's motives or apparent success, as long as the cross of Christ was proclaimed (Phil. 1:18).

When it came to the content of his preaching, Paul virtually eliminated everything else from his proclamation. He wore no Greek attire, he used no Greek rhetoric or logic, and told no stories. In the first two verses of 1 Corinthians 2, Paul virtually repeats his statement made to the Galatians: "It was before your eyes that Jesus Christ was publicly portrayed as crucified" (Gal. 3:1). In the cross, the wisdom and power of God are made manifest. Therefore, Paul will preach Christ crucified and nothing else. To preach the cross (in the Pauline sense) is to describe the work of Christ so vividly and graphically in his preaching, that it were as though Christ had been set before the audience on a billboard.

This declaration should serve as the basis for all subsequent Christian preaching and witness to non-Christians. God's wisdom and power are not manifest in tips for practical living (application-based or moralistic preaching), nor in therapeutic preaching (i.e., "God wants you to be happy."), in motivational preaching ("Get out there and be a champion for Christ!"), nor in the wisdom of the sages or the eloquence of the orators (the reason why people like Joel Osteen pack out basketball arenas turned-churches). God demonstrates his wisdom and power in the preaching of the scandalous message of Christ crucified, wherein Christ's righteousness, holiness, and redemption are revealed for all to see.

First Corinthians

Paul's assertion is remarkable because, apparently, the apostle was coming under a fair bit of criticism from the Corinthians because he was not keeping people on the edge of their pews during his sermons. Paul was not particularly eloquent, nor was he able to impress people with his own wisdom. He was not a charismatic man, nor an exceptional leader. In 2 Corinthians 10:10, Paul confesses that "they say, 'His letters are weighty and strong, but his bodily presence is weak, and his speech of no account.'" As Paul himself puts it, "And I was with you in weakness and in fear and much trembling, and my speech and my message were not in plausible words of wisdom, but in demonstration of the Spirit and of power, that your faith might not rest in the wisdom of men but in the power of God" (2 Corinthians 2:3–5).

Paul admits to being nervous, and was probably physically sick and certainly weary in body when he had been among the Corinthians earlier. This explains his reference to weakness and fear (1 Cor. 2:3). Paul had preached in Thessalonica, Berea, and Athens and was forced to flee to Corinth for his life. When he first arrived in the city, he was in need of rest. Throughout all of this (as recounted in Acts 17–18) we see that Paul did not fear men because he feared God. Nevertheless, Paul was human. He struggled with fear and human weaknesses just like everyone else. But it was in Paul's weakness that the power of God was made manifest.

Everything we know about Paul's life and ministry seems to indicate that Paul was not a particularly impressive speaker, and that he was painfully aware that people were criticizing him. His poor speaking style and lack of personal presence was what gave his enemies an open door to challenge his doctrine and his apostolic authority. In this, Paul was just like Moses (perhaps Israel's greatest historical figure), who likewise worried about his own unfitness to confront the Pharaoh as recounted in Exodus 4:1ff., only to be reminded that God's ability to do as he promised did not depend upon Moses' eloquence. In fact, Moses' difficulty in public speaking only made it all the more evident that God's power did not depend on human efforts! Just as this was true for Moses, it was true for Paul. Paul may not have been an impressive figure or a dynamic speaker. But he did know the gospel of Christ crucified, and he knew God's power to convert sinners was tied to that message.

A Demonstration of the Spirit's Power

Therefore, Paul preached a very specific message (the cross of Jesus Christ). Even though he was not worldly wise, and he did not seek to tickle the ears of the Greeks in places like Corinth, nevertheless, Paul can speak of his preaching as accompanied by "a demonstration of the Spirit and of power." Readers of 1 Corinthians have long debated what Paul means by this. The context tells us that Paul does not mean by this demonstration of the Spirit's power what we might call "signs and wonders," as some contemporary Pentecostals contend.[6]

No doubt there were signs and wonders in the apostolic age. There may have been signs and wonders when Paul first came to Corinth. Paul will even mention signs and wonders later on in this letter in connection to the gifts of the Spirit (chapter 12). But signs and wonders are not mentioned in Luke's account of Paul's arrival in Corinth in Acts 18. Luke merely says that Paul went first to the synagogue and preached Christ to the Jews gathered there. Neither is there any hint that this is what Paul means here when he speaks of the demonstration of the Spirit's power.[7] Remember that while we live in the age of the

---

6. Stanley M. Burgess and Gary B. McGee, eds., *Dictionary of Pentecostal and Charismatic Movements* (Grand Rapids: Zondervan, 1988), s.v. "Gifts of the Spirit."

7. Contra Fee, *The First Epistle to the Corinthians*, 95. Fee correctly regards this as conversion, but thinks it is primarily evidenced by speaking in tongues as a demonstration of power.

Holy Spirit, the wonder of Pentecost is not that those assembled in the upper room spoke in tongues (as dramatic as that was). Rather, the wonder of Pentecost is that through the preaching of a mere fisherman (Peter), God converted some three thousand people. The same holds true here.

What, then, does Paul mean when he speaks of a demonstration of the Spirit's power? As he just said, the Spirit's power is manifest in the fact that Jews and Greeks, who were dead in sin, and who could never understand God's wisdom if left to themselves, have now been united to Jesus Christ through faith. The demonstration of the Spirit's power was such that through the message of the cross, God exposed the worldly wisdom of the Greeks which kept people from the kingdom of God. The demonstration of the Spirit's power is seen in the fact that there is a growing church in Corinth. Through the scandalous message of the cross (where God's wisdom and power are revealed and wherein the Spirit manifests his power), God called many Jews and Greeks to faith in Jesus Christ. This is how the power of the Spirit is made manifest. The dead are raised, given new life, and granted faith in Christ through the preaching of the cross.

When, in verse 5, Paul writes "that your faith might not rest in the wisdom of men but in the power of God," we learn the reason as to why this is so. Because Paul's preaching is not centered in human wisdom, eloquence, or persuasion, the Christian faith rests upon the person and work of Christ (the historical facts of the gospel), where God's wisdom and power are clearly revealed. Our faith rests upon God's power (his election and calling of sinners), his gift of faith, and the subsequent justification and sanctification of sinners, as demonstrated in the power of God who raised Jesus Christ from the grave. To put it simply, the preaching of the gospel of a crucified Savior is the demonstration of the Spirit and the power of God. It is through the preaching of a crucified Savior that God gives life to the dead and saves the guiltiest of sinners. What the Greeks mock, God uses to save sinners.

There are three points of application we should take with us from this passage. First, we are surprisingly like the Greeks of Paul's day. We too love worldly wisdom. Because we do, we too tend to evaluate preachers and sermons based upon how they make us feel, rather than whether or not the minister was faithful to the text he was preaching. We live in an age when people think preaching is boring, and many Christians are not really interested in doctrine or the teaching of Scripture. To avoid this lack of interest (and when using worldly wisdom), preaching is often transformed into another form of entertainment. We hear comments such as, "Was the preacher funny?" "Did the worship service keep us entertained?" "Were there practical tips for living a better life?" "Did I experience something which stirred my emotions?" These are the criteria of worldly wisdom. This is the very thing going on in Corinth and for which Paul was taking the Corinthians to task. We need to be discerning. But we must use the proper standard of evaluation, which is God's Word.

In light of Paul's point, certain questions arise which we should ask concerning those who preach to us. "Was the sermon clear and did I understand what the minister was saying?" "Was there appropriate application drawn from the text upon which the sermon was based?" "Did the sermon (even if based upon an Old Testament text) ultimately point me to the saving work of Jesus Christ, in his three-fold office of prophet, priest, and king?"

But if we are to expect certain things from those who preach to us, there are things those who preach to us should expect from those who listen. "Do we pray for those who bring to us the words of life?" "Do we prepare ourselves to listen carefully to the sermon by reading the text for the sermon in advance and meditating upon it?" "Do we complain that the preaching is not 'practical enough' or that the sermons are boring when what we really want is not to be confronted with the difficult things the Bible expects us to believe, think, and do?" We may be more like the Corinthians than we are willing to admit.

Second, for Paul, everything centers upon the content of his message—Jesus Christ, and him crucified. Whenever the Word is opened and proclaimed, we are hearing wisdom from God, not mere opinion. This is not an excuse to turn a sermon into a lecture, nor is it an excuse for the minister to be boring or ineffectual as a communicator. But it is to say that the preaching of Christ is the means God himself has chosen to be the primary means of evangelism, and the means of creating faith in the hearts of his people. If you are concerned about evangelism, then focus on telling people the facts associated with the doing and dying of Jesus. This is what Paul did. This is what Paul tells us to do. You do not need to be a great speaker or a charismatic person to engage in evangelism with your neighbors, coworkers, or even family. All you need to know is that God saves sinful people through the proclamation of this particular message. And if God's saves sinners through the story of a crucified Savior, then the real question is, "Do you know the message well enough to communicate it to others?" Chances are, you do! It really does come down to this; "Are we confident that, through the work of the Holy Spirit, God will bless the communication of the gospel to others, even if we do not see immediate results?" If we are to learn anything from Paul in the opening verses of 1 Corinthians it is that eloquence and rhetorical skill count for little. The gospel is the power of God unto the salvation of sinners. That fact alone liberates us to engage in the work of evangelism without being crippled by fear of criticism or failure.

Finally, the message of Christ and him crucified is certainly a test of orthodoxy and the basis for Christian preaching and evangelism. But that is not all it is. Whenever the cross of Je-

Jesus Christ and Him Crucified

sus Christ is proclaimed, God will summon his people to trust that the sacrificial death of Jesus saves us from our sins. When we hear the message of Christ and him crucified, we are being summoned by God to trust in Jesus Christ. Through the life and death of the suffering Savior, God promises to forgive our sins and grant us eternal life. But God demands that we respond to this summons in faith. There is only one thing which spares us from the wrath of God on the day of judgment, and that is Jesus Christ and him crucified.

So, only one question remains. "Do you trust God's promise that the death of Jesus will save you from the wrath of God sure to come?" "Will you give up seeking human folly disguised as wisdom and instead place your trust in Jesus Christ, the crucified Savior?" As the hymn writer Toplady so wonderfully describes this act of trust in the third stanza of the famous hymn *Rock of Ages*: "Nothing in my hand I bring, simply to thy cross I cling; naked come to thee for dress; helpless look to thee for grace; foul I to the fountain fly, wash me Savior, or I die."

5

For the Spirit Searches Everything

1 CORINTHIANS 2:6–16

But we impart a secret and hidden wisdom of God, which God decreed before the ages for our glory. None of the rulers of this age understood this, for if they had, they would not have crucified the Lord of glory. But, as it is written, "What no eye has seen, nor ear heard, nor the heart of man imagined, what God has prepared for those who love him"—these things God has revealed to us through the Spirit. For the Spirit searches everything, even the depths of God. For who knows a person's thoughts except the spirit of that person, which is in him? So also no one comprehends the thoughts of God except the Spirit of God.

If people are dead in sin, and the message of Christ crucified comes to them as either foolishness or a stumbling block, why is it then that the Apostle Paul insists so strongly on the proclamation of the cross of Jesus Christ? The reason is simple. Paul knows that it is through the preaching of Christ and him crucified that the Holy Spirit calls those whom God has chosen (whether they be Jew or Greek), creates faith in their hearts, and then unites them to Christ. Although this message causes Jews to stumble and confounds Greeks, it is through the preaching of Christ crucified that we see the demonstration of the wisdom of God and the power of the Holy Spirit. The great paradox laid out by Paul is that what the world regards as wisdom, God regards as foolishness. And what the world regards as foolishness is the same message through which God reveals his wisdom and power.

As we have seen, a huge gap exists between Christian and non-Christian thinking. Realizing this fact helps us understand why it is that God must grant us understanding of spiritual things. If not, the cross will remain foolishness to us. This is why a true understanding of the gospel must be revealed to us by God, since the gospel can never be discovered by human wisdom. If the Corinthians fail to grasp this point, the church in Corinth will continue to struggle with the same kind of issues facing them: schism and division, sexual immorality, lawsuits, and improper conduct in worship.

We come to an important question raised by Paul in the closing verses of 1 Corinthians 2. If true wisdom comes from God, and yet is seen by Greeks as foolishness, how is it that people come to faith in Jesus Christ? This, Paul says, is the work of the Holy Spirit.

The Rulers of This Age

In verses 6 and 7 Paul writes, "Yet among the mature we do impart wisdom, although it is not a wisdom of this age or of the rulers of this age, who are doomed to pass away. But we impart a secret and hidden wisdom of God, which God decreed before the ages for our glory." In these verses, Paul contrasts the wisdom of men and true wisdom (i.e., that which comes from God). When, in verse 6, Paul speaks of the wisdom of this age (true worldliness), he ties such wisdom to the rulers of this age.

For the Spirit Searches Everything

But what does Paul mean when he connects the wisdom of this age to those who rule?

The mention of rulers (*archontes*) may be a reference to principalities and powers—demonic influences—as mentioned in 2 Corinthians 4:4, Romans 8:38–39, and Colossians 1:15. Since Paul has not mentioned demonic influences earlier in this epistle, but has repeatedly referred to human wisdom, it is far more than likely his reference to "rulers" points to Jewish and Roman authorities—such as Pilate and Caiaphas (cf. Acts 3:17; 4:5, 8; Rom. 13:3)—men who, in the wisdom of this age, put God's wisdom incarnate (Jesus) to death (cf. 2:8 below).[1] These rulers may exercise temporal power, but like everything else associated with this present evil age (cf. Gal. 4:4), their rule is destined to perish and will come to nothing. The irony is that one day they will bow the knee before the same Savior they have crucified.

Christians speak forth true wisdom among the mature (*teleioi*). When making this point, Paul refers to those who have reached their aim or goal. The irony is that those who are not wise, powerful, or of noble birth, but who trust in Christ, actually reach their goal, which is the discovery of true wisdom. They have been called to faith through the preaching of the gospel, in which the wisdom of Christ is revealed. But none of the "wise" sages, compelling orators, or brilliant philosophers of this age will ever find this wisdom or discover it on their own. The irony is that the worldly wise never do find the true wisdom they claim to be seeking.

Paul describes this true wisdom as "secret wisdom from God." Such wisdom is unlike the wisdom of this age because it had previously been hidden, yet is something which God has destined for our glory before time began. God's wisdom has been a mystery (something hidden until revealed, and therefore

---

1. Morris, *1 Corinthians*, 53–54.

"secret" in this sense), not something enlightened philosophers and sages can uncover through divination, speculation, or any other occult or magical practices typical of Greco-Roman religion. Until the coming of Christ, God's wisdom was hidden in the types and shadows of the Old Testament, rather than *kept* from God's people as the word "secret" seems to imply. The sense here seems to be that when the fullness of time came, God sent forth his Son (cf. Gal. 4:4), revealing that which had been hidden. To put it another way, God's wisdom is hidden from the world until it is revealed in the person of Jesus Christ.

With the coming of Jesus Christ, Paul believes a new eschatological age has dawned (the "age to come"). That which was hidden in the Old Testament (the wisdom and power of God, now manifest in the true righteousness, holiness, and redemption that is in Christ) is now fully revealed, or brought out into the open. With the coming of Christ, the wisdom of "the age to come" (the eternal) now stands in contrast to the "wisdom of this age" (the temporal). The connection between the coming of Christ and the revelation of what had previously been hidden means that Christ's person and work, along with Christ's relationship to the end times, are at the very heart of Paul's theology.[2] This explains why Paul speaks of the fact that what was revealed was foreordained by God for our well-being. God did this to bring his people to glory, which is the final state of maturity.

This also explains the rather stark declaration about human wisdom we find in verse 8. "None of the rulers of this age understood this, for if they had, they would not have crucified the Lord of glory." God's wisdom can only be known and understood through divine revelation. The rulers of this age (i.e., Pilate and Caiaphas) did not and could not understand God's

---

2. Ridderbos, *Paul: An Outline of His Theology* (Grand Rapids: William B. Eerdmans, 1975), 44–57. See also: Geerhardus Vos, *The Pauline Eschatology* (Grand Rapids: Baker Book House, 1979), 1–41.

wisdom, therefore, they crucified Jesus Christ, the Lord of glory. Recall that at the time of his crucifixion, Jesus said: "Father, forgive them, for they know not what they do" (Luke 23:34). The fact that the rulers of this age crucified wisdom incarnate is further proof that these leaders are rebellious sinners who have no clue as to what true wisdom actually entails.

Either these rulers did not understand the gospel because it centered in the cross (a scandalous message), or because they could not conceive of God in human flesh (how can God, who is pure spirit, take to himself a human body?).[3] The rulers of this age could not understand why God would save sinful people through the means of a cross—an instrument of torture reserved for the worst of criminals. Because human sinfulness and divine grace are often discussed using the categories of the wisdom of this age, it is no wonder that non-Christians often operate on the mistaken assumption that good people will be rewarded and bad people will be punished. This is the fundamental religious principle of modern western culture, just as it was in ancient Greece.

Sadly, this false conclusion is where human wisdom leaves us. The irony is that through the gospel, God saves repentant bad people, like tax-collectors, prostitutes, and other "sinners" to whom God reveals his Son as wisdom incarnate, while condemning the prophet, the sage, the wise man to whom these things remain hidden. A crucified Savior is a contradiction to someone who thinks that they are basically a good person. Recall, it was the self-righteous religious people who hated Jesus the most (cf. Luke 15:2). Yet for anyone who knows themselves to be a sinner before a holy God, a crucified Savior is our only hope of heaven and eternal life.

The "Lord of glory" is one of the most exalted titles applied to Christ in the whole of the New Testament. Throughout the

---

3. Barrett, *First Epistle to the Corinthians*, 70.

Scriptures, glory is closely connected to God the Father (cf. Acts 7:2; Eph. 1:17). Paul sees Christ as sharing in that glory, assigning to Christ a glory equal to that of YHWH. To call Jesus the "Lord of glory" is but another way of identifying Jesus as God in human flesh. If the Jews and Romans had even remotely grasped Christ's true identity, Caiaphas and Pilate would have never put him to death. They acted in ignorance because they were blinded by human sinfulness.

The contrast between how the rulers of this age and those to whom God's wisdom is revealed, could not be any greater. Paul sets this out in verse 9. "But, as it is written, 'What no eye has seen, nor ear heard, nor the heart of man imagined, what God has prepared for those who love him.'" The formula "it is written," is often used to indicate a direct citation from the Old Testament, but what follows is not a direct citation of a single verse, but is likely a paraphrase of Isaiah 64:4, with allusions to Psalm 31:20, or Isaiah 52:15 and 65:17.[4]

Regardless of the source of the quotation, its meaning is clear. In Isaiah 64, the prophet is describing the uniqueness of YHWH. He is not known by those who do not trust in him. God's way of salvation was hidden from unbelievers, but God has prepared this plan of salvation from before the foundation of the world for those whom he loves. The human eye cannot conceive of it, the ear cannot hear it, the heart cannot understand God's plan regarding it. Paul's use of heart (*kardia*) is worth notice. For a Greek, the heart was not just the seat of emotions, but was the whole of the inner life.[5] Paul's point is that God's plan of salvation cannot be grasped by human thinking, human emotions, or human willing. Yet, God is working out his plan, and the cross is not some random accident of history. The incarnation of Jesus and his death on the cross was

---

4. Hays, *First Corinthians*, 44.
5. Morris, *1 Corinthians*, 56.

For the Spirit Searches Everything

God's purpose from the very beginning. That this is saving truth is something God must reveal to those who trust in him. Unbelievers will never understand this while they still employ the categories of the wisdom of this age.

True Wisdom is Revealed by the Holy Spirit

In the next few verses (10–13), Paul emphasizes a single point—that which cannot be discovered by human wisdom, and which was hidden (the fact that God will save sinners through the cross of Jesus Christ), must be revealed by the Holy Spirit.

> These things God has revealed to us through the Spirit. For the Spirit searches everything, even the depths of God. For who knows a person's thoughts except the spirit of that person, which is in him? So also no one comprehends the thoughts of God except the Spirit of God. Now we have received not the spirit of the world, but the Spirit who is from God, that we might understand the things freely given us by God. And we impart this in words not taught by human wisdom but taught by the Spirit, interpreting spiritual truths to those who are spiritual. (v. 10–13)

In establishing this point, we now see the huge gulf which exists between Christian and non-Christian ways of thinking. God's wisdom cannot be discovered by philosophers and sages. Such wisdom must be revealed by God. Since it must be revealed by God, it can only be truly comprehended by faith. And this is the role of the Holy Spirit, illuminating our minds so that we understand what God says and that we accept what God says as truth.

In verse 10, Paul draws another sharp contrast between God's wisdom and human wisdom. The philosophers and sages did not discover these truths, but God revealed it to those of us whom the world regards as foolish. The agent of this revelation is the Holy Spirit. Paul's stress clearly falls upon the fact that God "reveals" his wisdom through the gospel. This emphasis can be seen in the fact that Paul mentions the Holy Spirit six times in verses 10–14. The Holy Spirit not only reveals these things to us, but the Spirit searches the deep things of God, because no human is capable of fathoming the innermost depths of the divine being.[6] Since the things we need to know to be saved must be revealed to us by the Holy Spirit, this precludes the possibility of people coming to faith by any other means than the preaching of the gospel—not through human willing, nor human goodness. The Holy Spirit must reveal these things to us.

There are strong parallels in Paul's discussion here with Jesus' discussion of the Holy Spirit in John 16:8–15. There Jesus says that the Holy Spirit will teach the disciples certain truths about him which, otherwise, they could never learn— that the Holy Spirit will convict the world of sin, teach God's people about Christ's righteousness, and then warn the world of judgment. We find God's wisdom about how he will save sinners revealed in the Scriptures and nowhere else. While much can be learned through general revelation, such as God's invisible attributes and divine nature, (cf. Rom. 1:20), as well the moral law, (cf. Rom. 2:14–15), the gospel cannot be learned from nature.

Part of the problem in Corinth was a proto-gnosticism in which sages, philosophers, and false religions all claimed to have discovered "wisdom," which they, in turn, were willing to reveal.[7] There is no real secret wisdom apart from the Spirit's revelation of the mind of God. God reveals his wisdom when-

---

6. Morris, *1 Corinthians*, 56–57.

7. According to Thiselton, "Certainly there are points of affinity with later Gnosticism," but notes that problems dating the rise of a system of Gnosticism are notoriously difficult. See Thiselton, *The First Epistle to the Corinthians* NIGTC, 92.

For the Spirit Searches Everything

ever Paul or someone else preaches the word of the cross.[8] The gospel is public (cf. Gal. 3:1ff.), not private, or secret. God announces to everyone how he will save them. This is why the gospel is "good news" which must be announced to people through preaching and evangelism.

Paul further explains this point by using an analogy in verse 11. As we know our own minds (self-consciousness), so the Holy Spirit knows the will of God. No philosopher, sage, or wise man knows the mind of God. But the Holy Spirit, who is God, knows the mind of God. Unless this knowledge is revealed to us, we cannot figure out what God is doing. Unless God reveals himself and his purposes to us through the Holy Spirit in his word, we have nothing but the "spirit of the world," or, as Paul put it earlier, the "wisdom of this age." If all we have is "the spirit of the world," then all we have is folly.

In verse 12, the contrast between Christians (the "foolish") and unbelievers (who think themselves wise) continues. Unlike the rulers of this age and those who are influenced by them, who have the spirit of the world and who think like non-Christians, we have God's Spirit, who reveals these things to us freely. Some take Paul to mean that the spirit of the world is connected to Satan or the demonic (cf. Eph. 2:2 where Paul says "in which you once walked, following the course of this world, following the prince of the power of the air, the spirit that is now at work in the sons of disobedience," or in a passage such as John 12:31—"Now is the judgment of this world; now will the ruler of this world be cast out"). While this interpretation is possible and supported by other Pauline texts,[9] since Paul is opposing human wisdom (the so-called "wisdom of this age" in v. 6), not a satanic or occult form of wisdom, I think it better to understand Paul to be speaking of human wisdom in contrast

---

8. Barrett, *Epistle to the Corinthians*, 74.
9. Barrett, *Epistle to the Corinthians*, 75.

to the wisdom of God. God's wisdom comes without cost. We need not pay a sage, a wizard, or a consultant for such wisdom, because God's wisdom is freely given in the gospel. From this perspective, worldliness is thinking like a pagan—"good people go to heaven, bad people go to hell," or "the purpose of life is to gain pleasure and to avoid pain," and so on.

Christians, who are indwelt by the Holy Spirit, think in a certain way and use a certain set of categories to interpret the world. Calvin speaks of the Word of God supplying the spectacles through which the Holy Spirit brings things into focus.[10] Non-Christians, on the other hand, think in a worldly-wise manner because all they know is the spirit of the world. This is not a question of one's intelligence or education. Paul does teach us in Ephesians 4:17–19 that sin clouds human thinking about eternal matters. The gulf cannot be bridged by human wisdom, but only by divine revelation and illumination. The Holy Spirit is the only one who can bridge this gap. This is why many pastors include a prayer for illumination prior to the reading and preaching of God's word. It is vital that the same Spirit who breathed forth the Word of God written, enable God's people to understand it when it is read or proclaimed to them.

Obviously, this has profound ramifications for Christian evangelism and apologetics, theology, and ethics. We cannot argue someone into saving faith, although we can show them that their unbelief is irrational and that there are good reasons to embrace the gospel. We cannot expect non-Christians to fully understand Christian theology (the facts perhaps, but not the substance). Nor can we expect non-Christians to live lives of gratitude before God and perform genuine good works, although, through general revelation and common grace, non-Christians can and certainly do live outwardly moral lives (a civic righteousness). But non-Christians cannot understand the

---

10. Calvin, *Institutes*, 1.6.1.

wisdom of God made manifest in the cross which is freely given to God's people through the work of the Holy Spirit.

Spiritual Truths

Paul's preaching of the cross, which may not have been as motivational, as exciting, or as entertaining as that of other preachers familiar to the Corinthians (criteria based upon worldly-wisdom), nevertheless, is that which God has revealed in the person and work of Christ. Therefore, in verse 13, Paul can state that in the gospel he preaches, "We impart this in words not taught by human wisdom but taught by the Spirit, interpreting spiritual truths to those who are spiritual." Those truths revealed by God in his Word are to be proclaimed and taught to others. Human words entertain, motivate, and excite. They contain worldly wisdom. But God's word reveals his wisdom as to how a holy God can justify the wicked (Rom. 4:5). The cross is therefore a spiritual word, which must be spiritually discerned. Since the wisdom of God is seen in the cross, the true meaning of which must be given by the Spirit, to preach the cross of Christ is to preach "spiritual words," not secret words. The gospel is that "good news" which non-Christians cannot accept unless the Spirit enables them to do so.

The contrast between believer (the spiritual man) and unbeliever (the natural man) comes to full relief in verses 14–16. It is the work of the Holy Spirit which determines whether someone is an unbeliever or not. This has nothing whatsoever to do with human wisdom, intelligence, or ability. This, of course, presents great problems for all forms of Arminianism, semi-pelagianism, and views of decisional regeneration in which it is argued that sinners have it within themselves the ability to take that first step toward God. Paul says something quite different. "The natural person does not accept the things of the Spirit of God, for they are folly to him, and he is not able to understand them because they are spiritually discerned. The spiritual person judges all things, but is himself to be judged by no one. 'For who has understood the mind of the Lord so as to instruct him?' But we have the mind of Christ."

In verse 14, Paul makes his point with great clarity. That person who does not have the Holy Spirit (the *psychikos* man) does not "accept" the things (the wisdom or word) that comes from God, through the Holy Spirit. The Greek word to "accept" (*dechomai*) means something like "welcome."[11] The cross remains "foolishness" to an unbeliever because they are not able to determine the cross's saving efficacy apart from the work of the Spirit. As we have been saying, this idea has profound ramifications for our doctrines of salvation and ethics, and should inform all attempts to interact with non-Christians in any evangelistic or apologetics context. Our confidence should not be in our personal testimony or in our power to persuade. Our confidence should be in the wisdom of God and the power of the Holy Spirit revealed in the gospel.

Non-Christians do not understand the gospel because the meaning of the cross is spiritually discerned. To them, God saving "sinners" while rejecting "good" people constitutes an injustice. The fact is that God saves whom he will save through the death of his Son. The self-righteous cannot see this. But the Christian (the *pneumatikos*) makes judgments upon all things, because through the work of the Holy Spirit, he sees things through the lens of Holy Scripture.

A Christian sees things in light of God's wisdom, and not in the dim light of the wisdom of this age. A Christian is no longer subject to the foolish judgments of the sages and philosophers, who call God's wisdom foolishness, all the while God mocks their wisdom as foolishness. As Christians, we have the mind of Christ (illumination), because we are indwelt by the Holy Spirit,

---

11. Morris, *1 Corinthians*, 58.

For the Spirit Searches Everything

who knows the mind of God, and who has revealed to us God's wisdom in the cross.

Paul does not mean we know all things, or even that we know all spiritual things infallibly. Since we are indwelt by the Holy Spirit, we view things from the perspective of Christ crucified. In other words, we have a Christian perspective on things grounded in God's wisdom from the age to come, which the apostle now speaks of in terms of having the mind of Christ. As Christians, we see things in light of biblical categories, not in the light of pagan wisdom. We think like Christians, not like unbelievers, because the Holy Spirit has given to us the mind of Christ. It all comes down to the simple fact that God's ways are not our ways and that his thoughts are not our thoughts (Isa. 55:8). Non-Christians look for God in all the wrong places, and they reject that very message (the cross) wherein everything they need to know to find true wisdom is revealed.

As but one example of the contrast between God's wisdom and human wisdom with which we are apt to be familiar, whenever Christian parents present their children at the font for baptism, it is because they believe God's covenant oath, "I will be your God and you will be my people." In doing so, they seek to ratify that oath through the baptism of their child. But the non-Christian will say, "This doesn't make any sense. The child is not old enough to decide for themselves. Why should the parents force their religion on their child—shouldn't the child be free to choose for himself?" Christian parents do this because God once said to Abraham, "As for you, you shall keep my covenant, you and your offspring after you throughout their generations. This is my covenant, which you shall keep, between me and you and your offspring after you: Every male among you shall be circumcised'" (Gen. 17:9–10).

First Corinthians

Here is the point—infant baptism (which has replaced circumcision under the new covenant) is not about the child deciding anything. It is about God promising something—to keep his covenant promise. If this is the case, then we see God's wisdom in requiring the baptism of children of believers, precisely because infant children of believers cannot yet do anything in relation to God. Baptism is tied to Christian parents believing God's promise. Yet this is the very thing lost to those who think in worldly categories. God's wisdom and power are manifest in the presence of human weakness and sin. A child is not wise, noble, or powerful. His parents are not worldly-wise, noble, or powerful. We are not wise (on pagan terms), noble, or powerful. That is the whole point.

Sadly, the degree to which we fail to grasp this point will be the degree to which we are tempted to replace the wisdom of God with our own. Worldly wisdom directs us to find that place where the action is. Such "wisdom" tells us to look for the "buzz" surrounding the latest Christian celebrity or fad. Worldly wisdom tells us that biblically-based sermons about Jesus which don't have much to do with my latest personal trial or difficulty at work are probably to be avoided. Worldly wisdom tells us that we should pick a church based on the kind of programs offered for our kids, or on the fact that the praise band sounds a bit like the band I just saw in concert. Worldly wisdom is fascinated with fame, celebrity, and power. It is the very antithesis of that which Paul instructs us to seek, for the wisdom of the world does not trust God's ways nor does it find them "relevant."

If we are in Christ, we are indwelt by the Spirit of God. Therefore, we have the mind of Christ. This is why we are to look for the wisdom of God and a demonstration of the Spirit's power precisely in those places where we are weakest. This is why Christianity will always remain foolishness to a Greek

For the Spirit Searches Everything

and a stumbling block to Jews. God reveals his wisdom and power in the cross, that message through which the Spirit of God demonstrates his power. But this means giving up much of what we hold dear and what we prefer. It also means admitting that God's ways are right and ours are wrong, and this is never easy.

6

The Foundation

1 CORINTHIANS 3:1–15

According to the grace of God given to me, like a skilled master builder I laid a foundation, and someone else is building upon it. Let each one take care how he builds upon it. For no one can lay a foundation other than that which is laid, which is Jesus Christ. Now if anyone builds on the foundation with gold, silver, precious stones, wood, hay, straw—each one's work will become manifest, for the Day will disclose it, because it will be revealed by fire, and the fire will test what sort of work each one has done. If the work that anyone has built on the foundation survives, he will receive a reward. If anyone's work is burned up, he will suffer loss, though he himself will be saved, but only as through fire.

Although we are reluctant to admit it, many of us raised in church can identify certain passages of the Bible that we would rather not hear preached, or that we do not enjoy reading or studying. This does not come about because of a disdain for the Word of God, or because we do not want to be convicted of sin. This reluctance comes about because at some point in the past, these passages which now trouble us have been misinterpreted or misapplied by someone who turned the passage into a source of fear or discomfort. It is my guess that Paul's discussion of being "saved through fire" is such a text for many.

Although Greeks see the cross of Christ as foolishness, and Jews stumble at the thought of a crucified Messiah, Paul has made his case that the cross of Jesus Christ is the revelation of the wisdom of God as well as a demonstration of the Holy Spirit's power. In this third chapter of his second letter to the Corinthians,[1] Paul addresses the specifics of what is going wrong in the church in Corinth. The Corinthians still heavily rely on human wisdom instead of that wisdom revealed by God through the preaching of the gospel. This reliance on human wisdom has led to a host of problems in the Corinthian church, beginning with the formation of various factions. As Paul will remind the Corinthians, the sole foundation of the church has already been laid through the preaching of the gospel. The question the apostle now puts to the Corinthians is, "What kind of church are they building on that foundation?" As good Greeks, the Corinthians love human wisdom. Although Corinthian Christians seem to understand the gospel, there is an intellectual struggle going on in this church as these new Christians are slow in learning to think like Christians. At the same time they are having trouble leaving their pagan ways behind.

In this section of his letter, Paul makes his case that the Corinthians are immature. Paul rebukes the Corinthian church for this lack of maturity using two vivid metaphors: adults (mature) vs. infants, and solid food vs. milk. Paul uses these familiar figures of speech to illustrate the false assumption on the part of the Corinthians that they are making real progress in the Christian life, when in fact they are not making much progress at all.[2] The

---

1. First Corinthians is actually the *second* letter Paul sent the Corinthians (1 Cor. 5:9). See my discussion of this on pp. xxx–xxxi of this volume.

2. Hays, *First Corinthians*, 48.

behavior of many in this congregation demonstrates that they are anything but mature. The reality is they are behaving like spiritual infants. The wisdom of God has not sufficiently informed their thinking or their conduct.

Time to Move on to Maturity

In the first verse of chapter 3, Paul addresses the problem with the Corinthians' failure to fully understand the source of true wisdom. "But I, brothers, could not address you as spiritual people, but as people of the flesh, as infants in Christ." Paul softens the coming rebuke a bit by referring to the Corinthians as "brothers," a term of endearment. These are people with whom he lived and labored for some time. Despite Paul's deep and abiding personal affection for these people, the congregation is about to receive a strong apostolic rebuke.

When Paul had been with the Corinthians earlier, he could not speak to them as "spiritual" (*pneumatikoi*), or mature (adults), but as "worldly" (*sarkinoi*), a term which literally means "fleshy." As new Christians and mere babes in Christ, the Corinthians were still conformed to the non-Christian patterns of this age in their thinking about the Christian life and related issues. It is hard to unlearn non-Christian attitudes and ways of thinking. When people become Christians, it takes time to stop thinking like unbelievers. Paul, no doubt, carefully considered this when he began to instruct them previously. He knows this is a struggle for the Corinthians. It is all too clear to the apostle that the Corinthians should have made much more progress than they have.

Paul reminds the Corinthians in verse 2 of how he had taught them personally. "I fed you with milk, not solid food, for you were not ready for it. And even now you are not yet ready." Since the Corinthians were infants and unable to digest solid food, Paul gave them milk. Milk is a metaphor for the basic doctrines of the Christian faith which are taught to new Christians—doctrines such as the Trinity, the deity of Christ, justification by grace alone through faith alone on account of Christ alone. The practice of teaching such doctrine to new Christians is what we commonly identify as catechesis, or "instruction." It was not the Corinthians' fault that they were infants. Paul took them as he found them, and fed them accordingly.[3]

The current situation in Corinth reflects the same level of immaturity in which Paul had found them when the initial members of this church came to faith in Christ. The Corinthians should have grown up by now. Sadly they have not. In fact, says Paul, these people still are not ready for solid food! The reason why their growth is so badly stunted is given in verses 3–4. "For you are still of the flesh. For while there is jealousy and strife among you, are you not of the flesh and behaving only in a human way? For when one says, 'I follow Paul,' and another, 'I follow Apollos,' are you not being merely human?"

Instead of showing signs of maturity, the Corinthians are still fleshy. That said, it is important to notice that the new Christians in Corinth could not help being *fleshy* because they were new Christians after all. Yet, the Corinthians should be moving toward maturity, and they are not. Their conduct is characterized by behavior typical of non-Christian Greek pagans, the same behavior they exercised before their conversion. For Paul, the "flesh" (*sarkikoi*) is a characteristic way of speaking of the sinful human nature which lies at the heart of what Paul has been calling "worldliness." The contrast which Paul sets out is between those who have the mind of Christ (*pneumatikois*) and who have matured in their thinking, with those who still act like pagans because they still have the mind of this age (i.e., the

---

[3]. *The Heidelberg Catechism* (1563), as but one example, was written for the purpose of providing doctrinal instruction for children and new converts in the central teachings of the Bible, as well as establishing a common theological language and ethos within the church (even among the mature).

fleshly).[4] It is those who demonstrate such immature behavior who come under Paul's rebuke.

This immature and "fleshy" mindset (characteristic of non-Christians) manifests itself in the following behavior. There are factions forming in the Corinthian church, with two of the most significant factions, apparently, centered around Paul and his close associate, Apollos. The members of these factions were now openly quarreling with each other, and apparently, each group was jealous (envious) of the other. This divisive behavior, Paul says, is that of mere men—i.e., people who conform themselves to the wisdom of this world, not the wisdom of God manifest in the cross. Instead of focusing upon God and his purposes made manifest in the preaching of Christ crucified, the Corinthians are focusing upon their personal and selfish agendas. This kind of immaturity is nothing but a manifestation of the flesh.

Christian Ministry Entails Service

To stop the formation of factions in the church, Paul must address the subject of what Christian ministry truly entails—service. A minister is called to serve the whole church, not to lead or encourage that portion of it who are attracted to him or to his teaching. Paul must also address the nature of the church itself and the foundation upon which it is built, the person and work of Jesus Christ.

To form factions around Paul and Apollos is to completely misunderstand what Paul and Apollos were actually doing. Paul and Apollos are not sages or philosophers, nor are their individual personalities and teaching/preaching styles what ultimately mattered when it came to their effectiveness. Rather, both men are servants of Jesus Christ, called to specific offices (church planting v. instruction in the faith). Paul exposes the immaturity

---

4. See Barrett, *Epistle to the Corinthians*, 80, on the point that *pneumatikoi* should be understood as "mature."

of the Corinthians by using one of his characteristic rhetorical questions in verse 5. "What then is Apollos? What is Paul? Servants through whom you believed, as the Lord assigned to each."

It is important that we notice that Paul does not ask "who" are Paul and Apollos, but "what" are Paul and Apollos. It is the immature person who focuses upon the personalities involved ("the who"), while Paul sees the office ("the what") to which he and Apollos have been called to be the critical issue. Paul and Apollos are mere servants (*diakonoi*) of Christ. The word (servants) is translated elsewhere in the New Testament as "deacons," which became a distinct office within the church devoted to the ministry of mercy (cf. Acts 6:1–7). Here Paul uses the term to refer to the fact that in one sense, all ministers are servants. How can servants be put up on a pedestal and made to be leaders of divisive factions? It is through the differing ministries of Paul and Apollos, that many in the Corinthian church came to faith in Christ. Paul and Apollos are merely the sinful human instruments that God has used to create and build the church in Corinth.[5] Yet, this is what the Corinthians failed to grasp and this remains an issue today when people treat leaders in the church as celebrities, or when they pit them against one another, seeking to see factions form around them.

Since it is the Lord who called them to their unique offices, Paul uses the following analogy in verses 7–8: "I planted, Apollos watered, but God gave the growth. So neither he who plants nor he who waters is anything, but only God who gives the growth. He who plants and he who waters are one, and each will receive his wages according to his labor." Botanical metaphors are used elsewhere by Paul. One of the most important is in Romans 11:11–24, where Paul speaks of Christ as the righteous root and Jews as natural branches, and Gentiles as wild

---

5. Barrett, *Epistle to the Corinthians*, 84.

The Foundation

branches. These metaphors made perfect sense in the first century Mediterranean world which was an agrarian society.

Paul and Apollos clearly have different callings. Paul is the evangelist/church planter. He plants the seed (founds the churches). Apollos, on the other hand, does the work of caring for the Lord's vineyard through teaching and instructing. He waters the seed Paul has planted, ensuring by God's grace that it grows. Paul and Apollos are only ministers (Christ's servants). Paul and Apollos are allies in this cause, and not rivals, as their followers were making them out to be. It is God who creates churches by his Word and Spirit through his called ministers, and it is God alone who brings about the growth of these newly-planted through these ordained means. Paul and Apollos may have different roles, but they only have one goal.

Since it is God alone who grants the increase, why divide into factions over the style and abilities of God's servants who merely plant and water? Paul and Apollos are nothing. It is God who causes all things to grow. Although Paul and Apollos have different callings (and different styles and abilities), since God is the one who grants the increase, Paul and Apollos actually have one common purpose. Church planting and evangelism are not more important than catechizing and shepherding God's flock. The critical thing to consider here is that God will reward his servants not according to their worldly success, but according to their faithfulness.

The Church as God's Garden and Temple

The conclusion in verse 9 naturally follows from what has gone before. "For we are God's fellow workers. You are God's field, God's building." In the original Greek, the word *theos* is placed first in the three clauses as a point of emphasis. It is God who reveals Jesus Christ to us, and who calls us to place our trust in him. It is God who gives us his Holy Spirit, and it is God who grants the increase when churches are founded, non-Christians are evangelized, and then Christians are grounded in their faith. This means that the church, and all who are in it, are God's garden. Because the church is Christ's, people are not free to cause division and form their own factions. Paul and Apollos, along with all those in the church, are fellow workers. We are all part of God's field (garden), and therefore, we are all in need of care and cultivation. We cannot uproot ourselves at will and create a new garden. Nor should we view our ministers as Christian celebrities who lead their own factions. Ministers are servants, who preach the word, administer the sacraments, and provide pastoral care for the churches.

Notice that Paul introduces a new metaphor which he will use throughout the balance of the chapter. He points out that we are all part of God's building (the temple of which he will speak in verses 16–17). Those who have the mind of Christ realize the organic nature of the church, while those who are fleshly see the church through the same lens as do non-Christians. For such people, personalities, self-interest, and false standards of evaluation such as "was the worship and the sermon entertaining?" are more important than God's purposes and the faithful preaching of Christ.

Following the change in metaphor from a garden to a building, (no doubt, based in part upon the theological connection between Israel's temple and the church), Paul reminds his immature readers that the foundation of the church is none other than Jesus Christ himself. The language used by Paul echoes various Old Testament descriptions of the temple (specifically in terms of how it was built and consecrated). One such passage to which Paul is probably alluding is 1 Chronicles 29:1–5, where the high quality and quantity of the gold and silver used in the temple's implements is mentioned, along with the desire God's people have to consecrate themselves to the Lord in response

The Foundation

to the grandeur before their eyes. Paul's point is that if Christ is building his temple (the church), and we are part of that temple, then who are we to destroy what Christ himself is building? Furthermore, who are we to build a building of our own upon another foundation? This is why the Corinthians must exercise both care and caution in the building of the church. The Corinthian church is Christ's, not theirs! The same goes for us today.

For Paul, the building of the church and its organic unity must be seen in relationship to the grace of God (v. 10–11). "According to the grace of God given to me, like a skilled master builder I laid a foundation, and someone else is building upon it. Let each one take care how he builds upon it. For no one can lay a foundation other than that which is laid, which is Jesus Christ." First and foremost, Paul's labors and success have come about because of the grace of God. God has enabled the apostle and the other servants of the gospel who have served the Corinthian church (e.g., Apollos) to do what he has done.

Take Care in Building God's Church

Paul describes himself as a skilled builder—literally a "wise" builder (*sophos*), or one who supervises the construction of a building (*architektōn*). Through the preaching of the cross, Paul has laid the foundation, which is Christ. Someone else (presumably Apollos) is now building upon that same foundation by instructing the Corinthians in Christian doctrine. Since the foundation is Christ (specifically the message of the cross, foolishness to the Greek, stumbling block to the Jew, but to those who are being saved the very power of God), men who build upon that foundation must be very careful. Just as Israel brought the best gold and silver into the house of God to be used for the vessels and implements in the temple, so too the Corinthians should be careful about how they seek to build the house of God (the church), on that foundation which Paul has already laid.

First Corinthians

This is, no doubt, a warning for the church to maintain sound doctrine, and for Christians to avoid being conformed to the pattern of this age. As Paul reminds the Ephesians (cf. 4:4–6), "There is one body and one Spirit—just as you were called to the one hope that belongs to your call—one Lord, one faith, one baptism, one God and Father of all, who is over all and through all and in all." Sound doctrine must be taught, and immature Christians must become mature. Indeed, since the foundation of the building (temple) which God is building is Christ and him crucified, there can be no other foundation than the one that Paul has already set down when he first preached the gospel in Corinth.

In verses 12–15, Paul warns the congregation (and her ministers):

> Now if anyone builds on the foundation with gold, silver, precious stones, wood, hay, straw—each one's work will become manifest, for the Day will disclose it, because it will be revealed by fire, and the fire will test what sort of work each one has done. If the work that anyone has built on the foundation survives, he will receive a reward. If anyone's work is burned up, he will suffer loss, though he himself will be saved, but only as through fire.

Unfortunately, this passage is often used to terrorize Christian consciences. "If you have not done enough for Christ and his church, you will suffer loss." Sadly, this misses the point of the apostle's warning.

Although there is but one foundation (Jesus Christ), there are any number of various building materials with which a building may be built. There are materials of great worth (silver, gold, and costly stones). There are materials which are ultimately worthless (wood, hay, and straw). The workman may try to build a building worthy of the foundation (using God's wisdom

The Foundation

to do it), or else he may build a cheap and useless edifice upon a precious foundation (using human or worldly wisdom). One either builds the church through the preaching of the cross and through instruction in sound doctrine, or else one attempts to build the church through the wisdom of men which inevitably creates factions and division. One is worthy of the foundation, the other is not. One of these buildings will survive the struggles sure to come, the other will not. As Hodge puts it, "False doctrine can no more stand the test of the day of judgment, than hay or stubble can stand a raging conflagration."[6]

Paul is clear that one day there will come a time of testing. Most likely, "the day" is a reference to the day of judgment (cf. 1 Thess. 5:4). This is when the works of God's people are judged and accepted in Jesus Christ, whose wisdom is then vindicated in the transformation of his people along the lines expressed in Ephesians 2:10—"For we are his workmanship, created in Christ Jesus for good works, which God prepared beforehand, that we should walk in them." Paul speaks of fire consuming the efforts of those who build with wood, hay, and straw upon the foundation of Christ, while those who build with silver, gold and precious stones, will be rewarded (literally, "be given his wages"). Those who utilize flimsy building materials will barely escape judgment, and their efforts to build Christ's church will be seen as futile and not worthy of the glorious foundation upon which they have been laid.

In light of the way this passage is often interpreted, it is important to point out that Paul is not warning Christians that they had better make more progress in their sanctification, or else they will perish. Paul is not telling Christians that unless they give their all (i.e., gold, silver, and precious stones), and stop being half-hearted (wood, hay, straw), they risk perishing on the day of judgment. Rather, Paul's point to the Corinthian

---

6. Hodge, *I & II Corinthians*, 57.

church is that human wisdom is mere wood, hay, and straw, which are not at all worthy of the foundation (Christ and him crucified) Paul laid down through the preaching of the gospel.

Building a church on human wisdom inevitably leads to division and factionalism. Rather, Paul warns, we must adopt God's ways, grounded in God's wisdom, in our effort to build Christ's church. This is what Paul means when he speaks of gold, silver, and precious stones. These things withstand both difficult times and divine judgment. God's wisdom is worth far more in this building process than any materials we can come up with on our own.

We also need to carefully consider Paul's warning about the seriousness of factions and schism within the church. The church is Christ's—it is not ours. To divide his body into factions, or to treat Christian leaders, pastors, and teachers as though they were celebrities to be followed by groupies and adoring fans, is to demonstrate gross spiritual immaturity. Instead, Paul exhorts us to see those who labor among us as servants who minister the word of Christ to us. This is why we need to see the church as the body of Christ, and not someone's personal empire or property. The entrepreneurial spirit is the engine of capitalism (and that may be a good thing), but it does not work well in the church. The church is not the place for men to build monuments to themselves. The church is that place where men serve Christ by applying God's wisdom to the fundamental human problem—our sin. The solution to this problem is, as Paul sees it, the continual preaching of Christ crucified.

Finally, Paul reminds us that the foundation of the church is Jesus Christ as he is preached in the true gospel. The content of the gospel then is the foundation upon which the church is built, and this message reveals to us the wisdom of God and its application to the various aspects of the Christian life. Through the preaching of Christ, God has called us to faith, and united us to-

The Foundation

gether into one body, one church, with one common faith. We are God's garden. We are God's building—God's temple as Paul puts it later in the chapter, indwelt by God's Spirit. There are no other foundations, and there is no other gospel. God calls some of us to plant, some of us to water, some of us to tend the garden in various ways. This is why we take such great care about how we build on the one foundation. By laboring together, we are building a church from gold, silver, and precious gems. By centering everything we do upon Christ and him crucified, each one's work will be manifest, and our labors will withstand both the trials of life and the judgment of God.

This is true because Jesus Christ shed his blood for all of our sins, fulfilled God's law through his perfect obedience, so that trusting in Christ alone we need never fear the wrath of God again. It is only in the gospel of Jesus Christ that we have the unshakable foundation upon which to build Christ's church. This glorious promise should comfort the people of God and encourage them to rely more and more on the wisdom of God and the cross of Christ. It is a shame that this passage has been used to terrorize the consciences of tender-hearted Christians when its true purpose is to point us to that foundation which cannot be shaken—the saving work of Jesus Christ.

7

You Are God's Temple

1 CORINTHIANS 3:16–23

Do you not know that you are God's temple and that God's Spirit dwells in you? If anyone destroys God's temple, God will destroy him. For God's temple is holy, and you are that temple.

Growing up in independent Bible-church fundamentalism, I recall hearing a number of sermons stressing the fact that our bodies are a temple of the Holy Spirit. While this was the reason usually given as to why we should not smoke cigarettes or drink alcoholic beverages, we were never told what it means to be the temple of the Holy Spirit, nor were we told how this doctrine should inform our view of the church. For Paul, the fact that Christ's church is the temple of the Holy Spirit (who indwells each one of us) must be fundamental to our conception of the nature of the church. Seeing Christ's church in this light explains why the divisions and factions in the Corinthian church were so destructive. To divide Christ's body (God's spiritual temple indwelt by the Holy Spirit) is to attempt to destroy that which God is building through the preaching of Christ crucified. Paul warns the Corinthians of the serious consequences of tearing apart that which God is building in their midst.

First Corinthians

Paul has been using irony to make a point. The Greeks think Paul's message of a crucified Savior is foolishness. The cross makes no sense to someone steeped in Greco-Roman culture. Yet Christians know that Christ's cross is the power of God unto salvation. In the preaching of Christ crucified the wisdom of God is revealed. It is this revelation of God's wisdom which exposes the so-called wisdom of the pagans for what it truly is—foolishness. In making this point, Paul has skillfully exposed the fact that the Greek quest for wisdom is not a quest for wisdom at all. Rather, the philosophers, prophets, and sages reject the very wisdom they claim to be seeking. They claim to be seeking the truth. Yet, the reality is that they are suppressing the truth in unrighteousness (cf. Rom. 1:18).

The new Christians in Corinth must understand that God's wisdom is revealed through the proclamation of the cross of Christ, even though that message offends Greek sensitivities. Paul sees the root of the problem in the fact that many of the Corinthians were still devoted to the worldly wisdom of their recent past. It was this typically Greek love of celebrities, entertaining public speakers, and philosophers who had all the answers to life's problems, which led the Corinthian Christians to devote themselves to those individuals in the church who had taught them when they first came to faith (Paul, Apollos, and Peter).

Sadly, the Corinthians quickly divided into cliques centering around their favorite teachers—even though those who taught them would never have encouraged the slogans being heard in the Corinthian church. "I follow Paul." "I follow Peter." "I follow Apollos." According to Paul, this mindset demonstrates the sad fact that even though the Corinthians may have thought themselves to be mature and making good progress in the Christian life, the reality is that this behavior actually demonstrates their spiritual immaturity and proves how deeply pagan ways of thinking and doing still dominate this church.

You Are God's Temple

In the opening chapter of his letter, Paul exhorted the Corinthians, "I appeal to you, brothers, by the name of our Lord Jesus Christ, that all of you agree, and that there be no divisions among you, but that you be united in the same mind and the same judgment" (v. 10). The Corinthians are to be united around a common faith and common doctrine. As Paul fleshes out his point in the next several chapters of this letter, he reminds us in the first half of chapter 3 of the organic nature of Christ's church. Christ's church is not a club, or some sort of voluntary society, like one of the pagan guilds which dominated Corinth. According to the inspired Paul, we are all part of God's garden of which Christ is Lord. Some are called to plant the seed, some are called to water the seed once planted, while others are called to tend various portions of the garden.

At this point in his letter, the apostle introduces the metaphor of the church as a building, making a theological connection between the temple as that place where God dwelt in the midst of his people under the old covenant, and the work of the Holy Spirit, who indwells believers, forming us into a living temple under the new covenant. This spiritual temple has been built upon the unshakable foundation of the cross of Jesus Christ, that foundation which Paul laid down when he first arrived in Corinth and preached the gospel to them. As Paul puts it in verse 11 of chapter 3, "For no one can lay a foundation other than that which is laid, which is Jesus Christ."

Since the foundation has already been laid, Paul exhorts the Corinthians to consider the fact that human wisdom is only so much wood, hay, and stubble. Any attempt to build Christ's church upon the sinful expectations of human wisdom, is to build a church that cannot withstand hard times, nor the judgment of God. Instead, Christians must build on the foundation of the gospel, using those elements given by God which reflect the wisdom of God (i.e., silver, gold, and precious stones). These are the things which withstand both difficult times as well as the judgment of God.

In the closing verses of chapter 3 (vv. 16–23) Paul now makes explicit what was implied in the previous portion of his argument. The building of which he has been speaking is the temple of God, which is the mystical body of Jesus Christ. This spiritual temple (the church) is that place where God's Spirit dwells with his people.

Jesus Christ: The True Temple of God

Throughout Paul's epistles, whenever he speaks of the temple, he is referring to Christ's church.[1] This is quite remarkable when we consider that when Paul wrote this letter to the Corinthians in the mid-fifties of the first century, the Jerusalem temple was still standing. The temple was not destroyed by the armies of Titus until AD 70, another fifteen years or so after Paul composed this letter. When Paul points out that the church—not the building, but its members who are indwelt by the Spirit—constitutes the true temple of God, this must have come as quite a shock to those Jews who may have heard Paul's preaching.

For Paul, the coming of Jesus Christ has changed everything. In light of the doing and dying of Jesus, God's people understand that the earthly temple, and the tabernacle which preceded it, were not an end in themselves, as Jews had come to believe. Rather, these physical structures should have served to point Israel ahead to the age of the new covenant in which God will dwell in the midst of his people in a way that transcends anything found in the Old Testament.

For a Jew, however, the Jerusalem temple was at the very center of Jewish religious life. The temple was that place where the high priest offered the sacrifices in the Holy of Holies, and

---

1. See the discussion in: G. K. Beale, *1–2 Thessalonians: IVP New Testament Commentary Series* (Downers Grove, IL: InterVarsity Press, 2003), 207–208.

You Are God's Temple

that place to which the faithful journeyed during the annual Passover. Not only that, but the Jerusalem temple was also the political and cultural center of all of Israel—like Big Ben in London, or the Eiffel Tower in Paris. The Jerusalem temple was a magnificent building that dominated the entire city. To say, as Paul does, that the temple was no longer that place where God was present with his people, was to challenge one of the fundamental tenants of the Jewish religion. To say that the Jerusalem temple had been superseded by a crucified Messiah, was a huge stumbling block to any Jew.

Yet this is exactly what Paul had been preaching. The Jerusalem temple was superseded by the coming of Jesus Christ, who declared himself "greater than the temple" (Matt. 12:6). No matter how magnificent, the building in Jerusalem had been rendered obsolete (cf. Heb. 8:13). In fact, Jesus even went so far as to proclaim that he was the true temple. In John 2:18–22, we read of the following exchange between Jesus and the moneychangers in the temple.

> The Jews said to him, "What sign do you show us for doing these things?" Jesus answered them, "Destroy this temple, and in three days I will raise it up." The Jews then said, "It has taken forty-six years to build this temple, and will you raise it up in three days?" But he was speaking about the temple of his body. When therefore he was raised from the dead, his disciples remembered that he had said this, and they believed the Scripture and the word that Jesus had spoken.

As John points out (John 2:22), this point did not became clear to Jesus' disciples until after his resurrection and Pentecost, when the Holy Spirit was poured out on all flesh. In light of the events associated with the Day of Pentecost as recounted in Acts 2, Christians have now become living stones in a spiritual temple. As we read in 1 Peter 2:4–5, "As you come to him [Jesus], a living stone rejected by men but in the sight of God chosen and precious, you yourselves like living stones are being built up as a spiritual house, to be a holy priesthood, to offer spiritual sacrifices acceptable to God through Jesus Christ." Christ's church is that spiritual house, composed of living stones, those who are indwelt by the Holy Spirit.

If Paul's doctrine that Christ was the true temple was a shock to Jews, this point is also an important response to the paganism which dominated Corinth. The Corinthians lived in a city filled with pagan temples which were dedicated to the individual members of the pantheon of pagan Greek or Roman gods. These temples were shrines to that particular "god" for whom they were named, and they were places where those who worshiped a particular god went to make the obligatory sacrifices to receive the blessing and protection of that deity. Paul responds to this notion that the "gods" were like super-humans who resided in these holy spaces built for them by their followers. He does so by pointing out that the true and living God is not bound to a particular building or place. God dwells in us.

In verses 16–17, Paul writes, "Do you not know that you are God's temple and that God's Spirit dwells in you? If anyone destroys God's temple, God will destroy him. For God's temple is holy, and you are that temple." From a Christian perspective, God, who is everywhere, resides with his people whenever and wherever they assemble for worship. This fact not only separates Christian worship from Judaism—Christians need not have a geographical center for their faith—this also distinguishes Christianity from paganism, who view their gods much like the super-heroes of American pop culture. The pagan gods are petty and angry, and must be placated through the offering of sacrifices (food, incense, coins, etc.). They must be venerated (or placated) through the building of elaborate temples and through the performance of very specific ceremonies and rituals. Paul's doctrine of the omnipresence of God undercuts all of this. Our God dwells within and among his people whenever we assemble for worship. We (his people) are his temple.

Living Stones in a Living Temple

The history of redemption reflects Paul's point. After God delivered his people from Egypt, and when he made a covenant with his people at Mount Sinai, he commanded Moses to build a tabernacle in which God would be present in the midst of the Israelites. As we read in Exodus 40:34–38, after Moses finished building the tabernacle,

> Then the cloud covered the tent of meeting, and the glory of the Lord filled the tabernacle. And Moses was not able to enter the tent of meeting because the cloud settled on it, and the glory of the Lord filled the tabernacle. Throughout all their journeys, whenever the cloud was taken up from over the tabernacle, the people of Israel would set out. But if the cloud was not taken up, then they did not set out till the day that it was taken up. For the cloud of the Lord was on the tabernacle by day, and fire was in it by night, in the sight of all the house of Israel throughout all their journeys.

The presence of God is seen in the pillar of fire (the cloud) and reappears on the Day of Pentecost when what looked like tongues of fire appeared over the head of each believer (Acts 2:3).

According to 2 Chronicles 7:1ff., when Solomon completed the first temple in Jerusalem, and after the ark had been brought in and the temple had been properly furnished, we read,

> As soon as Solomon finished his prayer, fire came down from heaven and consumed the burnt offering and the sacrifices, and the glory of the Lord filled the

> temple. And the priests could not enter the house of the Lord, because the glory of the Lord filled the Lord's house. When all the people of Israel saw the fire come down and the glory of the Lord on the temple, they bowed down with their faces to the ground on the pavement and worshiped and gave thanks to the Lord, saying, "For he is good, for his steadfast love endures forever."

Under the new covenant, all believers are living stones who make up God's temple when we assemble for worship. As God's glory now fills the spiritual temple when we assemble together to hear the word and receive the sacrament in the power of the Holy Spirit, we are to worship the Lord and respond with hearts of gratitude, because "he is good!"

When Paul begins verse 16 with a question, "Do you not know?" he is offering a bit of a rebuke. The question itself implies that what Paul is about to ask the Corinthians should be common knowledge, but they still are not grasping his point. All believers are part of God's temple, not just those who teach (i.e., Paul and Apollos). Believers compose the temple of God, because the Holy Spirit lives in them, since he indwells each member of Christ's church. We should notice that "temple" is singular, but the "you" is plural. We should not think that the individual by himself is God's temple (although Paul does speak that way in 1 Corinthians 6:19). Rather, his point here is that believers are all indwelt by the Holy Spirit, and together form the temple of God. There is an organic nature to the church, and it is important that we not overlook this point because it explains why the divisions and factions within the church are so serious. Division and schism rip apart Christ's spiritual temple. For Christians to divide into factions centered around those who teach and preach to us is a dangerous thing. It does great harm to Christ's church.

You Are God's Temple

Division in the Church Is Sinful

As Paul puts it in verse 17, such things and the individuals who participate in them, destroy the temple. The consequences of this are grave. God will destroy all those who bring about such division! If anyone destroys God's temple, God will destroy him. This is a very serious warning. Jesus reminds us in Matthew 16:18 that the gates of hell will not prevail against his church. Yet, it must be pointed out that such destruction may not refer to eternal punishment—after all, Paul has just told us in verse 15 that such people escape through the flames. However, this warning certainly indicates that there are serious consequences for all those who create division and form factions in the church. At the very least, their efforts will be frustrated by the Lord of the church himself. God's temple (the mystical body of Jesus Christ) is holy, and Paul warns that all who bring harm to it, will indeed, be punished by God.

Having made his point that believers form God's temple, in the closing verses of the chapter, (vv. 18–23), Paul returns to his main focus that the divisions in the Corinthian church are sinful because they stem from worldly wisdom, which, in actuality, is from God's perspective only foolishness. Paul began his discussion of true wisdom vs. false wisdom back in 1:18, and although he will refer back to that theme later on in this epistle, this section brings this discussion of wisdom to a conclusion. As one writer reminds us, "The things of God are not to be estimated in accordance with the rules of the philosophers."[2] This faulty perspective, of course, has been the root of the problem in Corinth. Church members are viewing spiritual things from the perspective of the philosophers—that is, from the perspective of this present evil age.

---

2. Morris, *1 Corinthians*, 68.

Paul warns in verse 18, "Let no one deceive himself. If anyone among you thinks that he is wise in this age, let him become a fool that he may become wise." Paul exhorts the Corinthians to realize the importance of seeing things related to the church from God's perspective, not from the perspective of the world. The verb "to deceive" (*exapatatō*), is used six times by Paul, but is not found anywhere else in the New Testament. The apostle issues this command here, emphasizing the fact that some of the Corinthians were deceiving themselves by hanging on to the wisdom of this age after coming to faith in Christ, and this self-deception must stop. The way this stops is to focus upon Christ and him crucified.

Those who are deceived, Paul says, are using the standards of "this age" to evaluate the way things ought to be done in the church. This error is what the Corinthians must grasp. For this present age is evil (that is, it is fallen), is dominated by Satanic deception, and it and everything associated with it is destined to perish (cf. Gal 1:4; 2 Cor. 4:4). The sad fact is that the wisdom of this age is still serving as the lens through which many of the Corinthians viewed Paul's gospel. Sadly, this is the lens through which many of our contemporaries still view Paul's gospel.

Paul's response to this matter is to exhort those doing this to see things from the perspective of the age to come (and therefore, to view the church and their behavior in the light of God's wisdom as revealed in the cross through the power of the Holy Spirit). The Corinthians must do this, even though the world will regard such wisdom as foolishness. They must face their pagan past and the temptation to return to that past, a temptation which is always present. But they must leave these things behind in order to move on to maturity. And so too must we.

Paul elaborates on this further, in the following verses (vv. 19–20). "For the wisdom of this world is folly with God. For it is written, 'He catches the wise in their craftiness,' and again,

You Are God's Temple

'The Lord knows the thoughts of the wise, that they are futile.'" In 1 Corinthians 1:20, Paul already asked the rhetorical questions, "Where is the one who is wise? Where is the scribe? Where is the debater of this age? Has not God made foolish the wisdom of the world?" Now he makes the very same point a second time. God mocks the wisdom of this age. Although the Corinthians may be impressed by it, God sees it for what it is: foolishness, futile, craftiness. To become truly wise, Christians must embrace the very thing the philosophers they admire regard as foolishness. True wisdom is found in God's revelation of a bloody Savior hanging upon a cross, and not in the so-called wisdom of this present evil age. As Christians, the only way we live lives of gratitude before God is to see things through the lens of the age to come, and not through the distorted vantage point of this present age.

Citing from Job 5:13, and then in verse 20, from Psalm 94:11, Paul understands full well that while the craftiness of men may fool others (they may have even fooled themselves), they have not fooled God. The Lord knows their thoughts and the outcome of their thinking. He knows the result of their thinking is futility (literally, "fruitless"). Like everything else associated with this age, such thinking is destined to perish. Why, then, should Christians remain so attracted to it? It only brings damage to the church.

Boast Only in the Lord

In light of this, Paul issues the following instructions in verses 21–23, "So let no one boast in men. For all things are yours, whether Paul or Apollos or Cephas or the world or life or death or the present or the future—all are yours, and you are Christ's, and Christ is God's." The first thing we should note is that Paul instructs the Corinthians that there will be no more boasting about mere men, apostles included. To pit Paul against Apollos, Peter, or others, as the Corinthians were doing, is to be deceived by the worldliness and foolishness of which Paul has been so critical.

However, there is an acceptable form of boasting for Paul, which he has already spelled out in 1 Corinthians 1:31. "Let the one who boasts, boast in the Lord." The question here is, "Why limit yourselves to boasting about those who teach you, when, in Christ, all things are yours" (cf. Rom. 8:32–39)? Indeed, we are heirs of all of the blessings which God has promised us in Christ Jesus.

So, Paul says to the Corinthians, do not boast about Apollos, Cephas, Paul, or anyone else. A Christian possesses all things, present and future, a veiled reference, no doubt, to possessing all the blessings of the age to come, even now, because we are in Christ. Since we are in Christ (literally, "We are Christ's"), we possess all that he has and is. As Paul puts it, "Christ is of God," and therefore, if we are in Christ, we also are of God. And since this is the case, there is no basis whatever for dividing into factions which form around specific individuals. The church is Christ's and we are his. This is why division and schism is so serious to the health and well-being of the church.

In light of Paul's assertion that Christians are the temple of God, what are the implications for us? How do we avoid repeating the errors of the Corinthians? When Paul speaks of the church as the temple of God it is hard for us to realize the shock waves such an assertion sent throughout Judaism. This was also a powerful apologetic against paganism. Even though the Jerusalem temple was still standing when Paul wrote this letter, after the events of Christ's death, resurrection, ascension, and the outpouring of the Holy Spirit at Pentecost, it is clear that one greater than the temple has come. When Jesus died upon the cross for our sins, when he was raised for our justification, when he ascended to the right hand of God and then baptizes each of us in the blessed Holy Spirit, the true purpose

You Are God's Temple

of the Jerusalem temple (the earthly building) can now be seen. The Jerusalem temple was designed to point us to the heavenly temple and to the kingly, prophetic, and priestly work of Christ. This is what Jesus meant when he told his disciples that it was good that he leave them and send to them the Holy Spirit (cf. John 14:25ff.).

This means that no longer is God's presence tied to a building or to a particular place. God is present with his people wherever we gather because we are God's temple. With the coming of Jesus, the earthly temple has been superseded. It is obsolete. This temple is not static-bound to time and space. It is composed of living stones and will extend into all the earth. We are that temple because God's Spirit dwells in us.[3] When we assemble on the Lord's Day to hear God's word and receive his sacraments, we are those living stones in whom God's Spirit dwells. This is why it is so important to devote ourselves to Lord's Day worship—not only because of the benefits God promises to us, but also because the assembly of God's people is a testimony to the watching world of the fruits of the saving work of Jesus Christ. God is building his temple using sinful people called from every race, socio-economic background, and status within the community. Let those in our communities around observe what kind of temple God is building!

Paul's point applies to the pagan religions in Corinth as well. God does not dwell in temples made by hands. He is not capricious nor arbitrary as were the so-called "gods" of the Greco-Roman religion. God does not require puny sacrifices or ceremonies to placate his anger. Because God is both holy and gracious, he has already poured his anger upon his own Son,

---

[3]. We might ask our dispensational friends the following question, "If Christ's body is the true temple—as Paul puts it, "For we are the temple of the living God" (2 Corinthians 6:16)—what use remains for a future literal temple?" That to which the temple had pointed, is now a reality through the work of the Holy Spirit. Why return to the type and shadow?

who has taken away the guilt of our sins and turned aside his holy wrath. Not only that, he has poured out his Spirit upon his people. The Corinthians need not make an offering in the temple of Zeus or Aphrodite to appease the gods. The wisdom of God in dealing with sin is seen in the cross. In Christ's crucifixion, God's anger has now turned to blessing and favor. And because Christ has died for us and because God has given us his Holy Spirit, Paul can say to the Corinthians and to all Christians, "You are God's temple." What a glorious promise and wonderful privilege! As Calvin expresses it, "We should consider it the great end of our existence to be found numbered amongst the worshippers of God. . . . Therefore, we should avail ourselves of the inestimable privilege [of being part] of the stated assemblies of the church."[4]

---

4. John Calvin, *Commentary on the Book of Psalms*, trans., J. Anderson, *Calvin's Commentaries*, reprint edition (Grand Rapids: Baker Academic, 1996), II.318.

8

For the Kingdom of God Does not Consist in Talk but in Power

1 CORINTHIANS 4:1–21

I do not write these things to make you ashamed, but to admonish you as my beloved children. For though you have countless guides in Christ, you do not have many fathers. For I became your father in Christ Jesus through the gospel. I urge you, then, be imitators of me.

One of the vivid memories that many of us share from our collective childhoods is that of our exasperated mother telling us, "Wait till your father gets home." In 1 Corinthians 4, we have the apostolic equivalent, "Wait until your apostle returns." Paul is in Ephesus when he composes 1 Corinthians. He is hundreds of miles and a sea away (the Aegean Sea) from Corinth. Although in the providence of God, Paul probably never returned to Corinth, he considers himself to be the father in the faith to the Corinthians. It was Paul who first preached the gospel to them which established the Corinthian congregation. In this section of his letter, Paul admonishes the Corinthians to imitate his behavior, because it is apparent that Paul does not seek favor with men, but only seeks the favor of Christ, who is Lord of his church. As the spiritual father of the Corinthian church, Paul hopes to return to Corinth to see his spiritual children. When he returns, the apostle hopes that the immature who are acting arrogantly will have humbled themselves and that he will be able to come in a spirit of gentleness.

We now take up Paul's discussion of the nature and authority of his apostolic office. Up to this point, Paul has been speaking in rather general terms. Now he gets very specific. The pastoral gloves come off, so to speak. In the first five verses of chapter four, Paul confronts those who have been judging him using the standards of worldly wisdom discussed in previous chapters. In verses 6–13, Paul addresses those in the church boasting about their own false perception of their own wisdom and stature. Paul then speaks fondly as a father speaking to his children in verses 14–17, before closing out the chapter with a very stern warning to those who reject the authority of his apostolic office (vv. 18–21).

In this chapter, we get a rare glimpse of Paul. The apostle is a bit sarcastic as he scolds the church which he helped to found. Paul has suffered greatly. He has sacrificed much. He hates to see this congregation facing division and schism, fighting among themselves, solely because they have not been able to leave pagan wisdom and categories behind. In this chapter, Paul sounds very much like a disappointed father getting word that his children are misbehaving. He also seems a bit exasperated, warning them that he is coming home after work, to either discipline or commend them, depending upon how they behave. Paul is clearly vexed, and more than a little frustrated.

Paul's Ministry Vindicated

Having completed his discussion of true and false wisdom, and having told the Corinthians that the time has come for them to

The Kingdom of God Does Not Consist in Talk

move on to maturity, Paul turns his focus to the way in which God vindicates Paul's ministry. As an apostle, Paul is a chosen servant of Christ. He is not just another faction leader.

In verse 1, Paul writes, "This is how one should regard us, as servants of Christ and stewards of the mysteries of God." What follows in the next five verses is the application to be drawn from the preceding discussion regarding the foundation laid down in the gospel. When believers assemble together, they make up the temple of the Holy Spirit. Given the fact that ministers are servants of God, certain things must follow. Whatever worldly wisdom is still adored by the Corinthians must play no role in evaluating that which God reveals. God alone can give a true and valid judgment of those who serve in Christ's church. In doing so, Paul returns to the theme of servanthood, first introduced in 1 Corinthians 3:5. Only this time, he does so with a new slant. God's servants are accountable only to God. Ministers and their ministries are not to be evaluated from a worldly point of view, but from a biblical one.

Paul's first point is that ministers are not to be regarded as anything but servants of Christ. The Greek word Paul uses is not *diakonoi* (i.e., table-waiters, from which we get our word "deacon") but *hyperetes*, which refers to an "under-rower," that is, an oarsman on the lower deck of a large ship.[1] Ministers are servants of God, called to a position of service which the world regards as lowly.

Ministers of God have been entrusted with the secret things of God. Although the world regards what they do as lowly "bottom deckers," God has called them to a very unique and important task. The word translated as "stewards" in the ESV is *oikonomois*, which refers to someone who supervises a large estate, as a manager or an administrator. This term should make us

---

1. Morris, *1 Corinthians*, 71.

think of one who functions as a chief of staff.[2] The *oikonomous* ran the master's estate, cared for the property and animals, supervised the laborers, and procured supplies. But the *oikonomous* was always subservient to the owner of the estate. Usually this individual was himself an indentured servant or a slave, but was a master over others of the same status. This is how we must view a minister (and his fellow office-bearers). Such men care for the church which is not theirs. It is Christ's, even though such men take a special pride in it.

The reference to secret things (*mystēriōn*) is an important one. Paul has already defined these secret things in 1 Corinthians 2:1, 7, as those things connected to the revelation of the gospel, a mystery throughout the Old Testament until the coming of Jesus Christ. Paul reminds us that these secrets have been entrusted to the ministers who are now to proclaim them. Ministers are administrators or stewards of these mysteries as they are revealed in God's word. That which was hidden is to be made plain. This is why only ordained ministers can preside over the sacraments, and matters related to keys of the kingdom (i.e., the "binding and loosing" associated with the preaching of the gospel, cf. Matt. 16:19).

Because they are entrusted with the mysteries of God's revelation, ministers are held to a higher standard than other members of the church. Paul spells this out in verse 2. "Moreover, it is required of stewards that they be found trustworthy." Those who have been given the job of supervising the master's estate must do their duties faithfully. Those who do not demonstrate themselves to be trustworthy disqualify themselves from such service.

In verse 3, Paul gets to the point of this brief exhortation. "But with me it is a very small thing that I should be judged by you or by any human court. In fact, I do not even judge myself." Paul has a completely different understanding of this than do

---

2. Hays, *First Corinthians*, 65.

The Kingdom of God Does Not Consist in Talk

the immature in the Corinthian church. The various ministers in the Corinthian church were servants to the Corinthians. The Corinthians are not the masters of Paul, nor any of others who had taught them. God is Paul's master. Since God is Paul's master, the apostle makes it very clear that he does not necessarily care what the Corinthians think of him. Paul does not stop and continually judge himself in light of the complaints against him from the immature among the Corinthian congregation. Rather, Paul knows that God is the final and ultimate judge of his teaching, so even if he is personally hurt by the criticism of the Corinthians, he will not change his methods or approach because of it—unless and until God instructs him to do otherwise.

In light of Paul's exhortation, ministers must be very careful not to preach so as to be popular or well-liked, or to preach to the so-called "felt needs" of a congregation. Ministers are to concentrate upon communicating the meaning of the biblical text—explaining the mysteries to which they have been entrusted. Likewise, the way in which the people in the pew should evaluate a sermon is not by whether the sermon was entertaining, motivational, and so on, but along the lines of "did the minister clearly and simply explain and apply the biblical text." Does the minister draw appropriate application from the text? This is what Paul has done because Christ has revealed to him the gospel, which Paul, in turn, has been entrusted to proclaim in those churches he has helped to found. But this is what the immature do not yet understand.

As Paul states in verse 4, "I am not aware of anything against myself, but I am not thereby acquitted. It is the Lord who judges me." Because Paul knows that God is his judge, his conscience is clear. He has done his best to be faithful. As he recounts in Philippians 3:4b-11, God has covered all his sins with Christ's perfect righteousness. Since God is Paul's judge, Paul's own efforts do not acquit him. Paul wisely leaves this matter in God's hands where it ought to be left. He is not going to allow those judging him by worldly standards to thwart his divinely-appointed mission.

Paul also knows that a final judgment is coming and that he is clothed with the righteousness of Christ himself. As he tells the Corinthians in verse 5, he will wait for the judgment for final vindication. "Therefore do not pronounce judgment before the time, before the Lord comes, who will bring to light the things now hidden in darkness and will disclose the purposes of the heart. Then each one will receive his commendation from God." Paul exhorts his readers to concentrate on being faithful, but to leave the outcome of these things in God's hand. The appointed time, for which we are to wait, is the second advent of Jesus Christ. On that day, all things will be brought out into the open, including those things we hide in darkness—a metaphor for sin—such as the motives of our hearts. On the day of judgment, God will deal with all of this, including the matter of whether or not Paul has been faithful in fulfilling his own calling as apostle to the Gentiles.

Paul's Rebuke of the Corinthians

There are two issues raised in the following verses. One is the work of Paul and Apollos among the Corinthians. The second has to do with the trials endured by the apostles in which Paul contrasts his lowly state with the self-important status found among the Corinthians. Paul's remarks in this regard have been called "an impassioned and incisive piece of prose, with irony so biting that some have felt that Paul can scarcely be addressing the church as a whole."[3] In the absence of any limitations attached to these words, we must assume that these remarks are addressed to the church as a whole. They constitute what we might call a stern fatherly rebuke.

---

3. Morris, *1 Corinthians*, 76.

The Kingdom of God Does Not Consist in Talk

We begin by addressing the issues related to Paul and Apollos in verses 6–7. "I have applied all these things to myself and Apollos for your benefit, brothers, that you may learn by us not to go beyond what is written, that none of you may be puffed up in favor of one against another. For who sees anything different in you? What do you have that you did not receive? If then you received it, why do you boast as if you did not receive it?" Paul uses a figure of speech ("applied") which means something like "to transform." He does this to make the point that he and Apollos are illustrations of what true servanthood should entail. Paul and Apollos have done all this for the benefit of the brothers, continuing to use affectionate language. Because of their example, the Corinthians are not to elevate men over God's purposes, by continuing to take pride in the factions which they had created.

Paul asks the Corinthians to consider the obvious; they are no different from anyone else. Everything they have comes from God, including the gospel which has been taught to them by both Paul and Apollos. The Corinthians are not to go beyond what is written. I take this to be a reference to the sufficiency of Scripture. God has revealed to us everything in his word which we need to know so as to trust in Christ and live the Christian life. Paul's words echo certain Old Testament passages, such as Deuteronomy 4:1–8, which speak of God's written word as authoritative, to which nothing should be added. Since these things come from God, on what basis then can the Corinthians boast? When using worldly categories, the Corinthians may have been able to boast. But when viewed from God's perspective, Christians have nothing to boast about but God and his sovereign grace, because all that we have has been given us by him.

The effect of Paul's rhetorical questions should put those who boast in worldly wisdom in their place. It were as though Paul were saying to those who boast, "Who do you think you are?"[4] To take credit for a gift from God is the height of worldliness and a most foolish act when viewed from the perspective of the cross. The ironic nature of what follows should not be missed. Perhaps these words actually reflect what some were saying in Corinth, although we cannot be sure. In any case, what follows (in verses 8–13), is a stinging rebuke to the Corinthians.

In verse 8, Paul reminds his readers, "Already you have all you want! Already you have become rich! Without us you have become kings! And would that you did reign, so that we might share the rule with you!" The Corinthians have all they want. They are fully satisfied. They think of themselves as rich, and as kings. This, of course, is the problem with the church in Laodicea as reported in Revelation 3:17. Jesus says to the Laodiceans, "For you say, I am rich, I have prospered, and I need nothing, not realizing that you are wretched, pitiable, poor, blind, and naked." The Corinthians face the same rebuke from Paul. They think they have all they need. They are secure and self-sufficient, which in actuality, is a dangerous state to be in, but probably quite typical of the influences of Stoic philosophy.[5] Because of the influence of pagan philosophy, the Corinthians fail to see that they are not rich at all.

The actual conditions faced by the apostles are quite different than the erroneous estimation of things being made by the immature among Corinthians. Paul spells these out in verses 9–13.

> For I think that God has exhibited us apostles as last of all, like men sentenced to death, because we have become a spectacle to the world, to angels, and to men. We are fools for Christ's sake, but you are wise in Christ. We are weak, but you are strong. You are held in honor, but we in disrepute. To the present hour we hunger and thirst, we are poorly dressed

---

4. Hays, *First Corinthians*, 69.
5. Morris, *1 Corinthians*, 76.

The Kingdom of God Does Not Consist in Talk

> and buffeted and homeless, and we labor, working with our own hands. When reviled, we bless; when persecuted, we endure; when slandered, we entreat. We have become, and are still, like the scum of the world, the refuse of all things.

Paul is not complaining in these verses, but he is pointing out that preaching the gospel has not brought fame, success, or fortune as the world regards fame, success, and fortune. In fact, he endured a number of horrible things while in Ephesus, from where he is presently writing to the Corinthians (recounted in Acts 19:23ff.). But this position of weakness and depravation enables Paul to preach the gospel for what it is—the power of God for salvation of all who believe. Paul cannot dare trust in his own abilities (which he knows, humanly speaking, are lacking). Therefore, he must trust in the power of God. This is to his advantage.

The number of things mentioned by Paul which he has had to endure is utterly remarkable. He has felt like an exhibit brought into the arena to be mocked and thrown to the animals. He has been put on display for the whole world to watch (both men and angels). His gospel is considered foolishness, he is weak and dishonored, while the Corinthians see themselves as wise, strong, and honored for behaving like pagans while still using the wisdom of "this age" to make sense of heavenly things. Paul has suffered great economic deprivation. He has been hungry, homeless, has no material possessions, and is often brutalized. He works as hard as humanly possible. He blesses those who curse him, while at the same time enduring the persecution to which the Lord has called him. He is slandered and does not respond in kind. Paul is regarded as something to be swept up and thrown out like trash, so that the world will be rid of him and his foolish message. Paul is regarded by both Jews and Greeks as contemptible. There are some who think that getting rid of him and his message would cleanse the earth.

The gap between the Corinthians' self-estimation (rich and kingly) and the reality faced by Paul (persecution) could not be greater. To avoid Paul's plight, the Corinthians are choosing to make peace with the world. Paul appeals to them not to see things from their distorted perspective, but from the reality that Paul sees—not only in a theological sense, but in a practical one. Although Paul warns his readers in what follows, at the same time he exhorts them to learn about the kingdom of God, which comes in the power of the Holy Spirit (through the message of Christ crucified). Christ's kingdom does not come through the flattering speech of sinful men and women seeking to avoid persecution.

Paul Speaks to the Corinthians as a Father

In verse 14, there is a marked change in Paul's tone as he speaks of the members of this church as his children. Having sternly rebuked the congregation and speaking somewhat sarcastically, Paul's language now becomes quite affectionate and tender. These are people Paul knows, and he obviously cares for them no matter how exasperating their behavior might be. Paul is angry with them, but his anger will not have the last word. "I do not write these things to make you ashamed, but to admonish you as my beloved children" (v. 14). Paul does not want to shame these people, but admonish them of the consequences of their immaturity.

At this point in the chapter, Paul assumes the role of a father, speaking firmly but tenderly to a disobedient child. "For though you have countless guides in Christ, you do not have many fathers. For I became your father in Christ Jesus through the gospel. I urge you, then, be imitators of me" (v. 15). The Corinthians may have a thousand guardians (*paidagōgous*) referring to the

The Kingdom of God Does Not Consist in Talk

slaves who took their charges to school, making sure that they fulfilled their assignments, but they have only one father in the faith.[6] Paul is not merely one who scolds the Corinthians using corporal punishment so that they comply. Rather, Paul is like a father who exercises firm but loving discipline. He is the first to have preached the gospel to them. He is the one who led them to Christ. It is because of the gospel he preached to them—the glorious message that Christ's death is sufficient to save sinners—that Paul is their father.

Because this is the case, Paul urges the Corinthians to imitate him. In doing this, Paul does not mean that the Corinthians should drop all their factional allegiances and simply follow him as the true faction leader. Rather they should imitate him, making sure that everything they do is done in the light of the gospel (and the age to come). The Corinthians must move on to maturity and leave behind the categories and patterns of this present age which produce their immature and selfish behavior.

Since he cannot come to Corinth in person, Paul will send someone who will come and help the Corinthians to move on to maturity. Paul explains in verse 17, "That is why I sent you Timothy, my beloved and faithful child in the Lord, to remind you of my ways in Christ, as I teach them everywhere in every church." We do not know much about Timothy's visit to Corinth, but Paul is obviously quite comfortable with the young Timothy's capabilities. Timothy will bear witness not only to the fact that Paul's life is consistent with his theology, and that what he is teaching the Corinthians is the same as he has been teaching all the churches—focusing upon the the proclamation of Christ crucified through Word and sacrament. Timothy can inform the Corinthians that Paul is dealing with them the same way he would deal with any church. Paul is not demanding anything of

---

6. Morris, *1 Corinthians*, 80.

the Corinthians that he would not demand of others. He is not treating the Corinthians unfairly.

Timothy will also confirm that Paul is willing to come to Corinth when he can, something the following verse indicates is a problem. "Some are arrogant, as though I were not coming to you" (v. 18). Some in the congregation are "puffed up," telling others that Paul would not come to Corinth, and behaving as though he would not come to address the issues in the congregation. "Paul doesn't care about us enough to come, why should we not follow someone else?"

In verse 19, Paul makes his intentions quite clear that this is absolutely not the case! "But I will come to you soon, if the Lord wills, and I will find out not the talk of these arrogant people but their power." It is clearly Paul's desire to return to Corinth, yet the Lord had other plans. One thing is certain, the immature among the Corinthians are all talk. They have no power. For the power of God is not revealed in mere human opinion, in mere talk, but in the gospel. This becomes plain in verse 20, when Paul writes, "For the kingdom of God does not consist in talk but in power." The kingdom of God is the rule of God, manifest in the person and work of Jesus Christ. When the kingdom comes, the power of God is manifest when the lame walk, the blind see, the deaf hear, the unclean (lepers) are healed, and even the worst of sinners are forgiven. This kingdom is not in any sense connected to this present evil age. Rather, the kingdom of God comes with power because it is the manifestation of the age to come. Like the Corinthians, we too are prone to expect the kingdom to come by "talk" and flash, not by the faithful preaching of the cross of Christ which is the true demonstration of God's power.

Paul ends his rebuke by giving the Corinthians a very clear choice. "What do you wish? Shall I come to you with a rod, or with love in a spirit of gentleness?" (v. 21). If the Corinthians move on to maturity Paul can come to them like a father visit-

The Kingdom of God Does Not Consist in Talk

ing his children who have moved away from home. If the Corinthians continue on in their present course, Paul will come as a father who must exercise discipline over disobedient children. The choice is up to the Corinthians. A rod? Or a gentle spirit? Wait till your apostle comes home!

In many ways, this is a difficult section of the Corinthian letter to read and interpret because Paul is so frustrated with the Corinthians' love of worldly wisdom that he speaks in sarcastic terms. For Paul this not a personal offense (that the Corinthians are attacking him personally), but stems from the fact that their behavior amounts to a dismissal of the wisdom of God revealed to them through the gospel which Paul had preached to them. Through that gospel the power of God is revealed as sinners are made right with God, because they learn that God's wrath and anger toward them has already been poured out upon his own Son. Why would the Corinthians—indeed why would we—continue to evaluate the gospel ministry through the lens of worldly wisdom when the wisdom God gives through the preaching of Christ crucified is the very thing we need to move on to maturity? The more we focus upon the cross as the demonstration of both the wisdom and power of God, the greater our progress will be.

Let us strive to see in Paul's concern for the Corinthians the great danger of evaluating the preaching of Christ crucified through the categories of our own age. We have heard people say with the best of intentions, "I'm a good person, I don't need a Savior. God just wants me to do my best, therefore Jesus is just an example for me to follow. All religions basically say the same thing, so can't we tone down all the focus on sin and blood? Can't we talk about me and the things I am interested in? Christianity is so divisive."

Paul reminds us that despite the fact that a crucified Savior offends us, it is through the gospel that God saves us from our sins. This is a message which our contemporaries hate just as much as did the Greeks in Corinth. Through the gospel, the kingdom of God comes with power. Everything else—especially the complaining of the immature who still think like unbelievers—is only so much talk. We must stop listening to those who can only talk, and know not the truth and power of the gospel. As we learn to do this and concentrate upon the glories of the gospel, we will see the power of God in our midst, and only then we will begin to move on to maturity in Jesus Christ. And as we mature, we will grow to appreciate the instruction and exhortations in God's word, God's promises confirmed in the sacraments, and in the fellowship with the saints. The foolishness of this world will become apparent and less attractive to us.

9

God Judges Those Outside

1 CORINTHIANS 5:1–13

I wrote to you in my letter not to associate with sexually immoral people—not at all meaning the sexually immoral of this world, or the greedy and swindlers, or idolaters, since then you would need to go out of the world. But now I am writing to you not to associate with anyone who bears the name of brother if he is guilty of sexual immorality or greed, or is an idolater, reviler, drunkard, or swindler—not even to eat with such a one. For what have I to do with judging outsiders? Is it not those inside the church whom you are to judge? God judges those outside. "Purge the evil person from among you."

Reformed Christians consider church discipline to be one of the three marks of a true church. For example, the Belgic Confession (1561) states:

> We believe that we ought to discern diligently and very carefully, by the Word of God, what is the true church—for all sects in the world today claim for themselves the name of "the church."

First Corinthians

We are not speaking here of the company of hypocrites who are mixed among the good in the church and who nonetheless are not part of it, even though they are physically there. But we are speaking of distinguishing the body and fellowship of the true church from all sects that call themselves "the church."

The true church can be recognized if it has the following marks: The church engages in the pure preaching of the gospel; it makes use of the pure administration of the sacraments as Christ instituted them; it practices church discipline for correcting faults. In short, it governs itself according to the pure Word of God, rejecting all things contrary to it and holding Jesus Christ as the only Head. By these marks one can be assured of recognizing the true church—and no one ought to be separated from it.

As for those who can belong to the church, we can recognize them by the distinguishing marks of Christians: namely by faith, and by their fleeing from sin and pursuing righteousness, once they have received the one and only Savior, Jesus Christ. They love the true God and their neighbors, without turning to the right or left, and they crucify the flesh and its works.

Though great weakness remains in them, they fight against it by the Spirit all the days of their lives, appealing constantly to the blood, suffering, death, and obedience of the Lord Jesus, in whom they have forgiveness of their sins, through faith in him.

As for the false church, it assigns more authority to itself and its ordinances than to the Word of God; it does not want to subject itself to the yoke of Christ; it does not administer the sacraments as Christ commanded in his Word; it rather adds to them or subtracts from them as it pleases; it bases itself on men, more than on Jesus Christ; it persecutes those who live holy lives according to the

God Judges Those Outside

Word of God and who rebuke it for its faults, greed, and idolatry.

These two churches are easy to recognize and thus to distinguish from each other.[1]

The reason for this insistence upon church discipline as a mark of the church is found in the fifth chapter of 1 Corinthians, where Paul commands the Corinthians to remove (excommunicate) a man from their midst who was professing faith in Christ, while at the same time, openly engaging in an activity which even Greco-Roman pagans regard as shameful. While the church is to be a hospital for sinners, and while there should always be sufficient grace for anyone struggling with sin, those who insist upon living as a law unto themselves, and who harden their hearts and are unrepentant when confronted, must be removed from the church, with a view to sincere repentance and restoration in the future. Yet, in 1 Corinthians 5, Paul does something quite unexpected. He cautions the Corinthians *not* to judge unbelievers and idolaters outside the church (the world)—because they do not know any better. At the same time, he warns those who profess faith in Christ that once they trust in the Savior they cannot live as they did when they were ignorant.

If the subject of church discipline troubled the Corinthians, it certainly troubles Americans. Many churches are so large and so loosely organized that people can live as they please without anyone in leadership even knowing who its members are, much less what they do. Many churches are fearful that church discipline might lead to litigation. Others find this distasteful because exercising discipline is not only a difficult thing to do, but church officers are fearful of being perceived as being judgmental. The flip side is that many American churches and Christians are perceived as being judgmental and unreasonable towards those outside their flocks, all the while tolerating hy-

---

1. Cf. *Belgic Confession*, Article 29.

pocrisy within. This subject requires careful consideration of Paul's discussion.

In chapter 5, Paul addresses a series of things going on in Corinth which had come to his attention and which are causing serious problems in the church. The first of these is the case of a man in the Corinthian church who is co-habiting and sexually involved with his father's wife (his stepmother). Somehow word had gotten to Paul while he was in Ephesus that this was going on back in Corinth, and that no one in the church was doing anything about it. It is important that we notice that Paul speaks much more sternly about the church's lax attitude toward the issue, than he does about the guilt of the individual offender, who is never named even though, presumably, everyone knew who this person was. What Paul condemns in the passage is the conduct of the church—the elders have failed to discipline the offending party. The fact that Paul says nothing about the woman involved may very well mean that she is not a Christian, and not a member of the church, or else she too would be subject to discipline.

Public Scandal and the Church

Paul is typically blunt and gets right to the point in verse 1. "It is actually reported that there is sexual immorality among you, and of a kind that is not tolerated even among pagans, for a man has his father's wife." It is easy to read between the lines and assume a fair bit of anger and disappointment on Paul's part stemming from the fact that the responsibility for dealing with this issue has been avoided by the pastors and elders of the Corinthian church. The word translated sexual immorality is *porneia* and comes from the root (*porne*) "harlot." By Paul's time, the term probably referred to any form of sexual immorality (in a moral sense) or sexual misconduct (in a legal sense). The specific issue is that the man in question *has* his

God Judges Those Outside

father's wife, which likely means that the woman in question is the man's step-mother. John Murray is certainly correct when he points out that Paul's "exasperation underlies the grossness of the wrong involved."[2]

The most likely scenario is that the man in question has seduced his father's wife or concubine, which implies—although Paul does not specifically state this fact—that the man's father had divorced the man's biological mother (or else the biological mother had died), and married someone younger, closer in age to the man in question. It is also possible that the man's biological father had died, and then the son took his widowed step-mother as his own wife (or concubine). In either case, it is clear that the fact of the man's relationship with his step-mother was widely known throughout the church and regarded as utterly scandalous even by the pagans. Yet the Corinthians did nothing.

The behavior of the man in question was so offensive that this kind of relationship was probably condemned by Roman law, and certainly by the Old Testament (cf. Lev. 18:8, 20:11; Deut. 22:30; 27:20). This was not conduct which fell into a gray area. Even the unbelieving world regarded such conduct as reprehensible.

There is a significant theological point made here which we may easily overlook because of the scandal involved. One scholar points out that "the word *ethnē*, translated by . . . most English versions as 'pagans,' is Paul's normal word for 'Gentiles' (i.e., 'Non-Jews'). His use of this term here offers a fascinating hint that Paul thinks of the Gentile converts at Corinth as Gentiles no longer (cf. 12:2, 13; Gal. 3:28). Now that they are in Christ, they belong to the covenant people of God, and their behavior should reflect that new status."[3] Paul doesn't speak of Gentile

---

2. John Murray, *Principles of Conduct* (Grand Rapids: William B. Eerdmans Publishing Co., 1957), 258.

3. Hays, *First Corinthians*, 81.

converts as "Gentiles." They *were* Gentiles (pagans). *Now* they are Christians. Paul's point is that Christians must make a complete break with their pagan past.

What was the attitude of the Corinthians toward this shameful behavior? Paul tells us in verse 2. "And you are arrogant! Ought you not rather to mourn? Let him who has done this be removed from among you." The Corinthians are proud, literally "puffed up." They are actually pleased with their own spiritual and material condition despite the fact that this was going on in their midst! Instead of being filled with grief and striving to remove the offending party from the church, they glibly tolerate this man's behavior. The Corinthians should be in a state of grief (literally "mourning") because of the need to excise one of the diseased members of their body like one removes a gangrenous limb.[4] Instead, they are proud of their accomplishments and high-standing in the community (royal, rich, and without need—cf. 1 Cor. 4:8). They see no need to take action. Paul will not allow the Corinthians to ignore this matter and do nothing.

The Offender Must Be Removed from the Church

In verse 3, he writes, "For though absent in body, I am present in spirit; and as if present, I have already pronounced judgment on the one who did such a thing." Even though Paul cannot be present with the Corinthians in person, he is certainly present with them in spirit. His attitude toward the situation stands in sharp contrast to theirs. Those elders present in Corinth have done nothing. Yet, the one who is absent (Paul) is taking action. Paul has already passed judgment on the matter, even though he does not name the offender (or the woman) by name.

In verses 4–5, Paul explains what must be done. "When you are assembled in the name of the Lord Jesus and my spirit is present, with the power of our Lord Jesus you are to deliver this

---

4. Morris, *1 Corinthians*, 83.

God Judges Those Outside

man to Satan for the destruction of the flesh, so that his spirit may be saved in the day of the Lord." However we understand the grammatical structure of the sentence, one thing is clear: Paul solemnly commands the Corinthians to remove this man from the fellowship (i.e., to excommunicate him). But this is not a mere judicial procedure. There are grave spiritual consequences resulting from this action. Once outside the safety of the church, the man in question is delivered over to the consequences of his sin and will now dwell in that sphere of life where Satan dominates.[5] Throughout Paul's writings, Satan is depicted as the destroyer (2 Cor. 4:4; 1 Tim. 1:20; 2 Thess. 2:9–10) and like a doomed animal, Satan awaits his final and appointed end (cf. 1 Pet. 5:8). The consequence of this act of excommunication is that the man's "flesh" might be destroyed and his spirit saved on the day of the Lord, i.e., on the day of judgment.

Obviously, the destruction of the man's flesh is a difficult concept. A number of possibilities have been suggested. One is that this is a reference to the destruction of the man's "lower nature." But this proposal raises the question as to how handing someone over to Satan has a purifying effect. Another interpretation is that the destruction of the flesh might refer to someone suffering from the weighty effects of excommunication, so that they put to death the deeds of the flesh and return to the church (cf. Rom. 8:13). Still others think this is a reference to physical destruction of the body and even death (cf. The account of Ananias and Sapphira in Acts 5:1–11). It seems best to say that the excommunicated person is allowed to suffer all of the consequences of their actions, physical, emotional, and spiritual, so that they will be convicted of their sin so that they repent and then are saved on the day of judgment.[6]

---

5. Morris, *1 Corinthians*, 85.
6. Hays, *First Corinthians*, 86.

However, it is vital to notice that even after the man is excommunicated and faces these severe spiritual consequences, Paul expects that the man will be saved on the day of judgment. This supports the idea that church discipline will ideally, if not inevitably, lead to the person's restoration, which, of course, presupposes repentance, restitution, and the forgiveness of the offender's sin. This is in line with Paul's instructions to the Galatians (6:1). "Brothers, if someone is caught in a sin, you who are spiritual should restore him gently. But watch yourself, or you also may be tempted." Church discipline must be exercised firmly, but incrementally, and pastorally, with the goal of seeing the disciplined party saved on the day of judgment (i.e., that the party repents and is restored). That church which does not exercise discipline, is a church which is being unfaithful to the Lord of the church. That church which exercises church discipline as a retributive punishment to merely shame (or embarrass) the sinner, is also not faithfully practicing church discipline. The goal is always restoration, and there is nothing as joyous as a sinner repenting (cf. Luke 15:7–10).[7]

Nevertheless, Paul insists that the prescribed action—excommunication—must take place. As he puts it in verse 6, "Your boasting is not good. Do you not know that a little leaven leavens the whole lump?" Paul is concerned that unless something is done about this man's outrageous behavior, the consequences of both his sin, as well as the church's failure to deal with this matter, will spread throughout the entire church with horrible consequences. Apparently, even the unchurched were watching, waiting to see what happened.

Even worse, this poison is spreading throughout the church while the Corinthians are still boasting about their spiritual ad-

---

[7]. The reader may wish to consult my essay, "The Fruit of Righteousness and Peace: Church Discipline," in Michael Brown, ed., *Called to Serve: Essays for Elders and Deacons* (Grandville, MI: Reformed Fellowship, 2006), 199–211.

God Judges Those Outside

vances. As Paul sees it, the issue is not merely that the Corinthians did nothing about this man's sin, but that they did nothing about a heinous sin, all the while boasting about their success. They were truly imitating the "wisdom" of this world. Using a common parable/figure of speech with both a cultural and a biblical basis, Paul now warns the Corinthians that even a small amount of yeast will work its way throughout the whole batch of dough. The Corinthian church is to be God's temple in Corinth, but cannot serve this function effectively with this kind of thing going on in her midst.[8]

While Paul's reference might be to the Corinthians' boasting—that it is their pride which will spread throughout the church—more than likely something much more serious is in view. To allow this man to remain in the Corinthian church is to allow this horrible situation to impact the entire church. Not only is toleration of one man's scandalous sin in view, but even worse, the failure to discipline this man will also affect the reputation of the entire church and the credibility of the gospel that its ministers proclaim. If the Corinthian church fails to excommunicate this man, not only do the man's evil actions go unpunished, but he will not be pressured to repent. In not protecting the church from evil, the entire church will be impacted. If the church does not exercise discipline, the signal is sent that no immoral conduct will be regarded as beyond the pale, and the Corinthian church will cease to be a true church (or a healthy church).

This is why Paul urges them, "Cleanse out the old leaven that you may be a new lump, as you really are unleavened. For Christ, our Passover lamb, has been sacrificed." Simply put, Paul is urging this congregation to get rid of the yeast (the sin of this particular individual) before it permeates the whole congregation. The reason for Paul's confident assertion that this congregation is a new lump (i.e., not yet fully permeated with yeast) is

---

8. Fee, *The First Epistle to the Corinthians*, 214–215.

spelled out in the second half of the verse. Christ has died for the Corinthian believers, removing the guilt of their sins. Paul's point is that Jesus Christ's death is to the Christian what the Passover was to the Jews.

Repentance and Restoration

In seeing Paul's words in this light, the redemptive historical implications become quite obvious. As recounted in Exodus 12, Israel was delivered from Egypt and all of its pagan influences on the night of the Passover. When celebrating the Passover, all yeast was removed from the house, a sign which pointed forward to the sacrifice of Christ removing the guilt and power of sin, as well as symbolically demonstrating Israel's rejection of paganism. The point is a powerful one—because Christ has delivered the Corinthians from slavery to sin through his death upon the cross, all yeast (sin) must be removed from their lives. The application is clear. While we are all sinners, and therefore forbidden from self-righteously judging others, the fact remains that all public and scandalous sins must be dealt with accordingly, either through the repentance of the sinner, or the removal of the sinner from the congregation should they refuse to repent and be restored.

Paul goes on to say, "Let us therefore celebrate the festival, not with the old leaven, the leaven of malice and evil, but with the unleavened bread of sincerity and truth." For the Christian, the Christian life is a continual festival (the "let us keep," meaning something continuous). There is also an implied reference to the Lord's Supper here as well. This fits both the context (the Passover typology), and situation, namely that the man who is expelled would presumably have been barred from the Lord's Table.[9] This act, called "silent censure" is usually the first step of church discipline.

---

9. Fee, *The First Epistle to the Corinthians*, 218.

God Judges Those Outside

The important point here is that the sins of malice (the strife which lead to factionalism) and the wickedness which led to a man taking his father's wife in a scandalous manner, are those things typified by old yeast. These are the things the Corinthians are to remove, so as to live in integrity and truth, as a new loaf, "bread without yeast." Once justified before God, because of the merits of Christ, received through faith alone, Christians are now to strive to live lives of gratitude and sincere obedience before God. The Corinthians, apparently, understand the gospel. Yet they do not seem very interested in living like Christians and not like pagans. This is the yeast (the consequence) of their immaturity and their love of worldly wisdom.

We also learn that Paul had already written to the Corinthians earlier to address some of these issues, and the Corinthians had, apparently, badly misunderstood his prior letter. Therefore, Paul addresses this misunderstanding directly. "I wrote to you in my letter not to associate with sexually immoral people—not at all meaning the sexually immoral of this world, or the greedy and swindlers, or idolaters, since then you would need to go out of the world." Paul has already told this congregation that they are not to associate (meaning "to be mixed up with")[10] with people who are sexually immoral—that is, with people who live by a Greco-Roman sexual ethic, rather than a biblical sexual ethic. Greco-Roman culture was characterized by what Christians consider to be sexual promiscuity. Among other things, men kept mistresses. Homosexual acts were widely practiced and tolerated. Many pagan religions were tied to temple prostitution. Then, as now, sexual promiscuity is the fruit of paganism—fertility rites, union with the divine, goddess worship, and so forth. Paganism often provides the needed justification to sin against nature.

The application for us should be obvious. We too live in a highly sexualized culture in which homosexuality is not only

---

10. Morris, *1 Corinthians*, 88.

tolerated, but is now seen as a noble challenge to our Puritan and "Victorian" past. Sex before (fornication) or outside of marriage (adultery) is commonplace, and pornography is available in every home *via* countless electronic devices. Throughout the Scriptures, Christians are commanded to live in purity, according to a biblical sexual ethic. In the Bible we are taught that homosexuality is not only a sin against God's law, but also against nature (cf. Rom. 1:19–32), which explains why the guilt attached to sexual sin is so deep (cf. 1 Cor. 6:18). Christians must abstain from all sexual relations until marriage. Christians believe that adultery is not only a sin but highly destructive of marriages and families. And Christians believe that pornography is a pandora's box to a host of sins, addictions, and psychological trauma. Christians endured this highly sexualized environment in Corinth while challenging pagans with the claims of Christ, even as we must do the same today.

God Judges Those Outside the Church

Obviously, one of the reasons why Paul is so direct in this letter (and even a bit sarcastic in the previous chapter) is because he has already told the congregation that its members should not be made up of people who still live and think like unbelievers. The Corinthians have not only failed to heed Paul's words, they have badly misunderstood his instructions. Some in the congregation have misunderstood Paul to be saying that they must have no contact whatsoever with any immoral persons (e.g., greedy, swindlers, or idolaters) in addition to those who are sexually immoral. Sadly, many Christians think this way today. If, as Paul says, he meant that Christians must avoid conduct with all immoral people, then they would have to leave the world because all people are immoral. Paul is not telling us to avoid non-Christians. He is telling us not to think and act like non-Christians once we become Christians.

God Judges Those Outside

Paul's clarification of this misunderstanding is spelled out in verse 11. "But now I am writing to you not to associate with anyone who bears the name of brother if he is guilty of sexual immorality or greed, or is an idolater, reviler, drunkard, or swindler—not even to eat with such a one." All of the items on this list are taken from so-called "exclusion texts" in the Book of Deuteronomy (cf. Deut 13:1–11; 17:2ff.; 22:21ff.). That conduct which God expected of the covenant community in the Old Testament, he still expects of his covenant people in the new. What Paul meant is that a Christian must not be associated with people who profess to be believers, but who still live like they are not. Paul is not talking about avoiding people who are struggling with sin. He is talking about people who continually self-justify their sinful conduct, and who show no signs of being concerned that what they do is an offense to God. There is no repentance. No godly sorrow.

Paul is also clear that Christians must avoid the appearance of evil, therefore they cannot even eat (associate directly) with those who profess faith in Christ but continue to be sexually immoral (who engage in adultery or fornication), greedy (dishonest gain), idolaters (syncretists), slanderers (liars), drunkards or swindlers (those who seize what isn't there). Some have taken the reference to eating to refer to the Lord's Supper. Paul is more than likely referring to table fellowship, which meant much more in the ancient world than it does in ours. To eat with someone in their home was to establish a bond with them.[11] And yet, Paul does not forbid Christians from eating in non-Christian homes (1 Cor. 10:27). Jesus ate with tax collectors and prostitutes (cf. Luke 15:2). Paul does forbid Christians from having direct and public association with people in the church who profess to be Christians but who still live as pagans.

---

11. S. S. Bartchy, "Table Fellowship," in *Dictionary of Jesus and the Gospels*, (Downers Grove: InterVarsity Press, 1992), 796.

First Corinthians

Indeed, as Paul goes on to say in verses 12–13, "For what have I to do with judging outsiders? Is it not those inside the church whom you are to judge? God judges those outside. 'Purge the evil person from among you.'" It is not Paul's place, nor ours, to judge those outside the church. God will take care of non-Christians. But the Corinthians (and we) are commanded to judge those within the church according to their life and doctrine, yet not in a self-righteous, "holier-than-thou" attitude. The bruised reed and smoldering wick—those who are weak in the faith and who struggle with their sins—must be nurtured and comforted with the promises of the gospel. But those who claim to be Christians, yet who live like pagans in complete indifference to the law of God, are to be expelled from the church unless they repent. Paul's words are not directed to struggling sinners, but to those who profess faith in Christ but then live as they please. The church cannot tolerate this kind of evil in its midst because it undermines the proclamation of the gospel. Christ died to save us from both the guilt of sin *and its power*.

There are two important points to be made. First, Paul's point bears repeating—the apostle tells us not to judge those outside the church. God judges those outside the covenant community. Since we are sinners who are saved by grace, and since all that we have is a gift from a gracious God, who are we to judge those who are not Christians? That said, it is our duty to continually confront non-Christians with the claims of Christ and of the gospel. While we are not to judge them, we are commanded to share the good news with them.

Second, Christ's church must be a disciplined church. If the truth were told, church discipline is that one area of church life which keeps ministers and elders up at night. Despite the difficulties associated with it, Christ commands it of us. An undisciplined church is not a healthy church. A church which practices discipline with a stern self-righteousness is not a hospital

God Judges Those Outside

for sinners. Again, the issue is not that there are sinners in the church. Sinners belong in church. The wonderful news in all of this is that Jesus Christ's death avails for sinners, turning aside God's wrath from them so that those who repent and believe need never fear God's judgment. Since the cross is the revelation of the wisdom and power of God, we undermine the credibility of that gospel we claim to love so much when we overlook those things which bring scandal to Christ's church, and when we fail to discipline those who claim to trust Christ, but act like the cross has no power whatsoever to break sin's hold upon us.

Leave those outside the church to God—he judges those outside. But let us strive to build churches which are a haven for sinners, yet which, at the same time, refuse to allow anything to bring shame to the cause of Christ, his church, and his gospel.

10

And Such Were Some of You

1 CORINTHIANS 6:1–11

Or do you not know that the unrighteous will not inherit the kingdom of God? Do not be deceived: neither the sexually immoral, nor idolaters, nor adulterers, nor men who practice homosexuality, nor thieves, nor the greedy, nor drunkards, nor revilers, nor swindlers will inherit the kingdom of God. And such were some of you. But you were washed, you were sanctified, you were justified in the name of the Lord Jesus Christ and by the Spirit of our God.

Only Americans could love Judge Judy—the famous television jurist and über-mom, as I call her, because of her matronly ability to make grown men look like disobedient children. I am sure that if the Corinthians had the technology we have, they would love Judge Judy also. The public airing of personal disputes makes for great theater. This explains Judge Judy's huge viewing audience in contemporary America. In Corinth, legal disputes were aired in large public buildings (basilicas) which were part of the city's forum. Whenever the court met, the public gathered around to take in the spectacle of well-known townsfolk accusing each other of all kinds of wrong-doing before the court, while a leading citizen who served as judge made his ruling. Although the public airing of personal disputes attracted large audiences in cities like Corinth, the Apostle Paul sees this as yet another manifestation of the wisdom of this age. Christians are to settle their disputes based upon the wisdom and power of God as revealed in the cross. Those who will judge the world, need to learn to settle their disputes in a God-honoring manner, and not resort to a public spectacle like that in the public marketplaces of Corinth.

Yet another strong indication of the spiritual immaturity within the Corinthian church can be seen in the fact that members of this congregation were taking each other to court to engage in civil litigation. Having spoken of the judgment to come upon those excommunicated in the previous chapter (v. 12), this brings to the apostle's mind the situation reported to him by members of Chloe's family (or others) regarding the fact that church members were suing each other in the city's courts.

In verses 1–6 of chapter 6, Paul rebukes the Corinthians for this immature behavior, while reminding them that Christians ought to be able to settle their own disputes without such litigation. In verses 7–8, Paul moves on to point out that church members were actually defrauding each other and cheating, a practice which Paul says must stop. Finally, in verses 9–11, Paul sets forth that conduct which excludes people from the kingdom of God so as to contrast this kind of prior conduct with the current status of Corinthian sinners who are trusting in Jesus Christ. Once again, it is important to note that Paul does not focus upon the particulars of these lawsuits, nor does he name any of the individuals involved. In fact, the focus really has not changed much from chapter 5. The issue in chapter 6 is still the failure of the Corinthian church to be the church.

And Such Were Some of You

Christians and Civil Litigation

Civil litigation among church members was a serious problem among the Corinthians. Apparently, members of this church were settling their disputes by suing each other in the civil courts of Corinth. Paul spells out the particulars in verse 1. "When one of you has a grievance against another, does he dare go to law before the unrighteous instead of the saints?" Paul is a realist—he knows full well that sinful people are going to have disputes with one another. The issue is "how should Christians settle these disputes when they arise?" Paul is emphatic that any personal disputes arising among members of the Corinthian church must be settled within the church, and not in the civil courts outside the church.

Some of the terminology Paul employs here is not only interesting, but very helpful in understanding his concerns. The word translated as "dare" (*tolma*) could be rendered something like "has the audacity." Paul is referring to conduct which is completely unacceptable for a Christian. The word for dispute (*pragma*) is a word which means "lawsuit" throughout secular Greek literature. The word translated "ungodly" is not *asebē* (cf. Rom. 4:5), but *adikōn*, which means "unrighteous" (not justified).[1]

Paul never says nor even implies that secular courts have no authority. But he does say they are composed of "the unrighteous" who do not consider matters affecting Christians from the perspective of God's word. It is not as though Christians cannot obtain justice in civil courts. Rather it is that Christians have no business taking their personal disputes before such courts in the first place. Paul's point is that these disputes need to be settled in the church along the lines prescribed by Jesus in Matthew 18:15–20, where Jesus prescribes that if a brother or sister sins against you, you seek them out personally, so as to

---

1. Morris, *1 Corinthians*, 90.

solve the matter before it goes any farther. Should that fail, Jesus prescribes additional steps, eventually taking the matter before the officers of the church. In that passage, we read,

> "If your brother sins against you, go and tell him his fault, between you and him alone. If he listens to you, you have gained your brother. But if he does not listen, take one or two others along with you, that every charge may be established by the evidence of two or three witnesses. If he refuses to listen to them, tell it to the church. And if he refuses to listen even to the church, let him be to you as a Gentile and a tax collector. Truly, I say to you, whatever you bind on earth shall be bound in heaven, and whatever you loose on earth shall be loosed in heaven. Again I say to you, if two of you agree on earth about anything they ask, it will be done for them by my Father in heaven. For where two or three are gathered in my name, there am I among them."

Throughout the Book of Acts, Paul repeatedly appealed to Caesar (and to the court) to protect him from physical harm from the Jews. In Romans 13:1–7, Paul speaks directly to the divine authority which underlies civil government, as well as the limitations God places on civil government. But Paul will not condone Christians taking other Christians to court over petty personal disputes. This was something Jews were particularly adamant about, and they avoided pagan courts altogether following the instructions given by Moses (in passages such as Deut. 1:9–18). Christians are to bring such disputes before the saints (the leaders of the church), not the world. In order to live in peace within the church and be a beacon to those outside the church, Christians must not air their dirty linen in public, so to speak.[2] No appearances on Judge Judy!

---

2. Barrett, *The First Epistle to the Corinthians*, 135.

And Such Were Some of You

There are a number of obvious parallels between Greco-Roman culture and our own. Civil litigation was common in Paul's time because the paganism of that age did not acknowledge transcendent absolutes. The citizens of Corinth believed in fate, or the arbitrary will of the gods. Just as in our own society, those of higher social standing took advantage of the courts since the judges were men from the same high strata of society. Those of the lower social status were at a decided disadvantage. In fact, one first century writer speaking about problems with the Isthmian Games, notes that Corinth and the surrounding area was filled with "lawyers innumerable perverting justice."[3] Since many in the Corinthian church were also from a lower social rank, no doubt, they too would have been at a decided disadvantage in the courts, should they be forced to litigate with someone of high social standing.

The same is true in our own day and age. The denial of moral absolutes produces a corresponding decline in personal moral responsibility. Given the vacuum regarding ethical and moral absolutes and personal responsibility, we see a corresponding increase in courts and lawyers, government power and intrusion into our private lives, and an increased emphasis upon lawyers, agents, managers, mediators, etc., who become the means of keeping order, since individuals have become increasingly incapable of keeping order themselves.[4] If people will not behave themselves, the police, the state, the courts will make them behave, and so we drown ourselves in a sea of laws, regulations, and litigation. Just as our culture is as highly sexualized as Corinth was, so too we live in a litigious society, as did the Corinthians.

---

3. Cf. Hays, *First Corinthians*, 93.

4. See, for example, the discussion of this in David F. Wells, *No Place for Truth* (Grand Rapids: William B. Eerdmans, 1995), 53–92.

Settling Our Disputes

In verse 2, Paul asks the first of six very pointed questions. "Or do you not know that the saints will judge the world? And if the world is to be judged by you, are you incompetent to try trivial cases?" The implication of Paul's question is that the Corinthians should know better than to do those things they were currently doing, including going to civil court, many times over trivial matters. Paul begins his series of questions by reminding the Corinthians that the reason they should take their disputes to the saints, rather than unbelievers, is the fact that "the saints will judge the world."

This certainly is an echo, in part, from our Lord's words in Matthew 19:28: "I tell you the truth, at the renewal of all things, when the Son of Man sits on his glorious throne, you who have followed me will also sit on twelve thrones, judging the twelve tribes of Israel." This particular judgment may refer to the present reign of the saints with Christ (cf. Rev. 20:4), or more likely to the final judgment. Paul's point is that if Christians are competent to assist in the judgment of the world on the day of judgment, are they not competent to judge in less weighty matters like settling disputes among Christians?

There is more in view here, however. "Do you not know that we are to judge angels? How much more, then, matters pertaining to this life!" (v. 3). Not only will the saints participate in the judgment of the world, they will even participate in the judgment of angelic beings, a statement found or implied nowhere else in Scripture. This may fit with subsequent comments Paul will make in 1 Corinthians 15:24–28 to the effect that all things are to be subject to Christ, "So that those who are in Christ will be placed over even the angels."[5] If this is true, how much more should Christians be able to judge the things of this life? Given

---

5. Hays, *First Corinthians*, 94.

the glorious final destiny of the church, the judgments we make about things in this life must be made in light of our participation in the age to come.

The solution is as follows (v. 4a): "So if you have such cases, why do you lay them before those who have no standing in the church?" Although this sounds like a hypothetical situation, the use of "if" carries with it the implication that such lawsuits should never arise in the first place. The Corinthians are submitting their personal disputes to those who are outside the church, people who do not have the mind of Christ in such matters. It is not a question of whether or not the secular judiciary is incompetent to judge. The fact of the matter is that Christians have no business taking their personal disputes outside the church. If we are suited to judge the world with Christ, then should we not be able to settle our personal disputes apart from a secular court? Of course, we can and we should.

In verses 4b-5, Paul raises this point for the following reason: "I say this to your shame. Can it be that there is no one among you wise enough to settle a dispute between the brothers." In 1 Corinthians 4:14, Paul stated that he did not want to shame his readers. "I do not write these things to make you ashamed, but to admonish you as my beloved children." Now the story is different, at least when it comes to those who are suing each other. The Corinthians prided themselves upon their great wisdom, yet Paul points out to them that given their attitude there may not even be one wise person in their midst.

By going to the secular courts, the Corinthians were subjecting themselves to judges who imbibed deeply from the well of the very same wisdom of this age which Paul is exhorting the Corinthians to reject. The word to "settle" (*diakrinai*) means something like "render a decision," and implies arbitration among believers, not litigation.[6] Paul is referring to arbitra-

---

6. Morris, *1 Corinthians*, 92.

tion (and not lawsuits) among "brothers," because he stresses the organic unity within the congregation, as in the next verse (v. 6): "But brother goes to law against brother, and that before unbelievers?" It is shocking to Paul that a brother would bring another member of the church family into a secular court to sue them. How can a Christian even bring such a matter out into the open in front of unbelievers? Paul is not asking us to hide our sins from unbelievers. He is asking us to demonstrate that the cross of Christ is God's solution to all of the problems associated with human sinfulness, including our disputes with one another.

Paul sternly admonishes the Corinthians that this must stop. In verse 7, the apostle puts this matter very directly: "To have lawsuits at all with one another is already a defeat for you. Why not rather suffer wrong? Why not rather be defrauded?" To take a brother into a secular court is already a defeat, whatever the outcome of the legal process. In fact, the outcome before the court really should not matter. There are no winners in such cases. One party loses the lawsuit. One party wins the lawsuit. But both parties end up bringing shame to the church. In fact, the real damage occurs not as result of the court's decision, but as a result of taking the matter outside the church. It would be better for an individual to be wronged or cheated than to risk dividing Christ's body by taking personal disputes before the unbelieving world.

The Corinthians never considered this point, apparently, because so many of them were involved in shady business dealings with each other. "But you yourselves wrong and defraud—even your own brothers!" (v. 8). Not only were members of this church engaging in wrong-doing, many were also the victims of cheating and fraud. The real scandal associated with the matter is that other church members were the ones inflicting the wrong-doing upon their fellow Christians! Christians should expect this of those outside the church, but certainly not from those within the church. Again, Paul does not give us the particulars of various situations, nor does he mention the individuals involved. But he does give us a general principle to follow—Christians should seek to settle personal disputes with other Christians without going to court.

Such Were Some of You

In verses 9–10, Paul makes a rather pointed statement, speaking in such a way as to imply that the behavior he's about to mention as excluding people from the kingdom of God, was common knowledge in the church. "Or do you not know that the unrighteous will not inherit the kingdom of God? Do not be deceived: neither the sexually immoral, nor idolaters, nor adulterers, nor men who practice homosexuality, nor thieves, nor the greedy, nor drunkards, nor revilers, nor swindlers will inherit the kingdom of God." This statement of the apostle fits well with the assertion that the critical issue in the Corinthian church is not confusion over the nature of the gospel, but rather with the inability to filter out pagan ways of thinking and doing.

Paul's use of the word "unrighteous" points to the status of the individuals involved before God. People who engage in such behavior without repentance will not inherit the kingdom of God. This list does not refer to Christians ("righteous") struggling with these particular sins as will become clear in the next verse (v. 11). But this list does indicate that this is the characteristic behavior of those outside the church, so the defrauding and cheating reflects behavior typical of pagans, not Christians. These are the same sins listed by Paul in 1 Corinthians 5:11. "But now I am writing to you not to associate with anyone who bears the name of brother if he is guilty of sexual immorality or greed, or is an idolater, reviler, drunkard, or swindler—not even to eat with such a one." And as previously noted, the items on this list are taken from the "exclusion texts" in the Book of Deuteronomy. The conduct God expects of the covenant community in the Old Testament, he expects of his covenant people in the new.

The linkage of various sexual sins with idolatry reflects the likely association of these practices with pagan worship, something typical of Greek religion and widespread throughout cities like Corinth. Yet, this is not the final word for the Corinthians. The final word is given in verse 11. Because the gospel has been preached to the Corinthians, the power of God has been manifest in their midst. The grace of God has wonderful results. "And such were some of you. But you were washed, you were sanctified, you were justified in the name of the Lord Jesus Christ and by the Spirit of our God." Paul's language suggests that there is a dramatic contrast between what the Corinthians *are now* because of the gospel, in light of what they *once were* before the gospel had been preached to them (i.e., when they were still pagans).

Some of the Corinthians *were* sexually immoral idolaters. Some *were* adulterers and prostitutes. Some *were* homosexual offenders. Some *were* greedy, partiers, drunkards, liars, and swindlers. Based upon this list, these people may have been deeply involved in paganism, either as practitioners or even as workers in the pagan temples. Some went before the city's courts, suing fellow church members to defraud them. Now these same people *have been* washed. They *have been* sanctified, they *have been* justified, in the name of Christ (the preaching of the gospel), through the power of the Holy Spirit manifest in that gospel. Paul's focus is on the contrast between what the Corinthians were (when they were living in unbelief) with what they are (in union with Christ by faith). Since this is what the Corinthians are by the grace of God, how can they continue to act like those who will not inherit the kingdom of God, by engaging in immorality (5:1–13), taking disputes before pagan courts (6:1–11), and engaging in fornication and adultery (6:12–20)?

The theological significance of this verse should not be overlooked. There is some discussion whether or not Paul sets out an *ordo salutis* (order of salvation) which places sanctification before justification, which is contrary to the order Paul sets out in Romans 8:28–30, which does not mention sanctification.[7] However, Paul is probably not speaking of a precise order of salvation, but has listed some of the many benefits which result from embracing the gospel by grace alone through faith alone.

The first of these benefits is "you were washed." The prefix (*apo*) points to the completeness of the act, while the aorist tense of the verb indicates that this is a completed and decisive act.[8] Many take this to refer to baptism since elsewhere the author of Hebrews says, "Let us draw near with a true heart in full assurance of faith, with our hearts sprinkled clean from an evil conscience and our bodies washed with pure water" (Hebrews 10:22). Baptism is the sign and seal of regeneration and the forgiveness of sins and echoes what Paul says in Titus 3:5: "He saved us, not because of works done by us in righteousness, but according to his own mercy, by the washing of regeneration and renewal of the Holy Spirit."

Paul does not mention baptism here in connection with "being washed." When he does mention baptism in other contexts such as Romans 6:1ff., Paul refers metaphorically to washing with the blood of Christ (cf. Rom. 3:35, through faith in his blood, 5:9, justified with Christ's blood). In any case, his main point is crystal clear. The Corinthians were washed (completely and definitively), and so now are clean. God no longer treats them as he did before this definitive act took place. His wrath

---

7. G. C. Berkouwer, *Faith and Justification* (Grand Rapids: William B. Eerdmans, 1979), 31.

8. Morris, *1 Corinthians*, 94.

no longer abides on them. Now, they are reckoned righteous and considered to be holy.

The second benefit listed by Paul is sanctification. Here too, Paul uses the aorist tense, meaning that all Christian believers have been set apart as God's for his own purposes. In 1 Corinthians 1:30, Paul wrote, "And because of him you are in Christ Jesus, who became to us wisdom from God, righteousness and sanctification and redemption." A believer in Jesus Christ receives all of Christ's saving benefits and has the guilt of their sin removed. Believers have been declared righteous because Christ's own righteousness has been credited to them through faith. Therefore, they are holy (*hagios*) by virtue of their union with Christ. They have received the perfect righteousness of Jesus Christ himself which has been imputed to them through faith. Can someone become "holier" through their own works after they already possess the perfect righteousness of Christ? The answer is, of course, "No." Christians are (*hagios*), they are "saints," or "holy." Yet sanctification does entail both mortification and vivification, the daily dying to sin and rising with Christ to newness of life (cf. Rom. 6:11).

The third benefit Paul mentions is justification. It too is spoken of in the aorist tense, meaning that all believers are now restored to a right-standing before God and regarded as righteous. Something definitive has already taken place which has restored sinners to a right-standing before God. It is unusual for Paul to speak of justification following sanctification. Perhaps the best way to explain this is that offered by Calvin. The reference to washing, sanctification, and justification, may be a reference to the same thing from three different angles. "Although these three phrases all refer, therefore, to the same thing, their variety, nevertheless, gives a great deal of force to what he says. For there are implied contrasts between washing and unclean things; sanctification and contamination; justification and guilt."[9] In any case, it is clear that all three of these blessings are associated with the "name of the Lord Jesus Christ." In other words, all of these blessings come to us by virtue of our union with Christ "and by the Spirit of our God" who effects a bond between all believers and their living head through faith. Those who were Gentile sinners are now the people of God who compose the living temple of the Holy Spirit. It no longer matters what they once did. Their former sins do not count against them. What now matters is they are "in Christ." Because they are in Christ, the Corinthian Christians are "washed," "sanctified," and "justified."

Don't Take Personal Disputes to Court

When Paul tells the church in Rome that even the Roman government is a minister of God (Rom. 13), he is informing us that there is a divinely-appointed role for both the civil and criminal courts. Yet, when writing to the Corinthians, Paul is dealing with a church composed of new Christians who are struggling to learn how to live as Christians. The Corinthian Christians were spiritually immature and still enamored with Greco-Roman wisdom. Many in the church had not yet learned one important aspect of biblical teaching—personal accountability for one's own actions. Like their contemporaries, many of the Corinthians had shady business practices and thought nothing of dragging people into court for the most trivial of reasons. Those who could afford a good lawyer (actually a skilled orator) could use the courts for personal gain by suing people for just about anything, hoping and expecting to prevail in court. Paul insists that the Corinthians cease defrauding one another, and that they follow the teaching of Jesus set out in Matthew 18 by settling personal disputes within the church, and not taking these personal matters out into the public courts before the pagans.

---

9. Calvin, *The First Epistle of Paul to the Corinthians*, 126.

First Corinthians

In a litigious society such as ours, Paul's words remind us of the importance of settling our disputes in the appropriate way. Yes, the courts have their place. When personal disputes arise, Christians need to seek resolution with each other first, and then take these matters before the church. No appearances on Judge Judy or in the People's Court! Christians are to settle their disputes among themselves.

Finally, in verses 9–11, Paul contrasts what the Corinthians were (sexually immoral, idolaters, adulterers, temple prostitutes, homosexuals, thieves, greedy, drunkards, revilers, swindlers) with what they now are in Christ: washed (forgiven), sanctified (holy), and justified (reckoned as righteous before God). The reason why this is the case is because the death of Jesus removes the guilt of our sin, and Christ's perfect righteousness is imputed to us through faith. There is no sin so bad and no sinner so vile that they cannot be redeemed by the blood and righteousness of Christ. When we are in union with Jesus Christ through faith, we must break with our pagan past and with all non-Christian ways of thinking and doing. We can no longer live our lives seeking pleasure and placing ourselves at the center of the universe. God graciously saves us from ourselves through the grace and mercy of Jesus Christ. But he also calls us to repent of our sin and leave behind our former way of life. If you struggle with the sins mentioned by Paul, hate what you do, and seek to cease living in sin, then be assured that God's kindness is indeed leading you to repentance (cf. Rom. 2:4). But if you seek to justify your sins, and if you make excuses as to why God loves you "just as you are" without requiring repentance, then please read through this section of Corinthians again. You have missed Paul's point

As with the Corinthians, such *were* all of us reading these words of Paul. But if we are in union with Jesus Christ through faith, we *have been* washed. We *have been* sanctified. We *have been* justified, through faith in Jesus Christ and through the manifestation of the Spirit's power. Thankfully, our fathers in the faith understood Paul's point quite well. As we read in questions 114 and 115 of the *Heidelberg Catechism*:

> **114. Can those who are converted to God keep these Commandments perfectly?**
>
> No, but even the holiest men, while in this life, have only a small beginning of such obedience, yet so that with earnest purpose they begin to live not only according to some, but according to all the Commandments of God.
>
> **115. Why then does God so strictly enjoin the Ten Commandments upon us, since in this life no one can keep them?**
>
> First, that as long as we live we may learn more and more to know our sinful nature, and so the more earnestly seek forgiveness of sins and righteousness in Christ; second, that without ceasing we diligently ask God for the grace of the Holy Spirit, that we be renewed more and more after the image of God, until we attain the goal of perfection after this life.

11

You Were Bought With a Price

1 CORINTHIANS 6:12–20

Flee from sexual immorality. Every other sin a person commits is outside the body, but the sexually immoral person sins against his own body. Or do you not know that your body is a temple of the Holy Spirit within you, whom you have from God? You are not your own, for you were bought with a price. So glorify God in your body.

No question, it was very difficult to be a Christian in first century Corinth. No question, it is very difficult to be a Christian in modern America. Corinth was a highly sexualized, promiscuous, and litigious society. So is ours. The Corinthians loved worldly wisdom, celebrity athletes, and superstitiously sought the blessings of the "gods." They were prone to depreciate the human body because of a pagan conception of the immortality of the soul, usually understood as a divine spark and the true essence of a person. Apparently, the Corinthian believers understood how sinners were justified, but they did not clearly understand the fact that Christians need to stop thinking and acting like pagans once they came to faith in Christ. Paul's solution to all of these matters is to press the Corinthian Christians to think about all of these issues in light of the cross of Jesus Christ. If we are bought with a price (the blood of Jesus), then we cannot do and think as we please. We belong to a risen Savior, who has not only purchased us, but who will raise us bodily from the dead.

In verse 12 of chapter 6, Paul makes a remarkable statement about Christian liberty which, apparently, was being cited out of context by some in the Corinthian congregation and turned into an excuse to indulge the flesh. Paul immediately and firmly sets the Corinthians straight. "'All things are lawful for me,' but not all things are helpful. 'All things are lawful for me,' but I will not be enslaved by anything." The phrase "all things are lawful for me" appears twice in this verse, and again in 1 Corinthians 10:23. There is some indication that these words had become a kind of motto within the Corinthian church, possibly based upon something Paul himself had said in response to Jewish legalism. These words are true, *if* understood in a particular way; we are justified by grace alone, through faith alone, on account of Christ alone, so we are now free to obey God and enjoy all of the good things which come to us from our heavenly Father.

Lawful, But Not Necessarily Helpful

By this statement, Paul does not mean that Christians are free from all rules and external constraints (i.e., the moral law), as some of the Corinthians were apparently contending. Understood properly, Paul's point is that the sacrificial death of Jesus Christ frees us from any form of legalistic scheme of self-justification based upon personal righteousness and obedience to the law of God (e.g., Jewish legalism). Since God has created all things and pronounced them "good," all things can be sanctified by prayer. This is why Christians are not forbidden from eating certain types of food; an issue in this congregation. This is

You Were Bought With a Price

what led Augustine to define the essence of the Christian ethic as, "Love God, and do what you will."[1] Understood in this way, a Christian can indeed affirm that "all things are permissible." In fact, this statement virtually echoes what Paul says in Galatians 5:13: "For you were called to freedom, brothers. Only do not use your freedom as an opportunity for the flesh, but through love serve one another." Paul's assertion, however, raises yet another question, "What is it that a Christian should desire to do?"

From what Paul says here, apparently some of the Corinthians had seized upon his phrase, removed it from its theological context, and then turned it into a slogan to justify their sinful behavior. "All things are lawful" took on new meaning for some in Corinth. "There are no limits." "I can profess faith in Christ but still live like a pagan!" This is why Paul reiterates that the phrase is true, but only with a very important qualification, "not all things are helpful." Christian freedom can be abused to the point that it becomes positively harmful to both body and soul. While all things are permissible (in a certain sense), not all things *ought* to be done. Peter puts it this way in his first epistle: "Live as people who are free, not using your freedom as a cover-up for evil, but living as servants of God" (1 Pet. 2:16). Reformed theologians have discussed the question of freedom and restraint under the heading of "prudence," which is the art (skill) of enjoying Christian freedom while at the same time engaging in self-discipline and discretion based upon godly wisdom and Spirit-enabled self-control.[2]

To reinforce the gravity of his original point, Paul reiterates the phrase yet a second time, but adds an additional qualification: "I will not be enslaved by anything" (v. 26b). Paul considers himself a bondservant of Jesus Christ (1 Cor. 7:22). He re-

---

1. Augustine, *Tractatus* VII, 8. (Homily 7 on the epistles of St. John). The Latin reads, *Dilige et quod vis fac*.

2. Michael S. Horton, "Recovering the Art of Christian Prudence," *Modern Reformation*, March/April 2000 Vol. 9, Num: 2.

fuses to allow himself to be mastered by anything other than Jesus Christ. There is a paradox of sorts here. Paul is a servant of Christ, and therefore free from Jewish legalism. While "all things" (rightly understood) are permissible to him, Paul is personally resigned not be bound by anything which he might otherwise be free to do. He is bound only to Christ. His fear is that a Christian (paradoxically) may unwittingly become enslaved to the very things he is now free to do.

That this is Paul's concern can be seen in verse 13, when, once again, Paul cites another slogan of the libertine party in the Corinthian church and responds to it. "'Food is meant for the stomach and the stomach for food'—and God will destroy both one and the other. The body is not meant for sexual immorality, but for the Lord, and the Lord for the body." From Paul's comment, it seems likely that some in the Corinthian church were using the slogan "Food is for the stomach" to justify their self-indulgence. This is a parallel of sorts to another slogan Paul cites in 1 Corinthians 15:32, "Let us eat and drink, for tomorrow we die." For many Greek pagans, the body does not really matter. It is the soul that counts. Taking Paul's words out of context and distorting his meaning, the libertines among the Corinthians were saying to themselves, "Let us indulge ourselves, and not only eat all kinds of things, let us enjoy them in great quantities!"

Paul must cut through the errors of Jewish legalism—that we are made right before God by obedience to works of law (cf. Gal. 2:16). He must also deal with Greek libertines for whom "anything goes," as well as with Greek Stoics, who sought to deny themselves any bodily pleasures. The critical theological error made by Corinthians is that gluttony and lust are merely "bodily urges." Biblically understood, these urges are manifestations of sinful and fallen human nature.

Many Greeks believed that the human soul was ethically pure (if not divine) and trapped in the prison house of the body. This way of thinking quite naturally led to the erroneous assumption that the body (not the soul) is the source of all sinful urges. This also leads to the belief that the body is not as important as the soul. Based upon this erroneous assumption, many first century Greeks believed that the body should be either abused to suppress its urges, or otherwise gratified and its urges indulged. This was thought to have little if any impact upon one's soul and spiritual condition.[3]

Other Greeks took the opposite route and denied any pleasure to themselves altogether. The former kind of thinking leads to gluttony and sexual immorality. The latter leads to abstinence from those things God permits us to enjoy. To the libertines, if the soul is all that matters, why not enjoy the pleasures of the flesh? To the Stoic Greek legalist, we must deny ourselves things which God says are good to keep the body from experiencing any pleasure.

The Importance of the Body

Paul's response to this two-sided misuse of Christian liberty is to remind the Corinthians of the importance of the body. Yet he does so in a way in which the Corinthians might not have expected. Contrary to the Greek assumption that the body is meaningless and that the soul is what truly matters, Paul reminds his readers that both food and stomach will be done away with. All such temporal things will be destroyed when this present age gives way to the age to come. This is Paul's point in Romans 14:17, when he writes, "For the kingdom of God is not a matter of eating and drinking but of righteousness and peace and joy in the Holy Spirit." Our bodies will be raised and transformed on the day of Christ Jesus, when God raises the dead with imperishable bodies.

---

[3]. Hays, *First Corinthians*, 103–104.

First Corinthians

Neither is there a necessary connection between hunger and gluttony. Bodily urges are good and natural. These urges are part and parcel of human existence. Gluttony, however, is sinful. Furthermore, our bodies were never made for lust, just as they were never made for gluttony. Our bodies were made for God, for his service, for his honor and glory.

Paul's assertion flies directly in the face of the gnostic impulse (and the corresponding depreciation of the material world) which was not only prominent in Corinth, but which is equally prominent in our contemporary society. It is paganism (and its corresponding dualism between spirit and matter) which leads to the depreciation of the human body. Paraphrasing C. S. Lewis, "God likes matter, he invented it."[4] Being a divine image-bearer, in part, entails bodily existence. Redemption from sin ultimately includes the redemption of our bodies (cf. Eph. 1:13–14). This is why Paul will go on to say in verse 20, "Glorify God in your bodies." The Corinthians need to understand this.

In light of Paul's concerns here, one of the sure signs of pagan influence upon our own thinking is any tendency toward the depreciation of matter in general, and the human body in particular. As for the Corinthians, this depreciation of the material aspect of human existence was yet another manifestation of the Corinthians' infatuation with pagan wisdom. In this, we see the spiritual and theological immaturity which plagues this congregation.

Paul's point in verse 14 is that God is concerned with the redemption of material things (including the human body). "And God raised the Lord and will also raise us up by his power." The resurrection of the body is one of the central themes of early Christian preaching and Pauline theology. In a display of his power, God raised Christ bodily from the dead. This was Jesus' own testimony in Luke 24:39: "See my hands and my feet, that

---

4. C. S. Lewis, *Mere Christianity* (New York: MacMillan, 1952), 91.

it is I myself. Touch me, and see. For a spirit does not have flesh and bones as you see that I have." The nature of the resurrection body will be described by Paul in great detail later on in this letter (1 Cor. 15:35–58).

Even as Jesus was bodily raised from the dead, so too shall we be raised. In 2 Corinthians 4:14, Paul writes, "Knowing that he who raised the Lord Jesus will raise us also with Jesus and bring us with you into his presence." Paul now takes the Corinthian slogan and turns it on its head to make a very important point (in v. 13). "Food is for the stomach and the stomach is for the body, and the end of both is destruction. The body is for the Lord and the Lord is for the body, and the resurrection is the destiny of both."[5]

The resurrection of our bodies is the Christian hope. God will redeem all of creation, including our bodily and material existence. Therefore, the pagan conception that the body is nothing, and that the soul is what really matters, flies directly in the face of Christian teaching, in which the person as a unity of body and soul is central to human life. The undoing of the unity between body and soul is why death is such a horrible thing. The unity of body and soul (which constitutes us as human persons), and which God has joined together when he gave us life, is now torn apart (cf. Psalm 139). This is why salvation from the consequences of our sin is such a great and wondrous thing. God will redeem both our bodies and souls, and in the resurrection he will reunite them, and then glorify the unity when reunited.

The Struggle with Sexual Immorality

As Paul points out, there is a direct connection between the depreciation of the body and sexual immorality. If the body is good, how can the Corinthian libertines continue to depreciate the body? Based upon Paul's prior instruction to them, the

---

5. Morris, *1 Corinthians*, 97.

Corinthians should have understood this. In verse 15, Paul appeals (for the fourth time) to his readers, asking them a question which implies that they should already know the answer. "Do you not know that your bodies are members of Christ? Shall I then take the members of Christ and make them members of a prostitute? Never!"

Paul asks the pointed rhetorical question, "Do you not know?" indicating that what follows is something his readers/hearers *should* know. Paul has already taught the Corinthians that all Christians are members of the body of Christ. Not only will Jesus raise our physical bodies (an indication that our bodies belong to Christ who is both our creator and redeemer), but we are even now united to the risen Christ through his indwelling Holy Spirit (cf. Eph. 1:3–14; 2:1–10). Just as we are married to our spouses, and therefore united to them, so too, we are analogously united to Jesus Christ, our heavenly bridegroom (cf. Eph. 5:22–32).

As Paul indicates, a sexual union with a prostitute is not strictly the same as a believer's union with the ascended Christ. But Paul does contend that sexual relations between a believer and a prostitute creates a bond between the two parties which certainly transcends an incidental act such as a handshake. To have sexual relations with someone is to be united to them in some sense beyond mere physical contact. Such a union is highly problematic for people with spouses, and for those who profess to be Christian believers. The fact that believers compose the body of Christ is discussed by Paul quite extensively later on this letter (1 Cor. 12:12ff., as well as in Ephesians 5:23ff.). Because of our inclusion in Christ's body, and because all believers are "in Christ," how then can it be proper to take those who are members of Christ's body and unite them with a prostitute in an idolatrous temple? Paul's answer is the emphatic *mē genoito*. "Never!"

You Were Bought With a Price

Of special importance here is the fact that Corinth was filled with temple prostitutes (both male and female). By engaging in sexual relations with such a prostitute, it was thought that the patron was united to the particular deity which the prostitute happened to represent. The holy—the Christian united to Christ—is now physically linked to the unholy. Given Paul's view of each Christian as a member of the body of Christ, as well as his stress upon the resurrection of the body to be set forth in 1 Corinthians 15, Paul recoils in horror at the very thought of such a union between Christians and pagans, especially when prostitution is directly tied to false worship and idolatrous religion. May it never be!

Not only are there connections to idolatry implied in the supposed union with a pagan deity through sexual relations, for Paul, to substitute an illicit sexual relationship (fornication, adultery, or homosexuality) for one sanctioned by God (marriage) has serious consequences (theological, moral, and emotional). Sexual sins are especially destructive. As Richard Hays points out,

> Sexual intercourse cannot be understood merely as a momentary act that satisfies a transient natural urge. Instead, it creates a mysterious but real and enduring union between man and woman . . . . The union of a member of the church with a prostitute . . . creates a real bonding with her; therefore, it creates an unholy bond between the Lord's members and the sinful world. The result is both defilement and confusion.[6]

In verse 16, Paul continues to make this point when he asks what seems obvious at this point. "Or do you not know that he who is joined to a prostitute becomes one body with her? For, as it is written, 'The two will become one flesh.'" Yet again, Paul

---

6. Hays, *First Corinthians*, 105.

asks a question implying Paul's readers/hearers should know the answer. To be frank, the Bible is not squeamish about sex, or sexual sins, and neither should Christians be squeamish about these things. We are sexual beings and sexual sins are part and parcel of church life. Such matters ought to be discussed frankly and openly as the apostle does. In fact, Paul's insights into this matter are exceptional by first century standards. Paul's question indicates that he had already taught the Corinthians about these matters in some detail. Since the sexual relationship involves two people becoming one flesh (as is taught in Gen. 2:24), the Corinthians must understand that such sexual encounters with prostitutes were hardly casual encounters without any theological, moral, or emotional consequences.

To engage in sexual relations with a temple prostitute is to become one (to form a spiritual union) with an individual in a relationship not sanctioned by God, and with someone who represents a deity directly opposed to God and to the gospel of Jesus Christ! To engage in this conduct is to set in motion a serious set of theological, moral, emotional, and physical consequences. For a Christian, there is no such thing as "casual sex." The many voices of contemporary culture may tell us that it is only natural to express our love for someone through sexual relations (if not married to them), or even that casual sexual relationships are actually a healthy expression of our sexuality. But Paul knows that sex before or outside of marriage is not only forbidden by God, when we do so, we are sinning against ourselves (our own bodies). And we cause our partner to do the same.

The theological implications of this are to be seen in light of Paul's point in verse 17. "But he who is joined to the Lord becomes one spirit with him." Believers are already united to Christ in a way analogous to a marriage between a husband and wife. As husband and wife become "one flesh," believers have already become "one spirit" with Jesus Christ by virtue of their union with him through faith. Because Christians are united to Christ in such a manner, how can the Corinthians substitute an illicit relationship in the place of one sanctioned by God (marriage)? Or, even worse, perhaps, how can they be united to a temple prostitute in the quest to become closer to a pagan deity? This is why paganism seeks to distort the natural order of things. To justify their practices, pagans must turn the unnatural into the natural, the immoral into the moral.

Verse 18 contains Paul's command (imperative) to the Corinthians. Paul also further develops the emotional ramifications of such sin. "Flee from sexual immorality. Every other sin a person commits is outside the body, but the sexually immoral person sins against his own body." It is important to notice that Paul does not command the Corinthians to resist sexual immorality. They are commanded to flee from it! There is a loud echo in Paul's words from the account of Joseph and Potiphar's wife in Genesis (cf. Gen. 39:12). The implication of Paul's imperative is that we must learn to flee from sexual sin. The person most likely to give in to sexual sin is the person who tries to resist sexual temptation. Paul's imperative is clear. Do not try to resist sexual immorality. Rather, flee from sexual immorality, because sexual temptation is so difficult to resist!

The reason for this command is that sexual sin affects us in a profound way. Not only is the temptation especially great, especially in a sexually promiscuous culture such as ours where we are continually bombarded with sexually explicit images, but so are the consequences. This does not in any sense mean that sexual sins are worse than other sins (in the sense that sexual sins make us guiltier before God than other sins). Paul's point is that sexual sins carry with them a sense of guilt and shame that other sins do not. This is why Paul can state that other sins are "outside the body," while sexual sins are sins against our own bodies. This may be a way of saying that sexual sins are sins against our own persons. It is also possible that the language "outside the body" may be another slogan from the libertine party in the Corinthian church.[7] Sexual lust arises for the sole purpose of self-gratification and is, therefore, one of the surest signs of how self-centered sin makes us. We will risk everything for that one moment of gratification.

This is why sexual sins are serious (psychologically speaking) for a Christian who is already united to Christ, and especially for a Christian who is married. Such sins not only carry with them a profound sense of guilt and shame, they often bring about serious consequences including: divorce, pregnancy, health issues, guilt and shame, etc. It is not uncommon for sexual sin to be connected with apostasy, depression, guilt, and self-destructive behavior. People who fall into sexual sin will often stop attending church. They often have doubts about whether or not Christianity is true. The inward and sinful pull toward sinful sexual behavior pulls us away from Christ. If someone wishes to live in sexual sin, they do not want to be reminded of what Christ has done for them, and that he is their spiritual bridegroom.

Our Bodies Are Temples of the Holy Spirit

Once again, in verses 19–20, Paul asks a question which reminds the Corinthians of something he has already taught them. "Or do you not know that your body is a temple of the Holy Spirit within you, whom you have from God? You are not your own, for you were bought with a price. So glorify God in your body." For the sixth time, Paul asks a question to which his readers/hearers should know the answer. Christians are united to the risen Christ through faith and are indwelt by the Holy Spirit. God's Spirit dwells in us, so that we (collectively) are God's temple: although at this point Paul does speak of each individual

---

7. Barrett, *First Epistle to the Corinthians*, 150.

You Were Bought With a Price

Christian being a temple. Because we are Jesus Christ's, we are indwelt by the Holy Spirit. Because we are indwelt by the Holy Spirit, we are no longer our own. We have been bought with a price, the shed blood of Jesus Christ.

The indicative (Christ purchasing us) precedes the imperative (glorifying God in our bodies). Instead of using our bodies as vehicles of self-gratification and engaging in self-destructive behavior (typical of paganism), Paul exhorts us to honor God with our bodies. We do this by living in modesty, chastity, and faith (the classical categories of Christian ethics). Christ shed his blood to redeem us from the things which destroy us. And since this is the case, why do so many still seek that which is so destructive? In this we see how deeply sin inheres in our fallen sinful nature, and why we must ever be on our guard, lest we too fall into sexual sin.

When Paul discusses the importance of Christian chastity, no doubt, his words at the end of this chapter must be read in light of the apostle's previous statement in 1 Corinthians 6:9–11 which precede this discussion.

> Or do you not know that the unrighteous will not inherit the kingdom of God? Do not be deceived: neither the sexually immoral, nor idolaters, nor adulterers, nor men who practice homosexuality, nor thieves, nor the greedy, nor drunkards, nor revilers, nor swindlers will inherit the kingdom of God. And such were some of you. But you were washed, you were sanctified, you were justified in the name of the Lord Jesus Christ and by the Spirit of our God.

Through the cross of Jesus Christ, God can and does forgive all sin—even sexual sin. If we are trusting in Jesus Christ, we have been washed, we have been sanctified, and we have been justified. If we trust in Jesus Christ, then he is preparing us to be his bride, as described in Ephesians 5:25–27. "Christ loved the church and gave himself up for her, that he might sanctify her, having cleansed her by the washing of water with the word, so that he might present the church to himself in splendor, without spot or wrinkle or any such thing, that she might be holy and without blemish." In Jesus Christ's eyes, we are all pure virgins. We are clothed in his perfect righteousness and cleansed from all our sins. It is only when we realize who we are in Christ (spotless) that our attraction to non-Christian views of sexuality begin to diminish, and we begin to gain both the strength and desire to flee whenever Potiphar's wife casts her gaze in our direction.

Because Jesus has bought us with a price (his blood), and will save even our bodies (in the resurrection), we have been truly liberated from bondage to sexual sin. How then can we attempt to justify living like we once did when we were non-Christians? We cannot. We have been bought with a price, so now we are to glorify God with our bodies. This means living all of life in light of the fact that our bodies have been redeemed by Christ and will be raised on the last day. We are his spotless bride, and he is our heavenly Bridegroom.

12

Each Has His Own Gift from God

1 CORINTHIANS 7:1–16

> *Now concerning the matters about which you wrote: "It is good for a man not to have sexual relations with a woman." But because of the temptation to sexual immorality, each man should have his own wife and each woman her own husband. The husband should give to his wife her conjugal rights, and likewise the wife to her husband. For the wife does not have authority over her own body, but the husband does. Likewise the husband does not have authority over his own body, but the wife does. Do not deprive one another, except perhaps by agreement for a limited time, that you may devote yourselves to prayer; but then come together again, so that Satan may not tempt you because of your lack of self-control.*

From a Christian perspective, pagan religion almost always leads to some form of self-indulgence. But paganism can also lead people to reject things which God has created and blessed, and which are intended for our use and enjoyment. If the soul is pure and trapped in the prison of the body, as the

Greek pagans were teaching, then the body is the source of both physical desires and sinful urges. If the body is inferior to the soul, then people will either indulge its every urge (as many in Corinth were doing), or else deny it any pleasure (even when that pleasure is ordained and blessed by God). This too is a problem in Corinth, especially when it comes to marriage, of all things. The Corinthians are confused about these issues and have written to Paul asking for clarification. Which he does.

In chapter seven of his letter to the Corinthians, Paul addresses the specific subjects about which the Corinthians had written him, requesting additional information and clarification (7:1). The first of these matters concerns marriage (chapter 7), before Paul moves on to address the subject of idolatry (beginning in chapter 8).

The Greco-Roman world was thoroughly pagan in terms of the prevailing sexual mores. The Greco-Roman denial of the biblical ethic usually took one of two directions. The first direction is toward sexual promiscuity (including fornication, adultery, and homosexuality). Not only was it common for men to keep mistresses, concubines, and engage in adulterous behavior (7:2), it was not uncommon for men to procure the services of temple prostitutes. Homosexual acts were commonplace. Paul has already addressed this topic in chapter 6, urging all Christians to flee from sexual immorality. He has also urged the Corinthian church to discipline those who engage in such behavior, but who refuse to repent and in doing so bring scandal to the church.

Another issue associated with pagan sexuality is asceticism and the repression of divinely-sanctioned human sexuality (in marriage). Celibacy was stressed in certain quarters in the Greco-Roman world because it was thought that those who mastered all bodily urges were able to keep their souls pure from earthly defilement. This is typical of a pagan dualism between

Each Has His Own Gift from God

spirit and matter. It is easy to see how the suppression of human sexuality would be an attractive option for Greeks who converted to Christianity, only to discover the biblical prohibitions against sexual immorality. This was clearly an issue among the Corinthians and, apparently, a number of them had questions about how celibacy relates to the biblical sexual ethic. Complete celibacy, even in marriage, was advocated by some as the norm for Christians.

Celibacy and Marriage

Paul informs the Corinthians that while celibacy is "good" under certain circumstances, and while there are certain advantages to remaining celibate, according to 1 Corinthians 11:11, Paul affirms that marriage is the normal human condition. Marriage can bring greater completeness while removing certain temptations. In 1 Corinthians 7:26, Paul speaks of the great distress in the church due to rampant sexual immorality, as the current climate in Corinth likely exacerbated sexual temptation for those who were struggling with sexual desire. As Paul sees it, celibacy is a gift from God and is one way of dealing with the pressures and temptations associated with pagan immorality. While Paul prefers to remain celibate himself (he is probably widowed by this time), he does not command celibacy. But he does recommend celibacy for those whom God has called to this status in life.

There are several common misconceptions about Paul's instructions which we will need to address before going through the details of the passage. Paul is not writing a systematic treatise on marriage. Rather, he is responding to specific questions posed by the Corinthians. Therefore, we must keep in mind that Paul is answering questions the Corinthians put to him, not those questions we may wish put to him which deal with issues in the modern world. This helps clarify a number of the issues which are addressed by Paul.

Paul's advice is remarkably common-sensical. His point is that people should remain in the condition they were in when the Lord called them. You cannot unscramble eggs. Those who are married should remain married, even if they are married to unbelievers. Those who are celibate by choice should remain celibate. There is no biblical command to marry, and there are certain advantages to celibacy. Those who are single and struggling with sexual immorality, should seek to marry, because it is better to marry than to burn with passion. The church should take people where we find them, and then seek to move them forward, rather than seek to undo all the mistakes and sins of the past, as some might advocate.

In verse 1, we learn that this discussion of marriage arises from correspondence sent by the Corinthians to Paul (while he was in Ephesus), and that at least some of the Corinthians approved of the following slogan and applied it even to marriage. Paul writes, "Now concerning the matters about which you wrote: 'It is good for a man not to have sexual relations with a woman.'" Therefore, the slogan in question, "It is . . . (good) for a man not to touch a woman" (v. 1) does not come from Paul, but from the Corinthians. This is not Paul's advice as some have understood this passage. Rather, it is a slogan coming from the lips of those who misunderstood Paul's reasons for celibacy.

The phrase as literally translated should be rendered, "It is good for a man not to touch a woman," which is a euphemism meaning to have sexual relations with a woman.[1] The expression (*haptesthai*) never means "to marry," and the reason some commentators and English translations (e.g., the NIV), interpret this as referring to marriage is because they mistakenly assume that Paul is generally endorsing the principle of celibacy, rather than refuting the erroneous notion held by certain peo-

---

1. Hays, *First Corinthians*, 113.

Each Has His Own Gift from God

ple in the church that even married people should abstain from sexual relations, as the slogan clearly indicates.[2]

This becomes clear when Paul writes in verses 2–4:

> But because of the temptation to sexual immorality, each man should have his own wife and each woman her own husband. The husband should give to his wife her conjugal rights, and likewise the wife to her husband. For the wife does not have authority over her own body, but the husband does. Likewise the husband does not have authority over his own body, but the wife does.

While Paul will point out that under certain conditions the avoidance of sexual relations is a good thing (e.g., someone called to celibacy, or someone waiting to be married), this does not apply to those already married, as some of the Corinthians were teaching.

Paul's point is very straight-forward. Since immorality is such a great problem, and the temptation to return to pagan ways is great and many people were giving in to it, married people should be clear about the fact that a husband and wife "have" authority over each other's bodies. This is not only a strong affirmation of monogamy, but because sexual temptation is so great, married couples must not heed this wrong-headed advice and abstain from sexual relations, since doing so only increases the temptation toward marital infidelity. Rather, it is the biblical duty of husbands and wives to enjoy the marital relationship (v. 3). Withholding marital relations is highly problematic, as Paul will go on to say in verse 10. The absence of sexual relations not only does great harm to the marriage and can lead to divorce (desertion), but it creates a situation where the temptation toward marital infidelity is greatly increased. John Murray bluntly reminds us of yet another potential problem here. "Failure to

---

2. Fee, *The First Epistle to the Corinthians*, 270–271.

co-operate in the use of the conjugal act becomes all the more reprehensible when it puts on the garb of piety. Then it becomes contemptible piosity."[3]

It is noteworthy, that in the ancient world (where wives were often regarded as property with few legal rights), Paul puts husband and wife on a parity of sorts. In Ephesians 5:22–33, Paul teaches that wives are to submit to the headship of their husbands, but he also teaches that the husband's body belongs to his wife (and vice-versa). The verb Paul uses in verse 4 of 1 Corinthians 7 (*exousiazei*) literally means to exercise authority over something, in the sense of "belonging to each other."[4]

Husbands and Wives

There are a number of important ramifications stemming from Paul's directive. Husbands and wives are sexual equals (which prevents one party from forcing the other party to do something offensive to them). This also reaffirms the point that sexual relations are indispensable to marriage (except in the case of distance or illness) and that those in the Corinthian church teaching that couples should abstain from marital relations within marriage are in error. Within the context of marriage, sexual relations do not defile the body. To teach otherwise is to adopt the pagan view that the body is evil and that the sexual urge is a "lower passion." We are created as sexual beings and God has given to us a wonderful context in which these natural desires can be fulfilled and enjoyed. Because husbands and wives "belong" to each other, we should cherish our spouses and enjoy one another sexually within the bounds of conscience.

There are times, however, in which abstinence from sexual relations within marriage is permissible, but only by mutual agreement. As Paul states in verse 5–6, "Do not deprive one an-

---

3. Murray, *Principles of Conduct*, 62.
4. Thiselton, *The First Epistle to the Corinthians*, 506.

Each Has His Own Gift from God

other, except perhaps by agreement for a limited time, that you may devote yourselves to prayer; but then come together again, so that Satan may not tempt you because of your lack of self-control. Now as a concession, not a command, I say this." Paul's command is clear—do not deprive each other, except by mutual agreement. This is so a married couple can devote themselves to a specific time of prayer. However, mutual abstinence should be practiced with great care, and for a limited duration so that spouses do not open the door to Satanic temptations (probably a reference to the connection in Corinth between temple prostitution and false religion) and because of a lack of self-control on the part of either party to the marriage. Paul does not command a period of abstinence, but he does permit it, provided there is mutual consent.

In the next verse (v. 7), Paul gives us some tantalizing hints about his own personal biography. "I wish that all were as I myself am. But each has his own gift from God, one of one kind and one of another." At the time of the writing of this epistle, Paul is single, probably a widower, since, according to the Mishnah, Jewish men were to be married and seek to have large families.[5] In Acts 26:10, we learn that Paul was closely associated with the Sanhedrin, and it is doubtful that a single man could have been made a member of the ruling council. Although it is possible that "Mrs. Paul" deserted her husband after his conversion (and remained behind in Jerusalem), it is far more likely that Mrs. Paul had died by this time and that Paul was now a widower. In any case, Paul states that he has the divine gift of celibacy and he wishes that others had it as well. This is probably a reference to the fact that many in the church were being told that celibacy was for all, and then found themselves burning with passion and falling victim to sexual temptation. Those with the gift of celibacy should remain

---

5. See the helpful discussion in F. F. Bruce, *Paul: The Apostle of the Set Free* (Grand Rapids: William B. Eerdmans, 1979), 269–270.

celibate. "To the unmarried and the widows I say that it is good for them to remain single as I am" (v. 8).

Widows and the Unmarried

Once the general rule of thumb has been established, Paul deals with specific cases, starting with the widowed and unmarried. If people in these particular circumstances have the gift of celibacy, then let them stay unmarried, as Paul now is. However, not everyone has the gift of celibacy, and those who do not have this gift should seek to get married. Some argue that Paul is referring here to widows and widowers (not unmarried people in general) whom Paul will specifically address in verses 25–38.[6] This would limit Paul's advice here specifically to those who have lost spouses to death. If true, this clearly points to Paul's own status as a widower, "as I am." While this interpretation has much to commend it, the word translated "unmarried" (*agamois*) is a broad term and includes all unmarried people. Paul is probably speaking to those who have lost spouses, as well as to those not yet married.

In verse 9, Paul addresses those who struggle with sexual temptation. "But if they cannot exercise self-control, they should marry. For it is better to marry than to burn with passion." For those who find being single a horrible burden and who struggle to control themselves in the face of constant temptation to sexual sin, it would be better to marry. Paul points out that marriage is better than struggling with the lusts of the flesh (lit., "burning with the fire of passion"). As Calvin wryly puts it, "It is one thing to burn, it is another to feel heat ... What Paul calls burning is not merely a slight sensation, but being so aflame with passion that you cannot stand up against it."[7] This is a command (imperative) for those who are "burning," rather than mere permission. Those who are widowed are permitted to remarry, and those who are

---

6. Hays, *First Corinthians*, 118–119.

7. Calvin, *The First Epistle of Paul to the Corinthians*, 144.

single (without the gift of celibacy) are exhorted to marry in the Lord.

Divorce

In verses 10–11, Paul now takes up the thorny subject of divorce. "To the married I give this charge (not I, but the Lord): the wife should not separate from her husband (but if she does, she should remain unmarried or else be reconciled to her husband), and the husband should not divorce his wife." Not everyone is, as Paul is, unmarried. To those Christians who were already married, and who were tempted to leave their spouses upon discovery that sexual relations (not celibacy) were mandatory, Paul passes along a command of Jesus ("not I, but the Lord").

Under limited certain circumstances, Roman law allowed a woman to instigate a divorce. But a Christian wife must not separate from her husband out of a desire to remain celibate. If she does, she must remain unmarried, or else be reconciled to her husband, who likewise must not divorce his wife for the same reason. Divorce is not a biblical option to escape from marital obligation. Should one party leave the other—in this case, to escape this obligation, or in the case of which Jesus was speaking, where someone divorces their spouse to marry another whom they prefer more—they must remain unmarried or else seek reconciliation with their current spouse.

There are several important issues at play here. This is one of the few places where Paul directly appeals to the teaching of Jesus (cf. 1 Cor. 9:4; 1 Thess. 4:15–17), which at this point was most likely a body of memorized sayings of Jesus (since the gospels were most likely not yet written). In Mark 10:2–12, Jesus addresses the subject of divorce directly—referring to Moses' provision for divorce in Deuteronomy 24:1–4. Paul does not mention the exceptional case (i.e., Jesus' permission of divorce in the case of adultery, Matt. 5:32; 19:9), or even divorce in the case of the desertion of a believing spouse by an unbeliever, a subject Paul is soon to take up in verse 15. No doubt, the early church (before the writing of the gospels) had access to the memorized teaching of Jesus through the apostles and those who actually heard Jesus preach.

It is also important to remember that Paul is not writing a systematic treatment on divorce or remarriage. Rather, Paul is dealing with the specific question raised by the letter to him from the Corinthians. In light of the specific question put to him, the case under consideration is that in order to remain celibate and not defile the body, some believers might consider (or had considered) divorce preferable to engaging in sexual relations. Paul does not speak to the case of the victim of adultery (as Jesus does, and as Paul will later on) or to the matter of desertion. Paul's specific concern here is to stop people from initiating divorce because they think the body and its passions are evil, and they prefer to remain celibate.

Before working our way through the substance of Paul's discussion of this matter, first, we ought to deal with the comment Paul makes about the authority of what follows: "I, not the Lord." Paul does not mean that what he affirms contradicts what Jesus has said. What Paul does mean is that Jesus did not speak to this specific situation in any known saying. What follows is grounded in Paul's own apostolic authority, which comports with that revealed by the Spirit of God (1 Cor. 7:40—"I think that I too have the Spirit of God"). The apostolic church was cognizant of the memorized sayings of Jesus, and that these sayings were authoritative. In those cases where there is no such oral tradition, Paul speaks with apostolic authority. "I, not the Lord."

The irony is that success of the Gentile mission created a whole series of pastoral problems including issues regarding divorce and sexual behavior. Paul must address a question which neither the Old Testament nor Jesus address, namely, "What is

Each Has His Own Gift from God

to be done in those cases where one party in a marriage converts to Christianity while the other does not? Should the Christian remain with a non-Christian spouse?" Paul will address the subject of a Christian who seeks to marry a non-Christian later in 2 Corinthians 6:14–7:1—"Do not do it!" But here he writes, "To the rest I say (I, not the Lord) that if any brother has a wife who is an unbeliever, and she consents to live with him, he should not divorce her. If any woman has a husband who is an unbeliever, and he consents to live with her, she should not divorce him."

Two Uses of "Holy"

This issue would have been a common one in Corinth, even as it can be in our own day. What happens in the case of those who marry before becoming Christians, and then later one spouse comes to faith in Christ while the other remains a non-Christian? If a Christian is married to an unbelieving wife, and she wishes to remain with her husband, Paul says, he is not to divorce her. The reverse is also true. If a woman has an unbelieving husband, she is not to divorce him because he is an unbeliever.

The question of what to do when one party of a marriage becomes a Christian necessarily raises the question about children of such marriages and their relationship to the covenant of grace. If believers are not to leave unbelieving spouses, does the unbelief of the one spouse render the children of such a marriage to be "unclean" and outside of the covenant? Not at all. As Paul states, "For the unbelieving husband is made holy because of his wife, and the unbelieving wife is made holy because of her husband. Otherwise your children would be unclean, but as it is, they are holy" (v. 14).

Paul's use of the term "holy" raises several important questions. He has just stated in the previous chapter that all Christian believers are "holy" (i.e., sanctified—*hēgiasthēte*) and have been set aside by God for his purposes (cf. 1 Cor. 6:11). In this instance, Paul refers to all those who have come to faith in Christ while married to unbelievers (*ho apistos*). Because the believer in the marriage has been sanctified (set apart) for God's purposes, this being "set apart" extends in some sense to the unbelieving spouse.

However, the "holiness" of which Paul speaks here cannot refer to the kind of sanctification as mentioned in 1 Corinthians 6:11. Paul specifically applies this particular "holiness" to the unbelieving spouse (who is not a Christian). The solution to this apparent contradiction is that Paul uses the term "holy" in two different ways. In the former instance (1 Corinthians 6:11), he is speaking of a Christian who is justified and sanctified through faith in Christ. But in this verse (v. 14), Paul is speaking of some sort of holiness which does not result from one's salvation, but from the salvation of their spouse. Furthermore, the fact that sanctification is emphasized in the sentence and is in the perfect tense (the "set-apartness" of sanctification is a continuing condition), means that the sanctification of a believing spouse extends not only to the unbelieving spouse, but also to the children of such a couple. If this were not the case, this would render the children "unclean" and, therefore outside the covenant of grace.

C. K. Barrett's comments are helpful here:

> In Paul's usage to be holy (*hagios*), or sanctified (*hagiasmenos*), is normally the distinguishing mark of a Christian. The Christians are saints (*hagioi*) and as such radically distinguished from the rest of mankind. To them he writes (v. 11) that notwithstanding their wicked past they have been sanctified in the name of Jesus Christ, and through the Spirit of God. By definition, the persons referred to in the present verse have not been sanctified in this sense, for they are unbelievers; as verse 16 shows they stand at present outside the realm of salvation, though there is hope that they may be brought within it. The verb "to sanctify,"

Each Has His Own Gift from God

and the adjective "holy" must therefore be used in this verse in a different sense differing from that customary in Paul.... The clue to the problem is found in the fact that Paul is still dealing with the antipathy, felt by at least some in Corinth, to sex and marriage in general. If marriage between Christians may be permitted, they argue, mixed marriages at least must be forbidden, for the Christian partner will be defiled by the non-Christian, and the children issuing from the marriage will be unclean. Paul answers that the truth is the reverse of what is suggested. The Christian partner has the effect of sanctifying the relationship (which, on his part, is the divine institution of marriage), and his partner in it.[8]

Paraphrasing Paul's words, Barrett concludes: "Otherwise... if the Christian partner did not sanctify the relationship, your children would be unclean, whereas in fact they are holy. Paul uses this truth, which he regards as self-evident, to clinch the matter ... The children are within the covenant; this would not be so if the marriage itself were unclean."[9] As Calvin points out, "The godliness of the one does more to 'sanctify' the marriage than the uncleanness of the other does to make it unclean."[10]

According to Paul, then, the children of such unions between one believer and an unbeliever are regarded as holy. Two important things must be considered in light of this assertion. The first is that Paul's comments about children being "holy" certainly points us in the direction of the baptism of infants. The children of a marriage with one believing spouse and one unbelieving spouse are not outside the covenant of grace. And if small children are in the covenant, how can we deny to them the sign and seal of that covenant, which is baptism? (cf. Col.

---

8. Barrett, *The First Epistle to the Corinthians*, 164–165.
9. Barrett, *The First Epistle to the Corinthians*, 164–165.
10. Calvin, *The First Epistle of Paul to the Corinthians*, 148.

2:11–12). The second consideration is that sanctification must be used here in its sense of "set apartness" or covenantal authority (when the head of the house exercises over those under his care)[11] and not in the sense which so many take it, moral purity. The "holy status" of the believing parent is not negated by the fact that one parent is an unbeliever—therefore, the children of such a union are still members of the covenant, and still eligible for baptism, even if one parent remains an unbeliever.

In verses 15–16, Paul addresses the case of what happens in the event that the unbelieving spouse chooses to leave the believing spouse, because of the believing spouse's faith in Jesus Christ. In verse 15, Paul writes, "But if the unbelieving partner separates, let it be so. In such cases the brother or sister is not enslaved. God has called you to peace." Paul's answer to this sad situation is very simple. If the unbeliever takes the initiative and leaves, the believing spouse is to let them do so, and no longer remains bound to them. The deserted party is free to remarry under such circumstances. The reason for this is that God has called us to live in peace. Believers are not to create situations in which they seek to dissolve their marriages. Since peace is the goal, believers are to remain with unbelievers if the unbelieving spouse does not desire to leave. But in those cases where unbelievers desert the believing spouse because the spouse is a believer, the believer is to keep the peace by letting them go. Paul says they are no longer bound.

Verse 16 raises another point of consideration which is important for the Corinthians to keep in mind. "For how do you know, wife, whether you will save your husband? Or how do you know, husband, whether you will save your wife?" There are two interpretations offered to this verse. One is the so-called

---

11. Meredith G. Kline, *By Oath Consigned* (Grand Rapids: William B. Eerdmans, 1968), 90–102.

Each Has His Own Gift from God

"optimistic view" in which it is held that the believer should remain as long as possible so as to bring about the conversion of the unbeliever. According to this line of thought, the sentence should be "understood as encouragement to the believing partner to stay in a marriage even if there is no receptiveness to the gospel."[12] While this view is grammatically possible (and desirable to a point), it seems to go against the context.

Paul has written that believers are not to seek to cling to marriages when unbelievers seek to end them. This is hardly in line with Paul's exhortation to keep the peace. Furthermore, God did not give marriage for the purpose of evangelism, although one partner's conversion does not nullify either the marriage, nor negate the requirement for marital relations to continue. All that Paul seems to be saying here is that the outcome regarding unbelieving spouses is uncertain. If they stay, they stay. If they leave, they leave.

Because the unregenerate do not have a biblical understanding of creation (that God made all things good), and because they do not have a biblical understanding of the fall (that Adam's sin brought the curse down upon the human race), they have no way to explain why human sexuality is a good thing, and yet why, at the same time, our sexuality is so easily turned into a source of sin and temptation. God has ordained marriage as that institution where men and women are to engage in sexual relations, and God sees fit to limit sexual relations to marriage. Those who are married are to remain married, give their spouse their marital due, and devote themselves to the preservation of the marriage. Should an unbelieving spouse leave a marriage because of their spouse's faith in Christ, Paul says "let them go."

But not all people are called to marriage. Some are called to be single and churches need to be careful not to stigmatize those who are are not married. In the case of those called to

---

12. Hays, *First Corinthians*, 121–122.

be single, they are to remain celibate, and if and when sexual temptation becomes too great, Paul says they should seek to be married. Whenever possible, people should seek to remain in that state in which they were in when they came to faith. After all, Paul says, "Each has his own gift from God" (v. 7). Part of sanctification is simply learning to be satisfied with our current station in life, and to realize that God has ordained these circumstances for our own well-being.

No doubt, Paul's doctrine of marriage reflects his view that Jesus has not only washed, sanctified, and justified all of us, but as he points out in Ephesians 5:22–33, marriage is a picture to us of Christ's relationship to his church. As Christians, and as members of Christ's church, we are Christ's bride, whom even now he is purifying in preparation for the great marriage supper of Christ the lamb (cf. Rev. 19:6–9). In order to answer the Corinthians' question, Paul ties creation and redemption together, because that same one (Jesus Christ) who created us as sexual beings and made us male and female, has also purchased us with his shed blood. This is why we glorify God with our bodies. This is why we are to be satisfied with our station in life and remain single if so called, or remain with an unbelieving spouse if this is what God has ordained. No doubt, these were important and difficult issues in Paul's day just as they are in ours. And this is why, like the Corinthians, we must deal with our questions regarding marriage and divorce in light of the fact that Jesus is our heavenly bridegroom who has given himself for us, his bride.

13

Do Not Become Bondservants of Men

1 CORINTHIANS 7:17–40

Only let each person lead the life that the Lord has assigned to him, and to which God has called him. This is my rule in all the churches. . . . Each one should remain in the condition in which he was called. . . . For he who was called in the Lord as a bondservant is a freedman of the Lord. Likewise he who was free when called is a bondservant of Christ. You were bought with a price; do not become bondservants of men. So, brothers, in whatever condition each was called, there let him remain with God.

Paul does not give us the specifics, but, in chapter 7, he speaks as though the Corinthian church is in the midst of some sort of serious crisis. While Paul has spoken in some detail about the pressing issues facing this church—the love of pagan wisdom, the rampant sexual immorality, the fact that Christians were suing each other in secular courts and failing to discipline erring members—Paul now speaks of unspecified dire circumstances confronting the Christians in Corinth. This crisis is the reason why Paul urges the members of this church to devote themselves to solving this matter, and why, in the meantime, the Corinthians should remain in their current social status until things are resolved.

Paul is still responding to a letter from the Corinthians in which they asked the apostle a number of specific questions about marriage and celibacy. In the opening part of chapter 7, Paul discusses marriage and the question of what to do when one party to the marriage becomes a believer while the other party remains an unbeliever. Paul moves on to address a Christian's social status at the time of their conversion. Three times in the balance of chapter 7, Paul affirms the general principle "stay as you were when called."

The issues here are very practical. When someone becomes a Christian, he is now a bondservant of Jesus Christ. How does this relate to their social standing? If they are uncircumcised, do they now submit to circumcision to avoid conflict with Jews? Should Gentiles begin to live as Jews? Should Jews seek to undo their Jewishness? Do the limits placed upon slaves by their masters infringe upon their freedom (standing) in Christ? What should slaves do once they become Christians? Must they stay slaves, or is slavery incompatible with Christianity? And what about young women, betrothed to be married, what should they do in the midst of the current crisis?

Remain Where You Are When Called to Faith in Jesus Christ

In verse 17, Paul turns his attention to these questions. "Only let each person lead the life that the Lord has assigned to him, and to which God has called him. This is my rule in all the churches." Paul has made the point that under certain circumstances—when an unbeliever deserts the believing spouse—the believer is not bound to the party who deserts them. Paul also asserts

Do Not Become Bond Servants of Men

that new Christians should ordinarily maintain their present state (vocation) after coming to faith. Paul is not referring to the initial call to faith in Christ at the time of conversion. He is referring to that calling (vocation) which a person had before coming to faith.

The phrase "lead the life" literally means "to walk." "To walk" is a favorite metaphor in Paul's writings for a person's course of life and implies progress in the faith. The main idea is that we should continue "the walk" which each of us had before coming to faith in Christ. God's call to faith in Christ is a gracious gift, and it completely eliminates social setting (or status) as having any kind of religious significance.[1] To put it another way, someone who comes to faith in Christ does not need to give up their secular job and get a "Christian" job or start a ministry.

Granted, due to sin, poor choices, the mysteries of God's providence, and so on, knowing what our own unique vocation entails can be a difficult thing. Finding our particular vocation, however, is not Paul's point. There are also people in the Corinthian church who were employed in jobs which would not constitute a legitimate calling (i.e., a temple prostitute), and who, once converted, cannot continue such work. Paul's main point should not be missed. We are to remain where we are when called to faith in Christ. Becoming a Christian does not mean that we are to withdraw from the world. God gives to us certain gifts and places us in certain situations. We should use the gifts God has given us and thereby fulfill our vocations. Paul lays down this general rule in all the churches—remain where you are when called. Do not quit your job!

In verses 18–19, Paul moves from the theoretical to specific situations. The first of these matters has to do with circumcision. "Was anyone at the time of his call already circumcised? Let him not seek to remove the marks of circumcision. Was

---

1. Fee, *The First Epistle to the Corinthians*, 311.

anyone at the time of his call uncircumcised? Let him not seek circumcision. For neither circumcision counts for anything nor uncircumcision, but keeping the commandments of God."

Circumcision was among the most divisive issues in the early church. Paul's Jewish readers would have been shocked by these words. The Epistle to the Galatians makes the gravity of this difference of opinion clear to all, since the coming of Christ fulfills that to which circumcision pointed (cf. Gal. 5:6). Jews regarded uncircumcised Gentiles as outside the covenant of God and therefore ineligible for all of God's covenant blessings. To a Jew, to be uncircumcised was to be unclean, and remain under God's wrath. To be circumcised was everything! It was the visible sign of an entire way of life which involved a certain diet and keeping both the Sabbath and feast days. But the situation was completely reversed for Gentiles. An enlightened Greco-Roman saw circumcision as an utterly barbaric practice, so much so that Jews were scorned for merely engaging in the process.

If someone is circumcised (a Jew) and becomes a Christian, Paul says, they should remain as they are. There are recorded instances of Jews disfiguring themselves to reverse or hide their circumcision. If someone is uncircumcised, they should remain uncircumcised. Echoing his comments in Galatians, Paul writes that God will judge us in light of his law (a point made by Moses in Deut. 6:16ff.), not based upon whether or not we have undergone a particular surgical procedure.

To make sure no one misses his point, in verse 20, Paul reaffirms the principle stated earlier in verse 17. "Each one should remain in the condition in which he was called." Because God has called us to our station in life (vocation), we should remain there once we are called to faith in Christ unless that vocation is inappropriate for a Christian (i.e., working in one of the pagan temples). In the words of Barrett, "A man

Do Not Become Bond Servants of Men

is not called . . . to a new occupation: [rather] his old occupation is given a new significance."[2]

What About Slaves?

In verses 21–23, Paul takes up the matter of slavery. "Were you a slave when called? Do not be concerned about it. (But if you can gain your freedom, avail yourself of the opportunity.) For he who was called in the Lord as a slave is a freedman of the Lord. Likewise he who was free when called is a slave of Christ. You were bought with a price; do not become slaves of men." If someone is a slave and then becomes a Christian, how does being a bondservant of Christ effect their relationship to their earthly masters? Paul advises such people not to be troubled. Again, his advice is exceedingly practical. Gain your freedom if you can, but if this is your station in life, you should serve Christ honorably while you serve your earthly master.

Some among the Corinthians may have been slaves (a significant segment of the Greco-Roman world were chattel slaves—i.e., someone's personal property) and therefore bound to an earthly master. This does not negate the fact that the slave has been freed from something far worse than their current plight. The Christian slave has been delivered from slavery to sin, slavery to the law, slavery to the world, slavery to the devil, and slavery to death (cf. Eph. 2:1–3). Slaves who come to faith in Jesus Christ, should view themselves as the Lord's freedmen. They are free from sin, from the law (cf. Rom. 10:4), and even from death (because they will be raised). Even people who occupy the lowliest stations in this life (slaves in Greco-Roman culture) are in actuality kings and priests in the kingdom of God. This perspective of such sinful institutions is what has led Christians (with a few shameful exceptions) to be so outspoken against the institution of slavery. As marriage is a picture of Christ's rela-

---

2. Barrett, *First Epistle to the Corinthians*, 170.

tionship to his church (cf. Eph. 5:22–33), slavery serves as an illustration of what sin does to us. This is why Christians exalt the institution of marriage and decry the institution of slavery.

Another irony is that even freedmen and women are slaves to sin, death and the law, unless they are set free from these tyrants by Jesus Christ. Having been set free from sin, the law, and death, the free man or woman is likewise a bondservant of Christ. In Romans 6:18, Paul speaks of this in terms of becoming a slave of righteousness since we have been buried with Christ and raised with him in baptism to newness of life (cf. Rom. 6:1–4). Both the believing freeman and the believing slave serve the same master—Jesus. In the kingdom of God, all class and social divisions are removed. There is no difference in the body of Christ between slave and free. As Paul tells us in Galatians 3:26–29: "For in Christ Jesus you are all sons of God, through faith. For as many of you as were baptized into Christ have put on Christ. There is neither Jew nor Greek, there is neither slave nor free, there is no male and female, for you are all one in Christ Jesus. And if you are Christ's, then you are Abraham's offspring, heirs according to promise." These are revolutionary words, not only to a Jew (who regarded Gentiles, slaves, and women as inferior), but to Greeks as well (since Greeks regarded slavery as shameful). In God's new society (the church), all of these societal distinctions are removed. We are all bond servants of Jesus.

The price of our freedom from sin (whether we be slave or free), the law, and death is the shed blood of Jesus Christ (cf. 1 Cor. 6:20). To be purchased by the blood of Christ is to be a freeman, never again to be slaves of sin. Since all believers belong to the Lord who bought them, they belong to no man and they are never again to be slaves to sin! Paul's point may even have served as an admonition to the Corinthian Christians that they should themselves own no slaves, and set free those

Do Not Become Bond Servants of Men

that they may have. While the institution of slavery is clearly an abomination on a number of grounds, Paul is probably speaking here in a metaphorical sense—Christians are to behave as freemen, never again to be slaves to the false religions of men which offer no relief from sin, the law, and death.

For the third time, Paul reiterates the principle already laid down (v. 24). "So, brothers, in whatever condition each was called, there let him remain with God." God has placed us in specific life situations (vocations) in addition to calling us to faith in Jesus Christ. Paul does not mean that we not seek to better ourselves, or that we cannot change vocations once we become Christians. His point is that unless God calls us to a new vocation, we are to remain where we are when called. As Leon Morris reminds us, "Conversion is not the signal to leave one's occupation (unless it is clearly incompatible with Christianity) and seek something more 'spiritual.' All of life is God's. We should serve God where we are until he calls us elsewhere."[3] When we come to faith in Christ, there is no reason to immediately quit our jobs and seek to enter the ministry. If what we are doing is not forbidden by the Word of God, we should continue to do it until God calls us to do something else. As Calvin reminds us, "Paul says it makes no difference to God what a person's means of livelihood is on this world."[4]

Advice to the Unmarried

In verse 25, Paul now discusses the unmarried. He writes, "Now concerning the betrothed, I have no command from the Lord, but I give my judgment as one who by the Lord's mercy is trustworthy." Given the previous discussion, a question emerges about whether the term "virgins" refers exclusively to unmarried young women, or to both male and female virgins. That

---

3. Morris, *1 Corinthians*, 111.

4. Calvin, *The First Epistle of Paul to the Corinthians*, 155

these are young women (and not young men) is clear based on the fact that of the five of the six times Paul uses the term, he uses the feminine article.[5] In Greco-Roman culture, whether or not a young woman married was usually determined by the young woman's parents (or guardian, in the case of slaves). She had no such right of self-determination regarding a spouse.

As used here, the term "virgin" (*parthenōn*—ESV "betrothed") is a young woman, still under the guardianship of parents. In the strictest sense, this does not refer to a single young woman who has decided not to get married, or who has delayed marriage until majority (legal age) as in contemporary western culture; although much of what is said here should inform how Christian singles conduct themselves. Since there is no saying of Jesus which specifically deals with this subject, Paul will speak (give a judgment) based upon his apostolic authority, which, as he now qualifies, arises from the Lord's mercy to him.

In verse 26, Paul speaks of the difficulties in Corinth. "I think that in view of the present distress it is good for a person to remain as he is." Given the difficult but unspecified circumstances facing these new converts to Christianity, (likely the struggle to live as a Christian in a pagan culture), the current situation, in Paul's estimation, has reached the level of a crisis. Some think this to be a reference to the imminent fall of Jerusalem, or even to the second coming of Jesus Christ.[6] Others think the crisis may be a reference to the famine during the reign of Emperor Claudius. Based upon the contents of the prior discussion, I think it far more likely that Paul is referring to the problems within this church mentioned earlier in this letter: A man sleeping with his father's wife and the lack of discipline in response (chapter 5), the matter of litigation among church

---

5. Morris, *1 Corinthians*, 112. Contra Fee, *The First Epistle to the Corinthians*, 325–328.

6. Barrett, *The First Epistle to the Corinthians*, 174.

Do Not Become Bond Servants of Men

members, Christians using prostitutes (chapter 6), as well as the questions now being put to Paul regarding the problems faced by married, widowed, and singles who have come to faith in Christ (chapter 7).

Paul's response to those who find themselves in this uncertain environment is simple: "I think that it is good for you to remain as you are." As one commentator quips, "When high seas are raging, it is not time to change ships."[7] Paul is not saying that people who are virgins when converted must remain unmarried for the rest of their lives. Rather, because of the current crisis facing those in the church, it is good (wise) for people to remain where they are, until such time as the Lord changes the present circumstances. You need not leave your job (cf. verses 17–24), your spouse, or change your status in life, because you have become a believer. Paul's advice is to tell people to remain where they are until such time as the crisis is over, when they can make an informed and rational decision about such important matters as marriage.

This becomes clear in the next verse. "Are you bound to a wife? Do not seek to be free. Are you free from a wife? Do not seek a wife." A man or woman who is married should not seek to end their marriage (literally "loose the tie") merely because their spouse remains an unbeliever—Paul has just spoken of this situation (vv. 12–16). Those who are widowed or virgins are not to look for a spouse, *if* they have the gift of celibacy. If they do not possess this gift and are burning with lust (and although it is not stated, but is certainly implied) and struggling with sexual sin, it is better for them to marry rather than continue to struggle with their sins (vv. 7–8). Otherwise, it is better for people to remain where they are.

Paul further qualifies this in the next verse (v. 28). "But if you do marry, you have not sinned, and if a betrothed wom-

---

7. Morris, *1 Corinthians*, 113.

an marries, she has not sinned. Yet those who marry will have worldly troubles, and I would spare you that." While Paul has encouraged those who, like himself, have the gift of celibacy to remain single, those who do not have this gift do not sin if they marry, despite what some in the Corinthian church may have been teaching. Paul believes that there is nothing sinful about marriage. In fact, it is the normal state for humanity, since only those who are given the gift of celibacy are able to do so without struggling with sexual sins. Yet in Corinth, where many were struggling with unlearning a pagan sexuality, it may indeed be a good thing to remain unmarried and to serve the Lord without distraction until reaching Christian maturity.

Ever the realist, Paul gives his reason for stressing that those who are virgins and widowed are to remain where they are, especially in times of crisis such as the Corinthians are now facing. Those who are married will face troubles in this life. Despite the many benefits of marriage, there are not only additional stresses facing those who are married, but these stresses are especially acute in difficult times. Marriage puts two sinful people together in the day to day struggles of life, with all the stress that goes with it. Married people face many struggles that virgins or widowed people do not, and it is Paul's desire to spare people from such troubles. These struggles can detract from the more urgent struggle facing the members of this congregation, many of whom are still thinking and acting like pagans.

The practical application is simply this: Those who are single or widowed and who think that getting married will solve all their problems are sadly mistaken. Marriage entails a whole set of unique difficulties—even in times not characterized as that of "crisis." Nevertheless, Paul teaches that marriage (not celibacy) is the normal state of life, and if entered into with "eyes wide open" and not in times of crisis (such as the current crisis in Corinth), it is an enjoyable and fulfilling state. We can only

Do Not Become Bond Servants of Men

wonder what the current divorce rate might be if we moderns considered Paul's caution more carefully, and did not marry so often on whim or impulse.

Those who have the gift of celibacy should not seek to be married, and Paul will tell us why in verse 29. "This is what I mean, brothers: the appointed time has grown very short. From now on, let those who have wives live as though they had none." There is an ongoing debate about the meaning of the phrase "The appointed time has grown very short." While Paul often speaks of the Lord's return, elsewhere he never gives this kind of counsel. In his Thessalonians letters and in Philippians, Paul exhorts Christians to live blameless lives, including family life (1 Thess. 5:1–11; Phil. 1:9–11). There is no reference in any of Paul's other letters to a crisis, such as that mentioned here. Those who argue that Paul is speaking of our Lord's second advent cannot explain why it is that those living at the time of the end should live differently from Christians who do not live at the time of the end.

Wait Until the Current Crisis Is Over

Therefore, I think it is best to understand Paul's comment as a reference to the present crisis in Corinth. As the Corinthian church becomes more established and deals with the issues it currently faces, the crisis will ease. Life will return to normal. In the meantime, people ought to remain where they are. In light of the fact that the crisis will eventually end, Paul gives the Corinthians a number of exhortations. The first exhortation is that those who are married are to live as if they did not have wives. By this, Paul does not mean that married men are to withdraw sexually from their wives, or else to live as they did before they were married. Paul is referring to the fact that the crisis this church faces is a matter of some urgency, and that people must devote themselves whole-heartedly to dealing with the matters facing the church, especially the disciplinary matters mentioned earlier.

There is an additional consideration mentioned in the following verses (30–34, especially v. 32):

> And those who mourn [should live] as though they were not mourning, and those who rejoice as though they were not rejoicing, and those who buy as though they had no goods, and those who deal with the world as though they had no dealings with it. For the present form of this world is passing away. I want you to be free from anxieties. The unmarried man is anxious about the things of the Lord, how to please the Lord. But the married man is anxious about worldly things, how to please his wife, and his interests are divided. And the unmarried or betrothed woman is anxious about the things of the Lord, how to be holy in body and spirit. But the married woman is anxious about worldly things, how to please her husband.

Those who mourn are consumed by their grief. Yet, there are important matters which need to be addressed now. Those who are happy are preoccupied with their present joyful circumstances. Yet, there are pressing matters with which this church must deal, now. Those who are consumers are enjoying their new possessions. There will be time for that later on—this church is presently in a crisis. There is also an eternal perspective on temporal things. Those preoccupied with the things of this world should not be engrossed by them because such things are temporal, in their present form are passing away. It is folly for believers to act like these things are permanent, for they will not last. While these things have their place in this life, they will pass away in the next. Christians need to consider that while temporal things are important, sometimes eternal things become more important—especially in times of spiritual crisis.

Do Not Become Bond Servants of Men

Because of this crisis, Paul advises the Corinthians to be free from such temporal concerns (cf. v. 27). Whatever concerns people have (marriage, grief, joy, possessions, preoccupation with things of the world, etc.) distract them from dealing with the issues at hand. Someone who is unmarried is not worrying about how to please their spouse, while a married man has other responsibilities. A married man's attention is divided. Someone who is a virgin or widowed is able to be more devoted to the Lord, in both body and spirit. While the time may come for them to marry later on, now is the time for them to remain as they are.

This is why Paul prefers celibacy to marriage. He is not distracted from the Lord's work at this most critical time. As he puts it in verse 35: "I say this for your own benefit, not to lay any restraint upon you, but to promote good order and to secure your undivided devotion to the Lord." Paul is not trying to restrict (harness) people from going about the affairs of daily life. He has already said that he does not want Christians to withdraw from the world. Nor is he saying that celibacy is superior to marriage (as those who depreciate the body might argue, and as monastics have done ever since). Rather, Paul is saying that those who have been given the gift of celibacy have certain advantages—they are not distracted during these difficult times because of the need to take care of a spouse.

In the rest of the chapter, Paul qualifies his comments about celibacy. Although he sees great advantages in remaining celibate, Paul is also clear that marriage is not to be despised. A virgin does not sin, if she decides to marry. "If anyone thinks that he is not behaving properly toward his betrothed, if his passions are strong, and it has to be, let him do as he wishes: let them marry—it is no sin." This is a very difficult verse to translate and interpret. My view is that Paul is referring to a situation (created by Greek paganism or misguided Christian asceticism), where people get engaged, but they still held to a pagan conception of the body (i.e., that all sexual desires and bodily passions were evil), and abstained from sexual relations even after marrying. They sought a spiritual union, not a physical one. In the situation described by Paul, the man (engaged, but unmarried) finds the strain too great and desires the woman (the virgin), acting unseemly toward her. In this case, Paul permits them to marry and cohabit, effectively refuting the erroneous pagan sexuality (focusing upon a spiritual and not physical union) which underlies such a relationship.

Additional Advice to Virgins and Widows

In the next few verses, Paul reiterates his view that virgins should remain unmarried but lists four very specific conditions before this advice be followed. "But whoever is firmly established in his heart, being under no necessity but having his desire under control, and has determined this in his heart, to keep her as his betrothed, he will do well." The four conditions are as follows: 1). The man must have settled this matter in his own mind: he must be convinced that this is the proper course of action. 2). He is under no compulsion, that is, there is no external contract (i.e., "a formal betrothal"). 3). He has control over his will (i.e., he is not a slave) and then, 4). He has made up his mind not to marry the woman. If these four things are in place, the man has done the right thing by keeping the woman from marriage.[8]

In verse 38, Paul adds, "So then he who marries his betrothed does well, and he who refrains from marriage will do even better." Someone who marries his betrothed does right, but only in light of the failure to meet conditions described in the previous verse. The man who does meet the conditions, and therefore waits to marry his betrothed until things improve does even better.

---

8. Morris, *1 Corinthians*, 119.

Do Not Become Bond Servants of Men

Finally, Paul discusses the status of widows in verses 39–40. "A wife is bound to her husband as long as he lives. But if her husband dies, she is free to be married to whom she wishes, only in the Lord. Yet in my judgment she is happier if she remains as she is. And I think that I too have the Spirit of God." In Paul's view of marriage, ordinarily partners remain bound until death—although there is the adultery exception taught by Jesus, and the desertion clause, mentioned above. Christians are not to seek divorce, although divorce may become necessary. However, if one spouse dies, the survivor is free to remarry, provided they marry "in the Lord," (i.e., they marry a Christian). And yet, Paul continues to see advantages (not superiority) in remaining unmarried. There is much that single folk can do when it comes to the service of Christ and his church which married people cannot. And as Paul sees it, his advice is that of an apostle because he has the Spirit of the Lord, something others in the congregation may have claimed as well.

While many of Paul's directives in chapter 7 are conditioned upon the fact that the Corinthian church was facing a serious spiritual crisis when Paul wrote this epistle, much of what Paul says was absolutely revolutionary in its day. Becoming a Christian did not change someone's current social status. Once in union with Christ, one's vocation and social standing no longer divides them, as these things did before they became Christians. Christianity is not a culture. Christianity transcends all cultures because it is concerned with the most fundamental human problem—we are sinners, enslaved to sin, and therefore under God's wrath. This is why, in the midst of a discussion of social mores (slavery, circumcision, marriage), and given the fact that Christians are to leave pagan ways of thinking and doing behind, Paul reminds the Corinthians one more time that they have been bought with the blood of Christ.

Therefore, they are not to become bondservants of men—a reference to the bondage foisted upon them by the false and pagan religions of ancient Corinth. Whether a Christian is a wealthy merchant or a lowly slave, in Christ these differences no longer matter. All believers are bondservants of Christ, purchased by his shed blood, and joint heirs to all the riches and treasures that are ours in Christ.

Paul's practical advice—which is remarkable for its common sense—is for the Corinthians to remain in the state they were in when they came to faith. In the meantime, they are to devote themselves to solving whatever crisis it was that the Corinthian church was currently facing. This makes perfect sense in Paul's day as well as in our own.

The underlying point is, however, becoming a Christian does not change (or negate) our callings and vocations in life. We need not seek to find a ministry or leave for the mission field (unless, of course we are called by God to do so). Rather, becoming a Christian changes how we are to understand our calling and vocation. We now see our current calling and vocation in a new and different light. Doing what we do in a God-honoring way brings glory to Christ as well as greater personal satisfaction that whatever we do to earn a paycheck matters to God. We are Christ's, therefore we should not be enslaved to sinful passions, pagan ways of thinking (i.e., that our bodies are bad), or rash and foolish behavior. Because we are Christ's, Paul exhorts us, "Do not become bondservants of men." This means self-consciously living as servants of Christ, no longer bound to the foolishness of pagan wisdom. It also means we need to stop thinking and acting like slaves to sin.

14

There Is One God

1 CORINTHIANS 8:1–13

Therefore, as to the eating of food offered to idols, we know that "an idol has no real existence," and that "there is no God but one." For although there may be so-called gods in heaven or on earth—as indeed there are many "gods" and many "lords"—yet for us there is one God, the Father, from whom are all things and for whom we exist, and one Lord, Jesus Christ, through whom are all things and through whom we exist.

I have heard of church members squabbling over doctrine, whether or not to add new programs at church, and even over whether or not the church's new carpet should be red or blue. But I have never heard Christians squabble over whether or not the meat someone brought to the church potluck had originally been used in a pagan sacrifice. Yet this matter had become a serious issue in Corinth. How do we as Christians interact with the non-Christian religions and rituals around us? Can we go to non-Christian religious ceremonies and participate in their rituals? Can we dress like pagans if they wear identifiable clothing associated with their views and practices? Can we identify in any sense with pagan elements in the surrounding culture?

And what about consuming any left-overs from ritual meals? Is doing such a thing participating in paganism, and a violation of God's prohibition of idolatry?

The following lengthy section of Paul's letter to the Corinthians (chapters 8–10) requires some background information to interpret properly, since the idea of sacrificing food to idols seems so foreign to us. It is easy for us to understand why Christians should have nothing to do with idolatry. Idolatry is clearly forbidden by the first three commandments and condemned in a number of Old Testament passages such as Deuteronomy 4:15–30. It is far more difficult to understand how food items can be so directly connected to pagan practices.

Pagan Sacrifices in the Greco-Roman World

As we work our way through this section of 1 Corinthians, there are several things we need to keep in mind. For one thing, there was no refrigeration in Paul's day, so once an animal had been butchered, it had to be eaten soon thereafter, lest the meat spoil. It was also common for people in Greco-Roman culture to eat meals in pagan temples or in trade guild dining halls dedicated to pagan deities. The latter were the forerunners of the modern restaurant. When people gathered together for such a meal, it was the usual practice to begin with a sacrifice to the deity to which the temple was dedicated, and then the diners would consume what was left of the sacrificial animal or other foodstuffs offered to the gods. Part of the butchered animal was burned as a sacrifice. The rest was placed upon the altar (the "table of the gods") where it was eaten by the priests and the participants in the festivities. If there was anything left over, the meat might be given to those in attendance, but, more often, was sold to local butchers for resale.[1]

---

1. Fee, *The First Epistle to the Corinthians*, 359.

There Is One God

Those in the upper levels of Corinthian society would have a difficult time avoiding such meals and places, since this was where virtually all of the social activities and commerce took place. Therefore, given the connection between the contents of the meal, and the particular pagan deity to whom the meal was dedicated, the question arises, "Can Christians participate in such activities?" It was the connection between the meal, the sacrifice, and the pagan deities associated with them, which created ethical problems for Christians throughout the Greco-Roman world. How could Christians justify eating in a pagan temple, or eating something which was offered as a pagan sacrifice? Apparently, a number of the Corinthians saw nothing whatsoever wrong with this practice.

There is also a related problem—perhaps even more difficult to assess. The poor of Corinth could not afford to purchase meat and so the only meat they could get (cheaply, or for free) was that left over from the pagan sacrifices. In fact, the pagan sacrifice was the location where most of the meat sold in the cities' shops was originally butchered. Merchants could buy it cheaply and then sell it for a profit. So, it would be very difficult for someone to know whether or not the meat they were eating was the leftover portion of an animal which had been sacrificed to some pagan deity.

Finally, Jews (and Jewish converts to Christianity) would have an especially difficult time in such circumstances, because the animals offered for these sacrifices would not be slaughtered in the proper way (i.e., according to Kosher practices).[2] This is why in most large cities with sufficient Jewish populations, Jews maintained their own markets and butcher shops.

---

2. Barrett, *First Epistle to the Corinthians*, 188.

What About Eating Food Sacrificed to Idols?

There are two important theological issues here. The first is whether a Christian can participate in pagan feasts. The second is what to do with what was left of an animal that had been sacrificed in a pagan temple, even though the meat may have been purchased from a butcher who got it from the temple.

Based upon the points Paul makes in response to the letter sent to him, some of the Corinthians continued to eat foods which had been used in pagan sacrifices, and they gave four reasons as to why they were able to do so. First, as Christians, they know that there is no reality behind the idols, so what difference did it make if they attended pagan temples and ate sacrificed food, since what the idols represent does not actually exist? Second, such people know that God made all things "good," and therefore food is a matter of "indifference" ("All things are clean if sanctified by prayer."). Third, if someone has been baptized, how can they fall into the temptation to worship idols? And then, fourth, does Paul even have the authority to forbid Christians from doing such things in the first place?[3] Throughout this section (chapters 8–10), Paul will respond to these objections in some detail.

This matter surfaces elsewhere in the New Testament, such as during the Jerusalem Council as recounted in Acts 15:28–29. Eating meat sacrificed to idols was one of the few restrictions placed upon the Gentiles by the leaders of the church. In Revelation, the churches of Pergamum and Thyatira are condemned by Christ for tolerating pagan practices in their midst (Rev. 2:14, 20). The fact that this is addressed in such diverse situations shows that the pressing problem—Christians participating in things connected to idolatry—was an issue faced by Christians of the first century on a daily basis.

---

3. Fee, *The First Epistle to the Corinthians*, 362.

There Is One God

When Paul addresses this issue in chapter 8, he begins by clarifying that love for our brothers and sisters in Christ lies at the heart of the Christian response to pagan idolatry. Although Paul will go on to forbid the Corinthians from going to pagan temples, he does point out that even though Christians know that paganism is not true (and therefore, in this sense there is no occult reality behind the idol), this does not necessarily give Christians the right to engage in conduct which causes others to stumble. Christians are to act in love and to avoid any conduct (even if they feel justified in doing so) which causes others to stumble. This is a foundation of Paul's ethical teaching.

Even though the first three verses begin abruptly and seem to have little to do with eating food sacrificed to idols, Paul is laying the groundwork for his discussion which follows in verses 4–13. The problem is that the goal of our faith is not knowledge for knowledge's sake, but love for our brothers and sisters in Christ. This explains the contrast between love and knowledge. Knowledge puffs up, *but* love builds up. If anyone thinks he has come to knowledge, he does not yet know as he ought to know. *But* if anyone loves God, they are known by God.

Paul addresses the problem of idolatry in verse 1 of chapter 8. "Now concerning food offered to idols: we know that 'all of us possess knowledge.' This 'knowledge' puffs up, but love builds up." In light of 1 Corinthians 7:1, Paul is answering yet another question put to him by members of this congregation. The phrase "all of us possess knowledge" is probably a statement used by the Corinthians in their letter to Paul. It is obvious to a Christian that there is no reality behind pagan idols. Christians know that God is the creator and sustainer of all things. Idols are nothing but a figment of the sinful human mind. This is tied to the Greek fascination with knowledge—the secrets of life, the mysteries of the fates, esoterica, and trivia. But this kind of knowledge can make people proud ("puffs up").

From what Paul says elsewhere in this letter, pride and boasting were significant problems in the Corinthian church. In 1 Corinthians 4:6, Paul writes: "I have applied all these things to myself and Apollos for your benefit, brothers, that you may learn by us not to go beyond what is written, that none of you may be puffed up in favor of one against another." In 1 Corinthians 4:18–19, he writes: "Some are arrogant, as though I were not coming to you. But I will come to you soon, if the Lord wills, and I will find out not the talk of these arrogant people but their power." And then in 1 Corinthians 5:2, Paul states: "And you are arrogant! Ought you not rather to mourn? Let him who has done this be removed from among you."

Love, on the other hand, builds up. To further explain his point, Paul uses a word which is normally used to refer to the construction of various buildings (*oikodomei*). Architectural metaphors are common throughout Paul's letters, including 1 Corinthians. Whatever conduct the Christian chooses, it must be based upon what is in the best interest of others so as to build them up. It cannot be based upon self-interest, which, in this case, is the knowledge that since idols have no reality we are free to eat anything, even if it offends others or causes them to stumble.

Reality Versus Perception

In verse 2, Paul fleshes this out a bit further. "If anyone imagines that he knows something, he does not yet know as he ought to know." Since we are creatures (finite and limited to time and space), our knowledge of something may be accurate, but is always incomplete. Paul is arguing that if we think we know all things, we really do not. The Corinthians, on the other hand, think they have knowledge. But Paul's response serves as an ironic reminder that one who claims to have such knowledge, by that very claim, reveals that he does not. There is no reason

There Is One God

for people who know that idols are false to be proud of such knowledge. Wisdom, on the other hand, always brings with it the element of humility—we don't know all things, so we should act in light of God's revelation, and even as we seek to learn, we should remain concerned for the needs of others.

Unlike the unbelieving world—whose knowledge is really foolishness—the Christian has a firm foundation, a point made in verse 3. "But if anyone loves God, he is known by God." While our knowledge is always transient and limited, love, on the other hand, comes from God. If Paul were using Greco-Roman categories (and influenced by some sort of proto-Gnosticism), we would expect him to say something like, "He who loves God truly has knowledge." Instead, Paul reminds us that our love for God is based upon the fact that God already knows us. As John says in his first epistle, we love only because God first loved us: "In this is love, not that we have loved God but that he loved us and sent his Son to be the propitiation for our sins" (1 John 4:10). The mutual relationship between God and those who love him is expressed in several biblical passages. In 2 Timothy 2:19, we read, "But God's firm foundation stands, bearing this seal: 'The Lord knows those who are his.'" In Galatians 4:9, Paul had spoken of this in similar terms. "But now that you have come to know God, or rather to be known by God, how can you turn back again to the weak and worthless elementary principles of the world, whose slaves you want to be once more?"

Despite the fact that there is no reality behind pagan idolatry, the Corinthians are not completely free to do as they wish (Paul's point in. v. 9). Such knowledge fails to act based on love for others in the body of Christ. Paul reminds the Corinthians that it is not knowledge which builds the body of Christ, but love which does not seek its own interests, and which truly considers the interests of others. We may be "free" to do something, but should we do it if it offends others? Is not the "loving" thing to do to consider the needs, feelings, and concerns of others before we act? This is a question the immature among the Corinthians were not asking, but it is one which all Christians must learn to ask.

In verse 4, Paul takes up the specific issues surrounding the practice of eating meat sacrificed to idols. "Therefore, as to the eating of food offered to idols, we know that 'an idol has no real existence,' and that 'there is no God but one.'" Paul is in full agreement with the point made by the Corinthians in their letter to him, namely that an idol is nothing. While Paul will go on to speak of an occult connection to idols later in this epistle (1 Cor. 10:20), the fact of the matter is that idols are nothing, because the "gods" of the pagans are nothing. What the Corinthians know is true, but this knowledge does not justify acting "puffed-up" and acting out of self-interest.

Idols are nothing. In words which echo the *Shema* (Deut. 6:4), Paul affirms that there is only one true God. Monotheism is as essential to Christianity as it is to Judaism. In making this assertion Paul also condemns all forms of polytheism and paganism. The problem in the Corinthian congregation is that because there is only one true and living God, members of this church were using this very point to justify eating in pagan temples, or eating meat sacrificed to idols. They are right about the facts—there is only one true God. But they are wrong about the application—they mistakenly think they are free to eat in pagan temples because there is no ultimate reality behind the idols.

So-Called "Gods"

This is an issue with which Paul must deal in verse 5–6. "For although there may be so-called gods in heaven or on earth—as indeed there are many 'gods' and many 'lords'—yet for us there is one God, the Father, from whom are all things and for whom we exist, and one Lord, Jesus Christ, through whom are all

There Is One God

things and through whom we exist." The so-called pagan gods are nothing.[4] Yet, Paul is fully aware that virtually everything in creation (heaven and earth) can be worshiped "as a god." This is because of human sinfulness (Rom. 1:18–25). Sinful people suppress the truth in unrighteousness, and then worship and serve created things instead of the one who created them and gives them life. For Paul, a pantheon of "gods" is not a sign of a culture's great spiritual insight or cultural achievement. Rather, this is a sign of its depravity.

There is also an important polemical point here. In Greco-Roman culture, it was quite commonplace to speak of the pagan deities as "lords" (*kurios*), which explains why Paul repeatedly affirms that Jesus Christ is truly Lord, not merely a so-called "lord."[5] While the "gods" and "lords" of paganism are but the figment of the sinful human imagination, Christians, on the other hand, know that there is but one God, who is not only our heavenly Father, but also the Father of the Lord Jesus Christ. In this, Paul affirms monotheism as clearly as he can, and at the same time ascribes the same divine attributes to Jesus as he does to the Father, namely that Jesus is the creator of all things and that one in whom we live. God is one, and the Christian lives for God. Jesus Christ is Lord, and the Christian lives for him as well. In these verses we find in very basic form the affirmation that there is one God, and that within the Godhead, there is Father and Son. Given the context—the false gods of paganism—Paul does not mention the Holy Spirit here, though he has already done so earlier in this epistle (1 Cor. 2:4–5) when he spoke of the Holy Spirit's power as God's power.

Since love builds up, Christians who are strong (those who know that idols are nothing), must act in such a way as to con-

---

4. These two verses are one sentence in the original language which is chiastic in its structure. See, for example: Fee, *The First Epistle to the Corinthians*, 372.

5. Morris, *1 Corinthians*, 122.

sider the situation of the weak (who think that eating meat sacrificed to idols is wrong). Paul makes this point in verse 7. "However, not all possess this knowledge. But some, through former association with idols, eat food as really offered to an idol, and their conscience, being weak, is defiled."

Paul has made the point that idols are nothing, but those who have recently come to faith in Christ from paganism still struggle with this matter. They may not fully understand that idols are nothing, and so, for them, eating certain foods still has a religious connotation. There was such a strong association between certain foods and idols (and those places and the manner in which the food was eaten) that some were still weak, in the sense that they didn't feel that they could eat certain things in certain places without defiling themselves. While the strong saw no problems with eating such food, the weak found it highly troubling when others did so. In the mind of the weak, to eat such things is to tolerate or even endorse paganism. Although eating meat sacrificed in pagan temples is not an issue for us, along similar lines many Christians today wrestle with the question of the consumption of alcoholic beverages (both in public and in private). It is often charged that those who do imbibe should not do so in the presence of non-Christians because it is supposedly a "bad witness" to them. As Paul is about to tell us, there are times when imbibing is perfectly okay (drunkenness is never okay), and there are times when Christians should gladly set their liberty aside for a time.

To Eat or Not to Eat

In verse 8, Paul comes to the heart of the issue. "Food will not commend us to God. We are no worse off if we do not eat, and no better off if we do." The eating of food belongs to the category of things "indifferent" (*adiaphora*). Food does not bring us close to God, nor does it bring us under God's judgment.

There Is One God

Whether we eat or do not eat, it is a matter of individual decision. Paul knew that Jesus pronounced all foods clean in Mark 7:18–19: "And he said to them, 'Then are you also without understanding? Do you not see that whatever goes into a person from outside cannot defile him, since it enters not his heart but his stomach, and is expelled?' (Thus he declared all foods clean)." Even though this is the case, the strong should not insist that the weak eat what they do. Nor should the weak insist that the strong abstain from things they would not eat themselves. The fact that the weak do so is a demonstration of their weakness.

Underlying Paul's comment here is a strong "mind your own business" doctrine which is a major plank in Paul's doctrine of the Christian life (cf. 1 Thess. 4:11–12; 2 Thess. 3:6–15). The Corinthians should eat what they eat with a clear conscience. They should not be concerned with what others are eating. Why should one Christian concern themselves with what others are doing or eating? Not only does this easily lead to gossip and create a climate of unbiblical judgmentalism, the tendency to worry about the state of someone else's sanctification often comes at the expense of interest in our own sanctification. If I was properly concerned with the state of my own sanctification, I probably wouldn't have time to worry about someone else's.

However, in verse 9, Paul adds an important caution: "But take care that this right of yours does not somehow become a stumbling block to the weak." The strong (who have knowledge that idols are nothing, so that they eat without a twinge of conscience), must also act in accordance with love toward the weak, who are their brothers and sisters in Christ. The strong may have the right to eat all foods, but exercising that right in the wrong way may end up causing the weak to stumble. This, Paul says, is unacceptable. When enjoying their liberty to eat or not to eat, the strong must not place obstacles in the way of the weak. The strong should know enough (if they have the knowledge they claim to have) that they assume all responsibility as to know when to set aside their liberty for the sake of those who, as of yet, do not fully understand, or who do not have the proper theological categories to think through these things biblically. While the strong are free in matters indifferent, that freedom carries with it the responsibility to act in love as far as the weak are concerned. Martin Luther's comment that "A Christian is a perfectly free lord of all, subject to none. A Christian is a perfectly dutiful servant of all, subject to all," captures the thrust of Paul's argument quite effectively.[6]

In verse 10, Paul describes in practical terms what might happen if the strong are not careful in how these use their freedom. "For if anyone sees you who have knowledge eating in an idol's temple, will he not be encouraged, if his conscience is weak, to eat food offered to idols?" Someone who is weak might actually be enticed or encouraged to eat in such a way as to violate his own conscience. While they may not fully understand that idols are nothing, they may go ahead and do something which they think to be wrong—namely to eat meat in the temple dedicated to a pagan god. In doing so, they become open to such false notions as thinking that they can be professing Christians yet still engage in certain pagan practices. Or their consciences become horribly and needlessly burdened over things indifferent, like food.

The Weak and the Strong

The solution, Paul says, is that the strong not flaunt their liberty (misuse their authority/freedom), but to turn the weak into the strong (build them up through love). According to verse 11, the strong must consider the situation of the weak, and treat them accordingly. "And so by your knowledge this weak person is de-

---

6. Martin Luther, "A Treatise on Christian Liberty" (Philadelphia: Fortress Press, 1957), 7.

stroyed, the brother for whom Christ died." The consequences of the strong not considering the weak are quite serious. The strong might actually create and bring about spiritual disaster for those who are weak. In effect, through their actions, the strong person is persuading the weak person to violate their own conscience so as to encourage them to sin. The language Paul uses ("destroyed" by your knowledge) does not refer to a Christian losing their salvation, but to someone whose spiritual development is severely damaged, because they do something they think to be wrong and struggle needlessly as a result. The key to seeing this correctly is to consider Paul's point, which is that Jesus Christ has died for such a person, therefore we too need to act toward them in a sacrificial way.

In verse 12, Paul states, "Thus, sinning against your brothers and wounding their conscience when it is weak, you sin against Christ." Paul's organic view of the church as the body of Christ (cf. 1 Cor. 12:12ff.) comes into view here. To cause (entice) someone to violate their own conscience is not only to sin against them, it is to sin against Christ who died for them. These people (weak as they may be) are as much a part of Christ's body as are the strong. To wound the conscience of the weaker Christian, is to sin against the Savior who died for them and incorporated them into his body.

This leads Paul to conclude, "Therefore, if food makes my brother stumble, I will never eat meat, lest I make my brother stumble." Paul sees the non-hindrance of the weak to be of such importance that he is perfectly willing to give up what he is free to do, so as to avoid the problem in the first place. The point is that the freedom enjoyed by the strong is misused if it causes the weak to fall (to be scandalized). While the strong must ensure that the weak do not undermine Christian liberty in the church, they must be very careful to treat the weak with love and due concern for their weakness. Although the strong must never give up Christian liberty in the face of Judaizers or Pharisees, the strong always should be willing to give up Christian liberty for the sake of the weaker brother who is struggling with leaving pagan practices behind. Furthermore, the strong must be engaged in catechesis (instruction) so that the weak become strong.

We know that there is one God and that Jesus Christ is Lord. We also know that paganism is false, and that idols are nothing. God made all things and pronounced them "good." Therefore, what we eat neither commends us before God, nor renders us guilty. Food is nothing. Christians are free to eat all foods. And yet being free to eat anything doesn't mean we *should* eat everything. We must be willing to set aside our liberty when love for our brethren requires that we do so.

In Corinth, those who had just left paganism behind needed to make a complete break with their past. Eating meat sacrificed to idols was a practice so tied to paganism that some Corinthians did not feel free to eat that meat without violating their consciences. Because Christ died for these people—demonstrating his sacrificial love for all members of his body—then stronger Christians who saw nothing wrong with eating this meat, should be willing to stop eating, whenever doing so stumbled someone who is weaker in the faith. Until such time as the weak become strong, the strong should be willing to give up their freedom until the weak learns the better way. The weak should never be tripped up and their consciences wounded, even though we know that God is one, Jesus Christ is Lord, and that idols are nothing.

15

For the Sake of the Gospel

1 CORINTHIANS 9:1–27

For though I am free from all, I have made myself a servant to all, that I might win more of them. To the Jews I became as a Jew, in order to win Jews. To those under the law I became as one under the law (though not being myself under the law) that I might win those under the law. To those outside the law I became as one outside the law (not being outside the law of God but under the law of Christ) that I might win those outside the law. To the weak I became weak, that I might win the weak. I have become all things to all people, that by all means I might save some. I do it all for the sake of the gospel, that I may share with them in its blessings.

Although we are two thousand years removed from the ancient Greek city of Corinth, we accept Paul's apostolic authority without question. For many of us, Paul is our favorite New Testament writer because he teaches so many of the doctrines we hold dear. It is hard for us to imagine that Paul had to defend his own apostolic authority in a church which he himself helped to found. Yet that is the case in 1 Corinthians 9. Paul cannot tell the strong among the Corinthians to act in a certain way toward the weak, if he himself does not practice what he preaches.[1] At this point in his letter, Paul must spell out his approach to dealing with Jewish and Gentile believers in the midst of a pagan culture.

In chapter 9 of 1 Corinthians, Paul continues to address problems arising from the practice of meat being sacrificed to idols. Apparently, some in the Corinthian church were using Paul's voluntary surrender of his liberty to eat all things as an argument that Paul's apostolic authority was limited. Even though Paul was free to eat all things, he realized that doing so might offend the weak, so in such cases, Paul abstained. As we saw in chapter 8, Paul explained that Christian liberty is not freedom to do whatever we want, but liberation to do as we ought. Love for our brethren trumps Christian freedom.

Paul's Apostolic Authority

Paul develops two basic lines of defense regarding his apostolic authority. These are stated in the form of a series of rhetorical questions. The first line of defense is Paul's assertion that he is indeed an apostle with all the rights and privileges thereof. The second is the fact that no Christian should use their liberty without due regard for the weak—as in the example Paul has set for the Corinthians. This is especially problematic given the fact that Paul apparently ate Gentile food in Gentile settings, even as he abstained in Jewish settings. It may have appeared to some that Paul is vacillating. So Paul defends his behavior. He has done nothing wrong or inconsistent with his apostolic calling. This is evident by the fact that he preaches the gospel voluntarily, even though he is entitled to be paid for his labor in the churches.

---

1. See, for example, the discussion in Conzelmann, *1 Corinthians*, 151.

For the Sake of the Gospel

Throughout 1 Corinthians 9, Paul asks a series of rhetorical questions, designed to prove the validity of the two main points just mentioned. In verse 1 of chapter 9, Paul asks, "Am I not free? Am I not an apostle? Have I not seen Jesus our Lord? Are not you my workmanship in the Lord?" As to the first question, Paul is free from the law (i.e., the Mosaic economy) because the Law of Moses belongs to this present evil age and has passed away with the coming of Christ (cf. Rom. 10:4). He is also free from the condemnation of the law because Christ has borne our condemnation in his own flesh (cf. Col. 2:13–15). If any Christian can rightfully claim such freedom, it is Paul (cf. 1 Cor. 9:19ff.). In Galatians 2:11ff. and 5:1, Paul argued that such freedom is a fruit of the gospel. As John Calvin put it, Christian freedom "is especially an appendage of justification and is of no little avail in understanding its power."[2]

Whenever this freedom is challenged by false teachers, Paul is the first person willing to defend Christian liberty, since such freedom is a corollary to the gospel. Yet, when it comes to the weak within the church, Paul is also the first to voluntarily give up his freedom to keep the weak from stumbling.

As to the second and third rhetorical questions, Paul is an apostle only because Jesus himself appeared to him while he was on his way to Damascus to hunt down and persecute Christians (Acts 9:1–31). The office of apostle is not something Paul had sought because of any sort of personal ambition. Paul's office as apostle has its basis and its authority in Christ's call since Paul is able to bear witness to Christ's resurrection, having seen the risen Christ. Paul's apostolic authority comes from none other than Jesus himself. It was the Risen Jesus who called Paul to his apostolic office.

Finally, it was through Paul's effort in preaching the gospel that the Corinthian church was born—it was the result of

---

2. Calvin, *Institutes*, 3.19.1.

Paul's work in the Lord. Paul "planted or founded the church in Corinth; he was its father in the sense that he was the instrument used by God."[3] The very existence of the Corinthian congregation is the proof. This is a point Paul made in 1 Corinthians 3:6: "I planted, Apollos watered, but God gave the growth."

As Paul points out in verse 2, "If to others I am not an apostle, at least I am to you, for you are the seal of my apostleship in the Lord." While others may have called Paul's apostolic credentials into question, the Corinthians ought to be the last to do so. They knew Paul. He had been in their midst for a significant period of time. The very existence of the Corinthian congregation constituted empirical verification of Paul's apostolic credentials. If the Corinthians deny the validity of Paul's call, they are, in effect, denying their own validity as a congregation.[4] The word translated as seal (*sphragis*), indicates a mark of authority or ownership. Paul is Christ's seal upon this church. The Corinthians should know who Paul is and what authority he possesses.

Paul's Defense of His Office

What follows in verse 3 gets at the heart of Paul's ministry as apostle to the Gentiles. "This is my defense to those who would examine me." Paul offers an *apologia* (a legal defense) against those who sit in judgment (also a legal term) upon his ministry. "Do we not have the right to eat and drink?" In 1 Corinthians 8:9, Paul had spoken of the rights (*hē exousia*) of the Corinthians to eat certain foods ("But take care that this right of yours does not somehow become a stumbling block to the weak"). At the very least, Paul is reminding the congregation that he has full rights to eat and drink all things, since all things have been created by God and can be sanctified through prayer.

---

3. Barrett, *The First Epistle to the Corinthians*, 201.
4. Conzelmann, *1 Corinthians*, 152.

For the Sake of the Gospel

However, the context indicates that the food and drink to which Paul is referring is that of having his personal needs met by the church in exchange for his service. Paul is speaking of personal sustenance and not Christian liberty. This conclusion is supported by the fact that Paul uses the plural ("we") indicating that this is true of all those who serve the church. Furthermore, the following verse makes this point plain. "Do we not have the right to take along a believing wife, as do the other apostles and the brothers of the Lord and Cephas?" While Paul assumes the right for apostles to be married (a bit of a problem for the Roman church and the notion of clerical celibacy), he argues that apostles have the right to travel with their wives at the church's expense while they conducted their apostolic ministries. Paul mentions Peter by name, indicating that Peter traveled with his wife to the area with the implication that it was common knowledge that the churches provided for Mr. And Mrs. Peter while he was conducting church business. Paul also mentions that other apostles and the Lord's brothers were married, the later is almost certainly a reference to Jesus' biological half-brothers and this, of course, means that Mary and Joseph had children together after our Lord was born.

In verse 6, the apostle pointedly asks, "Or is it only Barnabas and I who have no right to refrain from working for a living?" Paul and Barnabas, apparently, were two apostles who supported themselves by working, rather than rely upon support from the churches (therefore, the phrase "tent-making" ministries). To make his point, Paul asks several more questions. "Who serves as a soldier at his own expense? Who plants a vineyard without eating any of its fruit? Or who tends a flock without getting some of the milk?" These rhetorical questions illustrate the point that soldiers, vinedressers, and shepherds receive the fruit of their labors for their personal sustenance. The implication is obvious. The same thing should be true for the apostles, who should have their needs met by those whom they serve.

In verses 8–9, Paul bolsters this point by appealing to Deuteronomy 25:4. "Do I say these things on human authority? Does not the Law say the same? For it is written in the Law of Moses, 'You shall not muzzle an ox when it treads out the grain.' Is it for oxen that God is concerned?" The way the question is phrased indicates that Paul expects the reader to answer in the negative. The Law of Moses speaks directly to this subject. When a draft animal such as an ox smashed the heads of grain, the wind blew away the chaff while the grain remained behind. If the ox was not to be muzzled, the ox was to be able to sustain itself in its heavy labor by eating some of the grain that it had crushed. But muzzle the ox and it will eventually die.

When Paul asks the question, "Is God really concerned about the ox?" the rhetorical point is that "Yes, God is concerned about the ox," which is why this was included in the law. Yet, the principle Paul introduces goes beyond the needs of a beast of burden. If an ox is entitled to eat, then surely the man who labors in God's vineyard is entitled to the fruit of his labors. In this case, the apostles who labor to preach, teach, and plant churches, are certainly worthy of their labor. This is made clear in the next verse (v. 10). "Does he not speak entirely for our sake? It was written for our sake, because the plowman should plow in hope and the thresher thresh in hope of sharing in the crop." This time, Paul's rhetorical question is to be answered in the affirmative.

Those Who Labor Earn Their Wages

The illustration of an ox being able to eat from the grain it crushes supports the greater principle that those who labor are entitled to the fruit of their labor. As the plowman and the thresher eat what their fields produce, the same thing should

For the Sake of the Gospel

be true for those who labor in terms of the gospel, a point Paul specifically makes in verse 11. "If we have sown spiritual things among you, is it too much if we reap material things from you?" The question is phrased to indicate that the condition has already been fulfilled. If we have sown spiritual seed—and obviously, Paul and the others have done so—then like the plowman and thresher, those who labor in the gospel should reap a material harvest (i.e., their needs should be met).

And so in verse 12 Paul asks, "If others share this rightful claim on you, do not we even more? Nevertheless, we have not made use of this right, but we endure anything rather than put an obstacle in the way of the gospel of Christ." From Paul's comments, it is clear that others who have labored among the Corinthians had been supported by the church (Peter and Apollos have already been mentioned). Since Paul did not take any support, some had concluded that he was not entitled to support and that his apostolic authority was somehow less than that of the others. But if others were supported by the congregation, and Paul was the father (founder) of this congregation, should not Paul be every bit as entitled as the others? Paul did nothing to hinder the spread of the gospel. His sacrifice was voluntary and not in any sense an indication that his authority was less than the others.

The rhetorical question in verse 13 and the comment in verse 14 indicates that Paul's hearers should have known the answer to his questions. "Do you not know that those who are employed in the temple service get their food from the temple, and those who serve at the altar share in the sacrificial offerings? In the same way, the Lord commanded that those who proclaim the gospel should get their living by the gospel." In Leviticus 6:8ff., those who worked in the temple earned their livelihood by doing so, as do those who maintained the altar. Furthermore the Lord himself has commanded that those who preach should likewise earn their living through preaching. Although this is a touchy subject in some circles, Paul is clear that those whom God has called to serve as ministers of Word and sacrament are to be sufficiently cared for (i.e., sufficiently paid) by those whom they serve.

But Paul did not exercise his right to be supported, as he will now spell out in verses 15–18, when he acknowledges that he voluntarily gave up these rights. In verse 15, we read, "But I have made no use of any of these rights, nor am I writing these things to secure any such provision. For I would rather die than have anyone deprive me of my ground for boasting." While Paul is entitled to financial and material support, he has not taken anything from the congregation while preaching. Paul is not writing a fund-raising letter to the Corinthians to ask for support. In fact, he is so adamant about not taking any money that he even can state that he would rather die at this point than take anything from the Corinthians.

The apostle is obviously speaking rhetorically in this regard, but nevertheless, he is quite emotional about this point. "For if I preach the gospel, that gives me no ground for boasting. For necessity is laid upon me. Woe to me if I do not preach the gospel!" While Paul can boast about not taking support to which he is entitled, there is only woe for Paul if he does not preach the gospel. Preaching the gospel is Paul's calling. There is no reason for him to boast. This is what he lives to do, and he will not allow anything to get in the way of this task to which Jesus himself has called him.

Says Paul in verse 17: "For if I do this of my own will, I have a reward, but if not of my own will, I am still entrusted with a stewardship." This is a difficult verse both to translate and to interpret.[5] Paul probably means that even though he preaches the gospel freely and without pay, nevertheless he is entitled to

---

5. See the discussion in: Barrett, *The First Epistle to the Corinthians*, 210.

a reward (wage). Since Paul has been called by Christ (and is therefore a slave of Christ) he has no choice but to do as he has done. He is fulfilling that obligation which Jesus Christ has laid upon him. Paul is responsible to God and can do nothing else but preach Christ crucified. He asks, "What then is my reward? That in my preaching I may present the gospel free of charge, so as not to make full use of my right in the gospel" (v. 18). Paul has to preach, he can do nothing else. In a sense he is saying it is his proper pay to preach without being paid. While the gospel gives him certain rights (pay included), it is his personal privilege not to exercise these rights if he so chooses.

In the Service of the Gospel

If there is any one place in Paul's letters where he gives us a glimpse into his philosophy of ministry, it is here. Paul sees his role as placing himself in the position of his hearers so as to most effectively preach the gospel to them. This becomes clear in the following verses, especially v. 19. "For though I am free from all, I have made myself a servant to all, that I might win more of them." This is a very dramatic declaration that while Paul is free, he also regards himself as a slave. His reason for this is simple—to win as many people to Christ as possible. To "win people" is a Jewish notion, and reflects doing what is necessary to make it easy for people to convert, as Rabbis were frequently willing to do with proselytes.

Paul's reference to freedom might be the same as in 1 Corinthians 9:1, a theological reference to the law and its condemnation as part of the Mosaic economy. It might also be a reference to Paul's Roman citizenship, since Paul was a freeman. The point is that Paul regards himself as a slave to everyone, including the Corinthians.

Paul spells out how he understands his ministry in verse 20. To put it in modern terms, this is Paul's mission statement. "To the Jews I became like a Jew, to win the Jews. To those under the law I became like one under the law (though I myself am not under the law), so as to win those under the law." To start with, when it comes to his Jewish credentials and genealogical chart, Paul's background is impeccable. As he writes in Philippians 3:4–6, "Though I myself have reason for confidence in the flesh also. If anyone else thinks he has reason for confidence in the flesh, I have more: circumcised on the eighth day, of the people of Israel, of the tribe of Benjamin, a Hebrew of Hebrews; as to the law, a Pharisee; as to zeal, a persecutor of the church; as to righteousness under the law, blameless." Paul has a pedigree of which to boast. But he refuses to do so.

Although Paul is in union with Christ—who according to Paul in Romans 10:4 is the end of the law for everyone who believes—when approaching Jews to preach Christ to them, Paul lived like one under the law, to win those under the law. Paul was very careful about what he ate and respected Jewish traditions and customs (kosher) so as not to put obstacles in the way of his Jewish hearers considering the claims of Christ who fulfilled everything to which the Law of Moses pointed. This explains why Paul ordered that Timothy be circumcised in Acts 16:1–3, and why when in Jerusalem, Paul participated in Jewish purification rites (cf. Acts 21:23–26). Paul shows great respect for Jewish customs, so as to remove objections of antinomianism and to establish common ground with his people. Therefore, even though Paul is free from the law, he is perfectly willing to live as a Jew (as *if* under the law) to lead a Jew to faith in Jesus Christ.

For the Sake of the Gospel

Yet when Paul is with Gentiles, he is willing to live as a Gentile. "To those not having the law I became like one not having the law (though I am not free from God's law but am under Christ's

For the Sake of the Gospel

law), so as to win those not having the law" (v. 21). As he did with the Jews, Paul also met the Gentiles on their own ground. A good illustration of this can be seen in his various sermons to Gentiles (cf. Acts 17:22ff.). When Paul says he becomes as one not under the law, he does not mean that he is willing to behave lawlessly if and when the Gentiles do, since he is still under the law of Christ (i.e., the moral law).

Paul does mean that in the presence of Gentiles he does not live as a Jew (as one under the Mosaic economy) and probably ate Gentile food, and so on. Paul's comments are not a treatise on the relationship between the law and the gospel, but simply a follow-up to his previous comments. When Paul is with the Jews, he lives as a Jew. When Paul is with the Gentiles, he lives as a Gentile. He does so to avoid putting any obstacles in the way of the preaching of the gospel to either. Food (and related cultural issues) should not be an obstacle to evangelism.

At this point (vv. 22–23), Paul lays out what amounts to his philosophy of ministry. "To the weak I became weak, that I might win the weak. I have become all things to all people, that by all means I might save some. I do it all for the sake of the gospel, that I may share with them in its blessings." When Paul makes reference to living like a Jew or a Gentile, he does so for the express purpose of preaching the gospel to them, eliminating obstacles to faith. When he speaks of the weak, he is referring to people who are already Christians but have overly-sensitive scruples about certain things, such as food. Paul has already made plain his concern for these Christians whose consciences are burdened by things for which Christ has died and with which they should not be struggling.

When among the weak, Paul behaves as one who is weak, so as to win the weak and bring them to a position wherein they may become strong. Paul hopes to win new Christians (or the Christian who is still weak), so that their weak consciences would not overcome them causing them to leave the church. Paul respects such people's scruples about meat sacrificed to idols and seeks to do nothing to offend them. But his goal, certainly, is not to leave people in this weak position, but to strengthen them. The strong bear with the weak with the goal of helping them move on to maturity.

When Paul speaks of becoming all things to all men for the sake of the gospel, we must not take Paul to mean that he is an unprincipled pragmatist—that he will do anything which works so as to lead people to Christ. The end (evangelism) does not justify the means (watering down the gospel for the sake of a greater response). Paul never changes the theological content of the gospel he preaches, but he does change how he approaches those to whom he is preaching.[6] Paul does not adopt the crude speech of the local fishermen so as to witness to them. He simply tells them about Jesus in words they can understand. Paul does not become a brawler or a spectator of gladiatorial combat so as to reach those who attend the local games. He simply tells them about Jesus using athletic metaphors they all could understand. There is no evidence anywhere in the New Testament that Paul would let personal considerations and cultural differences to get in the way of his proclamation of Christ crucified to whomever he is currently preaching. Because his confidence is in that gospel Christ commissioned him to preach, Paul's speech is characterized by the love of Christ, the humility of being a justified sinner, and his conduct reflects the righteousness of Christ which has been imputed to him. Paul was able to see the big picture and not let non-essential things get in the way of his apostolic mission, which was to do everything possible so as to preach the gospel, so as that people will come to faith in Jesus Christ.

---

6. Fee, *The First Epistle to the Corinthians*, 432.

For the Sake of the Gospel

Running the Race

Paul concludes the argument begun back in verse 1 of this chapter with another illustration. Paul's readers were thoroughly conversant with athletic metaphors, just as people are in our own culture. The Isthmian Games were held every two years in Corinth, while the Olympic games were held nearby every four years. Paul's references to sporting events makes perfect sense in light of this widespread familiarity with the games and the athletic contests which composed them. In fact, because of the stress found in athletics upon personal sacrifice and self-control, referring to athletic events was a practice of philosophers as well as Jewish sources (i.e., Philo and 4 Maccabees).[7] Says Paul in verse 24, "Do you not know that in a race all the runners run, but only one receives the prize? So run that you may obtain it."

In foot races, which were the first events held in the pentathlon, there is only one possible winner. This is why runners not only have to be careful to prepare themselves beforehand, but also to pace themselves during the race. Paul's point is that Christians are to go about the business of the kingdom of God with the same deliberation as that of a runner preparing for a race. "Every athlete exercises self-control in all things. They do it to receive a perishable wreath, but we an imperishable" (v. 25). Competitors in such important races cannot be unprepared. They follow a strict training regimen. Olympic runners swore allegiance to Zeus that they would spend ten full months in preparation, during which they swore to live temperately during rigorous training. If they won their respective races, they received a pine garland or celery wreath, which lasted but several days.

---

7. Craig S. Keener, *The IVP Bible Background Commentary: New Testament* (Downers Grove: InterVarsity Press, 1993), 472.

Christians, on the other hand, are concerned with eternal things that cannot perish like a celery stalk. Whatever reward they receive (whether Paul means a literal crown or not is an open question) is one which will last forever (cf. 2 Tim. 4:8: "Henceforth there is laid up for me the crown of righteousness, which the Lord, the righteous judge, will award to me on that Day, and not only to me but also to all who have loved his appearing."). Paul is cognizant of this parallel in his own approach to ministry of the gospel and to the Christian life with that of an athlete. To be a faithful preacher of the gospel as well as a Christian seeking to persevere to the end in faith, requires the same determined attitude as that of someone preparing for a race. "So I do not run aimlessly; I do not box as one beating the air. But I discipline my body and keep it under control, lest after preaching to others I myself should be disqualified" (vv. 26–27). Boxing was one of the main features of Greek athletic games. A boxer must toughen up his hands so as to be able to endure a long fight. Shadow-boxing did not properly prepare a boxer. This took real-time training with a sparring partner.

Knowing what lies ahead, Paul understands exactly where the finish line is. Paul knows the direction he must go and how he must devote himself to the challenges ahead. Paul does not run aimlessly or beat the air. No, Paul has disciplined himself so that his body will not be consumed by those things which prevent him from competing effectively. Paul will not take the easy way out, seek pleasure at the expense of personal discipline, so that through his own actions (especially the sin of sloth), he does not disqualify himself from receiving the prize for which he has trained. In fact, he will later use the same kind of language when speaking to his young pastor friend Timothy:

> Be a good servant of Christ Jesus, being trained in the words of the faith and of the good doctrine that you have followed. Have nothing to do with irreverent, sil-

For the Sake of the Gospel

ly myths. Rather train yourself for godliness; for while bodily training is of some value, godliness is of value in every way, as it holds promise for the present life and also for the life to come. The saying is trustworthy and deserving of full acceptance. For to this end we toil and strive, because we have our hope set on the living God, who is the Savior of all people, especially of those who believe. (1 Timothy 4:6–10)

There are no shortcuts to the Christian ministry, only God's calling followed by hard work to prepare (a sufficient education) and then a life of service to Christ and the members of his church.

Contrary to some commentators, Paul's assertion that he might be disqualified from the prize has nothing whatsoever to do with his awareness that he risked losing his salvation *if* he did not persevere in his preparation.[8] Rather, this is a metaphor about how we should approach the Christian life and does not speak to the question of whether or not a Christian can lose their salvation.

Christians have been rescued from God's wrath by Christ's death upon the cross. Because we are reckoned righteous based upon Christ's righteousness which is imputed to us through faith, cultural issues surrounding food and drink become a matter of indifference (*adiaphora*). These things neither commend us before God nor condemn us before God. Such issues remain in the category of "things indifferent" only until someone thinks eating certain foods or drinking certain beverages is wrong, and then stumbles (by eating or drinking) when a stronger Christian flaunts their liberty in front of them. Christians must be willing to give up their Christian liberty so that a weak Christian can eventually become strong. But the strong should give up their liberty only for a time—until the weak become strong, and their

---

8. As in Barrett, *The First Epistle to the Corinthians*, 218.

consciences are no longer bound to things which God does not forbid. A proper understanding of our own sanctification entails (in part) learning how to responsibly enjoy that Christian liberty which has been won for us by Christ.

In evangelistic contexts, like Paul, we should always strive to become all things to all people for the sake of the gospel. This does not mean changing or modifying the gospel to make it more palatable or acceptable to people who may be offended by its contents. But this does mean not letting trivial or cultural things distract people from the key issue—that the law condemns us, and that we are saved by Jesus Christ through faith in his saving work. If people are offended (and many will be), let them be offended by the preaching of Christ crucified, and not because of matters of food and drink.

Paul was willing to do everything in his power to remove obstacles for the sake of the gospel, because he knew that food and drink are nothing, and that the gospel is the power of God unto salvation.

16

The Rock Was Christ

1 CORINTHIANS 10:1–13

For I do not want you to be unaware, brothers, that our fathers were all under the cloud, and all passed through the sea, and all were baptized into Moses in the cloud and in the sea, and all ate the same spiritual food, and all drank the same spiritual drink. For they drank from the spiritual Rock that followed them, and the Rock was Christ.

There is a serious issue facing many in the Corinthian congregation. How do we as Christians interact with pagan religions and pagan practices which seem to surround us? Can we profess our faith in Christ, go to church on Sunday, yet still participate in pagan practices or ceremonies outside of church life? Are we even permitted to attend pagan religious ceremonies and activities? What can we learn about this from the account of Israel's time in the wilderness? YHWH was present with his people, provided them with his word and sacraments (means of grace), yet the Israelites grumbled about God's prohibition against their participation in pagan ceremonies. In what way is the history of Israel, in this regard, an example to us?

First Corinthians

Paul has already spoken of his great concern for the weak in this congregation. The weak are those who cannot separate the eating of meat from idolatry, and who think that if they eat meat which has been used in a pagan sacrifice, they are somehow endorsing or participating in the same paganism they are striving to leave behind. Paul has gone to great lengths to defend his apostolic office and to make clear that he practices what he preaches. Paul has even voluntarily given up certain things to which he is entitled for the sake of the gospel. It is Paul's purpose to become all things to all men for the sake of the gospel, so by all means, some might come to a saving knowledge of Jesus Christ.

In typical Pauline fashion, Paul introduces an illustration from redemptive history to bolster this point about the damage done when the people of God continue to engage in idolatrous practices—turning from the true and living God to worship and serve created things, all the while professing faith in Christ. Throughout the Old Testament, Israel experienced countless blessings from God (including spiritual baptism, spiritual food and drink) only to have fallen into idolatry even when YHWH was present among his covenant people. The tragic result was that the generation of Israelites who left Egypt stumbled badly and did not obtain the promised inheritance. Countless Israelites died in the wilderness of the Sinai. Against the backdrop of Israel's own history, Paul's point is crystal clear. If, like Israel, the Corinthians continue to make peace with idolatry, they too may suffer the same fate as ancient Israel and come under God's judgment.

The Example of Israel

In the first 14 verses of chapter 10, Paul discusses Israel's history and then makes application to the current struggles facing the Corinthians. What follows is, in one sense, a powerful warning.

The Rock Was Christ

Whenever Paul states that he wants his readers to know something, this means the apostle is about to introduce something of great significance.[1] Professing members of the Corinthian church may find themselves coming under the awesome judgment of God.

In verse 1, Paul directs the Corinthians to consider one of the most amazing episodes in all of redemptive history. "For I want you to know, brothers, that our fathers were all under the cloud, and all passed through the sea." When YHWH led Israel out of their captivity in Egypt through the Red Sea on dry ground, he not only delivered his people from their bondage, he did so by leading the people through visible means—the cloud and pillar of fire (cf. Exod. 13:17ff.). Paul uses this event to explain how the Corinthians are to understand their own place in redemptive history. They have been rescued from their bondage to sin by the death of Christ, and like Israel did when in Egypt, they must resist the temptation to live like their unbelieving neighbors.

Although he is about to warn them in no uncertain terms, nevertheless Paul addresses the congregation as his brothers. No doubt, Paul is hoping that the warning of God's judgment will be heeded. Although he is writing to a congregation of Jews and Gentiles, Paul speaks of "our forefathers" in such a way as to indicate that Paul sees the Christian church as the true Israel—Israel's forefathers are the forerunners of a Jewish-Gentile church. The word "all" appears five times in this section, indicating that "all Israel," without exception, in some sense participated in these blessings from God, now enumerated by Paul. While not all members of the Sinai covenant were elect and therefore not all of them embraced God's covenant promise by faith, all of those who were members of the covenant did receive God's

---

1. Cf. Romans 1:13; 11:25; 1 Corinthians 12:1; 2 Corinthians 1:8; 1 Thessalonians 4:13.

blessing—even if only externally in the form of heavenly food (manna) and drink (water miraculously provided).

In Exodus 13:21–22, we are told that all Israel (i.e., "our fathers") passed through the cloud at the time the people passed through the sea as recounted in Exodus 14. Looking back at this event through the lens of Christ's fulfilling the promises and types of the Old Testament, Paul informs the Corinthians that it was Jesus himself who led his people through the waters of judgment, safely delivering them from their enemies through the same water which was poured out in judgment on Pharaoh's army. When that happened, "All were baptized into Moses in the cloud and in the sea." This act of passing through the sea, Paul says, "baptized" all Israel into Moses, a remarkable assertion.

Since Moses was the mediator of the Sinaitic covenant, Moses therefore, represented the people of Israel before God. In this office (as mediator) Moses served as a type of Christ's mediatorial office (cf. 1 Tim. 2:4). Even though all Israel passed through the sea on dry ground and were "baptized," remarkably they did not get wet. In fact, as Meredith Kline quips, the Israelites might "even have been a little dustier when they reached the far shore."[2] Obviously, Paul's assertion is quite problematic for our Baptist friends who argue that the essence of baptism is "immersion in water."[3] It was the armies of Pharaoh which were immersed in water, not the Israelites! Although the Israelites shared a common baptism into Moses by passing through the sea following the glory-Spirit (the cloud), this remarkable event rescued Israel from the clutches of Pharaoh, but did not prevent those within Israel who did not believe God's promises from eventually coming under God's judgment. And just as there were those among the Israelites and the Corinthians who appeared to be trusting in

---

2. Kline, *By Oath Consigned*, 70.

3. See, for example, Wayne Grudem, *Systematic Theology* (Grand Rapids: Zondervan, 1994), 967–969.

The Rock Was Christ

Christ, there are people today in our churches mistakenly counting upon their service, good works, denominational affiliation, and a host of other things to save them from the wrath of God. As Paul warns the Corinthians, so too he warns us to make our calling and election sure (cf. 2 Pet. 1:10). Are we trusting in the finished work of Christ, or is there some sense in which we are trusting in our own righteousness and good works?

Christ, the Rock!

Likewise, as all the Israelites were baptized, they all ate the same spiritual food (i.e., the manna). "And all ate the same spiritual food and all drank the same spiritual drink. For they drank from the spiritual Rock that followed them, and the Rock was Christ" (v. 4). Israel ate spiritual food and drank the spiritual water. Therefore, in some sense, Israel possessed the Old Testament equivalents of the two Christian sacraments (baptism and the Lord's Supper). The Israelites drank the same spiritual drink (the water from the rock: Exod. 17:1–7, Num. 20:2–13), which should have pointed them to that spiritual reality symbolized by that water, none other than Jesus Christ (the living water), who was present with the Israelites all along. It is noteworthy that Paul speaks of Christ as the "rock," affirming his pre-existence and using a term which was elsewhere applied to YHWH in the Old Testament (Deut. 32:15; Ps. 18:2). The use of language is found in connection with the sacraments of the New Testament, when the sign (i.e., water, bread and wine) can be spoken of as though it were the thing signified (i.e., "the washing of regeneration," cf. Tit: 3:5, or "Christ's body and blood," cf. Matt. 26:26–29).

In verse 5, Paul reminds the Corinthians of the outcome of Israel's journey through the wilderness. "Nevertheless, with most of them God was not pleased, for they were overthrown in the wilderness." This is a very sad and tragic assertion and refers to the episodes recounted in Numbers 14:1–14 and Numbers 25:1–9. Despite Israel's possession of spiritual baptism and spiritual food and drink, nevertheless, during the forty years in the wilderness the people of Israel came under God's curse because of their propensity to grumble and engage in idolatry. In fact, of all the men of Israel who left Egypt, only two of their leaders (Joshua and Caleb) entered Canaan, as the rest died in the desert of Sinai as a result of God's judgment.

Israel in the Wilderness

In making this point, Paul is reminding the Corinthians of one of the saddest episodes in the history of Israel. Paul does not do this as a mere history lesson, but as a direct warning to the Corinthian congregation. Like the Israelites, the Corinthians enjoy the same spiritual food and drink that Israel did (Christ), and the same covenant signs and seals that Israel enjoyed through type and shadow (baptism and the Lord's Supper), but now in their fullness. In light of God's gifts to his people (and especially so when we consider these gifts in the context of the covenant which God had made with Israel), it should be clear that Christianity is not in any sense compatible with idolatry, or with any sort of pagan rituals and feasting. To make peace with paganism, as some in the Corinthian church have done by participating in pagan feasting and rituals, even while at the same time they are receiving the same spiritual food and drink given them by Christ, may lead to the same consequences which came upon Israel in the Sinai—God's judgment.

In verse 6, Paul ties the example of Israel to the current situation facing this congregation. "Now these things took place as examples for us, that we might not desire evil as they did." Like the Israelites of old, some of the Corinthians were grumbling—not against God *per se*, but against the prohibitions from Paul (and perhaps others like Apollos) about their ongoing participation in paganism. In this case, the Israelites serve as an example

The Rock Was Christ

to the Corinthians. The word "example" (*typoi*) also can be used in the sense of a serious warning.[4] Paul is putting the Corinthians on notice to break all ties with their pagan past.

Those events which Paul recounts from Israel's history prefigure the realities that have now dawned in the messianic age. God did these things during Israel's journey through the wilderness to ensure that his purposes would ultimately be accomplished, and that redemptive history would reach its ultimate goal with the coming of the Messiah. These things happened then to keep the people of Israel from setting their hearts upon evil things (i.e., the idolatrous rites of paganism). Awareness of this fact is intended to remind the Corinthians of the danger of likewise setting their hearts upon evil things as some in their midst were already doing. It is a serious thing to profess faith in Christ yet still participate in paganism.

Paul issues the following warning by recounting four specific instances where Israel had done exactly the same thing. In verse 7, he writes, "Do not be idolaters as some of them were; as it is written, 'The people sat down to eat and drink and rose up to play.'" To make his point, Paul cites the incident of Israel and the golden calf in Exodus 32:6: "And they rose up early the next day and offered burnt offerings and brought peace offerings. And the people sat down to eat and drink and rose up to play." In the Exodus passage, eating and drinking are connected to pagan festivities, which, after the consumption of sufficient quantities of adult beverages frequently degenerated into debauchery, just as occurred among the Israelites at the foot of Mount Sinai.

Based upon Paul's warning, there is every indication that some of the Corinthians were doing exactly the same thing as the Israelites had done. It is important to remember that Paul does not condemn the eating of meat under all circumstances. The apostle has just said that eating certain foods and abstain-

---

4. Barrett, *First Epistle to the Corinthians*, 223.

ing from other foods does not commend us to or condemn us before God. What Paul does condemn is the eating of certain foods in so far as these foods and the manner in which they are eaten are connected to idolatry. Therefore, the Corinthians are to carefully consider the experience of Israel, who even in the midst of their own participation in God's mighty acts of redemption, were still prone to fall into pagan practices and engage in acts of idolatry. Paul's warning is direct and crystal clear. Do not be idolaters by engaging in pagan feasting, debauchery, and temple prostitution. *Stay out of pagan temples!*

This is not a matter of whether or not Christians are free to eat certain meats or consume certain beverages. Rather, the matter at hand is the absolute necessity that Christians not participate in any idolatrous practices. To do so risks bringing down the judgment of God. This was true of those Israelites who had walked through the Red Sea on dry ground behind the pillar and cloud, and who saw God's presence on Mount Sinai, and yet, despite personally witnessing these mighty acts, still engaged in an orgy at the foot of Mount Sinai so loud Moses could hear the Israelites while he was coming down off the mountain. It is also true of the Corinthians who have witnessed Christ's work in their midst through the preaching of the gospel and the administration of the sacraments, in and through the power of the Holy Spirit, but who think nothing of still participating in the various pagan rituals going on in the temples and banquet halls of Corinth.

Do Not Put Christ to the Test!

Paul spells out what exactly he means in verse 8. "We must not indulge in sexual immorality as some of them did, and twenty-three thousand fell in a single day." That Paul's warning concerns sexual immorality should not come as a surprise since this was an issue which was a serious problem facing this congregation.

The Rock Was Christ

Corinth was a city filled with pagan temples, and those temples were filled with prostitutes. Again, Paul turns to the Old Testament for an example of the point, this time the account in Numbers 25:1–9 in which some twenty-three thousand people died. Even as Israelite men began to indulge in sexual immorality with Moabite women and were soon engaging in the worship of Baal only to find themselves under the direct judgment of God, so too, Paul warns the Corinthians of the necessity of avoiding sexual immorality, especially since sexual immorality is so often connected to idolatry.[5] The connection between paganism, idolatry, and sexual immorality was found in Corinth, just as it is found throughout much of pop culture today.[6]

The broader application to be drawn by Paul is found in verse 9. "We must not put Christ to the test, as some of them did and were destroyed by serpents." This refers to the account of the Israelites grumbling against God and Moses because they were tired of heavenly bread and provision in the form of manna. The verb "to test" (*ekpeirazōmen*) has a secondary meaning of "to tempt." Paul's words have the sense of pointing out the futility of testing God to see how far a sinner can go before coming under God's judgment. In the Old Testament case, "testing God" referred to grumbling about the spiritual food and drink which God had so graciously provided, and which meant they could no longer participate in pagan feasting. Many of the Corinthians were now asking how far they could go in engaging in idolatrous practices while still professing faith in Christ. This is classic antinomian behavior. "Where is the line, so we can go right up to it, yet without coming under God's judgment?"

---

5. See the discussion about this in Morris, *1 Corinthians*, 141. The Numbers passage speaks of 24,000, while Paul cites the total as 23,000. The explanation is as simple as the fact that Paul may be allowing for those killed by the judges (cf. Numbers 25:5).

6. See, for example, the profound and helpful discussion of this in Peter Jones, *The God of Sex: How Spirituality Defines Your Sexuality* (Colorado Springs: David C. Cook, 2006).

First Corinthians

Paul's warning to the Corinthians makes plain that this desire to participate in pagan feast and at the same time enjoy the benefits of Christ is not an acceptable response. Any such professing Christian risks facing the same situation as that faced by the Israelites as described in Numbers 21:5–6. "And the people spoke against God and against Moses, 'Why have you brought us up out of Egypt to die in the wilderness? For there is no food and no water, and we loathe this worthless food.' Then the Lord sent fiery serpents among the people, and they bit the people, so that many people of Israel died." Just as Israel tested God and came under his judgment, so too the Corinthians need to be very careful about their own conduct. We need to remember that such divine restrictions do not come about because God is seeking to keep us from enjoying the good things he has given us, but rather to protect us from ourselves. Our God is a jealous God in that he zealously demands our absolute allegiance because he has saved us from our sins.

Paul's litany continues in the next verse when he tells the Corinthians not to "grumble, as some of them did and were destroyed by the Destroyer" (v.10). Paul is addressing the Corinthians directly. The Greek verb "to grumble" (*gongyzete*) is a word which appears throughout the Septuagint whenever the Israelites grumbled against God, and it is quite likely that anyone who read the Old Testament in Greek would have immediately picked up on Paul's point. Each time the Israelites grumbled (even after God had delivered them from Egypt and provided for all of their needs during the Exodus), God's judgment came upon them. The point should not be missed that the opposite of grumbling is gratitude. Paul has told the Corinthians to be satisfied with their stations in life, and he has made the point that in the gospel of a crucified Savior, God has given us everything we need to be delivered from the guilt and power of sin. But yet, so many of us want something *else*, or something *more*. Many want the church service to be more entertaining, more "relevant," and more reflective of the culture around us. But is this not what the Israelites wanted? Is this not what the Corinthians were doing?

Paul's reference to the destroyer—the term (*olothreutou*) occurs nowhere else in the Greek New Testament—probably refers to the judgment which fell upon the company of Korah as recounted in Numbers 16:1ff. Some believe that Paul's reference to the destroyer might be a reference to the Angel of Death[7] (cf. Exod. 12:23; 2 Sam. 24:16; Isa. 37:36), but this identification is not made by Paul, and Hays points out the difficulties of identifying Paul's precise reference.[8] Difficulties aside, we should not miss the obvious point that Paul is making. "Grumbling about God risks calling down divine punishment."[9]

Written for Our Instruction

In verse 11, Paul spells out the reason as to why these events are recorded in redemptive history, and this helps to explain in part, how we are to read and understand redemptive history (especially the Old Testament). "Now these things happened to them as an example, but they were written down for our instruction, on whom the end of the ages has come." The events cited by Paul are types (examples) of what is to come. Ultimately, all of these events point to Christ's Second Advent, but in the meantime they serve as warnings to us.

That said, we must not take these important events out of their redemptive historical context and treat them as timeless principles, like a Christian version of *Aesop's Fables*. There is much more to this than simplistically affirming that living the Christian life is merely avoiding the bad things people did in the

---

7. Cf. J. B. Phillips, *Translation of the New Testament*.
8. Hays, *First Corinthians*, 165.
9. Morris, *1 Corinthians*, 141.

past. Rather, we must view all of these events through the lens of the blessing/curse principle of covenant theology. In reminding the Corinthians of these events, Paul sets this down as the principle by which subsequent generations of Christians should seek to understand the history of Israel. Having saved us from our sins, we should be grateful and obedient to God because of what he has done.

When Paul speaks of Christ as that one upon whom the end of the ages has come, his point is that Jesus Christ is that one upon whom all of redemptive history centers. Paul is no millennarian. He does not understand the one thousand years described in Revelation 20:1–10 as a future period of time yet to unfold upon the earth. Rather, Paul sees Revelation 20 as the present period of time—the inter-adventual period (see his discussion of the man of sin in 2 Thess. 2:1–12).[10] Paul sees history as the successive unfolding of two eschatological ages ("this age" and "the age to come"), which hinge upon the person and work of Jesus Christ. Our Lord's first advent is the culmination of all that has gone before in the Old Testament. In this sense, Jesus has brought the end of ages (the *telos* of what has gone before) to fulfillment (cf 2 Cor. 5:17–6:2).[11] But we must also consider that our Lord's second coming will be the consummation of everything promised, which has not yet been fully realized. Jesus is the Lord of history, he is the one who will bring about everything promised by God.

Take Heed!

A more pointed warning is given in verse 12. "Therefore let anyone who thinks that he stands take heed lest he fall." The problem in the Corinthian church has been and continues to be

---

10. See my defense of this in Kim Riddlebarger, *The Man of Sin: Uncovering the Truth About the Antichrist* (Grand Rapids: Baker Book House, 2006), 117–134.

11. Fee, *The First Epistle to the Corinthians*, 458–459.

The Rock Was Christ

their pride. The Corinthians are viewing things from the perspective of this present evil age, instead of through the prism of the age to come. The fate of countless Israelites, who likewise were overconfident and filled with pride, should serve as a warning to the Corinthians. Whenever Israelites engaged in idolatry, they came under God's judgment. God did this to protect the covenant line to ensure the birth of the Messiah and the fulfillment of his redemptive purposes for his people.

So too, the Corinthians have been duly warned. God will purify his church as the means of presenting his Son with a spotless bride (Eph. 5:25–27). "Husbands, love your wives, as Christ loved the church and gave himself up for her, that he might sanctify her, having cleansed her by the washing of water with the word, so that he might present the church to himself in splendor, without spot or wrinkle or any such thing, that she might be holy and without blemish."

Therefore, the self-confident among the Corinthians need to be careful and consider Paul's warning just issued. It seems likely that the Christian who falls into such sin is the proud person who boasts that he will never fall into such sin. The other type of person who falls in this manner is the careless person who ignores the fact that such temptations inevitably will come, and makes no effort to be on the lookout for such temptations, failing to prepare a way of escape when temptation does actually come.

Ever the shepherd of his flock, Paul tempers his pointed warning with an important word of pastoral encouragement in verse 13. "No temptation has overtaken you that is not common to man. God is faithful, and he will not let you be tempted beyond your ability, but with the temptation he will also provide the way of escape, that you may be able to endure it." The Corinthians are not under some unique and extraordinary form of trial. Such things have been (and will continue to be) common to the people of God. In fact, these temptations are common to humanity in general. To be identified with Christ and his church is to be identified with the scorn which comes upon the people of God, as well as to face the ever-present temptation to return to pagan or worldly ways of thinking and doing.

Paul's primary point is that God is always faithful to his people when they struggle with those temptations common to humanity. God will not allow his people to be tempted beyond what they can bear, and he will always provide a way of escape. It is interesting to note that the word for "escape" (*ekbasin*) is a word which refers to "a mountain pass," a word of picturesque imagery to people familiar with Greek military history. God will always provide a means of escape, even when temptation seems as threatening and inevitable as does a defeat at the hands of a much larger army. God is always faithful to us, his people, especially when we must endure temptation.

This is, of course, the basis for our strength and hope whenever trials and temptations come upon us. As Calvin reminds us, there is good reason to be confident in God's promise offered to us by Paul, "God helps us in two ways, so that we may not be overwhelmed by temptation: He supplies us with the resources we need, and sets a limit to the temptation . . . God mitigates temptations to prevent their overpowering us by their weight. For he knows how far our ability can go."[12] We also know that Jesus himself understands what it is that we must endure. As we read in Hebrews 2, "For because [Jesus] himself has suffered when tempted, he is able to help those who are being tempted" (v. 18). God provides us with what we need to overcome temptation, he limits the temptation to what we can endure, and he has given us a Savior who knows our struggle. It is through keeping these things in mind, that whatever temptation we face will not overwhelm us.

---

12. Calvin, *The First Epistle of Paul to the Corinthians*, 214.

The Rock Was Christ

Paul appeals to the history of Israel to make two important points for the Corinthians to carefully consider. The first point is that just as God called the Israelites out of Egypt and provided them with the means of grace, God has done the same for the Corinthians, as well as for us. The same Lord Jesus who has washed, justified, and sanctified his people in Corinth was with Israel in type and shadow—the rock was Christ who followed them. The benefits that Israel enjoyed (hidden in type and shadow) pointed forward to the very realities that we as the people of God now enjoy in all their fullness. That which was promised to Israel is now a reality for us. Although hidden in type and shadow, Christ was the rock. For the Corinthians and for us, Jesus is the crucified one, now risen and ascended on high. Jesus is our blessed Savior who baptizes us in the Holy Spirit, who speaks to us through his word, and who gives himself to us in the sacraments (those means of grace which sustain that faith created in us through the gospel).

The second point Paul makes is that Israel coming under the judgment of God serves as an example to us that our God is a jealous God. Jesus is no longer hidden in type and shadow. We profess that we trust Jesus' death to save us from our sins. We see in Jesus the wisdom and righteousness of God. Because that is true, how then can we profess faith in Christ, yet still participate in non-Christian religious ceremonies or practices? We cannot. Since Jesus Christ has purchased us with his own blood, he will not share us with occult practitioners (like fortune-tellers or astrologists), with false religions (i.e., Islam or Buddhism), with heretical sects like Mormonism or Jehovah's Witnesses. He will not share us with popular religious hucksters like Deepak Chopra.

We are Christ's. Jesus has bought us with his shed blood. He has given his righteousness to us through faith. He has provided us with the means of grace, and even now he is preparing us to be his bride. Jesus will never give us more than we can bear and he will always provide us with a way of escape. And because all of this is ours—our glorious inheritance in Jesus Christ—paganism has nothing for us.

17

Do All to the Glory of God

1 CORINTHIANS 10:14–33

So, whether you eat or drink, or whatever you do, do all to the glory of God.

Despite popular opinion to the contrary, Christianity is not a religion centered in prohibitions—"Thou shalt not do this. Thou shalt not do that." Rather, Christianity is a religion centered in God's gracious plan to rescue sinners from the guilt and consequences of sin. Because God has saved us from our sins, he will not allow us to worship him while at the same time keeping our allegiances to any non-Christian religions or practices in which we may have been involved before we came to a saving knowledge of Jesus Christ. The Christians to whom Paul is writing in Corinth are struggling mightily to leave their pagan past behind. They have written to Paul asking him a series of questions about how their new faith in Christ impacts them as they continue to live in a city dominated by pagan temples and practices. Earlier, Paul exhorted them to put the needs of their neighbors above their own—to give up their liberty for the sake of others. Now he gives the Corinthians a very simple standard by which to live as Christians in the midst of a pagan world—"Do all to the glory of God."

The reason it has taken Paul so long to lay out his response is probably due to the fact that Paul is answering each of the points the Corinthians raised in their letter to the apostle in which they asked the question of whether or not it was acceptable for Christians to eat meat which had been sacrificed to idols. Paul has already explained that idols are nothing since there is one true and living God who has revealed himself in Jesus Christ. Paul has told the Corinthians that eating such meat, or not eating such meat, does not commend us nor condemn us before God. Paul is emphatic that the strong (those who see nothing wrong with eating meat sacrificed to idols) should be willing to bear with the weak (who think this meat should not be eaten) until the weak become strong. The strong must be willing to give up their freedom until such time as the weak outgrow their spiritual immaturity.

As we have seen throughout this section of 1 Corinthians (chapters 8–10), food was often tied to pagan forms of worship. It was commonplace for an animal to be sacrificed in one of the city's pagan temples. Part of the butchered animal was used as a burnt offering, some of it went to the priests and participants in these pagan rituals, but the remaining meat was often sold to local butchers or in the city's marketplace. It is one thing to go into a pagan temple and participate in the pagan ceremony which includes an animal sacrifice and the ritualistic consumption of its flesh. It is another thing to buy the leftover meat from these ceremonies from a third party when that meat had no religious significance other than it was to be eaten for dinner. Should Christians buy and eat this meat? Or should they abstain? What are you to do when someone offers you a meal and you do not know where the meat came from? What then?

Do All to The Glory of God

Flee from Idolatry

With that brief review in mind, we are now in a position to take up the conclusion of Paul's discussion of pagan feasting and the Christian's relationship to idolatry in verses 14–33 of chapter 10. In verse 14, Paul gives the Corinthians (and us) a direct prohibition regarding participation in idolatry. "Therefore, my beloved, flee from idolatry." That this verse is the conclusion to what has gone before is much more apparent in the original language than in the English translation. The word translated as "therefore" (*dioper*) occurs only two times in the New Testament (cf. 1 Cor. 8:13) and indicates that what follows is the logical conclusion to Paul's point that he has been making throughout this entire section.[1]

Paul continues to speak of his readers as "my beloved," (*mou agapētoi*) indicating Paul's personal concern for those to whom he is writing. These are people whom the apostle knows well and loves affectionately. In a similar tone, Paul has already urged the Corinthians to flee from fornication (1 Cor. 5:9; 6:18), now he strongly urges them to flee from idolatry. The flight from idolatry is to become the daily practice of the Corinthians. As Morris puts it, "There is to be no leisurely contemplation of the sin, thinking that one can go so far and be safe from going further. The only wise course is to have nothing to do with it."[2] The Christian is to *flee* from idolatry. Paul is worried about those among the Corinthians who do not seem to be able to sever all ties to their pagan past.

Even though Paul has just assured the Corinthians in verse 13 that God will be with them even in the midst of whatever temptations they may face ("He will also provide the way of escape"), nevertheless, the Corinthians must make every effort to avoid all forms of idolatry. The gravity and difficulty of this

---

1. Fee, *The First Epistle to the Corinthians*, 464.
2. Morris, *1 Corinthians*, 142.

exhortation is easy to overlook. Like other large Greco-Roman cities, Corinth was filled with pagan temples and prostitutes, trade-guilds which were dedicated to pagan deities, and public baths, which were filled with "art" which can only be described as the ancient equivalent of pornography. Paul's exhortation not only includes the avoidance of all places where idolatry is practiced (e.g., the pagan temples), but his exhortation most likely includes the avoidance of all things associated with paganism, such as temple prostitution and sexual immorality as well. Paul is not asking the Corinthians to do something which would have been easy to do. Paganism and all of its sexual perversion was everywhere on display.

Since the Corinthians prided themselves on their great wisdom, Paul puts their claim to the test. "I speak as to sensible people; judge for yourselves what I say" (v. 15). Surely, sensible people can see the obvious. Resisting temptation is a fool's errand. Instead of resisting temptation, we should flee from it (cf. 1 Cor. 6:18). Paul is right and the Corinthians should know that the apostle is telling them the truth—if they are truly as wise as they claim to be. Nothing good can come from a Christian's involvement in idolatry. Christians must flee from paganism.

Participation in the Body and Blood of Christ

This point is certainly reinforced by what follows as Paul raises important questions regarding a believer's intimate relationship with the risen Christ through the Lord's Supper. Those who come to the Lord's Table enjoy fellowship with Christ himself. Therefore, they cannot continue to participate in the demonic. In verse 16, Paul writes, "The cup of blessing that we bless, is it not a participation in the blood of Christ? The bread that we break, is it not a participation in the body of Christ?" Paul's reference to the "cup of blessing" is significant. This is clearly a reference to the Lord's Supper, as the following discussion here and in chapter 11 will make plain. The background to Paul's words is that Jesus referred to the third cup of the Passover meal as his own blood of the new covenant shed for the remission of sins. The prayer of thanksgiving was uttered over this cup as a means of both consecrating the wine and to humbly give thanks for what God has done for us to provide for the forgiveness of our sins.

From Paul's vivid language, it is clear that when a Christian drinks from the cup, they somehow participate (*koinōnia*) in the blood of Christ. In consuming the wine in this cup, believers are bound together with Christ in fellowship, i.e., a participation with the blood of Christ. As Calvin puts it, "The soul has as truly communion in the blood, as we drink wine with the mouth."[3] According to the *Belgic Confession* (Article 35), "This banquet is a spiritual table at which Christ communicates himself to us with all his benefits. At that table he makes us enjoy himself as much as the merits of his suffering and death, as he nourishes, strengthens, and comforts our poor, desolate souls by the eating of his flesh, and relieves and renews them by the drinking of his blood."

The reception of Christ's blood is spiritual (not physical or "carnal"), and nothing is said about how this reception takes place (i.e., the mechanics of it). We are only told of the fact that we participate in the blood of Christ. The same thing holds true of the bread as it does for the wine. The fact that Paul mentions the cup and blood before mentioning the bread and Christ's body, might be connected to the fact that in local pagan rituals of Corinth much was made of the shedding of sacrificial blood of the animal about to be consumed. Perhaps Paul mentions the blood first because of its significance in redemption.

Why would Paul introduce the subject of a Christian's participation in pagan feasting, if the Lord's Supper were but a

---

3. Calvin, *The First Epistle of Paul to the Corinthians*, 216.

mere memorial meal wherein what truly mattered was whether or not we feel sorry enough for our sins to come to the Lord's Table? Participation in Christ's body and blood implies spiritual eating and drinking, not merely remembering—although remembering what Christ has done for us is an essential aspect of the Supper (cf. Luke 22:19). We must also consider the fact that the worship of pagan deities is also involved in this kind of eating and drinking. Since the Lord's Supper is said to be a participation in the body and blood of Christ, how can the Corinthians simultaneously participate in pagan feasting? They cannot. Neither can we. Professing Christians cannot join the Masonic lodge and then come to the table of the Lord. Christians cannot attend Kabbalah classes seeking spiritual insight and participate in the body and blood of Christ. Christians cannot make life's decisions based upon their horoscopes or Tarot Card readings and then participate in the sacraments. If we follow Christ, we must leave these pagan things behind.

If Christians truly enjoy fellowship with Christ through his body and blood, how can they still participate in pagan practices and engage in fellowship with pagan deities, especially when they know that deity is in reality nothing? As he indicates in verse 17, "Because there is one bread, we who are many are one body, for we all partake of the one bread." Paul's stress on unity is important and often overlooked in connection to the Supper. Christian believers come from diverse backgrounds. Yet once joined to Christ, we all become members of Christ's spiritual body, which is the church. In the celebration of the Lord's Supper not only do believers participate in the body and blood of Christ, they are likewise united to each other as members of Christ's body (the church) even as they are fed by Christ's body in the Supper.

The Supper is not only a sacrament in which we feed upon Christ's body and blood through faith, it is also a sacrament in which that same Christ binds his people together as his spiritual body. This means that to participate in pagan feasting is not only to be unfaithful to Christ, it is to be unfaithful to the other members of the body of Christ. This is why the sacrament of the Lord's Supper is also the sacrament of Christian unity. We are one body who together partake of one loaf.

Idols Are Nothing

In verse 18, Paul once again returns to redemptive history to illustrate his point. "Consider the people of Israel: are not those who eat the sacrifices participants in the altar?" It is interesting that Paul literally speaks of "Israel according to the flesh" perhaps to distinguish national Israel from the new Israel which is the church. Says Paul, those who eat the sacrifices, participate (*koinōnoi*) in the altar, that is, they participate in all that the altar stands for. Paul is probably referring to the meals prescribed in Deuteronomy 14:22–27, in which the people eat the sacrificed food. By eating this meal, the people were bound together to YHWH and to each other.

In verses 19–21 Paul returns to the point made by the strong in 1 Corinthians 8:4—idols are nothing. "What do I imply then? That food offered to idols is anything, or that an idol is anything? No, I imply that what pagans sacrifice they offer to demons and not to God. I do not want you to be participants with demons." The dilemma that Paul is facing is simply this: If a Christian eats meat sacrificed to idols then he or she in some sense participates in the demonic. But if a Christian cannot eat such meat for ethical reasons, this seems to imply that idols are real, and appears to be the reason why Christians should avoid this food. Paul's rhetorical question, asked in verse 19 and then answered in verse 20, is designed to point out that not only are sacrifices made to idols nothing, but idols themselves are nothing.

First Corinthians

Although idols are nothing (there is no God but one), there is an occult (demonic) reality underlying idolatry. While the idols are nothing but wood and stone, demons use people's susceptibility to idolatry to make inroads into their lives through the means of deception. Some sort of bond is formed with demons through a fellowship meal associated with a pagan temple. Even though idols are in actuality nothing, people who associate with idols are not engaging in some neutral activity. There is an occult dimension so real that people who sacrifice to idols (which are nothing) are actually sacrificing to the demons themselves. Therefore, to share in the eating of food sacrificed to idols (which are nothing) is to form a bond of fellowship with demons (which are real). Idol worshipers do have fellowship with demons when they eat food sacrificed to idols. This is why someone who is in fellowship with Jesus Christ (and who participates in the Lord's Supper) must not continue to participate in the things which go on in these pagan temples. And this is why we, as the people of God, must understand that we belong to that one who bought us with his own blood. We cannot claim to love "Jesus" and then participate in "interfaith" events wherein the uniqueness of Jesus is denied. We cannot walk with one foot in Christ's church and one foot in the synagogue, the mosque, or the Masonic lodge.

This explains Paul's emphatic assertion in verse 21: "You cannot drink the cup of the Lord and the cup of demons. You cannot partake of the table of the Lord and the table of demons." When Paul speaks of the "table of the Lord" he is echoing a number of Old Testament passages (cf. Mal. 1:6ff.) which speak of the altar in the temple as the "table of the Lord." The altar occupied the central place in Israel's worship of YHWH. The unbelieving priests of Israel polluted the altar by offering improper sacrifices—blemished animals. As a result, they came under God's judgment. This is yet another illustration from redemptive history from which Christians can learn.

In the new covenant, the altar in the Jerusalem temple has been replaced by the "table of the Lord." No longer bound to a specific place, in every Christian church Christ gives himself to his people through bread and wine if they receive that bread and wine through faith, believing that they are receiving Christ's true body and blood.[4] This reminds us of the importance of the sacraments in general, and the Lord's Supper in particular, in the worship service of the apostolic churches. This is also the reason why the celebration of the Lord's Supper is tied to the preached word, and to be celebrated frequently, not infrequently, as is the practice of many Reformed and Presbyterian churches.[5]

Paul puts this matter in sharp relief. Christians cannot be participants both in the Lord's Supper and idol feasts. This is clearly an either/or choice. Christians cannot compromise on this matter. When we drink the cup of the Lord, we are spiritually participating with the blood of Christ. But someone who drinks the cup of a pagan ceremony somehow and in some way participates with the demonic. Those who participate in the Lord's Supper cannot take part in any pagan rituals—without risking God's judgment.

---

4. According to *The Heidelberg Catechism* Q & A 76. Q. "What does it mean to eat the crucified body and drink the shed blood of Christ? A. It means not only to embrace with a believing heart all the sufferings and death of Christ, and thereby to obtain the forgiveness of sins and life eternal; but moreover, also, to be so united more and more to His sacred body by the Holy Spirit, who dwells both in Christ and in us, that, although He is in heaven and we on earth, we are nevertheless flesh of His flesh and bone of His bone, and live and are governed forever by one Spirit, as members of the same body are governed by one soul."

5. Regarding the development of the biblical case for the frequent celebration of the Lord's Supper, see Kim Riddlebarger, "The Reformation of the Supper," in R. Scott Clark and Joel E. Kim, eds., *Always Reformed: Essays in Honor of W. Robert Godfrey* (Escondido, CA: Westminster Seminary California, 2010), 192–207.

Paul goes on to point out in verse 22 that there are serious consequences which may result from the Corinthians indifference or carelessness in this matter. "Shall we provoke the Lord to jealousy? Are we stronger than he?" Paul has pointed out at the beginning of this chapter that the Corinthians must be aware of the fate of ancient Israel—how the Israelites ate spiritual food and drink and yet came under God's judgment. He reminds the Corinthians that it is not a good thing to arouse God's jealousy. We are not stronger than God, and to mock him by participating in paganism is to risking coming under the covenant curse as described in 1 Corinthians 11:27–32.

> Whoever, therefore, eats the bread or drinks the cup of the Lord in an unworthy manner will be guilty concerning the body and blood of the Lord. Let a person examine himself, then, and so eat of the bread and drink of the cup. For anyone who eats and drinks without discerning the body eats and drinks judgment on himself. That is why many of you are weak and ill, and some have died. But if we judged ourselves truly, we would not be judged. But when we are judged by the Lord, we are disciplined so that we may not be condemned along with the world.

In verses 23–33, Paul returns to the subject he addressed previously in chapter 8, the eating of meat sacrificed to idols. The practical application of Paul's doctrine is set out in the balance of the chapter. As Paul puts it in verse 23, "'All things are lawful,' but not all things are helpful. 'All things are lawful,' but not all things build up." Paul has made this point several times before. While everything is permissible for him, not everything builds up the body of Christ. Christian liberty is to be defended at all costs against Pharisees and legalists, and yet at the same time Christian liberty must be exercised in such a way as not to cause the weak to stumble (cf. Gal. 5:1, 13). Just because I am free to do something, doesn't mean that I should. I might be free to enjoy a fine craft beer or bottle of wine with church friends, but in the presence of those who are weak and see such things as sinful, it might be better to abstain until such time as the weak Christian is properly instructed and then becomes strong.

Seek the Good of Our Neighbor

In verse 24, Paul reminds the Corinthians of one of the basic principles of the Christian life. "Let no one seek his own good, but the good of his neighbor." Because we are all members of Christ's body, we are not to place ourselves above others. Since we are to seek the good of others, we must be careful not to use our liberty as a way of justifying self-centered behavior. We are always to consider the weak, especially in the context of food. Food and drink should never divide the body of Christ.

This brings Paul to the very practical question of eating meat which has been sold in the market. What are we to do about this, especially if we do not know the origins of the meat? Once again, Paul's advice in verses 25–26 is simple and very practical. "Eat whatever is sold in the meat market without raising any question on the ground of conscience. For 'the earth is the Lord's, and the fullness thereof.'" While Christians cannot eat meat in a pagan context (e.g., at a pagan feast), there is nothing wrong whatsoever with eating meat which may or may not have come from a pagan temple. While the Jews would have been very scrupulous about this, Paul lays no such burden on the Gentiles. If we do not know where the meat came from, why worry about it? Eat and enjoy!

With a single sentence (the revolutionary nature of which we take for granted) Paul has just dismissed every world religion centered upon good works and religious rituals. Paul tells us to eat and not worry about it. Christians are not bound to superstition, nor to the rules of men who think themselves wiser than God. After all, there is no reality to the idol since the earth and everything in it is the Lord's (a citation from Psalm 24:1).

But what about meat which is offered to us in someone's home, when we may not know the origin of the meat? Paul's advice in verses 27–30 is simple and utterly practical.

> If one of the unbelievers invites you to dinner and you are disposed to go, eat whatever is set before you without raising any question on the ground of conscience. But if someone says to you, 'This has been offered in sacrifice,' then do not eat it, for the sake of the one who informed you, and for the sake of conscience—I do not mean your conscience, but his. For why should my liberty be determined by someone else's conscience? If I partake with thankfulness, why am I denounced because of that for which I give thanks?

The principle is very simple. As a matter of charity, the Christian is to eat whatever is put before them. But if the host announces that the meat comes from a pagan sacrifice, the Christian should not eat the food, both an example to the host that a believer's union with Christ prevents them from doing so, but also to avoid matters of which might disturb a weaker person's conscience.

According to Paul, the Christian is free to eat whatever he or she wants. Our liberty should not depend upon what others mistakenly think. But the weak Christian, or the non-Christian, needs to know that the Christian does not, and indeed cannot, sanction idolatry. Paul does not want Christians to offer a prayer of thanks over something which the strong is free to eat, but which the weaker party thinks is sinful, so they then denounce the strong. Paul wishes to avoid all such situations in the first place. Better not to eat if there are doubts. However, if nothing is said (the implication is do not ask), eat and enjoy!

Do All to The Glory of God

Do All to the Glory of God

This leads to the following guideline from Paul in verses 31–33 which serves as test as to whether or not to eat and drink: "So, whether you eat or drink, or whatever you do, do all to the glory of God. Give no offense to Jews or to Greeks or to the church of God, just as I try to please everyone in everything I do, not seeking my own advantage, but that of many, that they may be saved." If we do everything to the glory of God (i.e., we carefully consider that which exalts Christ and advances his kingdom), then we are free to eat and drink what we wish.

However, doing everything for the glory of God means that the strong must be careful in the presence of the weak and avoid doing any of those things which may cause the weak to stumble. Like Paul, we should all follow the example of Christ, and put the good of others before our own, so that we gain a hearing to preach the gospel, by which they may be saved.

Paul raises three issues in this section of 1 Corinthians. The first is that Christians are to enjoy their liberty in Christ. If our standing before God depends upon the merits of Christ (his death for our sins, his obedience providing us with a justifying righteousness which are received through faith), then what we eat and drink does not impact our standing with God. This means we are free to eat or drink whatever we wish (with moderation, of course). And yet, we must always be cognizant of the weak, and we must do nothing to cause them to stumble. We must put love for our brothers and sisters ahead of our freedom to eat or drink, or not.

Paul's second point is that idols are nothing—there is one God, who created and sustains all things. If people think the idols are real, then for all intents and purposes they are. The demonic comes into play through deception. Even though idols are nothing, demons are real. People may think they are worshiping Caesar Augustus, Diana, Mars or Jupiter or some other pagan deity, yet in doing so, they are actually serving demons. This is why Christians are to have nothing to do with idolatry. Paul is not worried about meat, he's worried about Christians unwittingly participating in the demonic.

Paul's third point is closely related to the others—Christ gives himself to us in the Lord's Supper. This is why the sacraments are essential to Christian worship, and are not something tagged on once in a while to the worship service. When we eat the consecrated bread and drink the wine, we are truly participating in Christ's body and blood. By faith, we take ordinary bread and wine (consecrated by prayer) as though they were the true body and blood of Christ. When we do this, the Holy Spirit ensures that we receive what is promised—Christ's body and blood. Paul's point is that if the reception of Christ's body and blood is a reality, how then can Christians receive Christ's true body and blood, yet still be willing to participate in the demonic? We cannot. This is why, Paul says, we must flee from idolatry. We must have nothing to do with idolatry in any of its forms, including those idols we encounter so often today: the love of money, the desire for power over and control of others, and the adoration of celebrity.

At the end of the day, Paul leaves us with two basic ethical principles to help us navigate our way through a pagan culture like that of our own. Because our salvation has already been accomplished for us by Jesus Christ through his death and resurrection, we must put the needs of our neighbor ahead of our own, and whatever we do, we must do all to the glory of God.

18

The Image and Glory of God

1 CORINTHIANS 11:1–16

Every man who prays or prophesies with his head covered dishonors his head, but every wife who prays or prophesies with her head uncovered dishonors her head, since it is the same as if her head were shaven. For if a wife will not cover her head, then she should cut her hair short. But since it is disgraceful for a wife to cut off her hair or shave her head, let her cover her head. For a man ought not to cover his head, since he is the image and glory of God, but woman is the glory of man. For man was not made from woman, but woman from man. Neither was man created for woman, but woman for man.

We live in a culture dominated by celebrities—people who are famous for being famous. The temporary glory of celebrity would be apparent if I were to list a few of the current ones, knowing full well in doing so, many, if not all of them would have been relegated to obscurity by the time someone reads this exposition even a few years later—fleeting glory is the very essence of the modern celebrity. Those who are currently household names do not always enjoy popularity because of their talent or accomplishments, but because of their ability to shock us by defying social convention. Sadly, our contemporaries are only interested in them *because* they offend our sensitivities.

Ironically, Paul is dealing with much the same thing in the Corinthian church. In an age in which women were not to be seen or heard, Paul recounts how what some have called a first century "woman's liberation movement" brought great distress to the Corinthian church.

Apparently, when composing their list of questions to Paul, the Corinthians asked the apostle about specific aspects of public worship. In light of these questions, Paul turns his attention to matters of proper conduct in worship (1 Cor. 11) before addressing spiritual gifts in chapter 12. After praising the Corinthians for holding fast to his teaching (v. 2), Paul raises the matter of headship to describe three important relationships: man/Christ, woman/man, and Christ/God, as the basis for his discussion of head coverings, or more likely, hairstyles (vv. 4–5a), specifically as these issues relate to male headship and the modesty of women in the churches.

Defying Societal Convention

The cultural background here is important. Unless we understand the cultural circumstances regarding appropriate clothing and hairstyles in first-century Corinth, we will not understand Paul's response.[1] While the general principles are clear and binding upon Christians in different cultures throughout the ages, the specific cultural issues Paul discusses are not always clear to us. The rebellion and immodesty which was symbolized by the long, flowing hairstyles in Corinth, may be symbolized

---

1. Helpful discussions of this can be found in Keener, *The IVP Bible Background Commentary*, 475–477 and Hays, *First Corinthians*, 182–190.

The Image and Glory of God

by another hairstyle in another culture. This is why we must not concentrate on the specifics of the Corinthian congregation in terms of application, but the general principles.

In Greco-Roman culture, a woman's hair was often the object of male lust. This is why in much of the Mediterranean world women were expected to cover their hair (or wear it up) as an expression of modesty and proper etiquette. In first century Greece, upper-class women would show off their social status by wearing their hair in provocative hairstyles. Paul must address this matter because this was causing great consternation among the Corinthians. Upper-class fashion and working-class sexual/social mores both coexisted in the Corinthian congregation. Now there was conflict. Further complicating things was the fact that Greeks often bared their heads in public, while Romans tended to cover their heads. Which was proper?

Upper-class women and female celebrities in Corinth were quite emancipated. Archeological evidence indicates that women even participated in the Isthmian games, competed in chariot races, the 200 meter race, and contests for lyre playing. Apparently, these women were well-known throughout the region and viewed as celebrities. These women set fashion trends and saw nothing wrong with going without a veil or a head-covering in public, while working-class women, Romans and Jews, all covered their heads in public, the Jewish women even veiling their faces. The conduct of these Greek women was seen as an offensive flaunting of social propriety. Paul will not allow such behavior to disrupt worship.

In verse 1, which is the conclusion to Paul's discussion of Christian liberty begun in the previous chapter (vv. 10–33), he writes "be imitators of me, as I am of Christ." If we do everything to the glory of God, we are free to eat and drink what we wish. However, doing everything for the glory of God means that the strong must be careful in the presence of the weak and avoid doing anything which may cause the weak to stumble. Like Paul, we should all follow the example of Christ, and put the good of others before our own, so that we gain a hearing to preach the gospel, by which they may be saved.

Maintain the Traditions

Moving on to a new topic, Paul reminds the Corinthians that Christians have no business flaunting public convention and causing disruption. As he states in verse 2, "Now I commend you because you remember me in everything and maintain the traditions even as I delivered them to you." Paul begins with a word of praise and refers to the fact that the members of this congregation thought of him often and prayed for him on a regular basis. They accepted his teaching ("the traditions"), which was the memorized oral tradition that had been given to Paul, which he, in turn, passed on to the Corinthians. This was not content Paul had invented, but "tradition" (the teaching of the apostles and the facts of the gospel) which was passed on to him and which he taught the Corinthians.

Paul continues in verse 3, "But I want you to understand that the head of every man is Christ, the head of a wife is her husband, and the head of Christ is God." As a mild form of rebuke, the sentence stands in contrast to Paul's compliment of verse 2. Paul sets out three representative instances of headship (man/Christ; woman/man; Christ/God), to illustrate the proper order of things. *Kephalē* (head) is a hotly debated term and probably means something like "source" as in the head of a river.

Throughout 1 Corinthians 11, Paul is probably not talking about a man's authority over a woman (headship as "authority"), but is instead referring to an event in redemptive history—that the woman was formed from the man as described in Genesis 2:21–22. The man is the source of the woman. This interpretation is confirmed by verses 8–9, when Paul returns to several terms of the analogy. Man was formed by Christ at creation. Christ derives his authority from the Father who sent him. Christ was not created, of course, but he was sent by the Father (in his incarnation) whose will is the source of Christ's redemptive work. We must not press the analogy too far, however, as none of these relationships are identical. Paul is concerned to show how certain relationships are based upon one party being the source of the other, and how shame coming upon one, therefore, brings shame upon the other.

Appearance Matters

Once we have considered this, we are in a position to explain why women must be careful about their appearance in public worship. As Paul says in verse 4, "Every man who prays or prophesies with his head covered dishonors his head." As we will see in verses 7–12, the order of creation lies at the heart of Paul's argument. Since the man was created first, Paul begins his discussion with men, whose heads must remain uncovered, or else they pray or prophesy improperly. While this might be a reference to long hair in the form of an androgynous hairstyle (perhaps associated with male temple prostitutes who decorated their own hair to be like that of fashionable women or to imitate female temple prostitutes), more likely Paul is referring to the practice of men covering their heads during prayer or preaching while pulling a toga up over the head, or perhaps wearing the Jewish prayer shawl.[2]

One possible application of this is that since man is God's image and glory (v. 7), men are not to veil that glory in worship. Another possible interpretation is that Paul wished to avoid Jewish practices (praying or preaching with a head covered by a prayer shawl) which would have presented a legalistic image to Gentiles who did not understand Jewish practices. Yet an-

---

2. Fee, *The First Epistle to the Corinthians*, 507.

other possible interpretation is that men covered their heads during the time of mourning, and Paul does not want men to pray and preach as though they were in mourning, when, in fact, Christ was raised from the dead and has ascended on high. Then, there is also the possibility that members of the Isis cult wore head-coverings and Paul wants Christians to avoid looking like cult members. Whatever was in view here, Paul's point is that for men to cover their heads while praying or preaching would bring shame to Christ (their head).

As for women, in verse 5 Paul adds, "But every wife who prays or prophesies with her head uncovered dishonors her head, since it is the same as if her head were shaven." The one thing which jumps out at us is that women prophesied in the Corinthian church as did men. Throughout the Mediterranean world and Greek culture in particular, women were not educated and certainly did not speak in public. Plutarch urged women to remain silent as a sign of modesty and virtue. Jews even regarded it a sin for women to participate in religious teaching. Yet, Jesus clearly allowed women to sit at his feet (cf. Luke 10:39–42). It is Christianity which advanced the cause of women, while paganism oppressed women, denying them education, treating them as mere sex objects or even as the property of their father or husband.

The fact that the Corinthians were allowing women to participate in religious instruction was itself quite remarkable, even more so that women could actually prophesy if they did so in an appropriate manner. Calvin asserts that such prophesying refers to "explaining the mysteries of God for the enlightening of those who hear,"[3] while Gaffin contends that Paul is referring to a Spirit-inspired utterance—not in the sense of insight into an existing biblical text or tradition—"but is itself the inspired,

---

3. Calvin, *The First Epistle of Paul to the Corinthians*, 230.

The Image and Glory of God

nonderivative word of God."[4] Without greater information about what this prophesying actually involved in the Corinthian church, I think it wise not to say more than that such prophecy entails "conveying the message of God to the hearers."[5] Clearly, Paul does not prohibit the practice of women prophesying, and he even describes how women should be dressed when doing so. While men are not to cover their heads (such would bring shame to Christ), women are not to uncover their heads (which brings shame to men).

Yet, Paul's comments here create an apparent problem later on in 1 Corinthians 14:34–35, because in this text Paul tells the Corinthians: "The women should keep silent in the churches. For they are not permitted to speak, but should be in submission, as the Law also says. If there is anything they desire to learn, let them ask their husbands at home. For it is shameful for a woman to speak in church." The solution to this apparent contradiction (women can prophesy, but can't speak in the church) may be as simple as the fact that in 1 Corinthians 11, Paul is speaking of women prophesying to other women, or prophesying on occasions other than the regular worship service on the Lord's Day. In any case, it is clear from what Paul teaches elsewhere that only males may be called to the office of elder and minister of word and sacrament (cf. 1 Tim. 2:11–15; 3:1–13). Whatever prophesying women did in Corinth with Paul's permission does not usurp the ruling and teaching authority of the male elders of the church, who must evaluate all such teaching.

Whenever a woman prays or prophesies in public, her head must be covered, or else she brings shame upon her husband. When that happens, it were as though her head were shaved, which is the ultimate sign of humiliation and shame for a wom-

---

4. Richard B. Gaffin, *Perspectives on Pentecost* (Phillipsburg: Presbyterian and Reformed, 1979), 59.

5. Morris, *1 Corinthians*, 169.

an in the Mediterranean world. The "uncovered" head may be a reference to "loosed hair" (which a woman allows to flow down her shoulders), which she normally would not have done in public, only in private. Since Paul goes on to say in verse 15 that a woman's long hair is her glory and her covering, as with his discussion of men in verse 4, he may also be referring to a head-covering of some type, but the reference is more likely to a provocative hairstyle.

Modesty is Critical

Paul is not talking about the length of a woman's hair, probably not even to her wearing something on her head (a hat, a covering) but wearing her hair in a shameful manner. Paul does not want women to do anything which causes disruption in the church, which is immodest, reflects an androgynous sexuality, or has overt stylistic ties to paganism and temple prostitution. Paul makes this point in verse 6. "For if a wife will not cover her head, then she should cut her hair short. But since it is disgraceful for a wife to cut off her hair or shave her head, let her cover her head." If a woman does not cover her head (wear her hair modestly) and so causes disruption, denies her gender, appears immodest, then she should just shave her head (which is the ultimate sign of shame) since her conduct has already brought shame upon herself.

The appropriate application to be drawn from this varies from culture to culture. Long hair may be a sign of modesty in one culture, and a sign of immodesty in another. But Paul's principle still applies in all cultures—women are to be modest, not hide their gender and appear as males, and are to avoid all stylistic connections to pagan religions or immoral activity. If temple prostitutes in Corinth covered their heads (or wore their hair in a bun), my guess is that Paul would have told the Corinthian women to wear their hair out, long and flowing. Paul does not want Christian

The Image and Glory of God

women or men to do anything to disrupt worship, cause strife within the church, or identify with paganism.

Man: The Image and Glory of God

Paul's argument in verses 7–16 is predicated upon his understanding of creation and the priorities which flow from the fact that the man was created prior to the woman. Paul establishes complementary roles for male and female to explain why men should have their heads uncovered in worship (so as not to bring shame to Christ) and why women should cover theirs (so as not to bring shame to men). As he states in verse 7, "For a man ought not to cover his head, since he is the image and glory of God, but woman is the glory of man." The reason for the point that Paul made back in verse 4—that a man should not cover his head while praying or preaching—is now given. Man is both the image and glory of God, which is a clear reference to the creation account (cf. Gen. 1:26–27).

Even though man's glory is not mentioned in the creation account, for Paul, God's creation of man as a divine image bearer is quite significant. Man exists to give glory to God, and, in fact, does give glory to God by being what he truly is, God's believing and obedient creature. As Paul sees it, before the Fall, Adam reflected the glory of his Creator, since Adam was created as divine image-bearer.

For Paul, the female-male relationship mirrors the image of the Christ-Adam relationship in that the woman reflects the glory of the man from whose side she was taken.[6] But we must be clear that woman is not made in the image of man but of God (cf. Gen. 1:26–28), although Paul does say she reflects the glory "of the man" (cf. Gen. 2:18–23). While woman is the glory of man, nevertheless she has her own unique role, although it

---

6. See M. G. Kline, *Images of the Spirit* (Grand Rapids: Baker Book House, 1980), 30, 34.

is different from Adam's in particular circumstances (such as childbearing, submitting to the headship of her husband, etc.).

This is why a man must not cover his head when he prays or preaches—presumably during worship, when the people of God are especially conscious of being in the presence of God—because the head of one who reflects the glory of his Creator is not to be covered. To cover his head would bring shame to his Creator. Therefore, in some sense, man remains an image-bearer and reflects the divine glory even after the Fall. And while he must not cover his head during worship, the opposite is true for women. Since the woman reflects the glory of man (from whom she was taken), she must have her head covered appropriately (more on this in verse 15), since God (and not man) is to be glorified during worship. It is when men and women deny the difference between the sexes (through appearances connected with hairstyle or fashion) and that they are the glory of God and man respectively, ironically, they fail to bring glory to God who created men and women as divine image-bearers with complementary roles in creation. We bring glory to God as males or females (as we were created), not as androgynous hybrids who seek to hide or deny our gender.

Creation and Gender

In verses 8–9, Paul directs us to the order of creation. "For man was not made from woman, but woman from man. Neither was man created for woman, but woman for man." According to the creation account, man does not come from the woman, but the woman comes from the man (a reference to the fact that Eve was created from a rib taken from Adam's side—cf. Gen. 2:21ff.). The reason why God created Eve is stated in Genesis 2:18: "Then the Lord God said, 'It is not good that the man should be alone; I will make him a helper fit for him.'" Man is incomplete without woman and woman is incomplete without man. Paul is not dis-

The Image and Glory of God

cussing the equality of the sexes as we moderns keep trying to get him to do. While Paul sees both men and woman as divine image bearers and equal in terms of their standing before God, nevertheless, Paul does speak of a complementary relationship between men and women.

In this complementary relationship, Adam has a redemptive-historical priority and thereby is given spiritual headship over the woman. Whenever Paul introduces the theme of male-female relationships, he is not thinking of Eve as *inferior* in any sense, but *complementary* to Adam, who was created first, and from whom she in turn is created. This is contrary to virtually all the thinking of Paul's age which subjugated woman and denied them even the most basic of rights, as well as those in our own age, who think that unless women can do everything men can do, women are still somehow inferior (symbolically).

This leads to the most controversial verse in this section, verse 10. "That is why a wife ought to have a symbol of authority on her head, because of the angels." Paul is not teaching that a woman was to cover her head in worship (with a hat, scarf, or veil) as a sign that she is subject to her husband, and therefore, an obedient wife. What Paul is saying that women are not inferior to men, as was commonly taught throughout the ancient world. As Paul sees it, in the new creation, distinctions which were formerly used to create division among the people of God, no longer apply (cf. Gal. 3:28).

Although women occupy different roles than men, the men of Corinth cannot view women as inferior as commonplace in Judaism and Greco-Roman paganism. Women were able to prophesy (v. 5) and for that they need a certain authority. By properly covering their heads with a modest hairstyle, unlike that of the emancipated female celebrities of Corinth, Christian women demonstrate that they too are under the authority of God, and that they are not submitting to other "gods," nor participating in idolatrous pagan practices and immorality. When Paul speaks of angels, he is probably referring to those angels in the presence of God which were thought to veil themselves before God (cf. Isa. 6:1ff.).

No doubt, Paul's comments are revolutionary and we must not overlook the fact that Paul's complementarian view (different roles but equal status regarding the sexes) would have been rather shocking at the time. In Judaism, women played a very minor role, and were not even counted as members of a synagogue. Much of the world of Paul's day regarded women as chattel, although in Corinth, there were many emancipated women associated with paganism or athletic competitions, who were establishing many of the styles creating such trouble in the churches, dividing the social classes, and causing identification with paganism. It is Christianity which liberates women from oppressive pagan and cultural views which deny that they too are divine image-bearers and thus under God's authority every bit as much as males.

This becomes clear in the following verse (v. 11). "Nevertheless, in the Lord woman is not independent of man nor man of woman." Paul clearly teaches that men and women have different roles (they are created for different, albeit complementary purposes). His point is that under the Lordship of Christ, and by virtue of the way in which things have been created, that neither sex exists without the other. Although man was created first, and has headship over the woman, this is not to be understood to mean that women are inferior to men, especially when it comes to matters of worship, the context for Paul's discussion here.

Complementary Roles

According to verse 12, "For as woman was made from man, so man is now born of woman. And all things are from God." Once again, Paul repeats his basic point, that woman came from man

The Image and Glory of God

(in creation), and that men are born through the woman as a result of woman's creation as Adam's partner. Since everything comes from God, all created things are not only to submit to God their Creator, but all things have the form and function assigned to them by God. Men and women have been created for specific purposes in redemptive history with complementary roles. Neither can exist independently of the other, and both are equal before God. I think we risk seriously misreading Paul if we attempt to read him through the lens of contemporary discussions of gender. Paul's argument provides no discrepancy whatsoever between holding to male headship in the home and in the church, while at the same time seeing women as equals before God in worship, and in terms of vocation in the civil realm. The first female President of the United States would still have to submit to the spiritual headship of her husband, if she be a Christian.

Paul returns to the theme that much of Christian conduct is to be determined in light of what is in the best interests of others and what will keep the peace of the church, which is the body of Christ. As he writes in verse 13, "Judge for yourselves: is it proper for a wife to pray to God with her head uncovered?" Paul again appeals to the Corinthians, who claim superior wisdom, to do what is right. A woman should not pray with her head uncovered, since to do so risks public identification with pagan religions and temple prostitution, and demonstrates a degree of immodesty which brings shame to men. Since a shaved head was a sign of shame for a woman in Paul's day, Christian women should never worship in shameful ways. Christian women are not to wear hairstyles (or clothing) which are identified with idolatrous practices, pagan religions, and with the rampant sexual immorality found throughout the city. The old-fashioned term for this is modesty. Modesty is not frumpishness, but is self-consciously humble and reverent behavior before God.

In verses 14–15, Paul continues to appeal to creation. "Does not nature itself teach you that if a man wears long hair it is a disgrace for him, but if a woman has long hair, it is her glory? For her hair is given to her for a covering." While there are a number of images in Greek history of men having long hair (the Spartans, and certain Greek philosophers and sages come to mind), most men wore short hair due to the nature of the work they performed, as well as to distinguish themselves from women (and their low social standing). If a woman's long hair is her glory, then her hair should be her covering (reflecting true modesty). She need not adopt the flamboyant hairstyles of pagan culture to attract undue attention to herself, and in doing so draw attention away from Christ.

Ultimately, the application for men has little to do with the length of hair, but with gender confusion. Paul's point is that men are not to dress nor wear the hairstyles of women, because God creates us as male and female. Transvestite and androgynous sexuality is highly problematic for Paul. Part of being a divine image-bearer is to be either male or female, and to deny our gender is to adopt a pagan conception of being human (with a confused sexuality) which brings shame to Christ.

To remind his readers that his basic point is not about the length of man's or woman's hair, but the peace and unity of the church, of which gender confusion and visible identification with paganism would have undone, Paul tells the Corinthians that Christian women are to be modest and demonstrate their submission to God through appropriate clothing and fashion. Men too are to reflect the divine glory by wearing appropriate styles and clothing which have no connection to paganism and idolatrous practices. Christians should avoid identifying with racial-identity groups (e.g., skinheads or Black Panthers), occultists (certain forms of "Goth," for example), or anarchists, in

The Image and Glory of God

their dress and attire. It is one thing to be fashionable. It is another to wear the "uniform" of those whose conduct rejects the teaching of Scripture.

As Paul states in verse 16, "If anyone is inclined to be contentious, we have no such practice, nor do the churches of God." Paul will not argue about this, and so he points to universal Christian custom. The Corinthians need to adopt those practices accepted by all of the other churches. This verse, in effect, is a foreshadowing of a specific exhortation he will give in 1 Corinthians 14:40: "But all things should be done decently and in order." Whatever Christians do, they cannot allow food, custom, or fashion to get in the way of the gospel, nor divide the body of Christ, nor disrupt Christian worship. Christian women need to be modest and not seek the attention of men, and Christian men need to be careful not to use the Lord's Day to advertise their favorite beer, sports team, or rock band on their clothing.

Paul, should he give us counsel today, would no doubt warn us about how easily celebrity antics negatively influence what is and is not proper for Christian worship and behavior. Women are to dress modestly and demonstrate proper submission to their husbands. Men are to demonstrate whole-hearted submission to Christ. Christians are forbidden from adopting styles for hair and clothing which overtly reflect or identify with pagan or idolatrous practices. The reason for this is simple. Men and women are divine image-bearers who have been redeemed by the blood of Christ.

How can we worship Christ, claim to trust his gospel, and then come to the heavenly table spread before us, while outwardly identifying with pagans, idolaters, the occult, or with immoral sexual behavior through our clothing and fashion? We cannot.

Paul is not some legalistic spoilsport. He is reminding us that while worship is a blessing and a privilege from God, there are covenantal responsibilities (blessings and curses) which come with entering into the presence of God to hear his word and receive his sacraments. Christians must be submissive to Christ, modest in their dress, and concerned for the needs of their neighbors. For we all are made in the image and glory of God, and we must do everything in our power to keep the peace in Christ's church.

19

Until He Comes

1 CORINTHIANS 11:17–26

For I received from the Lord what I also delivered to you, that the Lord Jesus on the night when he was betrayed took bread, and when he had given thanks, he broke it, and said, "This is my body which is for you. Do this in remembrance of me." In the same way also he took the cup, after supper, saying, "This cup is the new covenant in my blood. Do this, as often as you drink it, in remembrance of me." For as often as you eat this bread and drink the cup, you proclaim the Lord's death until he comes.

Have you ever wondered how much your church's Lord's Day worship service reflects the worship service of the apostolic church? In chapters 11–14 of 1 Corinthians, Paul gives us a fascinating account of what actually transpired during the worship service of an apostolic church. From Paul's account, it is clear that worship in the Corinthian church centered on the proclamation of Christ crucified, followed by the celebration of the Lord's Supper. The problem in Corinth is that the Corinthians were celebrating the Lord's Supper in such a way that the Supper had become virtually indistinguishable from one of the banquets held in a pagan temple or guild hall. Paul rebukes the Corinthians for this behavior in no uncertain terms. Yet in doing so, Paul also addresses the meaning of the Lord's Supper, as well as informing us why the Supper occupies such an important role in Christian worship.

In 1 Corinthians 11:17–34, we have the earliest account of the Lord's Supper in the New Testament. First Corinthians was probably written about AD 54, before any of the canonical gospels had been written. The Corinthian letter, therefore, gives us very important insight into the Supper as it was celebrated in churches from the earliest times. The Lord's Supper is the new covenant equivalent of the Jewish Passover, and like the Passover, was celebrated as part of a larger fellowship meal which followed what we might call the ordinary worship service.

It is important that we attempt to understand Paul's discussion of the abuse of the Supper against the backdrop of Greco-Roman culture, with its emphasis upon feasting and communal meals. Such meals were commonly celebrated in one of the pagan temples or guild halls throughout the city. On the one hand, the Corinthians would have been very familiar with communal meals like the one instituted by Jesus on his last night together with his disciples. Yet, on the other hand, the Corinthians would have dined only with those of the same social standing and profession, or with members of the same religious sect. The Supper, as instituted by Jesus, was intended to unite God's people around their common faith in Christ and his gospel promises, and not divide them along racial or socio-economic lines, as was apparently the case in Corinth.

Social Status and Division in the Churches

There are two critical issues at stake in Paul's directive. The first is that it would be difficult to get people from different ethnic groups and social standing to eat together at all since eating together in the first century Mediterranean world indicated that a bond of some kind had been formed. The rich did not eat with the poor. The Jews did not eat with the Greeks. And no one wanted to eat with the Romans. The second issue is that the Corinthians would quite naturally fall back into their old pagan habits and behave during the celebration of the Lord's Supper just as they behaved at the guild banquet, or as they did at the feast in the temple.

In fact, the Lord's Supper was being so badly abused in this congregation that Paul is now convinced that the celebration of the Supper was doing far more harm than good. The sacrament of Christian unity had become the source of more contention, and only served to reinforce the already-existing divisions within the church. Paul writes to correct these divisions and abuses.

Paul begins by addressing the shoddy treatment of the poor as recounted in verses 17–22. Paul identifies some of the abuses associated with the celebration of the Supper in the Corinthian church, before offering correction in the balance of the chapter. As we read in verse 17, "But in the following instructions I do not commend you, because when you come together it is not for the better but for the worse." Paul is very abrupt and emphatic in his directive to the Corinthians. The apostle has no word of praise for them (i.e., "I do not commend you"). His only comment is that the abuses of the Lord's Supper have created conditions in which their meetings (literally, their "gathering together" for worship) were doing more harm than good.

The Sad Fact of Division in the Corinthian Church

Paul goes on to mention some of the specific abuses in the next few verses. In verse 18, we learn: "For, in the first place, when you come together as a church, I hear that there are divisions among you. And I believe it in part." Paul has heard that when the Corinthian congregation gathers for worship there are divisions among the members. There are several things of interest and import here. First, it is highly likely that "the gathering together" of the church refers to regular Lord's Day worship services on the first day of the week. This means that when the Corinthians gathered for worship on the Lord's Day, they also celebrated the Lord's Supper. This is also the practice of the apostolic church elsewhere (i.e., Troas), as indicated in a passage such as Acts 20:7.

It is also important to note that Paul speaks of "church" (*ekklēsia*) without using the definite article (not "the" church). This would refer to "the gathering of God's people" (i.e., "the assembly") for worship, not necessarily to the church as an *institution*. The problem is that when the congregation assembles, there are "divisions" (*schismata*). Tragically, church members are divided, likely along cultural or ethnic lines. Although Paul has already spoken of division back in the opening chapter of the letter (1 Cor. 1:10—"I appeal to you, brothers, by the name of our Lord Jesus Christ, that all of you agree, and that there be no divisions among you, but that you be united in the same mind and the same judgment"), he may not be referring to the same thing here. Recall that, in the opening chapter, the issue was that people had allied themselves with particular teachers (Peter, Apollos, Paul, or others).

In this case, the division appears to be based on social standing (rich and poor) or racial-cultural divisions (Jew and Gentile). The particular issue seems to be that some have enough food to eat, and others do not. There is no mention here of alliances to particular teachers causing the problem, although these issues may in some way be related, say, if the Jewish believers identified with Peter rather than with Paul. Sadly, the unity Paul has just mentioned in 1 Corinthians 10:17 ("Because there is one bread, we who are many are one body, for we all partake of the one bread"), is not present when the Corinthians celebrate the "fellowship meal."[1] You cannot have true fellowship, if people are divided or mad at each other. It is hard to concentrate on the sermon, or prepare to come to the table of the Lord as members of Christ's one body, if you are preoccupied with how "so and so" (often a fellow church member) just slighted you, or why you would never do or say the thing you just saw the person sitting in front of you do.

When Paul says that he has heard that division is present (either mentioned in the letter sent to Paul, or information based on what Chloe's family in Ephesus disclosed to him), to some extent he believes it. Literally, he says he believes part of what he has heard. Apparently, the news which reached him contained exaggerated reports, and while Paul acknowledges that there were real divisions present, the situation may not have been as bad as he had heard.

Nevertheless, the reality is that there are divisions in the church, and the issue must be dealt with. As Paul states in verse 19, "For there must be factions among you in order that those who are genuine among you may be recognized." As Paul sees it, such divisions, while tragic, are a fact of church life. The word translated "factions" is an interesting word (*haireseis*) which refers to people who have chosen to go in a particular direction. In Acts 5:17, we read of the "party" of the Sadducees. In Acts 15:5, we read of the "party" of the Pharisees, while in Acts 24:5, 14, we read of the "sect" of the Nazarenes and "the way." In Galatians 5:20, Paul speaks of choosing to go the "way" of the flesh.[2] While the word means something similar to "divisions" (v. 18), the focus is upon the self-determination of the individuals involved. It is when people choose to go in a particular direction that those who have God's approval—and who withstand the test—demonstrate themselves to be in the right. When there

---
1. Barrett, *The First Epistle to the Corinthians*, 261.
2. Morris, *1 Corinthians*, 156.

are differences, those who withstand God's testing (that is, their teaching and practices are in accordance with God's word) will show that they have God's approval. In other words, time will prove who is right.

Regulations for the Lord's Supper

Yet according to verse 20, there is something very serious going on which needs Paul's immediate attention. "When you come together, it is not the Lord's supper that you eat." Because of these divisions, when this congregation assembles for worship, it is not the Lord's Supper (that is, the Lord's Supper as instituted by Christ) that they are eating. Instead of being practiced as instituted by Jesus and as taught to them by the apostles, the Supper as celebrated by the Corinthians has taken on the character described in the following verse—character sadly not unlike that of the pagan banquet hall they were supposed to have left behind.

In verse 21, Paul describes the problem. "For in eating, each one goes ahead with his own meal. One goes hungry, another gets drunk." The members of the Corinthian church would have clearly been familiar with communal meals, such as those associated with guilds and temples. But this meal was different. While the Lord's Supper was celebrated as part of communal meal (the so-called "love feast" mentioned in Jude 12), if it were being celebrated correctly, everyone who participated would be filled and no one would be drunk. More importantly, Christ would be exalted through the proclamation of his death. This is not the case in Corinth.

Based on what Paul describes, some of the members of these various factions were going ahead and eating without waiting for others. Perhaps those who provided the food consumed it before anyone else could get to it. Or perhaps there are even cultural issues involved, wherein certain ethnic foods were prepared which others would not eat. Such behavior is not only rude, but if one group ate all the food before others had a chance to eat this would have further exacerbated whatever divisions already existed in the church. Its bad enough to be divided, but imagine how deep those divisions could become when some were getting drunk and others were going hungry. If people are tipsy, or crabby because of low blood-sugar, no wonder there is trouble! Since it is difficult to become intoxicated from drinking grape juice, it is clear that fermented wine was used during communion.

We also get a hint at what was going on from what Paul says in verse 22, where it is implied that the wealthy provided the food and then ate it before the poor got a chance to eat the food which was supposed to be shared. Those who waited (out of charity and good manners) got nothing to eat. Those who ate first, we are told, consumed all of the wine and so were getting drunk, bringing further shame upon the church. Such behavior was turning the Supper into something very much like a guild or temple feast, and completely unlike the sacramental meal that Jesus himself instituted.

So, the problem is that people were not sharing their food during that which was intended to be a communal meal. Instead of becoming one body, certain people were acting selfishly, causing division. Some were eating and drinking without any regard for the true purpose of the Supper. The consequence, as Paul has already told them, is quite serious. "It is not the Lord's Supper you eat."

Questions for the Corinthians to Consider

To reinforce this point, in verse 22 Paul pounds away with a series of questions designed to expose the extent of the problem. "What! Do you not have houses to eat and drink in? Or do you despise the church of God and humiliate those who have nothing? What shall I say to you? Shall I commend you in this? No, I will not." If someone is hungry and prone to consume too much wine without proper manners or charity, Paul points out that they should indulge themselves at home, where they are free to behave as rudely as they wish. If Jews want to eat kosher foods at home, or if the rich wish to enjoy gourmet foods at home, so be it. If people do not want to share their food, or if they eat too much, that is fine at home. But such behavior should never be the occasion for division in the church.

When people behave this way in church, they are not only despising the church and its members (as the body of Christ), but those who provide the food and then consume it are humiliating the poor who are not able to bring anything and who have to wait to eat what the others do not consume. It is not improper to work backwards at this point and conclude that to belittle the poor is, in effect, to despise the church, since the poor are just as much members of the body of Christ as are the wealthy.

Paul is clearly exasperated with the Corinthians by this point. There is nothing more he can say. There is no word of praise for their conduct in this regard. In verses 23–26, Paul now turns to giving instruction into how the Supper is to be celebrated within the church. Paul begins his correction of the Corinthian practice of the Lord's Supper by reminding them of the Lord's words of institution, as well as including a command which we find nowhere else, namely that we are to celebrate this Supper until the Lord returns (v. 26), because when we do so we proclaim Christ's death.

Our Lord's Words of Institution

In verses 23–24, Paul writes, "For I received from the Lord what I also delivered to you, that the Lord Jesus on the night when he was betrayed took bread, and when he had given thanks, he broke it, and said, 'This is my body which is for you. Do this in remembrance of me.'" In discussing the meaning of the bread in verses 23–24, Paul begins with the origin of these words (remember, it is likely that the canonical gospels had not yet been written). Says Paul, "I received and delivered" which are both technical terms which refer to the receiving and passing along of oral tradition, in this case information Paul was given by none other than Jesus himself. Paul, no doubt, heard the facts of our Lord's last night from the other apostles and was instructed in the meaning of these events by the Lord himself. Paul refers to direct revelation from the Lord several places in other letters: 2 Corinthians 12:7 and Galatians 1:12; 2:2, for example.

As for Paul's theological point, Jesus instituted the Supper on the night he was betrayed by referring to the bread with the following words, "This is my body." Jesus does not say the bread *becomes* my body (as the Roman Catholic church argues). Nor does he say that my body is "in, with, and under the bread" (as with the Lutherans). Nor does he say that this bread "represents" or "symbolizes" my body (the Zwinglian/symbolic-memorialist view). Instead, Jesus says, "This bread *is* my body." In the following verses, Jesus does not refer to the wine as his blood, but as the new covenant in his blood. Neither Rome's notion of the sign (bread) being turned into the thing signified (Christ's flesh), nor the Zwinglian focus upon the essence of the Supper being a memorial meal in which nothing is received, can make proper sense of the New Testament's sacramental language. "This *is* my body."

When we discussed the first portion of chapter 10, we mentioned the fact that Jesus uses sacramental language when he speaks of the bread as his body and the wine as his blood, just as Paul has done back in 1 Corinthians 10:3–4 when he speaks of Christ as the rock, the manna as spiritual food, and baptism into Moses and the cloud as prefiguring Christian baptism. When we use sacramental language, we simply mean that there is a sign (bread and wine) and a thing signified (body and blood) and when sacramental language is used, the one thing (the bread) can be spoken of as though it were the other ("this is my body"). As we read in article 35 of the *Belgic Confession*,

> To represent to us this spiritual and heavenly bread Christ has instituted an earthly and visible bread as the sacrament of his body and wine as the sacrament of his blood. He did this to testify to us that just as truly as we take and hold the sacraments in our hands and eat and drink it in our mouths, by which our life is then sustained, so truly we receive into our souls, for our spiritual life, the true body and true blood of Christ, our only Savior. We receive these by faith, which is the hand and mouth of our souls.

It is also vital to notice that Paul emphasizes that Christ gives this body "for us." The essence of the Supper is that the same Jesus who gave himself *for us* on the cross, gives himself *to us* in the Lord's Supper. The sacrament is both the sign and the seal of his redemptive work for us, and is a covenant renewal ceremony in which God's promises are ratified anew. Through faith, and in the power of the Holy Spirit, we truly feed upon Christ (who has ascended into heaven—cf. Eph 2:6; Col. 3:1), since the bread is his body (understood sacramentally), given for the remission of our sins.

Furthermore, we are commanded to receive Christ's benefits on a regular basis. "'Do this' is a present continuous: 'keep on doing this,'" which at the very least seems to imply that we are commanded to do this remembering (*anamnesis*) on a regular basis.[3] The remembering of which Paul is speaking is not merely being sad upon considering the fact that Christ had to die upon the cross because of my sins—although my sorrow for my sin, and my repentance is certainly part of the process of preparing to come to the table. But "remembering" also means

---

3. Morris, *1 Corinthians*, 159.

recalling to mind and considering what the saving death of Jesus means for us, his people.

In verse 25, Paul turns his focus to the wine in the cup. "In the same way also he took the cup, after supper, saying, 'This cup is the new covenant in my blood. Do this, as often as you drink it, in remembrance of me.'" As Jesus took the bread, so too, he took the cup, and likewise invests it with new meaning, speaking of it as the new covenant in his blood, a clear reference to the new covenant prophecy of Jeremiah 31:31–34 and to the covenant renewal ceremony recounted in Exodus 24:1–18, where Moses and the elders of Israel, ate, drank, and saw the glory of God while up on Mount Sinai. Jesus is saying that the shedding of his blood will be the means by which the new covenant is ratified, the means by which our sins are forgiven, and the means by which the law is written upon our hearts. This "new" covenant is renewed every time we come to the table of the Lord.

Until Jesus Comes Again

In verse 26, Paul now adds an important element not found anywhere else in the New Testament. "For as often as you eat this bread and drink the cup, you proclaim the Lord's death until he comes." When we eat the bread and drink the cup, we receive what Jesus offers to us, namely, the forgiveness of sins—because his body was broken for us and his blood was shed for us. We also "show forth" (i.e., "announce" or "proclaim") the meaning of the death of Christ. The Greek word (*katangellete*) means something like to proclaim or announce, and is often used in connection to the preaching of the gospel.

The celebration of the Lord's Supper during the worship service is a vivid proclamation of the gospel. This is why Reformed Christians believe that the sacrament should be observed only in conjunction with the preached word, in a re-enactment of sorts of the Last Supper.[4] This is also why Calvin spoke of the Supper as the visible word—the outward sign of invisible grace. "One may call it a testimony of divine grace toward us, confirmed by an outward sign, with mutual attestation of our piety toward him."[5] What is promised to us in the gospel—the forgiveness of sin—is given us in the sacrament through those same elements Jesus instituted with his own disciples. We take in our hands the same elements Jesus handed to his twelve disciples on that night in which our Lord was betrayed. In faith, we take this ordinary bread and wine to be Christ's body and blood, and in believing Christ's promise, we receive the very thing promised; our Lord's true body and blood.

Notice too, there is an eschatological dimension here. Christ's death is not the end, it is the beginning of the end, which is why the Supper is to be celebrated by the church until the Lord returns as a testimony to, and in expectation of his return. We are to do this not only because the sacrament of the Lord's Supper nourishes us as Paul has said earlier, but because it reminds us every time we celebrate it of God's mercy to us in Jesus Christ. As Jesus has conquered death once and for all, our celebration of the Supper also points us to the Marriage Supper of Christ the Lamb at the end of the age (cf. Rev. 19:1–7). Indeed, all of God's covenant promises are ratified to us anew whenever we partake.

In 1 Corinthians 11:17ff., we learn a great deal about how the apostolic church worshiped. Paul taught the Corinthians to focus upon Christ's person and work as proclaimed in the gospel, and as ratified in the Lord's Supper. Although churches today practice the Supper differently than the apostolic church—we do not celebrate the Lord's Supper during a fellowship meal

---

4. John Calvin, *The Second Epistle of Paul to the Corinthians, and the Epistles to Timothy, Titus and Philemon*, trans. T. A. Smail (Grand Rapids: William B. Eerdmans, 1979), 79–80.

5. Calvin, *Institutes*, 4.14.1.

Until He Comes

after the regular worship service—nevertheless we do receive the same Christ and all his benefits which the Corinthian Christians received. Word and sacrament tie us to the apostolic church.

As Paul instructed the Corinthians, we are to center our worship in the proclamation of Christ's death until he comes. We come to church to hear words we can hear nowhere else—the gospel proclaimed by a minister who has been called and ordained by Christ to do this very thing. We come to hear that Jesus died for our sins. We come to be reminded that Jesus lived a perfect life to fulfill all righteousness, and that his righteousness becomes ours through faith. We assemble for public worship because the same risen and ascended Jesus who speaks to us through his word, offers himself to us at the table of the Lord. This is why we assemble together, because we are one body with one common faith and one common Savior.

All Jesus asks of us is that we believe his promises, that we take what he offers us in faith, and with gratitude, and as we do this, we consider both the blessing and the gravity of what it means to come to this table. At the table of the Lord, we are given but a brief foretaste of the glorious Marriage Supper of Christ the Lamb. This is why we are to proclaim Christ's death in the Supper "until he comes."

20

Let a Person Examine Himself

1 CORINTHIANS 11:27–34

Whoever, therefore, eats the bread or drinks the cup of the Lord in an unworthy manner will be guilty concerning the body and blood of the Lord. Let a person examine himself, then, and so eat of the bread and drink of the cup. For anyone who eats and drinks without discerning the body eats and drinks judgment on himself. That is why many of you are weak and ill, and some have died. But if we judged ourselves truly, we would not be judged. But when we are judged by the Lord, we are disciplined so that we may not be condemned along with the world.

In 1 Corinthians 11:27–34, Paul issues a warning which should give us all a moment's pause. Paul warns us that unless we examine ourselves before we come to table of the Lord, we risk coming under God's judgment, and as a result getting sick or even dying. Now that Paul has our attention, those of us who attend church services where the Lord's Supper is celebrated frequently need to consider the apostle's words with great care. But great care is not fear. Since Jesus has died for our sins (taking the covenant curse which we deserve upon himself), we need not fear coming to the table of the Lord because we are sinners and are struggling with our sins. We do need to examine ourselves in the matter prescribed by Paul. How do we properly examine ourselves before we come to the table of the Lord?

As we read through this entire chapter of 1 Corinthians, it is readily apparent that Paul is fit to be tied with many in the Corinthian congregation. Just as with the Jewish Passover, the celebration of the Lord's Supper took place within the context of a fellowship meal after the worship service had been conducted. But in Corinth, the church's celebration of the Lord's Supper had sadly degenerated into something like what went on in one of the city's pagan temples or guild halls. Some people were not waiting for others to be served and consumed all the food which had been prepared, leaving the poor without anything to eat. Others were drinking all the wine, getting drunk, and behaving in an unruly manner. Paul is disgusted by this behavior and rebukes the congregation accordingly. He has nothing good to say about this ("I do not commend you"—v. 17) and is even worried that the Supper is actually doing more harm than good. Things have gotten so bad, Paul can even say in verse 20, "When you come together, it is not the Lord's Supper that you eat," or at least as the Supper was instituted by Christ and taught to the Corinthians by Paul.

Eating Bread and Drinking from the Cup: The Language of Sacraments

After rebuking the Corinthians and exhorting them to eat and drink at home (if they cannot celebrate the Lord's Supper in an appropriate manner), Paul explains the words of institution which he received from Jesus himself and which the apostle, in turn, has passed along to the Corinthians. During the Last Supper, while distributing the bread, Jesus referred to it by saying

Let a Person Examine Himself

"this is my body." In verse 25, Paul tells us how Jesus went on to speak of the wine in the cup by saying, "'this cup is the new covenant in my blood. Do this, as often as you drink it, in remembrance of me.'" But what does Jesus mean when he speaks of the bread as his body and the wine in the cup as the new covenant in his blood?

Jesus is using sacramental language when instituting the Supper. There is a sign (bread and wine), and a thing signified (Christ's body and blood). When Jesus and Paul use sacramental language, the sign (the bread or the wine) can be spoken of as though it were the thing signified (Christ's body and blood). The same Savior who gave himself *for us* on the cross, also gives himself *to us* in the Supper. By faith, we take ordinary bread and wine (set apart and consecrated by prayer for this purpose) to be the body and blood of Christ. Through the work of the Holy Spirit we truly receive what Jesus has promised—his body and his blood.

The Lord's Supper is not in any sense a re-sacrifice of Christ to secure the forgiveness of sins as taught in Roman Catholicism.[1] Nor is the Supper merely a memorial meal in which the primary requirement for partaking is whether or not we are sufficiently sorry for all of our sins, or whether or not we have overcome all our sinful habits and behaviors. If, in the Supper, we are truly receiving Christ's body and blood through faith, then Paul's exhortation to "discern the body" means that we are to focus upon the body of the same Savior who gave himself for us, and who gives himself to us at the table of the Lord.

Paul speaks of that body in two ways in this passage. Paul not only refers to Christ's own true human nature which Jesus

---

1. Take, for example, one representative statement. "It is Christ himself, the eternal high priest of the New Covenant who, acting through the ministry of the priests, offers the Eucharistic sacrifice. And it is the same Christ, really present under the species of bread and wine, who is the offering of the Eucharistic sacrifice." See *The Catechism of the Catholic Church* (1994), sec. 1410.

gave for us on the cross and in which our Lord rose from the dead and ascended into heaven, Paul also refers to Christ's spiritual body, which is the church. This dual reference to Christ's body becomes apparent as Paul's discussion unfolds.

In verses 27–34, Paul informs the members of the Corinthian church how they should properly celebrate the Supper so as to avoid coming under the judgment of God. The Lord's Supper has been instituted by the Lord himself as the sacrament of his own body and blood and as a sign of the unity of Christ's mystical body, the church. Therefore, Paul will now drive home the point that the Supper can be properly celebrated only when we understand the nature of the Supper (Christ giving himself to us through bread and wine) and when we seek to build up Christ's body (the church) by avoiding those things which cause division in the church and which bring shame upon the congregation.

Eating in a Worthy Manner

In verse 27, Paul begins his discussion of the consequences of failing to observe the Supper in the appropriate manner. In verse 27, he writes, "Whoever, therefore, eats the bread or drinks the cup of the Lord in an unworthy manner will be guilty concerning the body and blood of the Lord." This is a significant warning. What follows is the obvious consequence of the failure to observe the Supper properly. Because the Lord's Supper involves the receiving of the body and blood of the Lord through faith, it is necessary to eat the bread and drink the cup in the proper manner (i.e., "worthily").

To partake in a worthy manner has a two-fold reference. The first point of reference is the proper consideration of what is being received through the eating of the bread and wine in faith (Christ and all his saving benefits). The second point of reference is our attitude toward our brothers and sisters in Christ, many of whom are from different races and from different so-

Let a Person Examine Himself

cioeconomic backgrounds. Christians are of one body, Paul says, who are to partake together from the same loaf of bread. The Corinthians must keep this in mind, lest the celebration of the Supper degenerate into something like a pagan feast.

While some interpret Paul's warning not to take the Supper in an unworthy manner to be directly connected to the current state of an individual's sanctification (i.e., the person is not at that moment "worthy" of receiving the Supper),[2] this is not the case, or else, if we were honest, none of us would be worthy to partake. If the Lord's Supper is celebrated in the proper liturgical setting, before we even come to the table, we have already confessed our sins, we have heard a declaration of pardon from the minister, and we have heard the promise of the gospel as the Word of God is preached. Although we are all "unworthy" to partake because we are all still sinful, nevertheless we confess our sins before we come to the table. We have heard and embraced the word of pardon, as well as considered Jesus' invitation for us to come and receive all the wonderful things he has for us (cf. Matt. 11:28). These considerations remind us that the Lord's Supper is for those who are weak in faith, those who are struggling with their sins yet who are also repentant, and for those who are seeking the strength to continue on with the Christian life so as to continue the war against the sinful nature (i.e., the flesh).

Therefore, if we are united to Jesus Christ through faith and believe the sacrament is what our Lord says it is—"this is my body," "this is my blood"—then we partake in the proper fashion ("worthily") by coming with repentant hearts, empty hands of faith, and simply receiving what is promised. As Calvin so wonderfully puts it,

> If you want to derive proper benefit from this gift of Christ, you must bring faith and repentance . . . . Indeed it is not perfect faith or repentance that is

---

2. See, for example, Barrett, *The First Epistle to the Corinthians*, 273.

> asked for. This is said because some people, by being far too insistent upon a perfection which cannot be found anywhere, are putting a barrier between every single man and woman and the Supper forever. But if you are serious in your intention to aspire to the righteousness of God, and if, humbled by the knowledge of your own wretchedness, you fall back upon the grace of Christ, and rest upon it, be assured that you are a worthy guest at this table. By saying you are worthy, I mean that the Lord does not keep you out, even if in other respects you are not all you ought to be. For faith, even if imperfect, makes the unworthy worthy.[3]

It is when we neglect to do this by not partaking in faith, that we sin against the body and blood of the Lord (i.e., we do not take the Supper as Jesus offers it to us, as his own body and blood). On the one hand then, the reference to the worthy partaking of the Supper has to do with recognizing Christ's body and blood offered to us through bread and wine. This is not a reference to someone being worthy to partake of the Supper because they are (for that moment) personally worthy of coming to the table.

The Nature of Paul's Warning

On the other hand, we have to consider that the stern warning that Paul gives to the Corinthians comes in the form of an exhortation not to fall back into their old habits acquired during years of feasting in a pagan context. Paul's warning is not so much a threat to the Corinthians that God is about to kill them all, but should be seen as the apostle calling them to behave as Christians should behave during the celebration of the Supper. The Corinthians need to remember that this meal was instituted by Christ himself, and is not in any sense connected

---

3. Calvin, *The First Epistle of Paul to the Corinthians*, 253.

Let a Person Examine Himself

to the pagan feasting of Greco-Roman culture. The rich must not shame the poor, the Jews must receive the Gentiles as members of the covenant community, Gentiles need to respect the dietary scruples of the Jews, and all the members of Christ's church must seek to be one, and not be divided along racial or cultural lines, or divided into factions because some of them follow a particular teacher (i.e., Peter, Paul, Apollos).

This means that we not only receive Christ's body and blood by eating the bread and wine in faith, but together we partake of Christ's body because we have a common faith, a common Savior, and are all members of Christ's church, despite our race, social standing, or wealth. Paul's warning about "partaking worthily" therefore applies to all those who do not discern Christ's body in the two-fold sense Paul describes here. There are those who do not take seriously the act of feeding upon Christ himself through faith. By this I am not referring to people who don't fully understand the mechanics of the Lord's Supper (i.e., how can we feed upon Christ if his human nature has ascended into heaven). I am referring, to people who partake but who do not believe the gospel, and who mock Christ by coming to this table in their own righteousness.

And then there are those among the Corinthians who seek to divide what Christ has made one—his spiritual body, which is his church, the members of which are purchased by his shed blood. People who are actively promoting factions, who exploit racial or cultural differences causing division, and who demonstrate contempt for others in the body of Christ not like themselves, are also not partaking worthily.

The need to discern the body of Christ (in this two-fold sense) is why Reformed and Presbyterian churches have historically "fenced" the table. Visitors, or those who are new to Reformed and Presbyterian churches, will often times take offense that elders request to interview visitors before admitting them to the Lord's Supper. The reason why Reformed and Presbyterian churches "fence the table" is because of the serious nature of Paul's warnings to the Corinthians, and thus to all Christians. We fence the table not because we are exclusive and think we are the only ones who are saved, because we are unfriendly, or because we are self-righteous and think ourselves better than others. We fence the table because we are protecting people in light of the serious warnings given us by Paul in this passage. The blessings found at Christ's table are great, but Paul's warning is very serious.

People who are under church discipline in one church should not seek to come to the table of the Lord in another church. People who are indifferent to church membership, who are unwilling to submit to a group of elders, or who refuse to embrace a particular doctrinal statement, who do not think that the doctrine which underlies the celebration of the Lord's Supper really matters that much, should not come to the table. But with those cautions before us, we must not forget that this is a table for sinners. It is a table for those who seek and desire the unity of Christ's church and who are striving to love their brothers and sisters even when they have different family trees, and live on opposite sides of the tracks. To put it another way, Paul's comments here presuppose that someone who partakes in such a way as not to sin against the Lord's body and blood believes the gospel, and understands that all their fellow church members are also members of Christ's one spiritual body. This is why the Supper must be celebrated with a proper reverence. This is a sacrament for repentant sinners who need to be reminded of the gospel promises.

If people have an agenda to divide the church, or if they reject the promise that Jesus died for our sins and then offers himself to us through the bread and wine, they do indeed risk coming under the kind of judgment described in the follow-

Let a Person Examine Himself

ing verse (v. 28). "Let a person examine himself, then, and so eat of the bread and drink of the cup." The word "examine" is the word "to test" (*dokimazetō*) and has its roots in the testing of metals as to their purity.[4] The Lord's Supper is no ordinary meal—like the church potluck. It is a sacrament instituted by Christ himself, who invests it with a very significant meaning. This is why participation in the Supper is a serious matter, and requires self-examination before partaking. Christians must confess their sins and give serious consideration to the spiritual eating and drinking about to take place. This is no meal to be eaten casually!

It is interesting to note that, in the previous verse, Paul speaks of sinning against the body and blood of the Lord, while here he speaks of eating bread and drinking from the cup. Not only does this effectively refute the Roman Catholic notion of transubstantiation (in the sacrament we eat bread, not Christ's body), but it is exactly what we would expect given the way in which sacramental language is used interchangeably of either the sign (the bread and wine) or the thing signified (his body and blood).

Discerning Christ's Body

The proper manner of self-examination is spelled out in what follows (v. 29). "For anyone who eats and drinks without discerning the body eats and drinks judgment on himself." To partake in a worthy manner is to discern Christ's body and blood in the two senses described previously. To partake in a worthy manner, we must understand what is received by faith (Christ's body and blood), and we must reject those sinful categories which tragically divide Christ's people (race, social standing, wealth). Failure to discern Christ's body (and by implication, his blood), risks God's judgment as described here by the apostle.

---

4. Morris, *1 Corinthians*, 161.

Although the words of institution define the body in view here (as Christ's), it is vital to notice that Paul uses the body metaphor in two ways. Again, there is Christ's body given us in the Supper, and there is Christ's spiritual body of which we are all members (i.e., the church). The particular sin of the Corinthian congregation was to forget the true significance of the meal, so that some were rushing ahead and consuming all the food or getting drunk, only exacerbating the divisions already present in the congregation. Paul has just told the Corinthians that they all partake of one loaf (1 Cor. 10:17) which is Christ's body. They are all members of Christ's spiritual body, so they are one (or should be one), even as Christ's body is one. What is in view (discerning the body) applies not only to what is received (Christ's body), but how it is received (through faith, and together as one body).

Failure to discern Christ's body in this two-fold sense has very serious consequences as made plain in verse 30: "That is why many of you are weak and ill, and some have died." The context for this seems to be Paul's discussion of the fate of the Israelites mentioned back in 1 Corinthians 10:5. That entire generation of Israelites who left Egypt wandered in the wilderness for forty years only to die in the Sinai desert because of their lack of faith in God's promise as seen in the grumbling and complaining. There are also echoes from the prophets (such as that found throughout the opening chapter of Isaiah's prophecy) who warned Israel about the sin in oppressing the poor, the alien, the widow, and the orphan, as well as mistreating the prophets God sent Israel to warn them of the consequences of their actions. As God's people, we must approach the Lord's Table in humility, with repentance, and with confidence that God truly invites and welcomes us as repentant sinners to his table. For it is here that he confirms to us the promises of the gospel.

Let a Person Examine Himself

In this meal, all the promises of the gospel are confirmed before our very eyes.

Self-Examination

The Corinthians were also familiar, as likely were all the members of the apostolic churches, with the account of Ananias and Sapphira as recounted in Acts 5:1–11. These two were struck dead by God because they lied to the Holy Spirit. Paul takes this occasion to remind the Corinthians that a number of them had gotten sick and a number have died, *because* they failed to discern Christ's body in the Supper. Paul's point is clear. While most illnesses have natural causes, in this case, some in Corinth have become ill, and some have died, as a direct result of sinning against the body and blood of the Lord.

While we must not think of the Supper as poisonous to a non-Christian, or even to a Christian who partakes in an unworthy manner, the fact of the matter is that those who do not take the Supper seriously (by examining themselves in the sense of reminding themselves that they are partaking of Christ's body and blood, or who are actively causing division) do indeed risk coming under Christ's temporal judgment, just as Israel did in the wilderness. Again, the gravity of this warning is an important reason to give instructions, exhortations, and warnings at the table. The gravity of the warning is also why we must examine ourselves before we come and eat, which we do, in part, through the confession of our sins and through accepting the declaration of pardon.

This is precisely the point Paul makes in verses 31–32. "But if we judged ourselves truly, we would not be judged. But when we are judged by the Lord, we are disciplined so that we may not be condemned along with the world." The verb "judged" in verse 31 (*diekrinomen*) means "to distinguish." It is in the imperfect tense, meaning that we are to make this judgment a regular practice. If we distinguish what we are (sinners), in light of what we are in Christ (righteous) then we will not come under God's judgment. We need to acknowledge and confess that we are sinners and confess that we cannot come to the Lord's Supper through our own righteousness or because of our good works. Rather, we come to this table as needy beggars, seeking the good things that God has for us (the body and blood of Christ), not because we are worthy to come, but because God is gracious to us in Christ, and Christ freely gives us what he has promised us. As Charles Spurgeon puts it in his wonderful communion hymn *Amidst Us Our Beloved Stands*, "What food luxurious loads the board, when at his table sits the Lord! The wine how rich, the bread how sweet, when Jesus deigns his guests to meet!"

If we fail to make such a judgment, and come to the Supper without regard for the body and blood of Christ and the unity of Christ's body, then we do indeed risk God's judgment. This is why confession and a declaration of pardon from sin should precede the celebration of the Supper, so that we come without fear and without any confidence in our own righteousness. The Corinthians, apparently, were doing little of this. For many of them, this was a chance to eat good food and drink good wine with little or no regard for the body and blood of Christ or the unity of the church. The Corinthians were not only mocking the redemptive work of Christ, they were giving no consideration for the poor, nor behaving properly in the church which is not a pagan banquet hall. That the judgment spoken of here is temporal and not eternal is likewise spelled out in these verses. God judges us in order to discipline us (as a loving father would), so that we will not be judged in the eschatological judgment which the unbelieving world will face on the last day.

Finally, in verses 33–34, we come to the conclusion to the problem set forth back in verse 21 ("For in eating, each one goes ahead with his own meal. One goes hungry, another gets drunk.""). Some people were not waiting for others and ate everything before others had a chance to eat. Some were getting drunk, acting rudely, and creating division. Such conduct was unacceptable. Paul writes, "So then, my brothers, when you come together to eat, wait for one another—if anyone is hungry, let him eat at home—so that when you come together it will not be for judgment. About the other things I will give directions when I come" (vv. 33–34).

Paul's advice is, once again, characterized by its utter simplicity and common sense. The purpose of the Lord's Supper is not to satisfy physical hunger. It is a spiritual meal meant to satisfy a spiritual hunger. Therefore, to avoid having people gorge themselves on the food before others can eat, thereby shaming the poor, Paul's advice is for people to eat at home *before* coming to church. That way people will not be hungry when they come to worship and they can properly reflect upon the true meaning of the Supper so as to avoid coming under God's judgment. This is why it is perfectly appropriate to celebrate the Supper as modern churches do, not in the context of a fellowship meal, but in the context of public worship, after sins have been confessed, pardon has been pronounced, and the gospel has been preached.

Paul wraps up this section of his letter by informing the Corinthians that he plans on coming to see them, and when he does so, he will give them further instructions about how to celebrate the Supper. But there is no evidence Paul ever made it back to Corinth. The Corinthians will have to get by on the instructions in this letter.

A Gospel Sacrament

The Lord's Supper is a gospel sacrament in which we show forth Christ's death until he comes again. Given the stern nature of Paul's rebuke of the Corinthians in terms of their selfish behavior and shameful treatment of the poor, coupled with the solemn warning Paul issues regarding discerning Christ's body before we partake of the bread and wine, many see in this exhortation a reason to fear coming to the table. Non-Christians should not come. Non-Christians should be afraid to come. But, as Paul points out, we need not fear *if* we examine ourselves before we come to the Lord's Table and partake of Christ's body and blood.

Proper examination begins with confessing our sins and receiving God's word of pardon. This table is for repentant sinners who are washed, sanctified, and justified through the death and resurrection of Jesus Christ (cf. 1 Cor. 6:9–11). Since Jesus died for all our sins, and since his righteousness is imputed to us through faith, we need not fear God's judgment because Christ has borne that judgment for us in his suffering upon the cross. But if we do not examine ourselves—and fail to acknowledge that we are sinners—then we mock God if we dare come to this table thinking we are worthy of coming to this table, and that we belong here without trusting in the shed blood and perfect righteousness of Christ.

We also properly examine ourselves by discerning Christ's body in the two-fold sense Paul spells out here. By faith, we receive Christ's body and blood through the bread and wine. And because we are Christ's, we discern Christ's body (his church) whenever we consider that we are part of that one body knit together by Christ, despite our racial, cultural, and socioeconomic differences. We partake together, as one people because we are Christ's body. Those who come to the Lord's Table while sowing seeds of division, spreading false doctrine, organizing factions, or profaning the table by their unruly conduct, should amend their ways, lest they find themselves coming under the judgment of God.

Let a Person Examine Himself

The blessings of the Lord's Supper are great. The same Savior who gave himself for us on the cross, gives himself to us through bread and wine. At the same time, the warning Paul gives to us is something we must consider. This why we all must listen to Paul, who exhorts us "Let a person examine himself" so that we are worthy partakers whenever we come to the table of the Lord. In this regard, the *Belgic Confession* (Article 35) reminds us,

> With humility and reverence we receive the holy sacrament in the gathering of God's people, as we engage together, with thanksgiving, in a holy remembrance of the death of Christ our Savior, and as we thus confess our faith and Christian religion. Therefore no one should come to this table without examining himself carefully, lest "by eating this bread and drinking this cup he eat and drink to his own judgment." In short, by the use of this holy sacrament we are moved to a fervent love of God and our neighbors.

21

Jesus is Lord

1 CORINTHIANS 12:1–3

Now concerning spiritual gifts, brothers, I do not want you to be uninformed. You know that when you were pagans you were led astray to mute idols, however you were led. Therefore I want you to understand that no one speaking in the Spirit of God ever says "Jesus is accursed!" and no one can say "Jesus is Lord" except in the Holy Spirit.

It is not uncommon for Christians to have questions about the person and work of the Holy Spirit. The Corinthians certainly had questions about the Spirit. And so in 1 Corinthians 12, Paul addresses the role of the Holy Spirit in the life of the church and its members. Paul has discussed the Holy Spirit earlier in this epistle, but not as comprehensively as he does here. Paul has explained that it was the Holy Spirit who brought the Corinthians to faith in Jesus Christ and then formed these individual believers into the living temple of God in which the Holy Spirit dwells. Because the church is the living temple of the Holy Spirit, no one should seek to divide it. This means that the factions which had formed in Corinth were not the work of the Holy Spirit, but a manifestation of that sinful behavior the pagans considered to be "wisdom."

Beginning in chapter 7, Paul addresses a group of questions put to him by the Corinthians in the form of a letter—to which this letter (which we know as 1 Corinthians) is Paul's response. Paul responds to these written questions by dealing first with the question put to him about the importance and the role of marriage. Then, from 1 Corinthians 8:1–10:22, Paul has been dealing with matters regarding the proper worship of God. Paul has forbidden the Corinthians from participating in any form of idolatry, like that which went on in any of the large number of pagan temples which filled the city. The apostle next dealt with several issues related to the worship then going on in the Corinthian congregation (chapter 11). One issue is the proper understanding of preaching (prophecy), and a second is the proper celebration of the Lord's Supper—requiring a stern rebuke from Paul about the way in which the Corinthians were abusing the Lord's Supper, to the point of risking the judgment of God.

The next section of this letter (1 Cor. 12:1–14:40) constitutes Paul's response to a third issue which has been raised by the Corinthians in their letter to him. This has to do with what it means to be spiritual—a subject especially important to a church such as the one in Corinth which was surrounded by pagan "spirituality." Although Paul does not tell us what the Corinthians said to him in their letter, from the subject matter in chapter 14, the primary issue seems to be the abuse of speaking in tongues. By working our way back from Paul's discussion there, we can see how Paul's comments in chapters 12–13 set the stage for what comes in chapter 14.

Pagan Spirituality Leads to Confusion

In Greco-Roman culture, it was commonly believed that certain enlightened individuals were in touch with the gods and endowed with unusual spiritual powers, like predicting the future, talking to the dead, pronouncing curses, etc. Given the close proximity of the Oracle of Delphi to the city of Corinth—a temple dedicated to Apollo where the faithful would receive direction from the gods—and given the large number of pagan temples in the city, the notion that certain individuals possessed great spiritual insight was no doubt widely held among the people living throughout the area. Many of those thought to possess these divine powers and abilities would offer up ecstatic utterances (like speaking in tongues), engage in religious frenzies, fall into trances, and so on. This was most often done during temple festivities. Among those religious groups we consider proto-gnostic (those looking for "secret knowledge" and the hidden keys to the meaning of life), such individuals were often designated "enthusiasts" and were characterized by their public outbursts and extreme religious practices.

Although Old Testament prophets were given revelation through dreams, visions, and other supernatural manifestations, Pentecost marked a new age in redemptive-history in which the Spirit of God was poured out upon all believers—not just upon a few enlightened individuals. In fact, the indwelling of the Holy Spirit is that which characterizes all those who are in Christ, since those in whom the Spirit dwells have been transferred from sin, death, and bondage to the law, to that freedom in Christ in which we are now seen as adopted sons or daughters of Christ and heirs to all the riches and treasures of heaven (cf. Eph. 1:13–14). While some Christians—especially the apostles—manifested sensational spiritual gifts after Pentecost (such as speaking in tongues, along with gifts of healing and miracles which confirm the preaching of the gospel), the primary manifestation of the work of the Holy Spirit was the production of the so-called "fruit of the Spirit" as mentioned by Paul in Galatians 5:22–23. The fruit of the Spirit stood in sharp contrast to the "works of the flesh" (Gal. 5:19–21), which characterized individuals prior to their conversion.[1]

It is not dramatic and sensational demonstrations of spirituality or "enthusiasm" which characterize the gifts of the Spirit, but more seemingly ordinary and mundane things that have more to do with the transformed behavior of individual Christians. In this section of his letter, Paul will explain that Christians are to view the "spiritual" through the lens of the age to come, not through the lens of this present evil age, which was tied to the so-called "wisdom" of the pagans. This would have been another area where Paul would need to correct the misconceptions of those who grew up with a pagan spirituality, and who were apt to simply transfer pagan behavior and spirituality into the church after converting to Christianity. This, perhaps, is why speaking in tongues has come to cause division in the church, and did not bring about the edification intended for the whole body of believers.

The Lordship of Christ

Remarkably, Paul's discussion of spiritual gifts begins with an affirmation of the Lordship of Jesus Christ. This may come as a surprise at first. As Gordon Fee puts it, "This opening paragraph seems quite unrelated to the topic at hand."[2] Nevertheless, the more we think about it, the more we should expect this of Paul. The apostle's focus is upon the Corinthians' former

---

1. There are several helpful works on this topic which the reader may wish to consult: Victor Budgen, *Charismatics and the Word of God* (Durham: Evangelical Press, 1989); D. A. Carson, *Showing the Spirit: A Theological Exposition of 1 Corinthians 12–14* (Grand Rapids: Baker Book House,1987); Richard B. Gaffin, *Perspectives on Pentecost* (Phillipsburg: Presbyterian and Reformed Publishing Company, 1979); J. I. Packer, *Keep in Step with the Spirit* (Old Tappen, NJ: Fleming H. Revell Company, 1984); Geerhardus Vos, "The Eschatological Aspect of the Pauline Conception of the Spirit," in Geerhardus Vos, *Redemptive History and Biblical Interpretation*, ed., Richard B. Gaffin (Phillipsburg: Presbyterian and Reformed Publishing Company, 1980), 91–125.

2. Fee, *The First Epistle to the Corinthians*, 574.

condition as spiritual idolaters in contrast to that freedom they now experience in Christ. Someone who does not submit to the Lordship of Jesus Christ does not manifest the gifts of the Spirit. Indeed, they cannot manifest the gifts of the Spirit. The Lordship of Christ, therefore, is Paul's starting point for all subsequent discussion of spiritual gifts. Understanding who Jesus is and what he has done for us is the key by which we determine whether or not these manifestations of "enthusiasm" are truly gifts of the Spirit.

While there are many gifts of the Spirit, Paul emphasizes that each one of these gifts contributes to the well-being of the mystical body of Jesus Christ (the church). But the most excellent of these gifts is love—Paul's subject in chapter 13. This means that as spiritual gifts are exercised within the church, these gifts are to be exercised so as to edify the body and build up the individual members of the church so that the church as a whole is the beneficiary. The tip-off that pagan wisdom is involved is when the supposed supernatural manifestation of the gifts of the Spirit benefits a particular individual (enabling them to show off their spirituality or their power), not the church as a whole.

No doubt, for Paul, the manifestation of sensational gifts has an important place in the church. But the preeminent role belongs to love, the greatest of these gifts. This, of course, would certainly differentiate Christianity from those pagan religions which stressed dramatic personal religious experience, while ignoring the corporate dimension of spiritual gifts which build up the church, enable us to love one another as Jesus has loved us, and which do not tear down what Christ has been building up in our midst.

The purpose of spiritual gifts—which are distributed among the members of Christ's body—is to bring glory to Jesus Christ through the building up of the church and through the edification of God's people. Given paganism's stress upon religious "enthusiasm" and a corresponding emphasis upon an individual's religious experience, such is absolutely detrimental to the health of the church because it disrupts the divinely prescribed order in the church. Those so-called "gifts of the spirit" which do not exalt Jesus Christ by building up his church, cannot be said to be true gifts of the Holy Spirit.

Concerning Spiritual Matters

In verse 1, Paul begins to address this matter. "Now concerning spiritual gifts, brothers, I do not want you to be uninformed." The opening words of this verse (*de Peri*—"now concerning") indicate to us that Paul is beginning another topic mentioned in the Corinthian congregation's letter to Paul (cf. 1 Cor. 7:1). We do not know exactly what the Corinthians asked of Paul in their letter, but Paul's rather lengthy response (which runs all the way from chapters 12:1–14:40) indicates that the issue they raised with Paul was a matter of pressing significance to the peace and well-being of the Corinthian congregation. This explains why Paul responds to these particular issues in such great detail.

Paul speaks of the "spiritual" (*tōn pneumatikōn*), but the word "gifts" is often added to most English translations (e.g., both the NIV and ESV render this "spiritual gifts"). This is because of the context. However, I take Paul to be speaking of "spiritual things" since the usual word for spiritual gifts is *charismatōn*, not *pneumatikōn*.[3] This means that Paul's topic in these three chapters is a proper understanding of spiritual things, of which the proper use of spiritual gifts plays a major role (especially the gift of tongues, which has caused such a problem in the Corinthian church). That Paul speaks of the Corinthians as "brothers" indicates that while Paul will have some words of rebuke and

---

3. Hays, *First Corinthians*, 207–209.

correction, nevertheless he is writing to people whom he knows well and loves deeply.

In any case, the primary reason for Paul's subsequent discussion is that he does not want the Corinthians to be ignorant about "spiritual things." The following discussion is not limited to spiritual gifts. Throughout Paul's writings, the phrase "I do not want you to be uninformed" indicates that what follows will be of some significance (cf. Rom. 1:13; 11:25; I Cor. 10:1; 12:1; 2 Cor. 1:8; 1 Thess. 4:13). Whenever we see this statement in one of Paul's letters, we know to pay close attention to what follows.

The Folly of Paganism

In verse 2, Paul reminds the Corinthians how far they have already come. "You know that when you were pagans you were led astray to mute idols, however you were led." Paul speaks of pagans (*ethnē*), using a word which is usually translated as "nations" or "Gentiles" (i.e., non-Jews). But the context indicates that Paul is speaking to his readers of a time before their conversion, therefore, "pagans" is a very appropriate rendering. Before coming to faith in Jesus Christ, these Gentile pagans were led astray by idols. From a Christian perspective, the essence of paganism is to be deceived by things that are not real. It is interesting that the verb and participle Paul uses here "led astray" (*ēgesthe apagomenoi*) are used elsewhere in the New Testament to convey the idea of a prisoner or a condemned person being led away under the control and direction of another (cf. Mark 14:44; 15:16). In other words, paganism held the Corinthians captive before Christ set them free.

When Paul portrays paganism as holding people captive to lifeless idols, he may be thinking of Israel's struggle with idolatry, since there are echoes in Paul's words here from Habakkuk 2:18–19: "What profit is an idol when its maker has shaped it, a metal image, a teacher of lies? For its maker trusts in his own creation when he makes speechless idols! Woe to him who says to a wooden thing, Awake; to a silent stone, Arise! Can this teach? Behold, it is overlaid with gold and silver, and there is no breath at all in it." Despite their great intellectual ability, the Greek pagans did not come to idolatry because of intellectual reasons—i.e., they were convinced of the truth of paganism. Rather, Paul treats them as people who do not know any better. This is hardly a compliment.

Notice yet again the great irony in Paul's point. Those who profess themselves to be wise are shown to be utterly foolish in light of the true wisdom which God has revealed in Jesus Christ. The wise are shamed, while those whom the world regards as "foolish" (the followers of Jesus) are those set free from being held captive by things not real. "Can this statue without breath teach?" Paul mocks these idols because they are "mute" (or dumb). Graven images are unable to speak nor answer the prayers of those who worship them. They can reveal nothing to those who come to them seeking wisdom and insight. The ultimate reality of the idol is the reflection back to us from the surface of the idol. Almost painfully, Paul again reminds his hearers that before they came to faith in Jesus Christ, they were being led to idols who could not speak, or provide any of the things idolaters were seeking. Why, then, would the Corinthians still be behaving as though the idols were real?

Jesus is Lord!

This leads Paul to his primary point in verse 3. "Therefore I want you to understand that no one speaking in the Spirit of God ever says 'Jesus is accursed!' and no one can say 'Jesus is Lord' except in the Holy Spirit." Thinking they truly understood spiritual things, the Corinthians actually knew nothing and were being led to seek speechless idols which could do absolutely nothing for them. The critical point is that what we affirm and confess

Jesus is Lord

about spiritual things reveals whether or not we are being led astray or have been given true wisdom.

In this first instance, Paul refers to someone who utters the phrase, "Jesus is accursed" (*anathema*). The circumstances behind this utterance are a matter of some speculation. Jews were known to have cursed Christians (as recounted in Acts 26:11), and the church historian Eusebius recounts that pagans often demanded that Christians curse Christ (i.e., renounce their faith), or else suffer persecution (being prevented from buying and selling, or worse).[4] Some believe that Paul's words are purely rhetorical in the sense that no one really uttered these words, but that Paul is making a point (i.e., the only way a true profession of faith can be uttered is through the work of the Holy Spirit).

Leon Morris offers a plausible take on this verse which may provide the answer. He is of the opinion that since the gospel entails Christ becoming a curse for us (cf. Gal. 3:13), someone speaking in an ecstatic utterance in the Corinthian church ended-up distorting the truth behind these words, and claimed to be doing so by the leading of the Holy Spirit.[5] The assertion, "Jesus was cursed by God while on the cross," became "Jesus is the accursed one," without the necessary qualifications. This makes a great deal of sense.

Although the underlying circumstances behind this utterance probably will never be known to us, Paul's point is simply that the words themselves (i.e., "on their face") prove that this utterance did not come from the Holy Spirit. While Jesus was accursed by God while suffering upon the cross (cf. Gal. 3;13), the resurrection proves that Jesus has been exalted to the right hand of his Father (Phil. 2:8–10). Jesus' acceptance by God (the

---

4. See, for example, Paul L. Maier, *Eusebius: The Church History* (Grand Rapids: Kregel Publications, 1999), Book 4, 135–164.

5. Morris, *1 Corinthians*, 165.

vindication of his saving work upon the cross, and fulfilling all righteousness through his obedience) means that Jesus is Lord over all things. The Holy Spirit would never deny the Lordship of Christ. In fact, the exact opposite is true. It is the Holy Spirit who leads us to affirm the Lordship of Christ, something the Corinthians could never do when they were being led astray by dumb idols.

While even Satan knows that Jesus is Lord and can utter the words "Jesus is Lord," Paul's point is that the expression "Jesus is Lord" becomes a true confession of faith only through the power of the Holy Spirit. It is the Holy Spirit who regenerates, creates faith, and who grants wisdom and understanding into those divine things which would otherwise be hidden. No Christian would ever say that "Jesus is accursed" with the intent to deny his Lordship. Only someone who becomes a Christian through the power of the Holy Spirit can utter the words "Jesus is Lord" with the full sense of meaning, and as a confession of faith in Jesus' redemptive work through which his Lordship is manifest. To confess that Jesus is Lord is to confess that Jesus is both Creator and Redeemer, as well as the supreme revelation of the wisdom and the power of God.

The assertion of Christ's Lordship then, is the basis for properly understanding the gifts of the Holy Spirit. For Paul, to confess Jesus as Lord is to be indwelt by the Holy Spirit. To be "in Christ" and "filled the with Spirit" are one and the same!

So then, what does it mean to confess that "Jesus is Lord"? As Christians, these words roll easily off our lips, but what do they mean? In order to understand spiritual things (the *pneumatikon*)—the main point of Paul's discussion of this section of Corinthians—we must understand that Jesus is the very Son of God, the second person of the Holy Trinity, his eternal glory now veiled in human flesh. If we want wisdom, we will find it in the person and work of the Son of God. We cannot find such

Jesus is Lord

wisdom anywhere else. We cannot find it in our culture, we cannot find it in secret principles of wisdom, and we cannot find it in the principles of a successful life, or even in discovering some sort of untapped human potential buried within. Our culture chases after these things—just as the ancient Greek and Romans did. When we confess that "Jesus is Lord," we are saying that in him, and in him alone, God has revealed everything we need to know about how to be saved from the guilt and power of sin, as well as that wisdom which God has revealed to rescue us from dumb idols which can do nothing to help us.

Since it is the Holy Spirit who enables us to make this confession, in these verses Paul sets forth one of the clearest declarations in all the Bible that the only reason any one of Adam's fallen children is a Christian is because the Holy Spirit enabled us to confess that Jesus is Lord. While the fallen children of Adam (non-Christians) can speak the words "Jesus is Lord" (so can the devil), the only way this becomes a sincere and heartfelt confession of faith is through the indwelling Holy Spirit—not just that Jesus is Lord, but that Jesus is *my* Lord.

To truly confess that Jesus is Lord is to be indwelt by the Holy Spirit. The sure sign that someone is indwelt by the Spirit, is their confession—"Jesus is Lord." Therefore, to understand spiritual things, we start with the person and work of Christ, just as the Apostle Paul did. When I confess "Jesus is Lord," I am confessing that Jesus is *my* Lord. And I can only do so because the Holy Spirit enables me to confess that Jesus is *my* Lord.

22

The Common Good

1 CORINTHIANS 12:4–11

Now there are varieties of gifts, but the same Spirit; and there are varieties of service, but the same Lord; and there are varieties of activities, but it is the same God who empowers them all in everyone. To each is given the manifestation of the Spirit for the common good.

The Corinthians were deeply confused about spiritual gifts and the role they are to play in the Christian life. Many of us have the same questions they had. When the Corinthians asked Paul a question about spiritual gifts and speaking in tongues, Paul answers their question by taking up a discussion of "spiritual things" (*pneumatikon*). Paul informs them that in order to understand spiritual things, a Christian must first confess that Jesus is Lord through the enabling of the Holy Spirit. A Christian must believe that Jesus is the Lord of all things and the very Son of God, whose death saves us from the guilt and power of sin, and whose righteousness is imputed to us through the instrument of faith. For Paul, knowing and confessing that Jesus is Lord is the starting point when it comes to understanding "spiritual things." In fact, we must understand spiritual things so that we understand "spiritual gifts" (the *charismata*), including the role of speaking in tongues.

Having affirmed the Lordship of Christ as the foundation for the discussion of spiritual things in verses 1–3 of chapter 12, Paul continues to deal with specific questions asked of him by the Corinthians. At this point, Paul takes up a discussion of spiritual gifts. While there is one Lord (Jesus) and one Holy Spirit, there are many spiritual gifts given to those within the church. Each of these individual Christians who is given a particular spiritual gift plays a vital role in the building up of the body of Christ because these gifts are given for the common good, as Paul puts it.

Spiritual Gifts and the Body of Christ

In verses 4–11 of chapter 12, Paul describes how genuine Christian unity is based upon the fact that there is one God, one Lord, one Spirit, and one common divine purpose for spiritual gifts. In light of this, the only way to make sense of spiritual gifts is to understand the unity of Christ's body, and consider how these gifts serve the purpose of building up that one body. This flies in the face of the pagan understanding of spiritual things which saw such "spirituality" as centering in someone's religious experiences, or in the ability to predict the future, speak to the dead, or pronounce or remove blessings and curses. Paul is reminding the Corinthians that any proper understanding of spiritual gifts should not focus upon Christians as individuals, but upon the well-being of Christ's church as a whole.

Yet there is the question of diversity here as well, as seen in the fact that the same Holy Spirit distributes a variety of spiritual gifts as he wills to various individuals within the church. Not everyone receives the same gifts since a multitude of different gifts make Christ's body as a whole that much stronger. There is one body, yet a diversity of gifts given that body. To put it another way, there is both unity (one body, one Christ, one Spirit, one purpose for spiritual gifts) and diversity in the church (each member of the body being given different gifts). In verses 12–26 of this chapter, Paul will address the subject of the body of Christ and focus upon the diversity among its members before he addresses the subject of certain offices in the church and how these offices relate to spiritual gifts in verses 27–31. Unless we understand the gifts of the Spirit in relationship to the body of Christ, we cannot understand either their purpose or the manner in which God's gifts are to be exercised.

Because chapters 12–14 is one long running argument, these chapters could be tackled as a whole. Unfortunately, we must address Paul's lengthy answer in small segments. You cannot talk about gifts of the Spirit (the *charismata*), without talking about the unity of Christ's body. And you cannot talk about spiritual gifts without understanding spiritual things (the *pneumatikon*). And you cannot understand spiritual things unless you understand that Jesus is Lord, and that the church is his body. These things are all inter-connected, according to Paul.

So, as we struggle to keep the big picture before us, in verses 4–11 Paul takes up the subject of the unity of Christ's body and diversity of the distribution of the gifts of the Spirit. In verse 4, Paul states, "Now there are varieties of gifts, but the same Spirit." The word the ESV translates as "varieties," comes from a root word which means to divide (*diaireseis*). The gifts of the Spirit are divided (we might say "divvied up") among the members of the church. These gifts of the Spirit are known as the *charismata*. The root of the word *charismata* is *charis* or "grace." The term refers to those extraordinary endowments which the Holy Spirit confers upon individuals within the church specifically for the purpose of building up of the body of Christ. While these gifts may be related to the natural abilities people already have (in the sense that spiritual gifts are a supernatural enhancement of our natural abilities), Paul's comments throughout this section emphasize the fact that the *charismata* are divine (or supernatural) endowments given specifically for the building up of the church and the edification of its members.

Given the pagan mindset of many of the Corinthian Christians who are now struggling to think like Christians, many Corinthians selfishly boasted about possessing God's gifts, or else used them in an inappropriate manner (as we will see Paul's discussion in chapter 14). An inappropriate manner is to call attention to oneself, to use these gifts as a pretense to divide the body (creating factions), or as a means of religious self-gratification. Perhaps you too have witnessed professing Christians engaging in all kinds of inappropriate behavior in public, and then claim to be doing so under the "guidance" of the Holy Spirit. The gifts of the Holy Spirit were intended to bring unity to the Corinthian church, and to build up Christ's body. Instead, they were becoming a source of sinful pride and division. Since the same Holy Spirit who gives these gifts also called the Corinthians to faith in Jesus Christ and included them in the church, the proper understanding and utilization of these gifts is to bring greater unity to the church, not more division.

Spiritual Gifts and Service

This issue becomes clear in the next verse (v. 5): "And there are varieties of service, but the same Lord." That there are different varieties of service points to the role and function of spiritual gifts, namely the service of others. The word for "service" (*diakoniōn*) is based on the same word from which we get our word "deacon" (one who serves). Paul's point is that while there are different ways to serve one another, we should never forget that there is but one Lord whom we all serve. Serving one another is the divinely-appointed result of the distribution of supernatural gifts among the members of the congregation. Therefore, we should not make the mistake that the Corinthians made and assume that the more spectacular the gift, the more important the person who possesses it. Since Jesus is Lord, the recipient of Christ's gifts cannot be greater than the Lord who gave him the gift.

If the end (goal) of these gifts (the *charismata*) is the service of others, then we should not depreciate what may appear mundane and unglamourous in the eyes of the world. This is exactly what the enthusiasts among the Corinthians were doing by belittling the service of others and boasting about their own gifts, claiming that it was the Holy Spirit who instructed individuals to disrupt the normal order of worship. The Greco-Roman fascination with individuals who possessed spectacular spiritual "powers" is what made the Corinthians so vulnerable to the so-called "super apostles"—a subject Paul takes up in 2 Corinthians 11:1–15.

Leon Morris reminds us of something quite important, yet which is easy to overlook. When Paul speaks of "the Lord," he is speaking of Jesus and affirming that Jesus is Israel's Messiah, as well as using the Greek word *Kurios*, which is the word used throughout the Septuagint to refer to God. While Paul does not formally affirm the doctrine of the Trinity in these verses, there are certainly Trinitarian ramifications throughout this entire section. Jesus is spoken of as on a par with the Father and the Holy Spirit. This really is a remarkable point and we can easily overlook it.[1]

The Spirit's Empowering

In verse 6, Paul continues this line of thought. "And there are varieties of activities, but it is the same God who empowers them all in everyone." Again, the gifts of the Spirit are directly connected to God's working (*ho energōn*, his "empowering"). The point is that God is the active party throughout, working in and through

---

1. Morris, *1 Corinthians*, 166.

these gifts of the Spirit to build up the body of Christ. Building up not only entails numerical growth (more people becoming Christians) it also means that the Corinthians are strengthened as individuals so that they are better able to resist pagan temptations, and they are also enabled to love one another so that they will serve one another. While these gifts are distributed among the members of the body, they all come from God, who works in and through those in his church. Therefore, the gifts of the Spirit should further God's purpose, not anyone's personal agenda.

The reason for God's activity and gifts is spelled out in the following verse (v. 7): "To each is given the manifestation of the Spirit for the common good." The church as a whole benefits from its members who have these different gifts. The gifts of the Spirit are given to "each one," which means that all of the members of the body of Christ are given at least one gift, and it is not unreasonable to conclude that no one individual receives all of them. The fact that these gifts are "manifested" (*phanerōsis*) emphasizes divine action—God gives these gifts as he wills, but gives them in such a way that the exercise of these gifts is evident to others. As Paul has been making plain, these gifts are given for the common good. This means that any exercise of the so-called "gifts" must have as its goal the well-being of Christ's church. Someone who is promoting themselves (in boasting about the greatness of the gift they have, or through religious self-gratification—talking about the sensational religious experiences they have had) is not manifesting the gifts of the Spirit, just as someone speaking by the Spirit cannot say that "Jesus is accursed."

In verses 8–10, Paul enumerates what these spiritual gifts are, and briefly touches upon how these gifts are to be used in the churches. The difficulty with these verses is that some of the gifts are not present (or normative) in the church today. As early as the time of church father Chrysostom (344–407), Christians were wondering about what these gifts entailed, since it was

The Common Good

thought that they had long-ceased to operate in the churches.[2] There are three interpretive options with what follows.

One approach is that taken by many Pentecostals who claim that all of these spiritual gifts are still normative in the church today.[3] My response to this claim is to ask a simple question. "How does what such people claim is a manifestation of the gifts of the Spirit in the church, actually match up with what we actually see going on in the New Testament?" Despite all the claims that are made by those who believe such things are normative today, where are the dramatic miracles, the instantaneous healings (along with accompanying medical verification), and so on? In the New Testament, the manifestation of certain of these miracles was quite public, and often occurred in the presence of unbelievers. If all the gifts are still operative (even the more dramatic ones), where and how are these gifts manifested today?

Another approach is to argue that miraculous gifts (the so-called "sign gifts" or "extraordinary gifts") ceased after the age of the apostles. This approach solves the problem of why these things do not go on in the church today, but raises questions about the continuity of redemptive history. Where does Paul say such miraculous gifts will cease? He does not. But he also does not say they are normative either. The key is that Paul does not ordain new apostles, but pastors, elders, and deacons, and these offices do become normative in the church. The miraculous gifts do not. According to B. B. Warfield, such gifts were "distinctly the authentication of Apostles. They were part of the credentials of the Apostles as authoritative agents of God in founding the Apostolic Church," and so these miraculous gifts, "necessarily passed way with [the Apostolic Age]."[4]

---

2. Cited in Morris, *1 Corinthians*, 167.

3. One thinks of John Wimber and the "signs and wonders" movement of the 1980s. See, for example, John Wimber and Kevin Springer, *Power Evangelism* (San Francisco: Harper & Row, 1986).

4. B. B. Warfield, *Counterfeit Miracles* (Edinburgh: The Banner of Truth

The third option is to define these gifts so that they are connected to things which occur in the church today, but making them far more ordinary and mundane than is often claimed. This approach means we must "de-supernaturalize" these gifts, and make them less miraculous and dramatic than they were during the New Testament era.

I contend that there is a bit of truth in both of the latter two options. Clearly signs and wonders accompanied the preaching of the gospel during the apostolic era in new areas of evangelism, specifically to confirm the truth of the message of the cross. There is no evidence, even in post-apostolic times (after the apostles had died), that these miracles continued on in the churches once they had been established. Since Paul makes the point rather emphatically that the purpose of these spiritual gifts is to serve others and build up the church, there is good reason to understand these gifts in terms of the more mundane activities of the church associated with service and love for one another. But, no doubt, this is clearly a difficult and divisive topic and we need to be cautious in some of our assessments.

Based upon what Paul says here, we can say for sure that these spiritual gifts are supernatural in origin—and although possibly enhancements of natural abilities, the emphasis falls upon the supernatural aspect of them. We can also say for sure that the purpose of these gifts is two-fold. One is for the common good of the church. The other is that these gifts are given to enable us to love one another as we labor together to build up the body of Christ. Therefore, if we stress continuity between our age and the time of the apostles, then we must assign the miraculous sign gifts primarily to the mission field so as to confirm the truth of the gospel when it is preached, and not make these gifts normative in established churches. If we stress discontinuity between our age and the time of the apostles then we must give some jus-

---

Trust, 1972), 6.

The Common Good

tification for certain gifts which were given for the common good not continuing in the post-apostolic age. The resolution to many of these problems is to concentrate upon the purposes these gifts served in the apostolic church. What role did these gifts play in the New Testament? Here we find some concrete answers to our contemporary struggle with application.

The Gifts of the Spirit Enumerated

In verses 8–10, Paul enumerates some of these gifts.

> For to one is given through the Spirit the utterance of wisdom, and to another the utterance of knowledge according to the same Spirit, to another faith by the same Spirit, to another gifts of healing by the one Spirit, to another the working of miracles, to another prophecy, to another the ability to distinguish between spirits, to another various kinds of tongues, to another the interpretation of tongues.

Paul mentions various gifts of the Spirit here, but the list here is not exhaustive because there are other such lists in Paul's letters, notably Romans 12:6–8 and Ephesians 4:11–12. There are profound echoes in this list of gifts from the second chapter of the prophecy of Joel (2:18–32), in which Joel predicts that the last days would be characterized by the work of God's Spirit poured out upon all believers, not just a few spiritual elites.

It is difficult to determine with precision what some of these gifts actually entailed, which makes the question of cessation of the gifts a difficult one. For one thing, it is just plain wrong-headed to do something with no biblical precedence—like a televangelist claiming to have "words of knowledge" about people watching their program at home—and then claim that what you are doing is offering a "word of knowledge" because Paul mentions this gift in 1 Corinthians 12. The use of these gifts in Scripture must define how we practice them today, not the other way around. This matter is further complicated by the fact that the difference between some of these gifts is not great (gifts of wisdom and knowledge, healing and miracles).[5]

The first gift mentioned by Paul is the "message of wisdom" (*logos sophias*) which likely refers to a spoken message of wisdom, in the sense of a Spirit-inspired insight into affairs of life. This gift reveals God's perspective on things, which the worldly wisdom of the Greco-Roman world cannot possibly discern or understand. Understood in this manner the "message of wisdom" refers to the Holy Spirit bringing to mind something found in Scripture (in this case, the Old Testament) and which the Holy Spirit now prompts us to mention to others.

The second gift listed is the word of knowledge (*logos gnōseōs*). This likely refers to a Spirit-given insight into the mysteries of God associated with the revelation of Jesus Christ. This, it would seem, would be connected to teaching, preaching, and spiritual counsel. It would be the exact opposite of paganism, which looked for hidden or secret knowledge. What God has done to save us from our sins and reveal to us his wisdom, he has done in public.

The next gift mentioned is faith. This gift is a bit tricky because faith is something that all Christians are given by the Holy Spirit. The difficulty lies in distinguishing this supernatural endowment of faith in light of the justifying faith possessed by all Christians. Since Paul goes on to list healing and miracles almost in the same breath, it is commonly thought that Paul is speaking here of that faith which is connected with the miraculous (either created as a result of the miraculous, or that faith which believes that God will perform the miraculous, thereby bringing it to pass). We cannot be certain.

When Paul speaks of "gifts of healing" (there is no article), he may mean different gifts of healing for different kinds of ill-

---

5. Gaffin, *Perspectives on Pentecost*, 51–52.

nesses, but again it is difficult to tell. We do know that elsewhere in Scripture (Mark 2:1–12; James 5:14–16), healing is directly connected with the forgiveness of sins. We also know that complete and total healing of all diseases and infirmities is promised to all of us on the day of resurrection, but not before. God can and does heal. He can and does allow some of us to be sick and suffer. Why one and not the other? Some are sick because of obvious reasons. Smokers get cancer, etc. In other cases, God simply does not tell us why one becomes ill and another does not. We can say that because Jesus Christ has died for all of our sins, the cruelest thing we can ever do is imply that some poor suffering saint must have done something which angered God and caused God to afflict them.

Miraculous powers are connected to those miracles which establish the gospel. Here, the Book of Acts should be our guide and these gifts may very well be connected to the mission field and the advance of the gospel. What modern faith-healers call "miracles" appear to have very little to do with what goes on in the New Testament. Jesus and the apostles performed miracles in public and in the presence of unbelievers to confirm the truth of the gospel—Jesus and the apostles did not perform so-called miracles in stadiums filled with thousands of excited followers hoping to see something highly dramatic.

In light of the apostolic preaching we find throughout the Book of Acts, prophecy is connected to preaching, and entails two related elements. The first is a Spirit-given insight into the meaning of the Old Testament (where Christ is hidden in type and shadow) as well as a supernatural boldness in proclaiming that gospel in the face of hostile opposition.[6] The second element is that the preacher proclaims the Word of God revealing new information about God's redemptive purposes in Christ. For an apostle, these elements were characteristic of his office. For a

---

6. Contra Gaffin, *Perspectives on Pentecost*, 59.

prophet, giving such prophetic utterances was an occasional and extraordinary circumstance. Says Hodge, "The difference . . . between the apostles and prophets, was, that the former were permanently inspired, so that their teaching was at all times infallible, whereas the prophets were infallible only occasionally."[7]

The discerning of spirits has to do with determining whether someone is truly a prophet or not. In 1 John 4:1, John warns Christians of the need to make such distinctions because there were false prophets everywhere present. Jesus warns us that the presence of false teachers will be one of the characteristics of the inter-adventual age (Matt. 24:11). John Owen saw this gift as especially important in the apostolic age because "the Lord graciously provided for his churches, that some among them should be enabled in an extraordinary manner to discern and judge of them who pretended unto extraordinary actings of the Spirit."[8] The standard here is relatively simple. Is what teachers teach and what preachers preach in line with the revealed Word of God? We know a false prophet to be a false prophet because he speaks lies. We know a false teacher based upon his false doctrine.

Finally, the ability to speak in tongues is often thought to be a divine enabling to speak a language the speaker does not know (a known language or a "heavenly language"), or else an ability to proclaim the gospel in a known language with great boldness. The gift of interpretation should be understood as a complementary gift (a supernatural ability to translate the language the tongue speaker does not know), or it may refer to someone who is able to translate what the speaker has said with a supernatural boldness so that the people of God might be edified (we will discuss this in more detail when we come to chapter 14 of 1 Corinthians).

---

7. Hodge, *I & II Corinthians*, 247.

8. John Owen, *The Works of John Owen* (Carlisle, PA: Banner of Truth Trust, 1965), III.35.

The Common Good

Unity and Diversity

Finally, in verse 11, Paul summarizes his prior point about the unity and diversity of these gifts. "All these are empowered by one and the same Spirit, who apportions to each one individually as he wills." All of these diverse gifts are from the same Holy Spirit. The Holy Spirit not only gives gifts to every Christian, he determines who gets what gifts and why. Since these diverse gifts come from the same source, they should have the same effect, to build up the body of Jesus Christ in which the Holy Spirit dwells.

There are two issues raised by this passage with which we must deal. The first issue is this: "If these gifts of the Spirit are still given to Christ's people today, how do I know which of these gifts I might have?" The answer is simple and comes in the form of a question. "What do you like doing, and what are you good at doing?" There is no question that these gifts are supernatural. But there is nothing indicated in the biblical text which tells us that someone who is afraid of public speaking suddenly will be called to preach. Or that someone who isn't comfortable around children will suddenly desire to become the Sunday school superintendent. If a Christian feels a desire to serve Christ's church in a particular area (an internal call) then they should pursue it. If someone enjoys an activity or serving, and discovers that they do it well, they have what we identify as an external call. This is how you know you have a particular gift of the Spirit. It may even be the case that other Christians, especially pastors and elders, call attention to particular skills and interests which you demonstrate in the life and service of the church and its members.

The second issue raised by this text is that the gifts of the Spirit are given to enable us to serve Christ's church for the common good—which is the building up of Christ's body. The gifts of the Spirit were not given to divide the church. When the charismatic movement swept through churches years ago, the first thing that happened was it divided the church into two camps—those who thought the gifts were for today and that everyone should use them, and the opposition which insisted that these gifts ceased when the apostolic era ended. As a result of a supposed work of the Spirit, the churches were divided. The Holy Spirit does not create schism in the body of Christ.

The gifts of the Spirit as enumerated by Paul are given for the service of others—for the common good—and for the building up of the body of Christ. The evidence that the Holy Spirit is at work is obvious when we think about this in biblical categories, but not obvious if pagan categories are our guide. Do God's people love one another? Is the coffee made? Are extra chairs set up if needed? Do people sing joyfully and faithfully participate in the worship? Is food provided and served during the potluck? To the poor and needy? Do people care for one another in times of need? Do they bear one another's burdens, like sending cards, making phone calls, and praying for one another? Do people long to see sinners come to faith in Jesus Christ? Do sinners repent? Is the gospel preached and do people desire to hear the Word of God proclaimed? Are the sacraments administered in accordance with the Word of God? Do people do these things without seeking to call attention to themselves?

If these things are present in the church, then we can be sure that the gifts of the Holy Spirit are being used to build up the body of Christ, for the common good and for the glory of Christ. But this starts with our confession that "Jesus is Lord," because he alone has saved us from our sins and included us in his body. It is Jesus our Lord who baptizes us in the Holy Spirit and who gives us "gifts of the Spirit."

23

One Body, Many Members

1 CORINTHIANS 12:12–26

> *For just as the body is one and has many members, and all the members of the body, though many, are one body, so it is with Christ. For in one Spirit we were all baptized into one body—Jews or Greeks, slaves or free—and all were made to drink of one Spirit.*

Almost all peoples and cultures have some sort of utopian dream—a world of universal peace and harmony yet to be realized. John Lennon's *Imagine* anyone? Yet, ours is a fallen race. And because we are a fallen race, we are divided along a number of racial, socioeconomic, political, and theological fault lines.

Much like the ancient Corinthians, we too struggle to find true unity in a world of diversity. Because of human sinfulness, the only way unity can be obtained is through force and coercion ("agree or else"), through deception (like that of a false religion or a political ideology), or through a superficial "herd" mentality. The bad news is there will be no earthly utopia this side of Christ's second coming. The good news is that God does provide us with a true unity based upon our common faith in Jesus Christ realized in the church through the person and work of the Holy Spirit. While this unity is imperfectly realized in this life, nevertheless, in Christ's church, God takes a host of diverse and different people, and then forms them into one body—the church of Jesus Christ in which his Holy Spirit dwells.

Throughout this entire chapter, Paul is addressing a question the Corinthians had asked him in their letter. Based on Paul's answer—which runs all the way from 1 Corinthians 12:1–14:40—the original question certainly had something to do with the role and practice of speaking in tongues (a subject addressed in some detail in chapter 14). In chapter 12, Paul begins to answer this question by laying the groundwork for how we should understand the gifts of the Spirit in general (the *charismata*). The apostle makes the case that unless we confess that "Jesus is Lord"—we confess that Jesus is Lord of all things, that he is the very Son of God, that he died for our sins and that he was raised from the dead for our justification—we cannot understand "spiritual things" (the *pneumatikon*).

But, says Paul, we cannot confess that Jesus is Lord except by the power of the Holy Spirit. It is the Holy Spirit whose gifts are given to those who are members of Christ's church, which is his body. In the previous section of this chapter (verses 4–11), Paul has made the point that God gives these gifts of the Spirit (which are supernatural endowments from the Holy Spirit) as he wills for the common good of the church. Although the Corinthians were struggling with the mistaken assumption that the greater the gift the more important the person who possessed that gift, Paul emphasizes that these gifts were not given so that people could boast about their spiritual prowess, or so that they could call attention to themselves, or even use these gifts as a pretense for dividing the church into factions. No, these gifts were given for the common good, the building up of the body of Christ.

One Body, Many Members

The Church as the Body of Christ

When it comes to the subject of spiritual things, Paul challenges those in the Corinthian church to think like Christians—and to cease thinking like pagans. But as Paul deals with the Corinthian preoccupation with pagan spirituality, Paul also challenges those among us who think of the church as nothing more than a voluntary assembly which we can join or un-join at our whim. Christ's spiritual body (the church) is indwelt by the Holy Spirit. Peter even speaks of the members of Christ's church as living stones in a spiritual temple in which God's Spirit dwells (cf. 1 Pet. 2:5). The church is not merely a list of names on the membership roll. The members of Christ's church are to assemble each Lord's Day to hear Christ's word, participate in the sacraments as Christ instituted them, exercise the gifts of the Spirit given to his church by Christ, and participate in the life of the local church, all for the common good and for the glory of Jesus Christ.

Paul's point is straightforward. If you are a Christian (and confess that Jesus is *your* Lord), you are part of Christ's body (the church). The body of Christ of which we are part is visibly manifest in a local church. We have been given gifts of the Spirit to be exercised in that local church for the common good, not for our own enjoyment or benefit. This means that there is no biblical justification whatsoever for the widespread tendency among evangelicals to confess that "Jesus is their Lord," but then fail to participate in the life of the church by joining a particular congregation. When we confess that Jesus is Lord, we do so in the context of the church, which is Christ's body. This is why the New Testament spends so much time on the marks of the church, the nature of the church, the mission of the church, and the way the church is to be governed. To put it another way, "unchurched Christian" is truly an oxymoron. The Reformed and Presbyterian confessions make this point when they affirm that "the visible church . . . consists of all those throughout the world that profess the true religion, together with their children, and is the kingdom of the Lord Jesus Christ, the house and family of God, out of which there is no ordinary possibility of salvation" (*Westminster Confession of Faith* 25.2).

In 1 Corinthians 12:12–26, Paul explains that the church is the body of Christ. As has been clear throughout this entire letter, Paul does not conceive of the church as a democracy, nor will he tolerate anarchy. This is because the church is the body of Christ. It is the Lord Jesus himself who adds diverse members to his one body. This explains why unity is so important to the health of the church, and why dividing the body of Christ is such a great sin. Paul's use of the body analogy also explains why there is so much diversity in the church in terms of its members and why such diversity is so important to the overall health of the body. The various members of Christ's body are given different gifts of the Spirit so as to benefit the whole. Although in the Greco-Roman world analogies drawn from the human body were rather common, Paul advances the analogy a bit by demonstrating that Christ adds diverse members to his own body so as to increase the strength of the whole, and so as to demonstrate that all individual members should strive for the common good.

One Body But Many Members

In verse 12, Paul begins his discussion of Christ's spiritual body (the church) which is made up of many members. "For just as the body is one and has many members, and all the members of the body, though many, are one body, so it is with Christ." A body is composed of many different members, each with vastly different functions. Legs, for instance, play a very different role than eyes, but both are very important. Although the members are different and have different purposes, there is a fundamental unity which transcends all the differences. Paul simply states, "So it is with Christ."

In Ephesians 5:23 and Colossians 1:18, Paul speaks of Christ as the head of the body. In the Corinthian letter, Paul's focus seems to fall upon our union with Christ. In 1 Corinthians 1:30, he writes, "And because of him you are in Christ Jesus, who became to us wisdom from God, righteousness and sanctification and redemption." Because all believers are "in Christ" and are currently united to Jesus (even though Jesus has ascended into heaven), all believers are members of Christ's body through the work of the Holy Spirit. This means that there is both unity (one body) and great diversity (many different members) in Christ's church.

Baptism and the Body of Christ

At this point, Paul addresses the means by which we are incorporated into Christ's visible body—baptism. In verse 13, Paul speaks of baptism in terms of the relationship of the sacrament to the unity of the body of Christ and to the indwelling of the Holy Spirit. "For in one Spirit we were all baptized into one body—Jews or Greeks, slaves or free—and all were made to drink of one Spirit." Given the sad fact that baptism has been a source of division in the Corinthian congregation (cf. 1 Cor. 1:13ff.—"I was baptized by so and so, therefore, I am a follower of so and so"), Paul reminds the Corinthians that baptism is what incorporates individuals into the visible body of Christ. Baptism is a sacrament of incorporation and unity. Lest we forget, the connection between baptism and union with Christ is prominent in Paul's writings. In Galatians 3:27, Paul writes, "For as many of you as were baptized into Christ have put on Christ." In Romans 6:3, he writes, "Do you not know that all of us who have been baptized into Christ Jesus were baptized into his death?" And in Titus 3:5, Paul states that God "saved us, not because of works done by us in righteousness, but according to his own mercy, by the washing of regeneration and renewal of the Holy Spirit."

Each one of the Corinthian Christians, regardless of what they were before coming to faith (Jew or Greek, slave or free) are baptized by the Holy Spirit into Christ's spiritual body. It is the Holy Spirit who takes these diverse individuals and makes them one through the sacrament of baptism. Since it is the Holy Spirit who performs this work of uniting these individuals into one body, Reformed Christians reject the idea that the act of applying water regenerates (baptismal regeneration), while at the same time affirming the importance of connecting the sign (the water of baptism) with the thing signified (the regenerating work of the Holy Spirit).

To state this connection in another way, where the sign is present (water), we believe that the thing signified is present (incorporation into the body of Christ). The water does not incorporate us into Christ, the Holy Spirit does. But we cannot see the work of the Spirit. Yet God is gracious, and in our weakness, God gives to us a visible sign (water) of the reality which we cannot see (the baptism of the Holy Spirit). This is what Paul is getting at when he says baptism is the means by which we are incorporated into Christ's body, which is the church.

This supports the point made earlier about someone professing faith in Christ, but not being a member of a local church. Biblically speaking, this makes no sense. Likewise, the New Testament has no category for someone who is a professing believer, but who is not baptized. The same thing holds true for children of believers. While baptism does not regenerate, it is the sign and seal of everything God promises to his people under the terms of the covenant of grace ("I will be your God and you will be my people). If we profess to be in that covenant of grace through faith in Jesus Christ, on what basis then do we reject the sign and seal of the covenant? And if our children are likewise in the covenant of grace (cf. 1 Cor. 7:14), how can we deny to them the sign and seal of that covenant which is baptism? This is, after all, what Jesus commanded his people to do in the Great Commission. "All authority in heaven and on earth has been given to me. Go therefore and make disciples of all nations, baptizing them in the name of the Father and of the Son and of the Holy Spirit, teaching them to observe all that I have commanded you. And behold, I am with you always, to the end of the age" (Matt. 28:18–20).

We All Drink of One Spirit

There are several echoes in Paul's discussion of unity and diversity drawn from messianic prophecies such as Isaiah 49:8–26 in which the prophet speaks of the way in which the Messiah will draw people from all nations (not just Israel) to participate in the blessings of God's covenant. The Messiah will call everyone from prisoners, to nursing mothers, to the oppressed, the afflicted, and the grieving. Kings will become servants, and God's blessing will extend to all those who confess that YHWH is the covenant Lord. This is what has happened in Corinth as well as in every Christian church where Jesus is confessed as Lord. God calls people from every race, tribe, and nation, and makes them one body, who together profess that "Jesus is Lord" because the day of salvation has come.

All of these individuals with their different social standings are said to "drink of one Spirit." It is the Holy Spirit who forms the body of Christ through creating faith in the hearts of those called by the gospel, and in creating the bond of our union with Christ who, although in heaven, is still present with us. If anyone is "in Christ," they are also "in the Spirit" and vice-versa. This bond cannot be broken—a true believer cannot be severed from Christ. But the unity of the body can be broken. This is the sad reality facing the Corinthian church which was plagued with division and factions, improperly celebrating the Lord's Supper (the sacrament of Christ's body) and selfishly misusing the gifts of the Holy Spirit. And this because the Corinthians were still thinking and acting like unbelievers.

Understanding the meaning and importance of baptism counteracts the kind of sinful thinking which creates divisions. Paul states in verse 14, "For the body does not consist of one member but of many." There is one body which we enter through baptism, but that body has many diverse members. Each member of Christ's body needs all of the other members of Christ's body, and since baptism unites us together, Paul is making the point that no single member of that body can exist on their own. No single member of the body is "the body." Just as no individual Christian is "the church."

An Analogy: Our Bodies and Christ's Body

At this point, Paul makes a number of points of application based upon the metaphor of the human body. As mentioned earlier, the use of such analogies was a common practice in the ancient world, especially in public speeches dealing with the peace and harmony of society. Although this was often done by men of power to keep subordinates in place—"Those of you who are feet, get to walking and realize that you are not the head!"—Paul takes the analogy in a different direction, discussing the relationship between unity and diversity in the church.[1] Every member of the body is equally important and essential to the well-being of the whole. The individual members of the body cannot simply opt out of the body, nor can they exist on their own, independent from the body. A severed limb is a *dead* limb. A body missing a limb is crippled by its loss.

---

1. Hays, *First Corinthians*, 213.

One Body, Many Members

Paul continues to make this point in verses 15–16. "If the foot should say, 'Because I am not a hand, I do not belong to the body,' that would not make it any less a part of the body. And if the ear should say, 'Because I am not an eye, I do not belong to the body,' that would not make it any less a part of the body." Apparently, the disputes among the Corinthians over spiritual gifts left a number of those with less-sensational and more mundane spiritual gifts feeling vastly inferior to those with more sensational and visible gifts.

This is what happens when spiritual gifts are applied using pagan or worldly categories of evaluation. Not only do Paul's words provide an important corrective to the false understanding of spiritual things so prevalent among the Corinthians (namely that spiritual gifts are not a matter of individual status, but are given for service and to equip us to love one another), but these words from Paul seem to be aimed at encouraging those who felt like they didn't measure up to those with more visible gifts. Your pinkie toe may not seem like much, but cut it off (or even stub it) and see what happens. This is also the case in the church. Where would we be without those with seemingly insignificant gifts? There are many folk in our church who quietly serve others, but prefer to do so "under the radar." It is not until they miss a Sunday or two that we realize how much they actually do. These are the folk who pray without ceasing, who call, correspond with, and visit the sick and the shut-ins. These are folk who bring dessert to share with others, who buy donuts, make coffee, set-up chairs, run the sound system, and so on. They do so not to call attention to themselves, but because they see a need and they take care of it.

As Paul says in verse 17, "If the whole body were an eye, where would be the sense of hearing? If the whole body were an ear, where would be the sense of smell?" Again, our place in the body of Christ is not a matter of personal status, nor personal attainment, but of God's sovereignty—a point which Paul emphasizes in verse 18: "But as it is, God arranged the members in the body, each one of them, as he chose." The fact of the matter is that God has sovereignly called and equipped each one of the members of Christ's body with these various gifts as he sees fit.

God Gives Spiritual Gifts According to His Will

Paul's emphasis upon the phrase "God arranged the members" is important. God is concerned with the health of the entire body, since he created this body and called its various members to faith in his Son. It is God who determines which of the Corinthians are the feet, the hands, the eyes, and the ears. God did this, Paul says, just as he wills and according to his purposes. Every member of the church and every gift which God gives these members are important to the well-being of the whole. We have been called by God and given specific gifts for the well-being of the entire body. Since these gifts are often tied to our interests and natural abilities, we should learn to identify these gifts and use them by asking a couple of simple questions. "What do I like doing?" "What am I good at doing?" That way, when a need arises, we'll know whether or not we are equipped to address it. Is the need something I feel compelled to address, and, realistically, will I be capable of doing so?

This brings Paul back to a discussion of the unity and diversity of the body in verses 19–20. "If all were a single member, where would the body be? As it is, there are many parts, yet one body." Obviously, a body is made up of many diverse parts with different functions. No matter how important any individual part of that body is, by itself, it does not compose the entire body. Nor can such body parts exist independently on their own. The individual parts (people called with their gifts determined by God) compose the one body of Jesus Christ. Therefore, the unity and diversity present in the body of Christ are necessary

One Body, Many Members

aspects of the church. We are all different, although brought together under one head, who is Christ.

At this point, Paul changes focus from those with less-spectacular gifts to those who are given more public and noticeable gifts. Paul goes from offering words of encouragement to those who may feel inferior, to offering words of caution (perhaps a mild rebuke) to those who may feel superior because of their more visible gifts. Notice that in verse 21, the focus shifts slightly to an emphasis upon the interconnectedness of the body's parts. "The eye cannot say to the hand, 'I have no need of you,' nor again the head to the feet, 'I have no need of you.'" Since God distributes spiritual gifts as he wishes for the well-being of the body, and since spiritual gifts are a matter of service not status, those with more spectacular gifts must not look down upon those with what they think are "lesser" gifts. An eye cannot look down upon the hand, nor can the head say to the feet, "Get lost." Those with spectacular gifts need those with less spectacular gifts because they are all part of the same body.

In fact, the members of the Corinthian church cannot get along without these members, hence the assertion Paul makes in verses 22. "On the contrary, the parts of the body that seem to be weaker are indispensable." Switching from the negative to the positive, Paul asserts that the weaker members (feet and ears) are every bit as indispensable to the body as "heads" and "eyes." This would have special significance to a culture struggling with issues of class and social status. The word Paul uses here (*asthenestera*, "weaker") comes from a word meaning "sick." Paul does not speak of these folk with weaker gifts as merely an addition to the body, or even as a "welcome" addition to the body. Rather, Paul says, these members are indispensable to the body, and the body cannot do without them.

This becomes clear when we consider how we treat the parts of our own bodies. "And on those parts of the body that we think less honorable we bestow the greater honor, and our unpresentable parts are treated with greater modesty, which our more presentable parts do not require. But God has so composed the body, giving greater honor to the part that lacked it" (v. 23–24). We dress up our feet with fancy shoes, and we cover our unpresentable parts so as to be modest. But our presentable parts get no special treatment—although in our culture it is hard to imagine any part of our body which is exposed to public view which doesn't get some special treatment in private before we go out in public.

If One Suffers, We All Suffer

God has taken all of these various parts (those with different spiritual gifts) and combined them into one body. The parts coexist as one body so that all the parts are honored. The reasons for this are spelled out in verses 25–26. "That there may be no division in the body, but that the members may have the same care for one another. If one member suffers, all suffer together; if one member is honored, all rejoice together." The goal of Paul's discussion is to point out how serious division in the body really is. All parts are to have equal concern for the others. If one part of the body suffers, all other parts of the body will likewise suffer. If one part of the body is honored, the whole body is honored. All body parts share a common source of life and this cannot, ultimately, be isolated from the other parts, for good or for ill. This is why the members of the local church should learn to watch out for their fellow Christians who are suffering, doing without, or in some sort of need. A kind word, a thoughtful note, a meal, yard work, baby-sitting, etc., go a long way to remind our brothers and sisters that there is a profound sense in which we are all in this together, and that when one of us suffers we all do.

In light of this understanding of the church as an organic whole, there is no justification whatsoever for causing division

One Body, Many Members

or striving to create factions. There is no justification for using the gifts of the Spirit for anything other than the building up of the body of Christ for the common good and for the glory of God.

Paul's discussion of the church as the body of Christ allows him to do several things. First, Paul stresses the organic nature of the church—in a profound sense Christ's church is an *organism*, not merely an *organization*. We are each a part of a living whole—the body of Christ. In making this point, Paul stresses the importance of the unity of the whole without at the same time sacrificing that diversity found in the fact that each of us are unique individuals who are given different spiritual gifts. This is a huge consideration for a church which was ethnically and culturally diverse as the church in Corinth. Christianity is not a culture to which we conform—like Islam. Although Christians come from different cultures, races, and socioeconomic backgrounds, together we confess our faith in the same Christ, and together we are members of his body. We are not identified as God's people by our dress, our appearance, what we eat, or our social standing. We identify ourselves as God's people through our common confession that "Jesus is Lord," and we become one body because we have all been baptized into our Lord's death and resurrection.

Paul's point also drives home the fact that in Christ there is a true unity which anticipates that great day after our Lord returns when all hints and traces of sin are gone, and together we become the glorious bride of Christ. This is not a forced unity, not a superficial or temporary unity, nor a campfire-"kumbaya" sort of unity. This is a true unity formed when we are baptized into Christ's body as the outward sign and seal of the invisible work of God's Spirit. God's people have been purchased by the shed blood of Jesus Christ. God's people are clothed with the perfect righteousness of Christ received through the means of faith alone. And God's people are given gifts of the Holy Spirit which enable us to work together to build up the body of Christ for the common good.

Called by Christ to membership in his church (his spiritual body), each individual believer is indispensable to the whole. This is why it grieves us when someone leaves the church, when they move away, or when they struggle during the trials of life. It troubles us when one of us experiences doubt or lacks assurance of salvation, or when we suffer illness or the loss of a job, or even when one of our own dies in Christ. Christ has made us one body with many members. When one of us suffers, we all suffer.

But we also rejoice as one body when one of us rejoices. There is good news as well: the birth and baptism of covenant children, new people joining our churches and professing their faith in Christ. People get new and better jobs, some get married, some graduate from school. You get the point. Yes, there is suffering and sadness. But there are many reasons to rejoice because there is one body with many members.

So, as members of Christ's church and important parts of the body of Christ, there is good reason to rejoice in the fact that Jesus has called us to faith, forgiven us of our sins, covered us with his perfect righteousness, given us gifts of the Spirit for the common good, and made us one body with many members.

24

Earnestly Desire the Higher Gifts

1 CORINTHIANS 12:27–31

> *Now you are the body of Christ and individually members of it. And God has appointed in the church first apostles, second prophets, third teachers, then miracles, then gifts of healing, helping, administrating, and various kinds of tongues. Are all apostles? Are all prophets? Are all teachers? Do all work miracles? Do all possess gifts of healing? Do all speak with tongues? Do all interpret? But earnestly desire the higher gifts. And I will show you a still more excellent way.*

It is very difficult to have a sane and thoughtful discussion about a hot-button theological topic when a doctrine has loyal and emotional adherents, a controversial history, has caused deep division, and lends itself to sensationalism. When this is the case, there is a natural tendency to seek to distance ourselves from those who abuse or distort that doctrine, instead of dealing with what Scripture actually says about it. If you have ever witnessed what takes place nightly on the set of the *Trinity Broadcasting Network* or have witnessed a revival meeting, you might just conclude that you want nothing to do with the gifts of the Spirit. Yet, Paul exhorts the Corinthians (and us) to "earnestly desire the higher gifts." What does Paul mean by this exhortation? What is the role and function of these higher gifts? How are they connected to the biblical offices in the church (minister, elder, and deacon)?

Given the length and complexity of Paul's three-chapter answer to a question the Corinthians had submitted to him about this topic, we have to unpack each of Paul's points in chapter 12 not only to understand why he will devote so much ink to a discussion of speaking in tongues in chapter 14, but also because the points Paul makes in chapter 12 are so important to the life and health of Christ's church.

Sadly, this section of Corinthians has been the source of great controversy, especially with the rise of the charismatic movement in the 1960's and 70's, and with Pentecostalism a bit earlier in the twentieth century. Charismatics and Pentecostals look to this section of 1 Corinthians for biblical support for many of their distinctive doctrines and practices. As we will see, the key to avoid the problems associated with Charismatics and Pentecostals (and their insistence that the manifestation of the *charismata* in the Corinthian church is to be normative in the church today) is to understand what these spiritual gifts actually entailed, as well as determining what role they actually played in the apostolic churches. One purpose of these gifts was to confirm the preaching of the gospel (this was especially the case with miracles and healing). Another purpose of these gifts was to equip each member for service in Christ's church for the common good. A third purpose was to enable a diverse group of believers to love one another because Christ has loved us first.

As Paul lays the groundwork in chapters 12 and 13 to answer the Corinthians' question about the role and purpose of tongue speaking in chapter 14, Paul reminds the Corinthians

Earnestly Desire the Higher Gifts

that in order to properly exercise the gift of tongues, the Corinthians first need to understand the role that spiritual gifts (the *charismata*) were to play in Christ's church. But we cannot understand the role of spiritual gifts without placing them in the broader category of spiritual things (the *pneumatikon*). In making a distinction between spiritual things and the gifts of the Spirit, Paul is able to contrast the pagan conception of "spirituality" with the way Christians should view the person and work of the Holy Spirit.

Paul's approach to spiritual things is completely unlike that of Greco-Roman pagans who understood spiritual things in terms of invisible forces which the spiritual elites among us learn to control and manipulate. The Greeks were especially fascinated with fortune-tellers, people who cast spells, and with those who spoke to the dead. They looked for spiritual superstars who were able to master these spiritual techniques to ensure good weather, good crops, and good fortune, as well as fertility. Paul has to convince the Corinthians to move beyond this pagan way of thinking and doing, for this is nothing but idolatry. Such beliefs are incompatible with their confession that Jesus is Lord, and with the biblical conception of spiritual gifts. The Corinthians must leave behind all these pagan practices, and so too must we.

The Holy Spirit gives some believers very visible and publicly-exercised spiritual gifts. The Holy Spirit also gives to others more mundane and seemingly "ordinary" gifts. But all of these gifts are given for the common good, for the service of others, and to enable us to love one another—the theme of chapter 13. Paul sees the church as the body of Christ. While not all the members of the body have the same function or purpose, each one of us is necessary to the well-being of the whole. This means that gifts are given for service, not for status. There are no spiritual elites in Christ's church, only justified sinners given gifts of the Spirit so that we might serve and love one another. We are appointed to our various roles in the church by Christ himself, for his purpose, our common good, and for his glory. As Calvin once expressed this point, "Even the least significant of believers does in fact bear fruit relative to his slender resources, so that there is no such thing as a useless member of the Church."[1]

Because Christ's church is an organism (Christ's spiritual body), and not merely an organization (although Paul will go on to emphasize proper order in the church), Paul reminds the Corinthians that when one part of the body suffers, the whole body suffers. When one part of the body rejoices, the whole body rejoices. This is why dividing the church is such a great sin, and why Christians have no business seeking to form factions. This is also why all members of the body are equally important. The church is Christ's body and he gives the gifts of the Spirit as he sees fit.

Offices in the Church and Gifts of the Spirit

In the closing verses of chapter 12 (vv. 27–31), Paul switches from the metaphor of the human body to the direct relationship between offices in the church and the gifts of the Spirit. As the apostle brings the body metaphor to a close, in verse 27 he concludes, "Now you are the body of Christ and individually members of it." In the Greek sentence, the "you" is placed forward in the sentence for emphasis and there is no article used with "body." This indicates that Paul is not talking about just any "body." Rather, Paul is referring to the body of Christ of which each of his readers ("you") are members.

In verse 28, Paul begins to discuss some of the ramifications of the way in which the gifts of the Spirit are related to the different offices within the church. Says Paul, "And God has appointed in the church first apostles, second prophets, third

---

1. John Calvin, *The Epistle of Paul to the Corinthians*, 269.

Earnestly Desire the Higher Gifts

teachers, then miracles, then gifts of healing, helping, administrating, and various kinds of tongues." Paul offers a similar list in Ephesians 4:11—"And he gave the apostles, the prophets, the evangelists, the shepherds and teachers." These lists of gifts indicate a priority of sorts, although given our prior discussion about the importance of every member of the body, we ought to be careful not to say more than Paul does. The list of these gifts and offices is probably representative rather than comprehensive. This is how some (not all) of the gifts, relate to some (not all) of the offices. Two points follow from this.

First, it is vital to notice the switch Paul makes mid-sentence from various offices (apostles, prophets, teachers) to various gifts of the Spirit (miracles, healing, and so on). I take this as an indication that the gifts of the Spirit are connected to the officers of the church—a point I will address below. There is an important set of assumptions in view here. Throughout the gospels, Jesus performs miracles. Throughout the Book of Acts, the apostles do the same to confirm the truth of the gospel they proclaim. This fact ties miracles directly to the office of apostle (or to the apostolic circle), and to the establishment of the first churches about which we read throughout the New Testament.

Second, the term "church" (*ekklēsia*) is used here in a universal sense, the universal church as the body of Christ. This is significant because throughout the New Testament, the term "church" is most often used of a local congregation.[2] This tells us that what follows is not only true of the Corinthian congregation, but of all the apostolic churches. God has appointed specific believers to these particular offices in all of the churches. God also gives those chosen for these offices the spiritual gifts necessary to equip them for their service in the church. This is why those who are given certain gifts of the Spirit are then called to the offices God has designed to rule his church in the

---

2. Morris, *1 Corinthians*, 174.

name of Christ. Those offices which Paul mentions here in 1 Corinthians 12 (i.e., apostles, prophets, and teachers) give way after the death of the apostles to those offices mentioned in 1 Timothy 3:1–13 and Titus 1:5–16, offices with which we are more familiar (minister, elder, and deacon).

The connection between certain spiritual gifts and church offices is often overlooked. However, once we make this connection, we can avoid much of the grief which arises from misuse of spiritual gifts. While there are no spiritual elites with insights into secret things (like the pagans believe), there is to be order in the church through the establishment of these three offices, which are filled by those men who have been equipped by the Spirit and called by the church to serve. Such men are called to these offices because the gifts given them by the Spirit (the so-called internal call) have been confirmed in them through their participation in the life of the churches (the external call).

Once the gifts of the Spirit mentioned here are tied to the three offices mentioned by Paul in his so-called pastoral epistles, we can immediately see the problem when someone claims to possess these gifts of the Spirit (such as miracles and healing), and then claims they are called to start their own "ministry" in which they exercise their "gifts" apart from the oversight of the local church. This entrepreneurial spirit produces the kind of lone ranger televangelist who starts his or her own ministry and who then runs amuck doing untold damage to the reputation of Christ and his church. Spiritual gifts are to be exercised in the church, for the common good, to build up the body of Christ. They are not to be used to build someone's fame and fortune.

The first two gifts mentioned by Paul (miracles and healing) clearly have a different (more dramatic and visible) significance than the other gifts. It is possible that God used those with the gifts of miracles and healing to establish the Corinthian church, though there is no mention of this in Acts 18:1–17, although mention is made there of Paul's preaching and teaching. It is also not an accident that Paul lists tongues as the least of the spiritual gifts. This is significant because the Corinthians valued the gift of tongues so highly that even though it was the least of the gifts, the way they were exercising that gift was causing much of the division among them. Whatever purpose speaking in tongues has, this gift does not establish the church, but it can divide it. That much is clear.

Apostles, Prophets, and Teachers

As for the offices mentioned by Paul (apostle, prophets, and teachers), according to Mark 3:14ff., apostles were men chosen and commissioned by Jesus himself to establish the churches after his ascension. The original twelve seem to have been supplemented by people like Barnabas, James, and Paul (what is often designated as the apostolic "circle"). These men were considered to have been guardians of the gospel given to them by Jesus himself, and they were among the eyewitnesses to Christ's bodily resurrection (or in Paul's case—a witness of the risen Christ). As the years go by, and more and more churches are established, the apostles begin to die off and any divinely-inspired writing (Scripture) become authoritative in their absence (cf. 2 Tim. 3:16, 2 Pet. 1:16–21). It is striking that the original apostles (or those in the apostolic circle) do not ordain new apostles. Instead, whenever they plant new churches they ordain ministers, elders, and deacons (cf. Acts 6:1–7; 14:23; 20:17, 28; Titus 1:5).

Almost from the beginning, the church spoke of the importance of bishops as men standing in direct continuity with the apostles. Bishop (*episcopus*) is but another word for elder.[3] After the Roman emperor Constantine's professed conversion to

---

3. See, for example, the discussion of this in David W. Hall & Joseph H. Hall, eds., *Paradigms in Polity: Classic Readings in Reformed and Presbyterian Church Government* (Grand Rapids: William B. Eerdmans, 1994), 5–6, 56–57, 80–82.

Christianity in AD 312 and Christianity became the official religion of the Roman empire, the office of bishop became a much more political and administrative office than it had been in the early church. Before Constantine's conversion, bishops tended to derive their authority from the fact that they preserved the true doctrine of the apostles as taught in God's word. After Constantine, bishops tended to see their authority arising from the office itself. It was not the continuity of the doctrine, but the continuity of the office which now mattered. This explains the Roman Catholic church's stress upon apostolic succession—an unbroken line of popes supposedly going all the way back to Peter. This is why Calvin and the Reformed churches reject apostolic succession, emphasizing instead the continuity of apostolic doctrine from the time of the writing of the New Testament to today.[4] Although the apostles disappeared, their doctrine did not. As Calvin so succinctly put it, "Wherein does [apostolic] Succession consist, if it be not in perpetuity of doctrine?"[5] This apostolic teaching is what prophets are to proclaim and what teachers are to make plain.

Prophets have nothing to do with Nostradamus. They do not predict the future. Biblically speaking, prophets are those men called to proclaim God's word (ministers), and are divinely enabled by the Holy Spirit to find Christ in the various books of the Old Testament. They were also enabled by the Spirit to proclaim the message of Christ crucified with a supernatural boldness, often times in the face of those who are hostile to Christianity. Recall that this was an age with no history of Christian reflection upon the events of the Old Testament. The canon of the New Testament was not yet completed, so there was a need

---

4. Hall and Hall, *Paradigms in Polity*, 5–11;

5. John Calvin, "The True Method of Giving Peace to Christendom and Reforming the Church," in *Selected Works of John Calvin: Tracts and Letters*, eds. Henry Beveridge and Jules Bonnet, Vol. 3, reprint edition (Grand Rapids: Baker Book House, 1983), 265.

Earnestly Desire the Higher Gifts

for the Holy Spirit to equip apostolic preachers to understand how Christ fulfilled the promises found in the Old Testament. The office of teacher is closely related to that of prophet, and more than likely refers to those engaged in catechesis (instruction in doctrine and refuting the claims of heretics and pagans), rather than proclamation. This difference is illustrated in the different ministries of Paul (with the gift of prophecy) and Apollos (the capable teacher).

From this point on in his discussion, Paul begins to speak of particular gifts of the Spirit, rather than the people who have these gifts, as he moves from a list of offices to particular gifts. Paul speaks of miracles and healings (which are fairly clear as to their meaning), before speaking of those with spiritual gifts which equip Christians to help others ("helping" in the sense of showing great compassion), as well as those who are able to administer (*kybernēseis*) the affairs of the church, a word which refers to someone who pilots a ship. What precise form, exactly, these gifts took in the Corinthian church remains a bit mysterious.

When he mentions apostles, Paul may have been speaking of those apostles who had visited Corinth (himself and Peter). When he mentions prophets, Paul may be referring to the prophets who preached in Corinth or those elders who taught them (like Apollos). When he mentions helps and administration, he may be referring to the unnamed men who served as deacons and to those who governed the church. In other words, Paul might have been speaking of the actual church officers who served in the church of Corinth, people whose names are now lost to us. In any case, the gift of tongues—which was causing the Corinthians so much grief—is clearly at the tail-end of Paul's list for a reason. As Paul states in 1 Corinthians 14:19, "In church I would rather speak five words with my mind in order to instruct others, than ten thousand words in a tongue."

God distributes these gifts as he wills, a point which is now hammered home through Paul's use of a series of rhetorical questions (a favorite technique of Paul's). In verses 29–30, Paul asks, "Are all apostles? Are all prophets? Are all teachers? Do all work miracles? Do all possess gifts of healing? Do all speak with tongues? Do all interpret?" The obvious answer to all of these questions is "No." These gifts of the Spirit are distributed to various individuals throughout the body for the greater good of the whole. While it appears from Paul's questions that all Christians receive at least one spiritual gift, his questions also make it clear that no one Christian receives all of the gifts of the Spirit. Everyone and their different gifts contributes to the well-being of the whole.

Seek the Greater Gifts

While Paul has repeatedly made the point that all gifts (even the lesser gifts) are essential to the well-being of the church, in verse 31, Paul exhorts the Corinthians to seek the greater gifts. At the same time he directs them beyond their preoccupation with spiritual gifts to something more far important. "But earnestly desire the higher gifts. And I will show you a still more excellent way." At first glance, this may appear to contradict what Paul has been repeatedly affirming throughout this section, that even the lesser (more mundane) gifts are essential to the well-being of the body as a whole. Now he says "earnestly seek the greater gifts." What does this exhortation mean?

It is not at all inconsistent for Paul to encourage the Corinthians to desire the greater gifts, given a proper understanding of spiritual gifts. God gives these gifts as he sees fit, and all of the gifts of the Spirit are essential to the well-being of Christ's church. Since these gifts enable us to serve one another in love, we should desire them, especially the greater ones. The desire for them reflects an internal call—that we desire to use our gifts

Earnestly Desire the Higher Gifts

for the service of others in Christ's church, and we are willing to receive whatever gift that God has for us because these gifts build up the body.

The temptation to misunderstand Paul's exhortation to seek the greater gifts—as though these gifts elevated those who have them to the category of spiritual elite—is also mitigated by what follows. Yes, Paul says, we should desire the higher gifts. But there is something far more important than seeking spiritual gifts, and that is love for one another within the body of Christ. "And I will show you a still more excellent way." The excellent way is spelled out in some detail in chapter 13, Paul's famous discussion of Christian love. This more excellent way ought to be the desire of everyone in the Corinthian congregation concerned with spiritual things. It should also be the desire of everyone who confesses that "Jesus is Lord."

Just as we have seen earlier in the chapter, Paul's "more excellent way" resounds with echoes from the prophecy of Isaiah, in which the prophet speaks of the blessings given by God's Spirit in the messianic age. Speaking through the prophet Isaiah (48:15–17), YHWH declares,

> "I, even I, have spoken and called him; I have brought him, and he will prosper in his way. Draw near to me, hear this: from the beginning I have not spoken in secret, from the time it came to be I have been there. And now the Lord God has sent me, and his Spirit. Thus says the Lord, your Redeemer, the Holy One of Israel: 'I am the Lord your God, who teaches you to profit, who leads you in the way you should go.'"

In chapter 13, Paul explains how the Lord led us in the way we should go—that more excellent way hinted at by the prophets. That more excellent way is to focus upon the love that we are to have for our brothers and sisters—a love which the Holy Spirit creates in our hearts.

First Corinthians

There are several things which we should carefully consider based upon Paul's exhortation to earnestly desire the higher gifts. First, Paul's exhortation only makes sense if we completely reject the pagan notion so typical of first century Greek religion (and of our own age) that there were spiritual elites who have access to all kinds of secret and esoteric information—the secret things which only the truly spiritual can grasp. Paul has refuted this notion by reminding the Corinthians that God gives the gifts of the Holy Spirit to every member of the church as he wills. The proper use of these gifts is for the common good, and to build up the body of Christ. There is nothing secret about them. These gifts are to be used in the day-to-day life of the church, in the service of their fellow members. The saints manifest these gifts each Lord's Day as the church assembles together. Think of all the labor and service that goes on in your church on any given Sunday! But the saints also manifest these gifts throughout the week in their service and care of others, or in their witness to their non-Christian friends and neighbors.

Paul is not telling us to seek these gifts so that we can start our own ministries and then attract a group of devoted followers. Paul is telling us to desire spiritual gifts for use in the church (especially the higher gifts) because this strengthens the body of Christ (the church).

We also need to remove from our thinking the idea that should God give us one of these "greater" gifts, the Holy Spirit will embarrass us by making us do something in public that we would not even think to do in private. Sadly, we may have witnessed people "laughing in the Spirit," people being "slain in the Spirit," people who claim to be "drunk" in the Spirit and so on. Understandably, after seeing such abuses we run the other way. But if the greater gifts are given to us by God for the common good and for the building up of the body, then we need not ignore them or fear them because abuses exist. Paul tells us to

Earnestly Desire the Higher Gifts

desire these higher gifts and exercise them as we see being done in the churches of the New Testament.

The stronger our members, the stronger our churches. The stronger our churches the greater our ability to identify pagan ways of thinking and doing, and the greater our resistance to heresy and schism, and the greater our ability to love one another. The stronger the church, the greater our ability to understand the gospel and the sufficiency of Jesus' death for all our sins, as well as the glories of his perfect righteousness which enables us to stand before God.

It certainly helps to keep before us the connection Paul makes between various offices and the gifts of the Spirit which are associated with these offices. Acknowledging this connection goes a long way in preventing the false teaching and the disruptive focus upon certain charismatic individuals who claim to exercise these gifts, but who use them for their own personal gain. Apostles are not around today, which explains why miracles and healings are not normative in established churches. Apostles established the first churches, miracles confirmed the truth of the gospel when it was preached, but then the apostles ordained ministers, elders, and deacons in those churches, and once established, the ordinary means of grace (preaching and sacraments) became normative. In our day, the Holy Spirit works in our midst through the preached word and the administration of the sacraments.

Therefore, when Paul tells the church in Corinth to "earnestly desire the higher gifts," he is actually exhorting us to see if we have an internal call within our hearts to serve in Christ's church. This refers to established church offices (desiring to be a minister, elder, or deacon), but is certainly not limited to these offices. In fact, the internal call is a simple thing. Do you see something that needs to be done, which you desire to do and which you are capable of doing? Then let one of your elders or pastors know of your calling, so that your internal call can be tested in the church (the external call), and so that your gifts can be exercised in such a way to strengthen the whole body.

This is why we all should earnestly desire the higher gifts for the good of our churches. Let us seek that more excellent way, so that if our churches are known for anything, it is our focus upon God's love for us in Christ and our love for each other. This is why we should earnestly desire the higher gifts.

25

The Greatest of These is Love

1 CORINTHIANS: 13:1–13

Love is patient and kind; love does not envy or boast; it is not arrogant or rude. It does not insist on its own way; it is not irritable or resentful; it does not rejoice at wrongdoing, but rejoices with the truth. Love bears all things, believes all things, hopes all things, endures all things.

What the Bible says about love, and the way most Americans think about love, are often two different things. Our culture thinks of love as essentially an emotional feeling, most often associated with romance. Pop culture's images of the hearts and cupids of Valentine's Day are ingrained in us from an early age. For those of us who grew up in the sixties and seventies, love is often tied to a utopian dream when people experience a powerful sense of brotherhood and unity. Remember Woodstock? Three days of peace and love?

Sadly, these contemporary images are far afield from the biblical meaning of love, which, as we will see, is an emotion which issues forth in action, and which arises neither from those romantic or sentimental images with which we are all-too familiar. The biblical understanding of love is tied to the good news of the gospel: the blood of Jesus Christ, shed on a Roman cross, redeems sinful people who are anything but worthy of the love God showers upon us in Christ's work of redemption. When the Bible speaks of love, we need to remove images of cupid's arrows, and reflect upon biblical texts like John 3:16. "For God so loved the world, that he gave his only Son, that whoever believes in him should not perish but have eternal life."

Chapter 13 of 1 Corinthians is one of the most familiar passages in all the Bible. As Gordon Fee notes, "This is one of the most beloved passages in the New Testament, and for good reason. It is one of Paul's finest moments: indeed, let the interpreter beware lest too much analysis detract from its sheer beauty and power."[1]

Love: The More Excellent Way

We have already noted that the church in Corinth was plagued by division and factions. This church was composed of new Christians who were struggling to leave their pagan ways of thinking and doing behind. When they asked Paul about the role and purpose of speaking in tongues—something which apparently was a source of ongoing division within the church—Paul answers their question in chapters 12–14. In the opening verses of chapter 12, Paul makes an important distinction between spiritual things (*pneumatikon*) and spiritual gifts (*charismata*), of which tongue-speaking was the least. According to Paul, you cannot properly understand spiritual gifts unless you first understand spiritual things. And you cannot understand spiritual things unless you confess that Jesus is Lord—Jesus is the only Savior from sin, the creator of all things, and whose death upon the cross takes away the wrath of God toward sinners. The cross is the picture of that love of which Paul now speaks.

---

1. Fee, *The First Epistle to the Corinthians*, 626.

The Greatest of These is Love

To make his case that all Christians are members of the spiritual body of Christ (the church) and are given gifts of the Spirit for the common good, Paul uses the metaphor of the human body. Every believer in Jesus Christ is a member of Christ's body (the church). Although not all members of Christ's body serve the same function (just as eyes are not toes), each member of that body is essential to the health and well-being of the whole. This is why Paul ties various gifts of the Spirit to the offices of the church before exhorting Christians to earnestly desire the higher gifts, so that the Corinthians will be stronger and better able to resist the temptations of their pagan past, as well as the sinful tendency to put our own interests ahead of others. At the end of chapter twelve Paul writes "but earnestly desire the higher gifts. And I will show you a still more excellent way."

This more excellent way is the way of love, the subject of chapter 13. While some have argued that chapter 13 is a digression from Paul's answer to the Corinthians' question, this is not the case. Throughout Paul's letters, whenever the apostle addresses the subject of gifts of the Spirit, he connects spiritual gifts to love for our brothers and sisters in Christ. Galatians 5:22 comes to mind, because in that passage Paul lists love as the first of the fruit of the Spirit. It is also worth considering that the word for love (*agape*) was not widely used before the New Testament era, yet the word *agape* is used 116 times in the New Testament. Paul uses the term 75 times, making *agape* the characteristic Pauline and Christian word for love. This is not a digression because *agape* is the more excellent way!

The problem we face today is that *agape* has a much different meaning in the New Testament than contemporary pop culture assigns to the word "love." According to Morris:

> Christians thought of love as that quality we see on the cross. It is a love for the utterly unworthy, a love that proceeds from a God who is love. It is a love

> lavished on others without a thought whether they are worthy or not. It proceeds from the nature of the lover, not from any attractiveness in the beloved. The Christian who has experienced God's love for him while he was yet a sinner (Romans 5:8) has been transformed by the experience. Now he sees people as those for whom Christ died, the objects of God's love and therefore the objects of the love of God's people. In his measure he comes to practice the love that seeks nothing for itself, but only the good of the loved one. It is this love that the apostle unfolds.[2]

Christ's love for sinners is the perfect picture of the love that believers are to have for each other. It is that which God requires of us in terms of loving our neighbor as required by God in his law, as we see, for example, in Leviticus 19:9–18. In order to truly understand the meaning of *agape*, we must look to the cross of Christ, as Paul himself directs us. "God shows his love for us in that while we were still sinners, Christ died for us" (Rom. 5:8). John makes a similar reference. "In this is love, not that we have loved God but that he loved us and sent his Son to be the propitiation for our sins" (1 John 4:10). Paul's point is that because *agape* refers to God's love for sinners, in turn, Christians are to demonstrate *agape* toward each other. *Agape* is not to be confused with *eros* (romantic love) or *philia* (brotherly love). *Agape* is the holy God's love for sinners like us, who can do nothing to earn God's love, and who are utterly unworthy of the love we receive.

Love and Spiritual Gifts

There is a long history of Christians using these verses out of context (because of their obvious beauty), sadly ignoring the obvious link Paul has drawn between the gifts of the Spirt, and love for our brothers and sisters earlier in this epistle. Although

---

2. Morris, *1 Corinthians*, 177.

The Greatest of These is Love

we often hear these verses read at Christian weddings, it is oftentimes based upon a confusion of *agape* with *eros* (romantic love). But at this point in his letter to the Corinthians, Paul is not talking about sentimental feelings or romance. Paul is talking about that love Christians are to have for each other because such love is not only the fruit of the Holy Spirit, but such love must govern all use of gifts of the Holy Spirit, including the gift of tongues.

Paul does not want people to stop using the gifts of the Holy Spirit, nor does he wish to depreciate their importance. But he does want a church divided by factions to be re-unified through a proper use and understanding of these gifts, since love for the fellow members of Christ's spiritual body (the church) is the ultimate purpose of the gifts of the Spirit.

Beginning in verse 1 of chapter 13, Paul makes his point using three conditional sentences (which begin with "if"), and which should have a sobering effect upon the Corinthians. Paul tackles the most divisive issue associated with spiritual gifts first (i.e., the speaking in tongues). "If I speak in the tongues of men and of angels, but have not love, I am a noisy gong or a clanging cymbal." While the phrase, "tongues of men and angels" may be a reference to the gift of tongues, the expression is broad enough to refer to speech in general, i.e., "the eloquence of men or of angels."[3]

Pentecostals often contend that Paul's reference to "tongues of angels" is proof that the gift of tongues entails speaking some kind of a heavenly language unknown by the speaker (i.e., the "tongues of angels," the language angels use to speak to one another). I am not convinced that this is Paul's point. According to Acts 2:6ff., people heard the gospel proclaimed in their own language (Greek) on the Day of Pentecost. Greek was widely spoken in all of the regions listed in Acts 2:7–11. Despite the

---
3. Morris, *1 Corinthians*, 177.

fact that there were diverse ethnic groups present in Jerusalem on Pentecost (each with their own local dialects) Peter's Acts 2 sermon was not interpreted by someone with the gift of doing so—which means Peter preached in Greek, the *lingua franca* of the time.[4] I take Paul's point here to be something much more mundane, yet quite relevant to his argument. He is not informing us that tongue-speakers literally speak the language of angels (i.e., a "heavenly language"), rather that no conceivable spoken language (whether human or angelic) eliminates the necessity of love for our brothers and sisters in Christ.

The issue at hand is that the Corinthians were used to being mesmerized by eloquent speech with flowery words. The Corinthians were unhappy with Paul, apparently, because the apostle was not a very captivating speaker. And yet, people who are eloquent in speech (perhaps some of those who were causing schism in the church) but who do not practice love, are nothing but noise-makers. Paul compares them (and himself, if he too does not practice love) to a noisy gong (literally "bronze vases" used for amplification in large buildings at the time), or a loud cymbal. According to God's Word, eloquent speech in any language, without love, is nothing but noise.

There is also every likelihood that there is a cultural reference here which goes beyond the making of noise. Although the Jews used cymbals in worship, cymbals and gongs may have been part of the temple worship practiced by Greek pagans, especially among the followers of Dionysus and Cybele.[5] Paul may be saying something like "words without action are as useless as the stuff that goes on at the local pagan temple." The gifts of the Spirit (including tongues) are given by God for service in

---

4. Robert Zerhusen, "A New Look at Tongues: A Linguistic Approach to Understanding Other Tongues in Acts 2," posted on the Alliance of Confessing Evangelicals, acessed Feb. 20, 2013. http://www.alliancenet.org/cc/article/0,,PTID307086_CHID560462_CIID1415640,00.html

5. Cf. Keener, *The IVP Bible Background Commentary*, 479.

The Greatest of These is Love

the church which is supposed to manifest itself in concrete acts of love for fellow Christians. Discussing the gifts of the Spirit, such as speaking in tongues, apart from the biblical connection to love for our brothers and sisters, risks distorting our understanding of any spiritual gift's true purpose.

Without Love, We Are Nothing

In verse 2, Paul continues this same line of thinking. "And if I have prophetic powers, and understand all mysteries and all knowledge, and if I have all faith, so as to remove mountains, but have not love, I am nothing." Continuing to correct non-Christian ways of thinking and doing, still widely-held and practiced by the Corinthian Christians, Paul takes aim at another Corinthian sacred cow, "knowledge." Yet before addressing the Corinthian misconception of knowledge, Paul first speaks of prophecy. Recall that in 1 Corinthians 12:10, Paul has mentioned that prophecy is ranked just below the office of apostle. Paul regards prophecy (preaching) very highly. Even the gift of prophecy, if not exercised in love, also amounts to nothing.

The same is true for understanding "mysteries" (Spirit-given insight into the things of Christ) apart from love. It amounts to nothing. The same holds true for knowledge. If a Christian has great faith but has not love, they are nothing. Even the possession of the greater spiritual gifts mentioned by Paul does not amount to anything in terms of personal status *if* the person who possesses these gifts does not manifest love for the other members of Christ's body. Without love for our brothers and sisters, we are nothing, no matter how many gifts of the Spirit we have been given.

Once again, Paul has turned the non-Christian concept of these things on its head. The purpose of spiritual gifts is not for the benefit, enjoyment, or status of the one who has given them. Gifts of the Spirit are given to us so that we might truly love one another and truly serve one another in love. Love is the prime fruit of the Spirit, and the presence of love among believers in the church is the proof that the gifts of the Spirit are operating in the church. If the gifts of the Spirit are being used properly, believers will love one another, just as various parts of the body work together as one. Paul even goes on to say in verse 3, "If I give away all I have, and if I deliver up my body to be burned, but have not love, I gain nothing." Even the person who sells all he has and gives it to the poor, but does not do it out of love, gains nothing. That one who voluntarily sacrifices himself in a spectacular fashion, but lacks love, gains nothing.

The Characteristics of *Agape*

For Paul, then, the gifts of the Spirit cannot be properly understood apart from their ultimate purpose. This, I think, gives us good reason to argue that the primary purpose of the gifts of the Spirit (from the greater gifts to the least) is to equip the members of the body of Christ (the church) so that we love one another. But all of this begs the question: "What are the characteristics of the kind of love of which Paul has been speaking?" These characteristics are now enumerated in verses 4–7 in familiar words which require little comment. "Love is patient and kind; love does not envy or boast; it is not arrogant or rude. It does not insist on its own way; it is not irritable or resentful; it does not rejoice at wrongdoing, but rejoices with the truth. Love bears all things, believes all things, hopes all things, endures all things."

The word for "patience" (*makrothymei*) is the opposite of being short-tempered. As used here, patience is directed to people, not circumstances. The next word, "kind" (*chrēsteuetai*), is used only one time in the entire New Testament (here). The word reinforces the idea that the work of the Spirit is to enable us to serve one another, since love is kind, or good, in re-

The Greatest of These is Love

sponse to those who treat us improperly. The love of which Paul speaks is not displeased with the success of others. Love is not a wind-bag (the literal meaning of the word translated "boast"—*perpereuetai*), nor is love proud, seeking to exalt oneself at the expense of others. Love keeps the needs and well-being of others firmly in mind. The word translated "rude" *(aschēmonei)* is taken from a word which means "proper form" (*schema*). Love does not act out of form, that is, contrary to its self-effacing nature. This calls to mind the example of our Lord as recounted by Paul in Philippians 2:5–11:

> Have this mind among yourselves, which is yours in Christ Jesus, who, though he was in the form of God, did not count equality with God a thing to be grasped, but emptied himself, by taking the form of a servant, being born in the likeness of men. And being found in human form, he humbled himself by becoming obedient to the point of death, even death on a cross. Therefore God has highly exalted him and bestowed on him the name that is above every name, so that at the name of Jesus every knee should bow, in heaven and on earth and under the earth, and every tongue confess that Jesus Christ is Lord, to the glory of God the Father.

Love does not seek its own way. Love is not easily angered. This is a reference to a self-righteous and sinful response to our neighbors, since anger is not necessarily a sin. In Ephesians 4:26, for example, Paul writes, "Be angry and do not sin." As Karl Barth once put it, "My neighbor can get dreadfully on my nerves even in what he regards as, and what may well be, his particular gifts. . . . Love cannot alter the fact that he gets on my nerves, but . . . it can rule out . . . my allowing myself to be 'provoked' by him."[6] Love does not keep a list of wrongs which

---

6. Karl Barth, *Church Dogmatics* (Edinburgh: T & T Clark, 1958), IV.2.834.

are eventually to be righted. Love does not delight in the sins and misfortunes of others, and this is one place where our bent toward sin almost inevitably surfaces. Love rejoices in the truth. And love speaks the truth, even when the truth hurts.

In verse 7, Paul lists some of the positive aspects of love—what love is, as opposed to what it is not. Love *always* bears, believes, hopes, endures. Love does not easily give up and circumstances do not allow it to change. Love protects (literally "covers"), in the sense of keeping things safe from public scrutiny. Love trusts, although it is not gullible. Love gives the benefit of doubt. Love hopes. Love is eschatological in the sense that it is forward looking, viewing things from God's eternal perspective, not merely through temporal circumstances. When Paul says that love perseveres, he means that love is steadfast and does not easily give up. Love will remain when everything else is gone.

The Abiding Character of Love

Throughout this discussion, Paul is continuing to give instructions about the true nature of spiritual gifts (to equip us for service and enable us to love one another), so as to place the Corinthians' preoccupation with the gift of tongues in the broader context of love of neighbor. Love has an abiding quality, because it is characteristic of Christians not only in this age, but also in the age to come where perfect love is finally manifest. The *charismata* are manifest only in "this present age" because of their equipping function. It is not that the *charismata* are unimportant. Let us not forget that Paul exhorts Christians to earnestly desire spiritual gifts precisely because they are so important to our present existence. But spiritual gifts are not permanent. Love is. This becomes clear in verse 8 when Paul points out that "love never ends. As for prophecies, they will pass away; as for tongues, they will cease; as for knowledge, it will pass away."

The Greatest of These is Love

As Paul understands the nature of love, its character abides—it will not fail (in the sense of collapsing). Love will abide both in this age and the age to come, while the *charismata* will not. At some future point then (i.e., "when the perfect comes," v. 10), prophecy, tongues, and knowledge will cease to exercise this equipping function characteristic of these spiritual gifts. Like this present evil age, the *charismata* will cease when the age to come is fully realized, when Jesus comes back to judge the world, raise the dead, and make all things new.

The transient nature of the gifts just mentioned is set forth in verses 9–10 when Paul states, "For we know in part and we prophesy in part, but when the perfect comes, the partial will pass away." While the meaning of Paul's assertion about the perfect coming is often disputed ("Is Paul telling us that these spiritual gifts cease when the canon of Scripture is completed? Or do these gifts cease when Jesus returns?"), Paul's comments make much sense in light of the already/not yet distinction he has already put before the Corinthians (cf. 1 Cor. 10:11).

In order to correct the misconceptions among the Corinthians, many of whom were enamored by the gifts of the Spirit for all the wrong reasons, it was important for Paul to point out that the very gifts which the Corinthians valued so highly were not of the same character as love. Love will remain, while prophecy, tongues, and knowledge will have no role once Jesus Christ returns at the end of the age. The word "perfect" (v. 10) is the Greek word *(teleion)* which refers to the predestined aim or end decreed by God. There is little doubt that Paul is referring to the second coming of Jesus Christ, and to the end of the age when he speaks of the perfect arriving.[7] In the presence of God, we will no longer need prophecy, the gift of tongues, or of Spirit-given knowledge. These things will pass away when this evil age passes away. They will no longer be needed.

---

7. Gaffin, *Perspectives on Pentecost*, 109.

Even through the means of divinely-given speech (prophecy) God does not reveal everything to us, since there are a number of things associated with the "not yet," which remain beyond our comprehension. But when we reach the end (when God brings all things to their divinely-appointed goal), at that time knowledge and prophecy will cease. These things will no longer be needed when we see things from God's perspective (i.e., "the age to come"), the point of the following verses.

Becoming Mature

Paul moves on to speak of maturity. The Corinthian church must grow up so as to see the purpose of spiritual gifts correctly. This means understanding that the exercise of love is of far more importance to Christian maturity (because it abides) than the gifts of knowledge, prophecy, and tongues (which will not). In verses 11–13, Paul employs yet another illustration. "When I was a child, I spoke like a child, I thought like a child, I reasoned like a child. When I became a man, I gave up childish ways. For now we see in a mirror dimly, but then face to face. Now I know in part; then I shall know fully, even as I have been fully known. So now faith, hope, and love abide, these three; but the greatest of these is love."

Children grow up and adults no longer think and act like children (or at least are not supposed to). While this is a process with an indiscernible time frame, the perfect tense points to the fact of a definitive break with our childish past ("when I *was*"). At some point, we become adults. We stop behaving as children. Paul's point is that the body of Christ will one day mature to the point where spiritual gifts are no longer needed—the gifts just mentioned will pass away, even as our childhoods do. To connect this maturity to the close of the apostolic era is a bit problematic, because Paul connects this to a time when we see face to face, when Christ returns. But there is no doubt that

The Greatest of These is Love

Paul's comment about childhood is a pointed reminder that it is time for the Corinthians to grow up. It is equally important that we grow up and leave behind those childish things which draw our attention away from Christ and his gospel. We must move beyond an immature preoccupation with ourselves (as children are apt to do), and learn to consider that love for and service of others is God's purpose behind all spiritual gifts. These gifts are not given to demonstrate how "spiritual" I am, but to enable me to serve others (especially my brothers and sisters in Christ) for the common good.

Paul's reference to seeing things poorly in the present is a reference to the fact that we live in this present evil age, awaiting the coming of the perfect and the age to come. Until Jesus Christ returns, at best we see things dimly, as a faint reflection of those glories which are to come. When the age to come dawns in its fullness when Jesus comes back, then we will indeed see face to face. The mirror metaphor makes perfect sense in the already/not yet eschatological categories used by Paul. In that day, we will not only know as we ought (the theology of pilgrims becomes the theology of the blessed—a long-standing theme in Reformed theology),[8] but we will be truly known (a knowledge which God has of us even now). Over against those things which pass away (prophecy, tongues, and knowledge), some things will remain, faith, hope, and love (all fruit of the Spirit). While all these things abide even now, love is the greatest of them all, the most excellent way and the distinguishing characteristic of the glorious age to come.

Paul's exhortation to the Corinthians to "grow up" and move on to maturity applies to Christians across the ages every bit as much as it did to the Corinthians of the first century. The Corinthians were fighting over how to exercise the gift of

---

8. Richard A. Muller, *Post-Reformation Reformed Dogmatics: Prolegomena to Theology*, vol. 1, 2nd ed. (Grand Rapids: Baker Academic, 2003), 259ff.

tongues during worship (ironically, the least of the gifts), and in the process were tearing the church apart. We too need to act like adults and not be so prone to belittle others through our speech and actions. In my estimation, the primary sin of Christians in our Reformed tradition is pride—we are convinced we are right about doctrine, so everyone else is looked upon condescendingly. We may be right about our doctrine, but we cannot forget Paul's words (also a doctrine!) to the effect that if we have not love for our brothers and sisters (even when we think them wrong), we are nothing but windbags and noisy gongs.

Paul's emphasis upon love for our brothers and sisters also reminds us that when biblically understood, love is not some vague feeling of unity or brotherhood. We must not confuse *agape* with *eros* or *philia*. *Agape* is not tied to cupid's arrows or Valentine's hearts. Love (*agape*) sees others—equally unworthy as we are—as redeemed by the blood of Christ. Because of this, love acts when we have brothers and sisters in need. Love empathizes with those who weep, mourn, and suffer. Love cooks food, provides meals, cleans house, visits the sick, makes phone calls, and sends cards of encouragement. Love prays for those in need, gives money to the deacons to help those in dire straits, and love places the interests of others above itself. Love is a fruit of the Spirit, and love should be the end result of God giving gifts of the Spirit to the church. According to Paul, any biblically sound discussion of gifts of the Spirit, must lead to the consideration that God gives these gifts to the church to enable us to love one another, even as Christ has loved us.

The best way to love our brothers and sisters as God commands of us, is to look to the cross, where Jesus died for all of my sins, including all those times I have failed to love my brothers and sisters in Christ as God has commanded us. Whatever love I show to my neighbor is to mirror that love which God has shown to me in the shed blood and wounds of my crucified

The Greatest of These is Love

Savior (Rom 5:8–9; John 3:16; 1 John 4:10). Love for my neighbor can arise only when I behold the cross of Jesus Christ, and consider his death for my sins.

As Paul has made plain in this wonderful chapter, the gifts of the Spirit will cease when the perfect comes and we finally reach maturity. "Faith, hope, and love abide; but the greatest of these is love."

26

Strive to Excel in Building Up the Church

1 CORINTHIANS: 14:1–19

Pursue love, and earnestly desire the spiritual gifts, especially that you may prophesy. For one who speaks in a tongue speaks not to men but to God; for no one understands him, but he utters mysteries in the Spirit. On the other hand, the one who prophesies speaks to people for their upbuilding and encouragement and consolation. The one who speaks in a tongue builds up himself, but the one who prophesies builds up the church. Now I want you all to speak in tongues, but even more to prophesy. The one who prophesies is greater than the one who speaks in tongues, unless someone interprets, so that the church may be built up.

One of the most divisive theological controversies of my lifetime was the charismatic movement of the 1970s and 1980s and its emphasis upon speaking in tongues. Whenever the charismatic renewal spread to a new church, it immediately divided the church into two camps—those who experienced what they claimed was a new work of the Holy Spirit which manifested itself in speaking with tongues, and those who thought such a thing was demonic and who did everything in their power to stamp out the movement before it could spread. Thankfully, in many places, this heated controversy has long since died down. It amazes me that we are able to tackle this subject with much less controversy, when, not that long ago, this was considered a very controversial and divisive subject.

In 1 Corinthians 14, Paul discusses speaking in tongues and proper behavior in Christian worship. It is clear from the apostle's discussion that the Corinthians were greatly divided about the role and purpose of tongue-speaking in public worship, and in their letter to Paul they asked him about this very thing. Although we do not have their original letter to Paul, so we don't know what exactly the Corinthians asked him, we do know that it takes Paul three chapters to answer the Corinthians' question.

In the opening verses of chapter 12, Paul began his answer by addressing the Corinthians' faulty understanding of spiritual things (*pneumatikon*) before taking up a discussion of gifts of the Spirit (the *charismata*) in which Paul uses the metaphor of the human body as an illustration of the church of Jesus Christ. In chapter 13, Paul pointed out that love of our brothers and sisters is the context in which any discussion of spiritual gifts must take place.

Tongue-Speaking and Controversy in Corinth

In chapter 14, Paul turns his focus to the specifics of the controversy causing so much consternation among the Corinthians, speaking in tongues during worship. It is clear from Paul's response that certain individuals among the Corinthians who had the gift of tongues thought themselves to be superior to others in the church who did not have this gift. Once Paul has estab-

Strive to Excel in Building Up the Church

lished the proper categories to discuss such things ("spiritual things" and "spiritual gifts"), Paul proceeds to discuss the specifics of the controversy plaguing the Corinthians. The Corinthians' question and Paul's answer deals with the way in which Christians properly exercise the gift of tongues, so that this gift strengthens the body and is exercised in love. As Paul has reminded them in the preceding chapter, those who claim to be spiritual must demonstrate love for others, or else they demonstrate that they are nothing but windbags.

In light of the Corinthians' letter sent to Paul, we need to keep in mind that Paul is addressing a specific problem in the Corinthian church. Paul is not writing a systematic treatise on what Christians should include in worship and how they should proceed to conduct their services. Rather, the apostle is answering a specific question put to him in writing by the Corinthians. In his response to their question, Paul must steer between two perilous shoals. On the one hand, Paul must confirm that tongues is a legitimate spiritual gift which has an appropriate function in the church. We should not see Paul as condemning tongue-speaking with faint praise when he says it is the least of the spiritual gifts.[1] On the other hand, Paul must also demonstrate that tongues is inferior to the gift of prophecy, and that what is important is that the entire congregation be edified, not divided, because love is the more excellent way. Love will abide long after spiritual gifts have passed away.

If love was the theme of chapter 13, the overarching theme of chapter 14 is the building up of the church, which is the reason why spiritual gifts are given to the church. In verses 1–5 of chapter 14, Paul continues his theme that love is paramount, and that Christians are to eagerly desire the greater spiritual gifts. This latter point is an important corrective to those Corinthians who regarded tongue-speaking as the greatest of gifts.

---

1. Hays, *First Corinthians*, 234.

Those tongue-speakers who thought of this gift out of proportion with its true significance, need to be reminded that this gift is inferior to prophecy.

In verse 1, Paul exhorts the Corinthians, "Pursue love, and earnestly desire the spiritual gifts, especially that you may prophesy." Literally, Paul says "pursue love without stopping." Paul also exhorts the Corinthians to eagerly desire "spiritual gifts." But the first gift on Paul's list is not tongues, but prophecy (Spirit-inspired utterance or "preaching"). This statement is clearly a gentle rebuke of those who thought too highly of themselves because they spoke in tongues. What gift should the Corinthians desire? Prophecy.

The reason why tongue-speaking is inferior to prophecy is that tongue-speaking is unintelligible to the congregation as a whole. In verse 2, Paul reminds the Corinthians, "For one who speaks in a tongue speaks not to men but to God; for no one understands him, but he utters mysteries in the Spirit." The one who speaks in a tongue is not speaking to others, but to God, since no one else in the congregation understands them. The tongue-speaker utters mysteries—things other people could not know unless God reveals them.

What Is "Speaking in Tongues"?

The critical issue to be addressed before we go any farther is this one: "What is the gift of tongues of which Paul is speaking?" Several answers have been proposed. The so-called "traditional view" is that tongues refers to known languages which are unknown to the speaker. The Holy Spirit supernaturally enables someone to speak a human language they do not know. The so-called "charismatic view" adds an element to the traditional view when it is argued that the gift of tongues is either a known language *or* a heavenly language (i.e., the tongues of angels mentioned in 1 Corinthians 13:1), which the speaker does not know. In this understanding, the Spirit enables someone to speak a human language they do not know, or else enables them to speak in a heavenly language. A third view, which I am calling the "alternative" view (and the view which I hold), contends that tongues refers to a known language (a local dialect) which the speaker knows, but the congregation does not (i.e., "someone's native language").

The traditional view is capably set forth by Leon Morris, who believes that this statement from Paul ("no one understands him") means that the gift of tongues operating in 1 Corinthians 14 is different from that in Acts 2 where the audience "understood the tongue." This, it seems to me, is one of the great weaknesses of both the traditional and charismatic views. But this is one of the strengths of the alternative view I am proposing, which contends that speaking in tongues refers to speaking in a language which the speaker himself knows (but others do not), and which, if not translated, does not edify the entire congregation.[2] According to the alternative view, the tongues of Acts 2 and 1 Corinthians 14 are the same thing—the speaker knows the language he is speaking. In Acts 2, everyone in the audience understood Greek, which is why the tongue spoken by Peter is not interpreted. Likewise, in 1 Corinthians 14, the tongue-speaker is speaking his native dialect. If not translated into Greek (through the gift of "interpretation" or "translation"), people who do not speak the speaker's native language cannot possibly understand him and be edified by what is said.

The Superiority of Prophecy

The superiority of prophecy derives from the fact that it is intelligible. Because such prophecy is understood by the people in the congregation, this gift strengthens, encourages, and com-

---

2. Robert Zerhusen, "A New Look at Tongues," originally published in *Biblical Theology Journal* (1996) Vol. 26, and "The Problem of Tongues in 1 Corinthians 14" which is also published in *Biblical Theology Journal* (1997) Vol. 27. Both articles have been reprinted on the webpage of the Alliance of Confessing Evangelicals.

forts all those who hear it, unlike an untranslated tongue which people do not understand because it is spoken in a language they do not know. This is clearly the case in verses 3–4 where Paul states, "On the other hand, the one who prophesies speaks to people for their upbuilding and encouragement and consolation. The one who speaks in a tongue builds up himself, but the one who prophesies builds up the church."

As long as the tongue is not translated, the tongue-speaker is speaking only to himself. The speaker alone is edified because they alone understand what they are saying. Yet Paul specifically says that the one who prophesies (i.e., who gives a Spirit-inspired utterance about an Old Testament text, or some new word from the Lord) edifies the entire church, since the prophecy is intelligible to all. One argument in favor of the alternative view can be framed in the form of a question. "If the tongue is unknown to the speaker (i.e., a tongue of angels, or tongues as a heavenly language, or a known language unknown to the speaker), how is the speaker edified, if what he is speaking is unintelligible to him?"

In verse 5, Paul's words are an echo of Numbers 11:16–30. In light of that passage, the apostle offers his own perspective on speaking in tongues. "Now I want you all to speak in tongues, but even more to prophesy. The one who prophesies is greater than the one who speaks in tongues, unless someone interprets, so that the church may be built up." Paul does not in any sense depreciate the gift of tongues. The apostle wishes that all Christians possessed this gift, just as Moses wished that all the Israelites were prophets. Paul would rather see Christians prophesy because those who do so are greater than those who speak in tongues. The reason for this superiority is the intelligibility of prophesy in light of the lack of intelligibility of tongues. But if the tongue is interpreted (translated), it is now on par with prophecy. Why? Because people understand the tongue and it edifies the entire church, not just the tongue-speaker.

Strive to Excel in Building Up the Church

In verses 6–12, Paul argues that when tongues are spoken in worship they need to be understood by the congregation. The problem with tongues as currently practiced by the Corinthians is that they are unintelligible (and not being interpreted). When tongues were spoken and not interpreted, this caused great disruption in the church. Whether the speaker knows the language of the tongue or not, the issue causing so much consternation is that the members of the church do not understand what the tongue-speaker is saying and mass confusion is the result.

The nature of the problem is described in verse 6. "Now, brothers, if I come to you speaking in tongues, how will I benefit you unless I bring you some revelation or knowledge or prophecy or teaching?" Once again, despite the rebuke, Paul speaks to the Corinthians with great affection, calling them "brothers." Whether Paul is speaking in this verse of an anticipated future visit, or whether he is offering yet another rhetorical question (typical of Paul's letters) is not clear. If Paul comes to Corinth and speaks in tongues, what good will it be? None. But if Paul comes and brings some revelation, word of knowledge, prophecy, or word of instruction (catechesis) then the church will be edified. Why? Because these things are all intelligible, while tongues are not (unless interpreted or translated).

Paul uses several analogies to make his point about the importance of intelligibility in verses 7 and 8. "If even lifeless instruments, such as the flute or the harp, do not give distinct notes, how will anyone know what is played? And if the bugle gives an indistinct sound, who will get ready for battle?" Again, if the bugle does not sound a clear call and just makes noise, chaos results on the battlefield. If there is no discernible tune, then these instruments are nothing but useless noise makers. The same thing holds true for the Corinthians. "So with yourselves, if with your tongue you utter speech that is not intelligible, how will anyone know what is said? For you will be speaking into the air." The tongue-speakers in Corinth are like flutes, harps, and trumpets making loud sounds, but not playing recognizable tunes. Even worse, they were certainly not playing the same tune at the same time! Unless a tongue is interpreted (or translated), no one will know what the speaker is saying, so the tongue-speaker is doing nothing more than speaking into the air, and chaos in the church is the result.

In verse 10, Paul makes mention of different languages. "There are doubtless many different languages in the world, and none is without meaning." While this verse is difficult to translate, Paul's point is very simple. There are many different languages in the world, but all of them have meaning to those who speak them. I understand Paul to be saying that the gift of tongues is not a heavenly or angelic language, but a known language which is therefore capable of translation.

The reason why unintelligibility is such a problem in the church is spelled out in verses 11. "But if I do not know the meaning of the language, I will be a foreigner to the speaker and the speaker a foreigner to me." Both the Greeks and Romans considered people they could not understand to be "barbarians" (foreigners). We know that as a merchant seaport, Corinth would be home to many immigrants, transient laborers, and traders who did not speak Greek as their primary language, although virtually everyone engaged in commerce in that period had to know enough Greek or Latin to conduct business. This is the case with the Corinthian tongue-speakers. Unless their tongue is translated, those speaking are like foreigners. The language barrier must be overcome so that people are not treated like barbarians.

Strive to Build Up the Church

In verse 12, Paul zeroes in on the issue. "So with yourselves, since you are eager for manifestations of the Spirit, strive to excel in building up the church." Since this is the case with the Corin-

Strive to Excel in Building Up the Church

thians, and the tongue-speaking renders them as foreigners to each other, the Corinthians should continue to desire spiritual gifts as they have been doing, but they should especially desire those gifts which build up the church (i.e., the greater gifts such as prophecy). The problem is not too much zeal for these gifts, rather their lack of zeal. The Corinthians should be eager to use their spiritual gifts to build up the church. Instead, they are treating each other like foreigners because they cannot understand the tongue-speaker. In doing so, they are behaving like the pagans they once were.

On a practical level, what does it mean to desire the greater gifts so as to build each other up? Paul will explain this in verses 13–19. Because an untranslated tongue is unintelligible (and therefore unable to edify those who do not understand it), people who pray in tongues should likewise pray that they be able to interpret that tongue. In verse 13, Paul writes, "Therefore, one who speaks in a tongue should pray for the power to interpret." Admittedly, this verse is problematic for the alternative view which sees tongues as a language known to the tongue-speaker, but unknown to the congregation. Why would someone who understood the language he was speaking need to pray for the gift of interpretation?

This objection can be answered by observing how tongues were to be used in the churches.[3] There are three important considerations. First, according to the list of spiritual gifts in 1 Corinthians 12:28, not all of the gifts of the Spirit mentioned require a dramatic supernatural manifestation (e.g., gifts of administration and helping others). The translation (interpretation) of tongues does not necessarily require a miraculous ability. Yet someone with this gift (the ability to translate a local dialect into clear and intelligible Greek), would have been of

---

3. Robert Zerhusen, "The Problem of Tongues in 1 Corinthians 14" also published in *Biblical Theology Journal* (1997) Vol. 27, (no page number).

great value to the church in the edification of others. The same thing can be said of those who were capable administrators, and who had a knack for helping the poor.

Second, verse 28 provides, in part, an explanation of verse 13. If the tongue-speaker is competent in his own language as well as in Greek, then they should go ahead and interpret their own tongue, so that the entire church can be edified. If they are not competent to translate their own tongue into Greek, (that is, his Greek is not good enough) then the rule set forth by Paul in verse 28 applies: "But if there is no one to interpret, let each of them keep silent in church and speak to himself and to God." In the case in which the tongue-speaker is not competent in Greek, the tongue-speaker should pray to acquire the language skills needed to be able to translate his own tongue (language) into Greek.

Finally, if speaking in tongues is a miraculous ability, then the situation described in verse 28 theoretically should never occur. Are we really to believe that God gives the tongue-speaker the supernatural ability to speak a language he does not know, yet the Holy Spirit does not provide the church with someone able to interpret the tongue which the Spirit just uttered? That circumstance makes little sense, and is why I think the alternative view makes the best sense of all the issues raised in this passage.

In verses 14–15, Paul goes on to describe his own practice regarding speaking in tongues. "For if I pray in a tongue, my spirit prays but my mind is unfruitful. What am I to do? I will pray with my spirit, but I will pray with my mind also; I will sing praise with my spirit, but I will sing with my mind also." Up to this point, Paul has been speaking of the Corinthian situation, but he now speaks of his own personal practice. When Paul prays in a tongue his spirit prays, but his mind *(nous)* remains "unfruitful."

Strive to Excel in Building Up the Church

The importance of this assertion should not be overlooked, because Paul assigns a prominent role to the intellectual life of a Christian (i.e., "the mind"). Pentecostals and charismatics commonly argue that speaking in tongues is a good thing because by exercising this gift we bypass the mind (the rational) so that our spirits speak to God directly apart from human rationality (i.e., the mind and thought process gets in the way of direct communion with God). This view is certainly not in line with what Paul describes here, and is much more akin to that ancient proto-Gnosticism found at that time in cities such as Corinth. Paul desires to pray and sing with his spirit and mind on the same page. Prayer and worship are to be intellectual activities, with mind and heart focused upon the same things. Where the mind goes, the heart will follow.

At first glance, Paul's comments in verses 14–15 seem to mitigate against the alternative view I am setting forth. If Paul says that his mind is unfruitful (*akarpos*) when he sings, prays, or speaks in a tongue, how then can he understand the tongue he is speaking? As one writer has argued, it is a mistake to think of "unfruitful" as passive ("inactive"). Rather the term is active and has the sense that "my spirit prays but my mind does not produce fruit in others."[4] In other words, Paul says nothing about whether he himself understands the words, only that they do not bear fruit in others if they are not intelligible.

Giving Thanks and Saying "Amen!"

In verses 16–19, Paul turns to the actual Corinthian practice of tongue-speaking. In verse 16, Paul points out that, "If you give thanks with your spirit, how can anyone in the position of an outsider say 'Amen' to your thanksgiving when he does not know what you are saying?" The key to understanding this verse is the meaning of the word *idiotai* (i.e, one who does not

---

4. Zerhusen, "The Problem of Tongues in 1 Corinthians 14," n.p.

know). How can people give agreement (say "Amen") when they don't understand what is said? Some think of this as a reference to unbelievers who are in the midst of believers, but it is probably better to think of this as people who are new Christians or inquirers, and who do not yet fully understand what is going on (whether they be new converts or unbelievers going through the process of conversion).

Regardless of the nuances of the word, Paul is saying that those who do not understand the tongue (because it is unintelligible), will say "Amen," but they don't fully understand what is going on. This is because an untranslated (i.e., uninterpreted tongue) is unintelligible. Such people (believers or not) do not know what is going on, or understand what is being said, so they just say "Amen" like everyone else in the congregation is doing. Paul concludes, "For you may be giving thanks well enough, but the other person is not being built up" (v. 17).

If you give thanks for what God has done, so be it. But those who don't understand the tongue remain unedified. They are saying "amen" to something they do not fully understand—not a satisfactory circumstance. This is why Paul goes on to state in verses 18–19, "I thank God that I speak in tongues more than all of you. Nevertheless, in church I would rather speak five words with my mind in order to instruct others, than ten thousand words in a tongue." While the gift of tongues has a very important role to play, if a tongue is uninterpreted, no one in the church is edified.

Paul is thankful he speaks in tongues. According to the alternative view, this is a reference to Paul's private worship, or to his preaching the gospel and participating in worship in a number of contexts where Greek was not spoken. There is much evidence for this throughout the Book of Acts. According to the traditional and charismatic views, this is Paul's speaking an ecstatic utterance in private worship using a language he does not know. How-

Strive to Excel in Building Up the Church

ever, in the public assembly which has gathered for worship (the *ekklesia*), how much better for everything to be understood. In fact, all three views of the meaning of tongue-speaking agree on this point. Five words which are understood are better than ten thousand words in a tongue which are not translated.

Throughout his answer to the Corinthians' question, Paul repeatedly focuses upon the work of the Spirit in giving gifts for the common good, equipping officers in the church (where the greater gifts are to be exercised) and reminding us that love is the more excellent way. While there were many good things associated with the charismatic renewal, it is hard to read these chapters and come away believing that a genuine work of the Holy Spirit would immediately divide Christ's church into two factions—those who speak in tongues and those who do not.

The problem in Corinth was that people were misusing the spiritual gifts (including tongues) and the result was chaos and division during worship and that certain individuals were proud that they had been given gifts of the Spirit. The application for churches today is that we too must seek the greater gifts for the common good, while at the same time doing everything in light of the more excellent way, which is love. Such love for our brothers and sisters will only arise within us only as we look to the love of God in Jesus Christ, and when we consider Jesus' suffering and dying for all of our sins.

Paul's exhortation to the Corinthians—"Strive to excel in building up the church"—applies to Christ's churches today. We do this by grounding everything we do in our confession that Jesus is Lord. We proclaim the finished work of Christ on behalf of sinners to everyone who will listen. We earnestly desire the higher gifts because we know this strengthens our church and helps us withstand the pagan temptations all around us. In light of the cross of Christ, we pursue the more excellent way of love, because love abides long after the gift of tongues is gone. We do this by focusing upon the clear proclamation of the Word of God (prophecy) in which we proclaim Jesus as Lord and Savior from Genesis 1:1 to Revelation 22:21. And in doing so, the message of the gospel is intelligible to all and Christ's church will grow strong.

27

Decently and In Order

1 CORINTHIANS: 14:20–40

If anyone thinks that he is a prophet, or spiritual, he should acknowledge that the things I am writing to you are a command of the Lord. If anyone does not recognize this, he is not recognized. So, my brothers, earnestly desire to prophesy, and do not forbid speaking in tongues. But all things should be done decently and in order

It has been said that the true creed of the Reformed and Presbyterian churches is Paul's assertion in 1 Corinthians 14:40: "Do everything in good order." While we may make light of the Reformed obsession with rules and proper procedure, we must not overlook the fact that this statement is Paul's concluding point in his lengthy response to the Corinthians' question to him about the role and proper exercise of the gift of tongues. Sadly, division and confusion reigned in the Corinthian church—as it often does today—and Paul is writing to correct a number of problems in the church, problems which led unbelievers to think the Corinthian Christians were out of their minds.

Paul is answering a question put to him by the Corinthians about the role and practice of the gift of tongues. Apparently, the way in which the Corinthians were exercising this gift was causing division in the church, as well as creating much chaos during Lord's Day worship services. Paul has emphasized the need for Christians to earnestly desire the gifts of the Spirit because these gifts are for the common good. They strengthen the churches, and they enable us to love one another (the more excellent way). Now, Paul gives explicit instructions as to how the Corinthians are to use this gift, as well as the gift of prophecy.

Throughout this chapter, Paul makes the point that while tongue-speaking is a true gift of the Holy Spirit, the gift of tongues is inferior to the gift of prophecy. The reason for this is that those who speak in a tongue (whether that tongue is known or unknown to the speaker) cannot be understood by the assembled church unless the tongue is interpreted, while those who prophesy (which is Spirit-enabled speech) speak in such a way that the congregation understands what is said. Therefore, the congregation is said to be edified by some word or revelation from God.

What Will Unbelievers Think?

In the last half of chapter 14, Paul addresses the effects of uninterpreted tongue-speaking upon unbelievers who may happen to visit the Corinthian congregation during worship. Believers remain unedified because they cannot understand what is being said. Non-Christians will be completely put off by the confusion and chaos created by uninterpreted tongues, and by many people attempting to speak at one time. Seeing the confusion and disorder in the service, visitors will think Christians are crazy! Or, even worse, visitors will think that Christians behave no differently than those who attend the pagan temples down the street.

This concern explains Paul's exhortation to the Corinthians in verse 20. "Brothers, do not be children in your thinking. Be infants in evil, but in your thinking be mature." Paul softens the

Decently and In Order

stern rebuke a bit by affectionately referring to the Corinthians as "brothers." But the force of the imperative (command) must not be missed—"stop thinking like children." To paraphrase Paul: "Grow up! Quit acting like children."

While the Corinthians should remain naïve (childlike) in regard to evil, Paul exhorts them to grow up (become mature) in an intellectual sense. This is so church members realize and correct their current behavior, which was utterly disruptive within the church and serving as an obstacle to unbelievers coming to faith in Jesus Christ. In verse 21, Paul uses an Old Testament passage to illustrate his point, citing from Isaiah 28:11. "In the Law it is written, 'By people of strange tongues and by the lips of foreigners will I speak to this people, and even then they will not listen to me, says the Lord.'"

When Paul uses the term "Law" (*nomos*), he is using it in the broadest possible sense as a title (i.e., "the Old Testament"—not just the Pentateuch or the Ten Commandments).[1] Paul makes a free citation from Isaiah 28:11. His words do not correspond with either the Hebrew text, or to the Septuagint, so Paul is probably citing this passage loosely from memory. Because Israel did not listen to God's messenger (Isaiah), the nation came under judgment in the form of men of strange speech (i.e., Assyrian invaders from the north who spoke a language which the Israelites did not understand).

Because the prophets of Israel prophesied in Hebrew, Isaiah's prophecy was intelligible. But when God's judgment came in the form of hostile invaders who spoke different languages, the Israelites could not understand what was said. Because the Israelites did not listen to God, they were oppressed by people of strange tongues (with unintelligible speech). The application

---

1. According to Calvin, Paul "means that the law covers the whole body of Scripture which existed until the time of Christ." See, Calvin, *The First Epistle of Paul to the Corinthians*, 296.

to be drawn from this is if the Corinthians continue to speak in uninterpreted tongues—even though the tongue-speaker will declare the wonders of God—people in the congregation will not be able to understand the words from God, even as the Israelites could not understand the Assyrians. Not being able to understand what is said is ultimately a form of judgment brought about by the people's failure to do things properly.

The lack of intelligibility is the basis for Paul's comment in verse 22. "Thus tongues are a sign not for believers but for unbelievers, while prophecy is a sign not for unbelievers but for believers." On the face of it, this verse seems contradictory, given what Paul said in verse 21, that true prophecy was intelligible and was therefore of great benefit to those who believed that the prophet was from God. On the other hand, the unintelligible language of Israel's conquerors was the result of the fact that the people of Israel did not believe God's promises and thus came under God's judgment in the form of unintelligible speech.

Like the Israelites, when the Corinthians prophesied (or spoke in a tongue which was subsequently translated) so as to be edifying to the church as a whole, this was of great benefit for those who believe the gospel. But when a tongue is not translated and no one can understand it, the confusion which results becomes a sign of God's judgment. No one can listen to God, because no one can understand what is being said. Because of their current practice, the Corinthian church risks becoming like Israel and held captive to a people who cannot be understood. According to A. C. Thiselton, "Paul portrays speaking in tongues as a sign which inexpert unbelievers (rightly or wrongly) associate with, and interpret as pagan . . . and thereby are pushed yet further away into judgment. On the other hand, prophetic speech brings genuine . . . conviction of the truth, and hence faith.[2]

---

2. Thiselton, *The First Epistle to the Corinthians*, 1126.

Decently and In Order

This explains the following point in verse 23. "If, therefore, the whole church comes together and all speak in tongues, and outsiders or unbelievers enter, will they not say that you are out of your minds?" When the Corinthian church assembles for worship and people are speaking in tongues without interpretation (a sign of judgment connected to unbelief), and people are present who do not understand what is being spoken, and witness the confusion, they will react accordingly. "You people are crazy!" It is very likely that they will come to the conclusion that this assembly is no different from the Greco-Roman mystery religions found throughout Corinth, whose religious assemblies where characterized by wild behavior and ecstatic utterances, much of it unintelligible.

Prophecy Leads to Conviction

However, prophecy (or an interpreted tongue) has a markedly different effect, now described by the apostle in verses 24–25. "But if all prophesy, and an unbeliever or outsider enters, he is convicted by all, he is called to account by all, the secrets of his heart are disclosed, and so, falling on his face, he will worship God and declare that God is really among you." The superiority of prophecy (preaching) is virtually self-evident in the effect that it has upon unbelievers. Although pagan religions emphasize religious experience and bizarre behavior, such should not be the characteristic of the church.

If the Corinthians focus upon prophecy, then the law and the gospel will be clearly proclaimed, so that when an unbeliever comes in, they will become aware of their sins, be aware that they are under God's judgment and that they cannot keep their sins hidden from God. And what will the sinner's response be? Instead of seeing the confusion of untranslated tongues as a sign of God's judgment upon the church and think the people to be crazy, they will hear the law and gospel in an intelligible way. They will know that they are sinners in need of a Savior. They will then say "God is really among you" (unlike the pagan religions). This is why prophesying and interpreted tongues are superior to an uninterpreted (untranslated) tongue, which is a sign of God's judgment.

What follows is a rather interesting section of this letter because Paul gives us a brief glimpse of the way in which the Corinthians conducted worship. This is the only place in the New Testament where we find such a description. While not describing the entire service, it does seem to indicate that the Corinthian worship services were far less structured than that of services conducted today, and this seems to be part of the problem. In Acts 2:42 we are given a brief list of those things which were central in apostolic worship (apostolic teaching, the breaking of bread, the prayers, and fellowship), but there is no mention in Acts of any order or manner in which these things were done. Based upon what we read here, worship services in Corinth were likely conducted in private homes or in public spaces not specifically designed for public assembly and the proper worship of God. It would be easy to associate these places with whatever pagan activities and feasting had been conducted there previously.

Christian churches, built and designed for worship, did not come until later in the post-apostolic period. The more orderly services with which we are familiar (with a carefully thought-out liturgy and with suitable seating, a pulpit, a communion table, etc.), are in many ways the consequence of Christians heeding Paul's exhortations to the Corinthians.

In verses 26–33, Paul takes up the matter of how tongue-speaking and prophecy should be conducted within the Corinthian church during corporate worship. In verse 26, Paul asks, "What then, brothers? When you come together, each one has a hymn, a lesson, a revelation, a tongue, or an interpretation.

Decently and In Order

Let all things be done for building up." When Paul speaks of the Corinthian church "assembling for worship," Paul indicates that everybody had something to contribute (although there is nothing to indicate that everybody participated with every gift in every worship service). Although Paul does not mention prophecy in this list—a matter of some surprise, since Paul has been speaking of the superiority of prophecy to tongues—"a revelation" may be the same thing (or similar) to prophecy.

A hymn (or song) refers to someone who sings (probably accompanied by instrumentation of some sort). There are a number of instances recorded in the New Testament of Christians singing during worship (see v. 15; Matt. 26:30; Eph. 5:19; Col. 3:16). When Paul says each one has a hymn, he is probably referring to someone who would sing a song which they themselves had composed, or else which was used by early Christians in worship.[3]

One Person at a Time

A word of instruction (*didache*) is some form of Christian teaching or instruction (catechesis). A revelation is probably a reference to something similar to a prophecy—God revealing how Christ is revealed in an Old Testament text (or similar—remember there was no New Testament yet). An interpretation, of course, refers to an interpretation of a tongue. Paul also lays out precise instructions for how the interpretation is to be handled in verses 27–28: "If any speak in a tongue, let there be only two or at most three, and each in turn, and let someone interpret. But if there is no one to interpret, let each of them keep silent in church and speak to himself and to God."

It was the misuse of this gift (tongues) which created much controversy among the Corinthians, so Paul takes up this matter first. Many of these issues he raises are merely matters of

---

3. Morris, *1 Corinthians*, 194.

practicality. Paul limits the number of tongue-speakers to two or three only. What is key here is that tongue-speakers are to speak one at a time, not simultaneously, which is, apparently, what had been causing so much of the trouble (confusion). And when someone spoke in a tongue (unintelligible) it must be immediately interpreted so that everyone present can understand what was being said. If there is no one there who can interpret the tongue, then the tongue-speaker is to keep silent and pray and praise God privately. Verses 27–28 make perfect sense on the alternative view (proposed above). Why would God give his people a supernatural utterance which they do not understand (a tongue in a language which the speaker does not know), yet withhold the gift of interpretation so that the person must remain silent? On both the traditional and charismatic interpretations, this question remains unanswered.

In verse 29, Paul now turns his attention to the use of prophecy. "Let two or three prophets speak, and let the others weigh what is said." Seeking to keep things orderly, Paul likewise restricts the number of those prophets who can speak to two or three people, and that the members of the congregation should listen very carefully to what the prophets have to say. If the Holy Spirit gives someone a particularly important revelation (the revelation of something previously hidden in God's word), then the situation described in v. 30 applies. "If a revelation is made to another sitting there, let the first be silent." Paul's point is not to stifle the Spirit, but to do all things in good order (see v. 33).

When the Spirit gives someone the revelation of a mystery regarding Jesus Christ, the speaker should allow the person who is sitting down (presumably listening—v. 29) to be given a turn to speak. The reason for this is spelled out in verse 31. "For you can all prophesy one by one, so that all may learn and all be encouraged." Again, the purpose for such precise instruction is to end the mass confusion which was leading to disruption in the worship service, and to provide an orderly procedure in which everyone present in the church might be instructed and encouraged (i.e., edified).

Just as tongue-speakers are to control their actions, so too are those with the gift of prophecy. This verse is problematic for those churches which conduct worship services in which public outbursts are tolerated and encouraged. This not only disrupts the worship service, it creates the kind of situation in which non-Christians do not hear the law and the gospel. "And the spirits of prophets are subject to prophets." Those who have the gift of prophecy can control its use, and are to do so, for the reason spelled in the first half of verse 33. "For God is not a God of confusion but of peace."

The Corinthians must not emulate the pagans and allow public assemblies (especially, Christian worship) to degenerate into a free for all, in which people indulge themselves in individualistic and inappropriate behavior. God desires peace, so that the members of the church be instructed, encouraged, strengthened, and edified. This is why the worship service is to be conducted along the lines suggested by Paul, with a suitable liturgy (including those things mentioned in the New Testament—cf. Acts 2:42) and so that everything is done in good order, as instructed in verse 40. As John Murray wisely reminds us, "Scripture in its total extent, according to the conception entertained by our Lord and his apostles, is the only revelation of the mind and will of God available to us."[4] This fact is the basis for the so-called "regulative principle" in worship, expressed for example in the *Heidelberg Catechism* (Lord's Day 35, Q & A 96) which instructs us that we do not "worship [God] in any other way than He has commanded us in His Word."

---

4. John Murray, "The Finality and Sufficiency of Scripture," in *Collected Writings* (Carlisle, PA: Banner of Truth Trust, 1976), I.19.

Paul has already addressed the question of the roles of women in the church (1 Cor. 11:2) and Paul reiterates here what was said earlier. Christian women are to be modest and not reflect the pagan mores of Corinth. Christians must not accept the pagan sexuality (androgynous, immoral, and immodest) increasingly found throughout the Greco-Roman world. Christian worship is to be orderly and Christian women are to be modest.

Modesty and Submission

In verses 33b-35, Paul lays down the same principle for the Corinthians that all the other churches follow. "As in all the churches of the saints, the women should keep silent in the churches. For they are not permitted to speak, but should be in submission, as the Law also says. If there is anything they desire to learn, let them ask their husbands at home. For it is shameful for a woman to speak in church." The standing principle of the churches to which the Corinthians must conform is that women are not to speak in the churches during worship. This principle is spelled out in Paul's first letter to Timothy when he instructs the young pastor to "let a woman learn quietly with all submissiveness. I do not permit a woman to teach or to exercise authority over a man; rather, she is to remain quiet."

In Greco-Roman culture, women did not speak or say anything in public (except to other women). To do so was to be considered rude, immodest, and disrespectful of one's husband (or father). It was the recent and ongoing emancipation of women in Corinth which had created the situation which Paul is writing to correct. Women in Greek culture were becoming increasingly immodest and unwilling to follow accepted social norms, much of it stirred by pagan religious practices and spirituality. To avoid identification with this pagan trend, Paul has already exhorted women to avoid wearing their hair in such a way as to identify themselves in appearance with temple pros-

Decently and In Order

titutes or devotees of goddess worship. Paul exhorts Christian women not to speak in the church (presumably he is referring to prophecy or tongue-speaking), as a sign of submission to their husbands (or fathers), the essence of public modesty.

When Paul refers to the law, the question is, "What part of the law?" Most commentators believe that this refers to the fact that the husband is to exercise headship over his wife (especially when it comes to theological/ecclesiastical matters) as stated in Genesis 3:16: "To the woman he said, 'I will surely multiply your pain in childbearing; in pain you shall bring forth children. Your desire shall be for your husband, and he shall rule over you.'" If this is the case, it explains why Paul exhorts women to ask their husbands questions at home, since to do so in public was considered a sign of disrespect. It may also have been the case that the early churches followed the practice of the synagogues, in which men and women sat on opposite sides of the room. If women were to attempt to talk with each other or with their husbands (across the room), it would have been very disruptive. That too may have been part of the problem in Corinth.

It is important that we remember that women of that era received no formal education. Jews still considered it a sin to teach a woman, and Jews had a higher view of women than most. Women were treated poorly in the ancient world and it must be pointed out that Jesus saw no problem in instructing women (Luke 10:39–42), a practice which carried over into the early churches. Christianity did not oppress women as many of our contemporaries would like us to believe.

A couple of points of application need to be addressed. As we have seen throughout our exposition of chapters 12–14, Paul is speaking to the subject of the importance of modesty and differentiating Christian worship from paganism in light of the particular problems in Corinth. Christians are to be modest and behave decently. The application of this command means women should be silent in worship (not disruptive) and submissive to their husbands. To do otherwise is to be immodest. Paul does not say here that women cannot say anything in public (only that they should not speak in worship). As Calvin points out, Paul forbids women to speak in public and not to teach or prophesy in worship, yet says the Reformer, "We should understand this as referring to the situation where things can be done in the regular way, or when the Church is well established. For a situation can arise where there is need of such a kind as calls for a woman to speak."[5]

If Anyone Thinks He Is Spiritual

Paul now brings the Corinthians his final words on the subject. Paul starts off in verse 36 by rebuking them for their pride. "Or was it from you that the word of God came? Or are you the only ones it has reached?" Once again it is difficult to know whether the Corinthians actually thought this to be the case, or whether Paul is being a bit sarcastic. Regardless, this demonstrates that the issue underlying most of the Corinthians' problems is pride. The Word of God did not originate with the Corinthians and they are not the only church God has established. Furthermore, they must give due consideration to making sure their practices are the same as that of other Christian churches.

In verse 37, Paul reminds the Corinthians of his apostolic authority to issue binding edicts about how worship should be conducted. "If anyone thinks that he is a prophet, or spiritual, he should acknowledge that the things I am writing to you are a command of the Lord." Since Paul is writing with the full authority of his office, even those who claim to be prophets and "spiritual" are obligated to obey Paul's command. If the gifts of the Spirit are to be used for the edification of the church, then these gifts must be used in the right way and in line with the

---

5. Calvin, *The First Epistle of Paul to the Corinthians*, 306.

apostle's instructions. In fact, there will be serious consequences if Paul's advice is not followed. "If anyone does not recognize this, he is not recognized" (v. 38).

If members of the Corinthian church fail to heed these instructions, they will be ignored during worship. Those who truly possess the Holy Spirit and exercise the gifts of the Spirit will not behave in such a way as to cause disruption. Because they are concerned for the church and they love their brothers and sisters, they will gladly heed Paul's instructions. Should someone fail to follow Paul's instructions, they demonstrate that they are not truly spiritual. And so Paul wraps up his argument in verse 39 when he states, "So, my brothers, earnestly desire to prophesy, and do not forbid speaking in tongues." Prophecy is superior, but tongues (when properly used and interpreted) should not be forbidden.

Decently and In Good Order

Paul finally brings to an end his lengthy answer to the Corinthians' question about speaking in tongues and order in worship with the very important exhortation in verse 40. "But all things should be done decently and in order." This is the key principle in light of which all public worship should be conducted. Content is important, but so is doing things in the proper way. Immodest, self-centered, and disruptive behavior has no place in Christian worship. According to Paul, everything should be done in a way which is fitting with God's purpose for public worship, which is that Christ's word be proclaimed, that the sacraments are administered properly, and so that everything which is done by God's people, serves the common good and brings him honor and glory. This is the ideal which the elders of the church are to pursue and enforce.

One way Reformed Christians do this is through a proper liturgy (which includes the content specified in Acts 2:42), which exalts prophecy (the preaching of God's word) and ensures the careful administration of the sacraments (as taught in Scripture). A properly ordered worship service does not permit disruption as we see in Corinth, either through outbursts of speaking in tongues, or even in idle conversation among church members while the service is being conducted. I can only imagine what Paul's response might be to someone's cell phone going off during worship, especially if they took the incoming call!

While we may chuckle about the Reformed and Presbyterian obsession with rules and procedures, it is an apostolic command to do things decently and in good order. This is so that nothing detracts from the proclamation of the gospel ensuring that everyone hears and understands the preaching of Christ crucified for sinners. This also ensures that Christian worship does not descend into chaos like that of paganism. In the Corinthian context, Paul will not allow the worship service to be dominated by particular individuals with gigantic egos and personal agendas. The only one who can dominate worship is Jesus Christ, the Lord of his church!

Scripture spells out several things which are to occur during Christian worship (i.e., the elements of worship). Take Acts 2:42 for example—the apostles' teaching, the Lord's Supper, fellowship with the risen Christ and with each other, and the prayers. How we do these things on Sunday morning is not specified, but it falls to the consistory or the session of the local church (the ministers and elders) to make sure that everything that is done during worship exalts Christ, is intelligible to all, serves the common good, is done from the motive of love, and done "decently and in good order."

28

The Gospel

1 CORINTHIANS: 15:1–11

For I delivered to you as of first importance what I also received: that Christ died for our sins in accordance with the Scriptures, that he was buried, that he was raised on the third day in accordance with the Scriptures, and that he appeared to Cephas, then to the twelve. Then he appeared to more than five hundred brothers at one time, most of whom are still alive, though some have fallen asleep. Then he appeared to James, then to all the apostles. Last of all, as to one untimely born, he appeared also to me.

If someone walked up to you and asked, "What is the gospel?" what would you say? If you cannot come up with the answer immediately, then carefully consider what follows. The gospel is that message which recounts what Jesus Christ did to save sinners. It is spelled out in concise form by the Apostle Paul in Corinthians 15:3–5. The gospel is called "good news" because it is the proclamation of a set of particular historical facts—Jesus suffered and died as a payment for our sins, and he was raised by God from the dead on the third day as proof that his death turned aside God's wrath toward sinners. And all of this is in accordance with the Scriptures. Apart from the good news of the gospel, we have no hope of heaven because we are sinners and cannot save ourselves. The gospel is a non-negotiable and fundamental article of the Christian faith.

We come to the last major topic addressed by Paul in 1 Corinthians—the bodily resurrection of believers. While I need to qualify what I am about to say by affirming that all of Scripture is God-breathed, and therefore profitable for teaching, rebuking, and training in righteousness (cf. 2 Tim. 3:16), Paul's discussion of the resurrection in 1 Corinthians 15 is one of the most important chapters in all the Bible. The reason for this assertion is simple. Paul defines the gospel in verses 1–11. He speaks of the fact of the resurrection in verses 12–19, and of the relationship of the bodily resurrection of believers to the second coming of Jesus Christ in verses 20–28. Paul goes on to define the importance of the resurrection for Christian living in verses 29–34 before addressing the nature of the resurrection body in verses 35–58. Each of these things matter because they deal with the very foundation of our faith. Virtually everything in this chapter is under dispute both in the church and outside the church in the surrounding culture.

Since the wages of sin is death, and since we are all sinners, death is an inevitability. Try as we will, we cannot escape the reality of death. Death has claimed many whom we know and love. Death will claim us, barring the return of Jesus Christ. Therefore, we ignore this subject to our own peril. In the face of this horrible foe, Paul anchors the Christian's hope in the resurrection of our bodies. Just as Jesus died and was raised from the dead three days later, so too we shall be raised on that final day when Jesus comes to judge the world, raise the dead, and make all things new. At death, our bodies and souls are torn apart. In the resurrection, God reunites them. This is why Paul's discussion of the resurrection body in 1 Corinthians 15 is so impor-

The Gospel

tant, since it is in this resurrected state that we will live for all of eternity in the presence of Christ on a new heaven and earth.

Christ's Resurrection Body and Greek Thought

The doctrine of the bodily resurrection was a serious intellectual obstacle for the Greeks in Corinth, many of whom believed that at death, the immortal soul (which was pure spirit and therefore untainted by sins or passions) was liberated from the prison house of the body (which was material, and therefore evil). To the pagans, death was considered to be a natural event, and enabled us to escape our bodies which are the source of bad habits and evil desires. Death was not seen as the consequence of Adam's act of rebellion against God, and a universal curse which God pronounced upon the entire human race. According to his comment in verse 12 of chapter 15 ("how can some of you say that there is no resurrection of the dead?"), Paul must address this matter with the Corinthians because a number of them, apparently, were laboring under the pagan (and mistaken) assumption that the resurrection is spiritual only, and that the dead will not be raised (bodily), but exist throughout eternity as disembodied spirits (eternal soul).

Paul had been a Pharisee and had been taught that human history culminated in a resurrection at the time of judgment (Daniel 12:1–4). According to Paul, to deny the bodily resurrection of Jesus Christ is to deny the Christian faith. Unless Christians are raised from the dead on the day of resurrection—even as Jesus Christ was raised from the dead on the first Easter—Christians are to be pitied more than all men. If Jesus Christ is not bodily raised from the dead, then Christ's death does not pay for our sins, nor does it reverse the curse (death). This means we are still in our sins. It also means that we are false witnesses about Jesus Christ, because we have been telling everyone that God raised him from the dead.

Therefore, Jesus Christ's bodily resurrection is fundamental to Christianity. As B. B. Warfield once put it, the resurrection is "the cardinal doctrine of our system: on it *all other doctrines hang.*"[1] If Jesus Christ rose bodily from the dead, then he is God in human flesh and Christianity is true. If Jesus did not rise from the dead then Christianity collapses and cannot be true. If Jesus' body still lies in an unknown tomb somewhere near Jerusalem, then it is "sex, drugs and rock and roll," to paraphrase Paul's point in verse 32. If the dead are not raised, "Let us eat, and drink, for tomorrow we die."

When Easter arrives each year, I always take a look at the religion section of the newspaper and examine the sermon topics and advertisements from local churches. I am amazed (and saddened) at how many local churches virtually ignore the biblical emphasis upon the empty tomb and the bodily resurrection of Jesus—which is both a fundamental doctrine of the Christian faith and an objective fact of history. Instead, many churches focus upon the so-called "Easter experience" of the apostles. If the focus of Easter is made to fall upon the experience and change of heart felt by Jesus' apostles—who first did not believe, but then did so—then Easter can be presented as another "experience" which we too can share with the early followers of Jesus. To redefine the resurrection and downplay the fact that Jesus was dead but was raised bodily to life, guts the resurrection of its redemptive-historical and biblical significance. The first Easter is not about an experience the apostles had in which we can share, but Easter is the apostles' account of Jesus being raised bodily from the dead. Because the tomb was empty, this means that his death was the payment for our sins, the new creation has dawned, and that God has conquered our greatest enemy,

---

1. B. B. Warfield, "The Resurrection of Christ a Historical Fact," in *Selected Shorter Writings*, Vol. 1, ed., John E. Meeter (Phillipsburg: Presbyterian and Reformed Publishing Company, 1970), 178.

The Gospel

death, by overturning the curse. Easter is not an experience in which we share; the bodily resurrection of Jesus is both a fact and a doctrine which we must believe.

The Gospel Paul Preached

For Paul, all of Christianity hangs upon the resurrection of Jesus Christ, a topic he addresses in verses 1–11 when he defines the gospel. Paul begins this section by connecting Christ's resurrection directly to the gospel which he first proclaimed to the Corinthians. Paul states in verse 1, "Now I would remind you, brothers, of the gospel I preached to you, which you received, in which you stand." As he did when writing to the Galatians (cf. Gal. 3:1), Paul reminds his readers of the gospel which he has already preached to them. The Corinthians received that gospel, and it is the gospel which is said to be the foundation of the church. Therefore, it is the preaching of the gospel which establishes the church—a point which Paul emphasizes again in the following verse. Get the gospel wrong, and we have nothing upon which to build a church.

The fact that Paul speaks of the Corinthians as "brothers" yet again shows how differently Paul views the situation in Corinth from that of Galatia. The Corinthians were struggling to work through those truths they had initially embraced. Unlike Galatia, this church was not plagued by Judaizers who were attacking the gospel by redefining it in Paul's absence. As recent converts to Christianity, the Corinthians were struggling with Christian maturity, trying to leave behind non-Christian ways of thinking and doing. Although Paul harshly rebuked the Galatians ("You foolish Galatians." cf. Gal. 3:1), Paul does not speak of the "foolish Corinthians." He warmly calls them brothers, despite their many struggles and the immorality present in the church. It is one thing for a church to be made up of struggling sinners. It is another thing entirely to deny the gospel or tolerate those who do.

In verse 2, Paul reminds the Corinthians of the message which he had preached to them and upon which the church was founded. "And by which you are being saved, if you hold fast to the word I preached to you—unless you believed in vain." This is a watershed verse in this epistle. "By this gospel" (literally, "through" *dia* this gospel), the Corinthians are saved. Not only is the verb in the present tense (giving the sense "you are being saved") but Paul also indicates that the Corinthians must hold fast to that gospel. When seen in light of verse one—the gospel was preached to the Corinthians and received by them—the point is that through the gospel (defined below as the saving work of Jesus Christ)—the Corinthians are being saved, provided they do not reject that gospel. The same thing is true for us.

The Corinthians must hold fast to that which Paul has already preached to them. This is not a proof-text indicating that a true Christian may fall away from Christ and be lost as some have argued.[2] Paul's point is that it is through the gospel (and only through the gospel) that the Corinthians will be delivered from God's wrath (i.e., "saved"), they must cling tenaciously to that message which Paul has preached and which they have received. There can be no deliverance from sin without holding fast to the gospel, since the gospel is the proclamation of the facts regarding Jesus Christ's dying for our sins and rising again from the dead. Those who are truly Christ's will heed this warning.

Should the Corinthians fall back into their old ways of thinking and doing (and trust in human righteousness and goodness to save them), then the gospel will be of no avail to them and they will suffer the fate of some among the Galatians (cf. Gal.

---

2. See, for example, I. Howard Marshall, *Kept by the Power of God: A Study of Perseverance and Falling Away* (Minneapolis: Bethany Fellowship, 1969), 99; Robert Shank, *Life in the Son: A Study of the Doctrine of Perseverance* (Minneapolis: Bethany House Publishers, 1989), 33.

The Gospel

5:4—"You are severed from Christ, you who would be justified by the law; you have fallen away from grace."). Those who have believed for a time (temporary faith) will find that the death of Jesus will not save them, unless they *remain* united to Christ through faith. Christians must persevere to the end to be saved. Let us not forget, however, that such perseverance is based upon Christ's preservation of his own, such as we read of the Good Shepherd in John 10:25–30. God's elect do persevere to the end because Christ preserves them to the end (1 John 2:1–2). Not one of his sheep will get away from his care. This is how we discern God's elect: they persevere and do not fall away. This is why Peter can exhort us in his second epistle, "Therefore, brothers, be all the more diligent to confirm your calling and election, for if you practice these qualities you will never fall" (2 Pet. 1:10).

Paul defines the gospel in verses 3–7. Throughout these verses, his focus is upon the objective, historical, and factual nature of what Christ has done on behalf of sinners. Paul had proclaimed these facts to the Corinthians (i.e., "he delivered"), those things he himself had received from Jesus and the other apostles. The language which Paul uses refers to the careful handling of sacred tradition (cf. Luke 1:1–4). From the very beginning of the apostolic age, the preaching of the church was centered in what Jesus Christ has done for sinners through his life, death, and resurrection. Paul sets out these facts as follows,

> For I delivered to you as of first importance what I also received: that Christ died for our sins in accordance with the Scriptures, that he was buried, that he was raised on the third day in accordance with the Scriptures, and that he appeared to Cephas, then to the twelve. Then he appeared to more than five hundred brothers at one time, most of whom are still alive, though some have fallen asleep. Then he appeared to James, then to all the apostles. (vv. 3–7)

First Corinthians

Many scholars have noted that verses 3–5 take the form of an early creed, or a confession of faith. There are two parallel double statements here which seem to confirm this point: "Jesus died, he was buried," and "he was raised up, and he appeared."[3] This structure shows the importance which Paul and the early church placed upon the bodily resurrection of our Lord. The bodily resurrection of Jesus Christ, as well as his post-resurrection appearances, are essential elements of the Christian faith and must be confessed as such—then and now. In fact, this is one of several such creedal formulations found in Paul's epistles (e.g., Rom. 10:9; Eph. 5:14; Phil. 2:6–11; Col. 1:15–20; 1 Tim. 3:16).[4] These biblical creeds provide the foundation for the later creeds, confessions, and catechisms of the church, designed to teach and defend the central doctrines of the Christian faith, as well as to instruct children and new converts in those doctrines taught in the Bible and confessed by God's people.

Christ's Death, Burial, and Resurrection

The first thing Paul does when it comes to defining the gospel is to make it clear that Jesus Christ died for our sins, according to the Scriptures. Since the New Testament (especially the gospels, which contain the historical account of the crucifixion) was not yet complete and the gospels had probably not yet been written when Paul writes this letter, much of apostolic preaching was done directly from the Old Testament, as seen throughout the Book of Acts (Acts 2:14–36; 3:11ff., etc.). To preach the gospel is to make a truth claim centered in the historical fact that Jesus Christ fulfilled messianic prophecy, and that Jesus was raised from the dead, and that this event was common knowledge in Jerusalem.

---

3. Conzelmann, *1 Corinthians*, 251–254.

4. W. J. Porter, "Creeds and Hymns" in Craig A. Evans & Stanley E. Porter, *Dictionary of New Testament Background* (Downers Grove, IL: InterVarsity Press, 2000), 231–238

The Gospel

For Paul, the essence of the gospel is clearly found in the saving death of Jesus "for our sins," which was long foretold by the Old Testament prophets and which has now been fulfilled through the events underlying the gospel. Apparently, apostolic preaching (prophecy) was centered in recounting the facts surrounding Christ's death and resurrection which were presented as events which fulfilled Old Testament prophecy. Paul explains in greater detail the meaning of the death of Jesus in other epistles such as Romans 3:25; 5:6–11; 2 Corinthians 5:14–21.

While the mention made by Paul in verse 4 of Christ's burial comes as a surprise to some ("Why would Paul place such emphasis on Jesus' burial?"), our Lord's burial is the proof that Jesus truly died. As the *Heidelberg Catechism* puts it in Question and Answer 41, "His burial testifies that he really died." Jesus did not merely "swoon," only to recover later and help perpetrate the hoax which founded Christianity. Having established that Jesus was really dead, Paul next addresses Christ's resurrection on the third day, an event foretold in very general terms in Isaiah 53:10–12 and Psalm 16:10.

From Paul's statement—"He was raised on the third day in accordance with the Scriptures"—it is clear that the resurrection entails the reanimation of a dead corpse which was buried in a manner, as recorded in the gospel account, and consistent with Jewish traditions. Paul says that Jesus "was raised" from the dead, which is probably a way of emphasizing that the Father raised Jesus from death to life and that Jesus' resurrection is a permanent state. The perfect tense is used in this way six times in this chapter of Corinthians, but only once elsewhere in the New Testament. Jesus is (not was) the Risen Lord! He will always be the Risen Lord.

According to the facts of the gospel and the messianic prophecy which underlies it, Jesus died in the ordinary sense of the term, and was brought back to life while still lying dead in the tomb. In fact, there is no way whatsoever to make sense of the gospel apart from Christ's bodily resurrection. The resurrection has nothing to do with an "Easter" experience on the part of the disciples—as a new sense of awareness or enlightenment which changed their lives. Nor was this resurrection faked by the apostles. Nor did it involve mass hysteria as argued by analytic philosopher Anthony Flew.[5] The tomb was empty because Jesus was raised bodily from the dead. On this fact (the bodily resurrection), the entire Christian faith stands or falls. As J. Gresham Machen once put it, "The great weapon with which the disciples of Jesus set out to conquer the world was not a mere comprehension of eternal principles; it was not an historical message, and account of something that had recently happened, it was the message, 'He is risen.'"[6] Indeed, if Christ be not raised from the dead, then we ought to eat, drink, and be merry, because this life is all that there is, and Christian preaching is but mere opinion if not outright deception.

Our Lord's Post-Resurrection Appearances

While the empty tomb is taken by many to be the essential proof of the resurrection (I am thinking of B. B. Warfield's comment that the empty tomb is sufficient to found Christianity upon),[7] Paul does not put the matter that way in 1 Corinthians 15:3–7. Because of his own experience of the risen Christ's appearance to him, Paul speaks of Christ's Easter appearances (not the empty tomb) to his disciples in the days before his Ascension as the primary proof of our Lord's resurrection. Paul recounts a number of these appearances for his readers.

---

5. Cf. Gary Habermas and Anthony Flew, *Did Jesus Rise Again from the Dead? The Resurrection Debate*, ed. Terry L. Miethe (San Francisco: Harper and Row, 1987).

6. J. Gresham Machen, *Christianity and Liberalism* (Grand Rapids: William B. Eerdmans, 1981), 28–29.

7. Warfield, "The Resurrection of Christ a Historical Fact," 190.

The Gospel

The resurrected Lord Jesus physically appeared first to Peter, then to the twelve (the other apostles who had assembled in the upper room according to John 20:19ff.), then to over five hundred people at once, most of whom were still living when Paul wrote this epistle. This may be the event referred to in Matthew 28:16–17. "Now the eleven disciples went to Galilee, to the mountain to which Jesus had directed them. And when they saw him they worshiped him, but some doubted." It is very likely that people who had seen Jesus both before and after the crucifixion were well-known in the early church.[8] In effect, Paul is saying, "These witnesses are well known, and if you don't believe me, go ask them." The resurrection is clearly a factual event and Paul appeals to those with knowledge of it, because they had seen the risen Christ with their own eyes (cf. the comments made by John in 1 John 1:1–3). All the Jews or the Romans had to do is produce Jesus' dead body and Christianity was over before it started. But they do not produce a body. Instead, the Jewish authorities called Jesus a magician and a deceiver (cf. Matt. 27:62ff.).

This also explains why the early church did not venerate Christ's tomb as a holy place or a shrine. From the beginning, Christians were aware of Christ's presence in their midst through word and sacrament in the power of the Holy Spirit. Jesus did not invite the disciples to come visit the tomb, rather, after walking out of it and leaving only his grave clothes behind, he appeared to them alive in a number of post-resurrection appearances (e.g., John 20:19ff.). Jesus is present with his people through word and sacrament, and not through pilgrimages to "holy" places. Jesus comes to us, we do not need to go to places where he once was in order to find him.

---

[8]. See Richard Bauckham, *Jesus and the Eyewitnesses: The Gospels as Eyewitness Testimony* (Grand Rapids: William B. Eerdmans, 2006).

Paul goes on to say that Jesus appeared to James (the Lord's brother) and other unnamed apostles which probably led to James' conversion, since neither James nor his brothers believed in Jesus during his earthly life (cf. John 7:5). But by the time the events recounted in Acts 1:11 occur, Jesus' brothers are numbered among the founders of the church. How did this happen? Jesus appeared to them after his resurrection and they believed that he was who he claimed to be. According to John 2:22, "When therefore he was raised from the dead, his disciples remembered that he had said this, and they believed the Scripture and the word that Jesus had spoken." Of course, the disciples believed the Scriptures while they were with Jesus before the resurrection. John's point is that after Jesus rose from the dead, the disciples understood the promises far better than they ever could have before. Now it makes sense.

Paul's Encounter with the Risen Christ

In verse 8, Paul now recounts to his own experience of the risen Christ while on the road to Damascus (spelled out in detail in Acts 9:1–31). "Last of all, as to one untimely born, he appeared also to me." Jesus appeared physically to all of the founders of the church, Paul being the last. The implication is that Jesus stopped appearing to people after he appeared to Paul (cf. Acts 1:11). When Paul speaks of himself as "abnormally born" he uses the Greek word for miscarriage or an abortion (*ektrōmati*). Paul is referring either to the abnormal way he was converted, or to the fact that he regards himself as completely unworthy of the call he has received.

That the latter is probably the case can be seen in verses 9–10. "For I am the least of the apostles, unworthy to be called an apostle, because I persecuted the church of God. But by the grace of God I am what I am, and his grace toward me was not in vain. On the contrary, I worked harder than any of them,

The Gospel

though it was not I, but the grace of God that is with me." Paul had not been among the disciples when Jesus was alive. We do not know if Paul ever heard or saw Jesus during our Lord's messianic mission. We do know that Paul had been a persecutor of Christ's church. Paul does not feel worthy of being an apostle, since the others are elsewhere described as being with Jesus from the beginning (cf. Acts 1:21–22). Yet Paul was personally called by Jesus to his apostolic office. Everything Paul is as an apostle he owes to the grace of God in Jesus Christ. Furthermore, Paul has given himself completely to his calling. He can state with a clear conscience that he (being energized by the grace of God) has worked harder than any of the others. Paul is not bragging, but making an important point.

Despite Paul's lowly status and given the gracious nature of his call to his office from the Lord of the church, Paul ties his message directly to that preached by the other apostles. In fact, Paul can affirm in verse 11, "Whether then it was I or they, so we preach and so you believed." Paul, Peter, Apollos, and the others, preached the same gospel—Jesus Christ's death, burial, and resurrection according to the Scriptures. As Paul says plainly, this gospel was sufficient to found the church in Corinth, just as it had been sufficient to found churches everywhere. Paul preached this gospel. The other apostles preached this gospel. And this gospel is what the Corinthians believed. Yet everything hinges upon the fact of Christ's resurrection, a point that Paul addresses in the next section (vv. 12–19), to which we will turn shortly.

What Is the Gospel?

One of the biggest shocks I have experienced as a Christian is witnessing the inability of professing Christians to define the gospel. Sadly, many professing Christians know very little about the basics of the Christian faith, including the gospel. People can repeat various Christian slogans they have heard, but since it is often assumed in church circles these days that people know what the gospel is, few talk about it, much less define it along the lines Paul does. So, it is no wonder that Christians often stumble badly when trying to define something so basic to the Christian faith, that you cannot even be a Christian without believing it. If you cannot define the gospel when asked, this must be remedied. All that is required is familiarity with 1 Corinthians 15:3–8!

As Paul makes plain in the first eleven verses of 1 Corinthians 15, the gospel is anchored in those historic events associated with the life, death, burial, and resurrection of Jesus Christ. Preaching the gospel, or sharing the gospel with a non-Christian (evangelism) involves recounting the basic facts that Paul sets out here (and which we find in the gospels—Matthew, Mark, Luke, and John). Therefore, we too should be able to communicate the facts surrounding the life, death, burial, and resurrection of Jesus in such a way that the people with whom we are discussing these things understand that we are speaking about things that really happened—historical facts. Because the gospel is true, it is our business to proclaim and share those facts with non-Christians. Let the facts speak for themselves, and then trust the Holy Spirit to create faith through the proclamation/communication of the gospel. This is how we do evangelism. We simply tell people who Jesus is and what he did. We tell people that these things are true—they really happened. We then ask them if they will trust that one who died for their sins and who was raised from the dead to save them from the wrath of God on the day of judgment.

Since the gospel is centered in these historical facts, Martin Luther was absolutely correct to speak of the gospel as being "outside of us."[9] Our relationship before God does not de-

---

9. Martin Luther, *Lectures on Romans*, trans. Wilhelm Pauck, (Philadelphia: The Westminster Press, 1961), 124–125.

The Gospel

pend upon how we feel about ourselves and our progress in the Christian life at any given moment. The gospel does not depend upon how sorry we are for what we have done, or not done, as the case may be. It does not even matter how sincere we are, or how many works we have done. Our salvation depends upon what Jesus did *for* us and in our place. Our salvation was accomplished for us on a Roman cross about two-thousand years ago one Friday afternoon a short walk outside the walls of Jerusalem. This is what we mean when we speak of the gospel as something grounded in the objective facts of history. Jesus died for our sins. He was buried. He was raised from the dead on the third day. Had you been there you would have seen these things.

Faith is our act of trusting in what Jesus did *for* us, to save us from our sins. But there can be no saving faith apart from the facts of the gospel. Faith can only be our response to the facts associated with the gospel. Can you answer that question, "What is the gospel?" More importantly, do you believe that what Jesus did saves you from your sins, and that he will rescue you from facing the judgment of God on the day of judgment?

This is the message Paul preached. It is the message we much preach, because this message tells us how God saves sinners, and that is why it is the foundation of the church of Jesus Christ.

29

Christ Has Been Raised!

1 CORINTHIANS: 15:12–34

For if the dead are not raised, not even Christ has been raised. And if Christ has not been raised, your faith is futile and you are still in your sins. Then those also who have fallen asleep in Christ have perished. If in Christ we have hope in this life only, we are of all people most to be pitied. But in fact Christ has been raised from the dead, the first fruits of those who have fallen asleep. For as by a man came death, by a man has come also the resurrection of the dead. For as in Adam all die, so also in Christ shall all be made alive.

Imagine the shock and panic you would feel upon hearing news that the body of Jesus had been found in a tomb somewhere near the city of Jerusalem, and that the remains were positively identified as those of the central figure of the New Testament. What would your reaction be? Fear? Anger? Would it even matter? Would you still call yourself a Christian? While we can be certain that no one is going to find the body of Jesus in a tomb near Jerusalem because Jesus was raised from the dead that first

Easter, nevertheless, the question is an important one because it pushes us to face a more fundamental question. How do we know that Christianity is true? Why are you a Christian? And why does any of this really matter?

In the previous chapter, we dealt with the opening verses of chapter 15 (vv. 1–11) in which Paul defines the gospel in terms of those historical facts associated with the death, burial, and resurrection of Jesus, according to the Scriptures. These facts compose the gospel which Paul preached, and which the Corinthians believed. It was this gospel which established the church in Corinth as well as churches throughout the Roman world. To preach the Christian gospel is to proclaim these facts to both Christians and non-Christians alike in such a way that everyone understands we are making a truth claim (i.e., that Christianity is true and all other religions are false). To preach the gospel is to communicate that we are speaking about our salvation being accomplished for us, by Jesus Christ, in ordinary human history, through the shedding of blood (which was Rh typable), on a Roman cross which would have given you splinters had you rubbed your hand across it. The gospel is a truth claim grounded in very specific historical facts. These facts must be believed and the Savior to whom they point is to be the object of our trust.

We also know that Jesus was raised from the dead the first Easter because the tomb in which he had been buried was empty despite a huge stone which sealed the tomb's entrance, and despite the fact that the Romans placed a guard at the tomb. We also know that Jesus was raised from the dead because the Risen Jesus appeared visibly to all the apostles, to over five hundred people at one time, and then finally to Paul, who considered himself completely unworthy of such an honor. Paul not only appeals to the fact that he himself saw the resurrected Jesus while traveling on the road to Damascus, Paul mentions that most of the five hundred people who saw Jesus were still alive. The implication of this latter point is that it is likely the Corinthians knew who many of these people were, and that the events associated with the gospel were not only true, they were common knowledge.

The Christian Truth Claim

The Christian faith therefore is a public faith. Christianity is based upon certain historical facts, which, if true, establish Christianity as the only true and viable religion, and which if false (i.e., these things did not happen) conversely demonstrates that Christianity cannot be true, no matter how many people claim to be followers of Jesus.

Having established that the Christian faith is necessarily grounded in these well-established historical events which are contained in the gospel, Paul addresses two related themes in this section of 1 Corinthians 15. First, Paul continues to speak of the fact of the resurrection (vv. 12–19), and then, second, turns to the related matter as to how the resurrection of Jesus Christ impacts the Christian life (vv. 29–34). In the next chapter, we will backtrack a bit and then take up the relationship of the bodily resurrection of believers to the second coming of Jesus Christ (vv. 20–28).

With that in mind, we turn now to Paul's discussion of the fact of the resurrection in verses 12–19. Since Christianity's basic truth claim is centered in historical events—the life, death, burial, and resurrection of Jesus Christ, there is the theoretical possibility of the falsification of Christianity. Although this may make some Christians nervous, the fact is that *if* Jesus did not rise again from the dead, then Christianity cannot be true.

This point explains why this is such a watershed issue, and why I think it important to consider questions just raised. If you deny the bodily resurrection of Jesus Christ, then you deny Christianity. If the body of Jesus is recovered in Jerusalem, then

Christianity cannot be true, because the gospel upon which apostolic churches were founded was grounded in Christ's bodily resurrection. Jesus was not only a crucified Savior, but he is also the Risen Lord. All the Jewish religious authorities or the Romans needed to do was produce Jesus' dead body and Christianity was finished before it ever started. Both the Jews and the Romans had the means, motive, and opportunity to prove Christianity to be false, but never produced a body or hard evidence that Jesus remained dead after his crucifixion. In fact, what little Jewish and Roman opposition to Christianity there was actually acknowledges that the first Christians based everything on their claim that Jesus had risen from the dead. As Machen reminds us, "If any one thing must be clear . . . it is that Christianity at the beginning was founded squarely upon an account of things that had happened, upon a piece of news, or in other words, upon a 'gospel.'"[1]

Paul spells out the precise nature of the Christian truth claim for his readers in verse 12. "Now if Christ is proclaimed as raised from the dead, how can some of you say that there is no resurrection of the dead?" From this remarkable assertion we can see the serious nature of the problem which Paul is addressing with the Corinthians. Those who have been preaching in Corinth (Paul, Peter, Apollos) have all been preaching that Christ was raised bodily from the dead. The fact of the Resurrection lies at the very heart of the gospel. How, then, is it that people in the Corinthian church have come to the conclusion that there is no resurrection of the dead?

A Bodily Resurrection

The reason why this is the case has to do with Greco-Roman culture and that form of pagan religion in which the Corinthi-

---

1. J. Gresham Machen, *What is Faith?* (Grand Rapids: William B. Eerdmans, 1962), 149.

ans were steeped. Both Greeks and Romans had a serious intellectual problem with the very notion of the resurrection of the body because pagan religion often held that matter itself (as opposed to pure spirit) is intrinsically evil. At death, Greek pagans believed that the human spirit (or the immortal soul) was at last liberated from the prison house of the body. The body was understood to be the source of all of our bad habits and desires because it was material, and therefore humans were inclined toward indulging or stifling these bodily passions. Death was seen as that moment when people were finally liberated from their material existence, which was often thought to be the source of many of humanity's problems.

Because Jesus conquered death and the grave in the resurrection of his body, Paul has been preaching that people will not live forever as disembodied spirits, but that God will reunite body and soul in the general resurrection at the end of history. As much as Paul—the former Pharisee turned apostle of Jesus Christ—looked forward to the resurrection of the body at the end of the age, this was a concept which did not give hope to Greek pagans, but confused them—given their pagan presuppositions. This also explains the tendency among the Corinthians to deny the bodily resurrection, and instead to favor some sort of spiritual resurrection or disembodied existence after death. Since the gospel was grounded in Jesus' bodily resurrection, Paul's teaching was completely foreign to them and completely contrary to what had they come to expect given their pagan background.

Therefore, the lengthy discussion of the resurrection of the body in 1 Corinthians 15 is, in part, Paul's corrective to the errors of Greco-Roman paganism. In fact, as Paul states in verse 13, to deny the possibility of the bodily resurrection, is to deny the resurrection of Jesus Christ, which is the foundation of the Christian faith and the very heart of the gospel. Paul minces no words. "But if there is no resurrection of the dead, then not even Christ has been raised." If the dead cannot be raised (because of the reasons we have just mentioned), then not even Jesus Christ has been raised from the dead. And if not even Jesus has been raised, there can only be one possible conclusion, spelled out by Paul in verses 14–18:

> And if Christ has not been raised, then our preaching is in vain and your faith is in vain. We are even found to be misrepresenting God, because we testified about God that he raised Christ, whom he did not raise if it is true that the dead are not raised. For if the dead are not raised, not even Christ has been raised. And if Christ has not been raised, your faith is futile and you are still in your sins. Then those also who have fallen asleep in Christ have perished.

For Paul this is an either/or situation. If Jesus Christ was not raised from the dead, then the preaching of the gospel is absolutely useless because the content of the gospel would be a falsehood. In fact, to preach that Jesus Christ was raised from the dead, *if* he was not raised, is to bear false witness. Not only is preaching the gospel bearing false witness (if Christ be not raised), the response of those who believed it (faith) is also in vain. If Jesus is not raised, Christians across the ages have believed a lie. We have placed our hope in a gigantic hoax. Those who have gone on before us are dead with no bodily existence, and even worse, those who have died do not live on in the presence of God awaiting the resurrection at the end of the age.

The bottom line is that we have placed our trust in a dead man, who cannot save us because he did not rise again from the dead. We are still in our sins and our faith is useless. There is no hope. This life is all there is. And if this life is all there is—to put it bluntly and directly—then it does not matter what we do, or how we live. We are free to sin with impunity, provided we can

Christ Has Been Raised!

get away with it. There is no reason to do good, no reason to love our neighbor, and no reason to deny ourselves any sort of pleasure. As the Russian novelist Dostoevsky put it, under such circumstances, "Everything is permitted and that's that."[2] Moral anarchy reigns. This is why so many of our contemporaries dismiss the Christian truth claim without consideration. If Christ be raised, they cannot do as they please.

If Christ Is Not Raised

Paul presses home the stark reality of a life lived without the hope of the resurrection from the dead in verse 19. "If in Christ we have hope in this life only, we are of all people most to be pitied." If Jesus Christ is still buried in a tomb, then we are to be pitied more than anyone else because we have staked our hope on something that is patently false. We have believed a lie, and we sacrificed much for no reason. While gospel singer Andrae Crouch can write a song *If Heaven Was Never Promised to Me*, in which he contends that being a Christian is such a wonderful thing that he would be a believer even if this life is all that there is, Paul, on the other hand, says to the Corinthians that if Jesus Christ be not raised from the dead then we are in an absolutely deplorable condition. Even worse, we are a laughing stock as well as liars. As far as Christianity goes, everything depends upon a resurrected Savior and the coming resurrection from the dead at the end of the age. If this is not true, we are still in our sins, Christianity is patently false, and we have no hope. We deserve to be mocked if we have based everything on a myth or a legend.

Yet, as Paul points out in verse 20, "But in fact Christ has been raised from the dead, the first fruits of those who have fallen asleep." This is a theme we will unpack in some detail in

---

2. Fyodor Dostoevsky, *The Brothers Karamazov*, trans. Richard Pevear and Larissa Volokhonsky (New York: Vintage Classics, 1991), 649.

First Corinthians

the next chapter of this exposition (30), but it is vital to realize that Christianity without Jesus' resurrection is inconceivable for Paul. At this point, we turn to the second (and closely related) issue raised by Paul in verses 29–34, the relationship between the fact of Christ's resurrection and the Christian life.

Baptism for the Dead?

In verse 29, Paul changes gears a bit, turning from his discussion of Christ's resurrection and its connection to our own resurrection at the end of the age (one of the main themes of New Testament eschatology), to address the inconsistencies of those among the Corinthians who deny the bodily resurrection. Some of those among the Corinthians who claim there is no resurrection of the dead are engaging in certain practices which clearly indicate that there will be a resurrection. This is self-contradictory, and Paul points out the obvious inconsistencies in their doctrine and practice.

In verse 29, we find one of the most peculiar verses in the New Testament. "Otherwise, what do people mean by being baptized on behalf of the dead? If the dead are not raised at all, why are people baptized on their behalf?" Paul's point is that if there is no bodily resurrection of the dead at the end of the age, why are people being baptized for the dead? This assertion makes little sense to us because we have no information about this practice, or the reasons why some in Corinth were doing such a thing. Paul's statement about baptizing the dead creates a major interpretive problem which has plagued the church from its beginning. What is, exactly, this business of baptizing people on behalf of those who have already died? This verse has been so problematic and its meaning so uncertain that one commentator has identified over two hundred interpretations of this passage.[3]

---

3. Morris, *1 Corinthians*, 215.

Christ Has Been Raised!

According to the second clause of the verse ("baptized for them"—*hupere*), people were being vicariously baptized in the place of those who had already died, presumably without having been baptized before death. It appears as though this particular baptism was being done so that the benefits of baptism would apply to people who had already died without themselves being baptized. It also appears to be the case that this practice occurs in the same circles where people were teaching that the dead are not raised bodily, therefore the inconsistency in their thinking is readily apparent.

The best answer as to why the Corinthians were doing this is that we simply do not know why people were engaging in proxy baptism, nor do we know with any precision what such baptism meant. Paul's comment is that it made no sense for the Corinthians to be baptizing dead people if there was no bodily resurrection.

Some heretical groups like the Marcionites of the second century, or the Mormons of today, have taken Paul's comment here as an endorsement of the practice of baptizing the dead through some sort of proxy baptism—someone is baptized on behalf of the dead person so that the dead person received the benefits of baptism they otherwise would have missed. The circumstances in Corinth may be like the confusion we see among the Thessalonians who wondered whether or not those who died before Christ returned might miss out on the resurrection (1 Thess. 4:13ff.). There is no other mention of this practice in the New Testament or any other Christian literature of the first century. The act of baptizing the living on behalf of the dead was never an accepted Christian practice anywhere else, and there is absolutely nothing here—other than Paul's mention of it—which even remotely implies that it is. Whatever else we may say about this, Paul does not endorse the practice merely by mentioning it in connection with an erroneous denial of the resurrection.

First Corinthians

The Resurrection and the Christian Hope

In verse 30, Paul now makes a much more general point about the gospel and its connection to Christ's resurrection. "Why are we in danger every hour?" Why would Christians risk great danger by professing faith in Jesus Christ, if there were there no bodily resurrection at the end of the age? What is it that gives Christians hope and courage in the face of great danger? It is the knowledge of the resurrection yet to come. We may die of sickness, accident, or even of old age. We may be killed at the hands of another. But God will raise us bodily from the dead on the last day. This is our hope. We base everything on the Resurrection. We know this to be true because God has already raised Jesus from the dead—the first fruits of the harvest at the end of the age.

This is why Paul will risk danger and persecution to preach the gospel—not because Christianity works (i.e., it changes lives, it provides people with a meaningful way to live, it makes them more moral, etc). Paul risks danger because Christianity's central claims are true. Jesus Christ has been raised bodily from the dead! Paul has seen the risen Christ with his own eyes, and his own encounter with Jesus was verified by the fact that over five hundred others saw the risen Christ at the same time.

As the apostle expresses it in verse 31, "I protest, brothers, by my pride in you, which I have in Christ Jesus our Lord, I die every day!" We know from Luke's account of Paul's missionary endeavors throughout the Book of Acts, that Paul's life was in constant danger. Paul faces danger and death every time he enters a new city, from angry Jews (who threaten to kill Paul, or who riot because of his preaching), or from Roman or local authorities (who want to keep the peace and who see Paul as a trouble-maker). Nevertheless, Paul boasts about and glories in what Jesus Christ has done among the Corinthians. There is a reason why the apostles were willing to lay down their lives if that would cause the gospel to spread. That reason is the hope of the Resurrection because they know Jesus' tomb was empty and that the Lord had shown himself to be alive. The crucified one is also the Risen One.

In verse 32, Paul presses this point home to its logical conclusion. "What do I gain if, humanly speaking, I fought with beasts at Ephesus? If the dead are not raised, 'Let us eat and drink, for tomorrow we die.'" When Paul speaks of fighting wild beasts in Ephesus, he is probably speaking rhetorically, as in "what if I did fight with wild beasts?" Paul was a Roman citizen and would have been exempt from being thrown to the wild animals or victimized in gladiatorial combat. Furthermore, people thrown to the beasts usually did not survive the encounter. So, more than likely, Paul is referring to the events described in Acts 19 and to the riots caused by the presence of Christian preachers arriving in Ephesus. Paul himself had faced the angry mob (who behaved like wild animals) when he first arrived in Ephesus, the city from which he wrote this letter to the Corinthians.

If the Dead Are Not Raised

The main point of the verse is Paul's lament. "If the dead are not raised, let us eat and drink, for tomorrow we die." This was a well-known slogan in Paul's day, and is even found in Isaiah 22:13. It is the ancient equivalent of the mantra repeated by many of my friends who survived the sixties and seventies: "sex, drugs, and rock and roll." If Jesus Christ is not raised from the dead, then what else is there but the pursuit of pleasure and self-gratification? To the ancients, this meant drinking too much and feasting to the point of vomiting. To the moderns, it is pure self-indulgence, altered consciousness, and the desire to be distracted from life's problems by entertainment and trivialities. If there is no resurrection, Christianity is a lie. What else is there but the pursuit of pleasure?

In the next verse (v. 33), Paul cites yet another well-known proverb to make the point that association with people who deny the resurrection (and therefore are prone to self-gratifying behavior) may lead Christian people into sinful behavior, and ultimately to a denial of the Christian faith. "Do not be deceived: 'Bad company ruins good morals.'" If people have no moral anchor in life, they are completely adrift with no basis other than opinion or gut feeling from which to determine what is right or wrong. When good people ("good" in the relative sense of a favorable comparison to societal norms—i.e., a "civic righteousness") associate in any sustained way with bad people (immoral), more often than not the bad corrupt the good, rather than the good elevating the bad. There are some who can pull this off, but the fact of the matter is that given our own sinful propensities, we are far more likely to fall to the level of those with whom we associate (if they fit Paul's description of "bad company"), than we are to see them rise to a higher level of acceptable conduct. The escalator of civic righteousness usually runs down, not up.

Paul is very clear about this either/or choice. If Jesus did not rise from the dead, then this life is all that there is, and we might as well seek as much pleasure as we can because "time is a wastin.'" Yet Paul is able to remind those among the Corinthians who mistakenly cast all caution to the wind, that there is a huge price to be paid for such behavior. The pursuit of pleasure places you in the circle of others seeking pleasure, and oftentimes they seek their pleasure at your expense. The Corinthians do not want to put themselves in such a dangerous place—especially because Jesus did rise from the dead, and therefore life does have meaning and purpose, despite the world's opinion to the contrary.

In verse 34, Paul makes a very pointed exhortation to those in the church who were acting like there was no resurrection

Christ Has Been Raised!

from the dead. "Wake up from your drunken stupor, as is right, and do not go on sinning. For some have no knowledge of God. I say this to your shame." The exhortation literally reads, "Sober up. Stop sinning." The Corinthians must stop following this false teaching, because it almost inevitably leads to sin.

If there is no resurrection, then everything is permissible because nothing is absolute. Because Jesus Christ has been raised from the dead, we have hope that we live on after death, and we know that everything we do in this life truly does matter! At its root then, the problem is that people are ignorant about God—a point which Paul makes to shame those of his readers who follow those who deny the resurrection of the body. God has raised Jesus from the dead, and this changes everything.

The Impact of the Resurrection

One of the great dangers we face in our day and age is the temptation to consider our standing with God based upon how we happen to feel at any given moment. When things are going well, we tend to feel more positive about God and our faith seems strong. But when things get tough, we may feel that God is distant from us, or that he is somehow punishing us. How many people have left the faith after suffering some trauma in life from which they conclude that Christianity is not true, or that Christianity does not work for them? We all know of people who have done this. We may even be thinking like this now.

This is what happens when we base our faith on the intensity of our experience, or how we feel at any given moment, or based upon our current circumstances, and not upon what God has done in history. When our faith is based upon the truth of Christianity—that what Paul and the apostles claim happened to Jesus of Nazareth actually happened—we are far less likely to be overwhelmed by the storms of life, or times of doubt. Our relationship with God was forever secured by a bloody cross and an empty tomb. Our standing with God does not depend upon our current circumstances, our experience, or our feelings, good or bad. This is truly good news, and the only place to find comfort, consolation, and strength during the trials and tragedies of life—the doing and dying of Jesus Christ, for us, and in our place.

The fact of the resurrection gives meaning and purpose to everything we do. We are not left with an ethic of "sex, drugs, and rock 'n' roll," because this life is all that there is. On the contrary, because God has raised Jesus Christ from the dead, death is not the end of our existence. The empty tomb means that this life is the beginning of an eternal existence in resurrected bodies living in the presence of God and of Christ on a new heaven and earth. Because Jesus Christ has been raised, all of God's promises are secured. We now live every moment of our lives in light of Jesus Christ's resurrection from the dead. We look back to Christ's cross and the empty tomb to see that our salvation was already accomplished for us. We live each new day struggling to die to self and live unto Christ who is our wisdom and righteousness from God. And we look ahead to that great and glorious day when the heavens will roll up like a scroll and all the promises of God are fully realized in the resurrection of our bodies and life eternal. This is our hope. This is our confidence. This is how we go on living in grateful obedience to a gracious Savior.

Because Jesus Christ has been raised from the dead, this means that Christianity is true whether people believe it or not. All non-Christians must live their lives attempting to deny or ignore what God has done in history. To escape the truth, they invent false religion, they turn Christianity into some sort of subjective religious experience, or they attempt to ignore the claims of God and Christ upon their lives. We do not need to prove to such people that Christianity is true, because it is true.

Christ Has Been Raised!

We do need to preach the gospel to them and let them feel the weight and guilt that comes with denying the truth.

How can we know that all of this is true? Jesus Christ has been raised from the dead! For a Christian, it is not the empty creed of "sex, drugs, and rock 'n' roll." Rather it is the triumphant expression of Easter Sunday: "He is risen!"

30

He Must Reign

1 CORINTHIANS: 15:20–28

But in fact Christ has been raised from the dead, the first fruits of those who have fallen asleep. For as by a man came death, by a man has come also the resurrection of the dead. For as in Adam all die, so also in Christ shall all be made alive. But each in his own order: Christ the first fruits, then at his coming those who belong to Christ. Then comes the end, when he delivers the kingdom to God the Father after destroying every rule and every authority and power. For he must reign until he has put all his enemies under his feet. The last enemy to be destroyed is death. For "God has put all things in subjection under his feet."

In the opening verses of this chapter (vv. 1–11), and in the section which follows this one (vv. 29–34) Paul has made his case that the Christian faith stands or falls based upon whether or not Jesus Christ has been raised from the dead. Paul reminds the Corinthians that the gospel he preached to them, and which they accepted as true, is grounded in the historical facts of Jesus Christ's death, burial, and resurrection according to the Scriptures. If Jesus Christ was bodily raised from the dead, then Christianity is true, and so is the gospel the Corinthians believed. But if Jesus did not rise again from the dead, then Christian preaching and teaching is false, and the Corinthians have believed that gospel in vain. A dead Savior cannot save anyone else, if he cannot even save *himself*. Because Jesus did rise again from the dead, Paul must address the relationship between Jesus Christ's own death and resurrection and our bodily resurrection at the end of the age. This brings us to Paul's discussion of the second coming of Jesus Christ, the resurrection of the dead at the end of the age, and the course of redemptive history in between (vv. 20–28).

Unlike the pagans, who see death as that moment when the soul is finally liberated from the body (and its bodily urges), Christians anticipate the resurrection of our bodies, when God rejoins body and soul which have been torn apart by death. It is here that we find our hope for the future. Not having such hope, pagans can only live for the moment reciting their creed, "Eat and drink, for tomorrow we die." In fact, Christians look ahead to that glorious day when Jesus Christ returns to judge the world, raise the dead, and to make all things new. We live our daily lives in light of that great event yet to come. This gives everything we do meaning and purpose.

Bible prophecy devotees run wild with all kinds of speculation about the Rapture, calculations about the identity of the Antichrist, the timing of the Battle of Armageddon, a hope grounded in a future millennial kingdom in which lions, supposedly, will lie down with lambs, and when Jesus rules the world from the city of Jerusalem. Yet, when Paul discusses the course of the future, none of these things are mentioned. For Paul, the Christian hope is grounded in Jesus Christ's resurrection from the dead, which is the first fruits of the great harvest yet to come, the general resurrection at the end of the age, when

He Must Reign

Jesus Christ returns and all of human history comes to its final and glorious climax.

Christ's Resurrection: The First fruits

At this point in our exposition of chapter 15, we will backtrack a bit to cover verses 20–28, in which Paul lays out the course of the future, beginning with the resurrection of Jesus Christ. Throughout the preceding verses (12–19), Paul set out a series of hypothetical situations to make his point. "If Jesus Christ is not raised then you are still in your sins, and we might as well 'eat and drink for tomorrow we die,' because this life is all there is." In verse 20, Paul answers these hypothetical questions by reminding the Corinthians of the fact of our Lord's resurrection. Jesus Christ's bodily resurrection from the dead constitutes the first fruits of a great harvest which guarantees the final harvest (resurrection) of all those who are his. Christ's resurrection from the dead, then, is the proof that his redemptive work (as the second Adam) overturns the effects of the curse resulting from Adam's fall into sin. For Paul, Jesus Christ is Lord over all things, even death. This is where we as Christians are to find our hope and purpose in life (cf. Col. 3:2).

In verse 20, Paul asserts what by now should be obvious to his readers. "But in fact Christ has been raised from the dead, the first fruits of those who have fallen asleep." Christians are not to be pitied more than all men. Far from it. Jesus' tomb is empty. Jesus has shown himself to be alive to all of the apostles, to over five-hundred people at one time, as well as to Paul himself. The resurrection of Jesus is an established fact. Therefore, Paul's argument in these verses stands in sharp contrast to the hypothetical assertions made in the previous verses. Jesus Christ has been raised from the dead. For Paul, this fact not only establishes the truth of Christianity but, as we will see shortly, our Lord's resurrection is the basis for many of Paul's distinctive doctrinal emphases.

Once again, Paul uses the perfect tense of the verb ("has been raised"—*egēgertai*) to make the critical point that Jesus Christ's own resurrection from the dead is an ongoing condition. Jesus *is* the Risen Lord (and continues to be) the Risen Lord because he has conquered death and the grave once for all. This explains why it is that Jesus Christ's resurrection plays such a major role in Paul's theology. The Resurrection lies at the heart of the gospel, and is therefore the foundation for Christian hope—just as our Lord was raised from the dead, so too, shall we. Furthermore, the Resurrection is the basis for Christian ethics—because Jesus has been raised, everything we do matters because we must live this life in the light of the next.

Paul makes three important points to strengthen his argument. First, Paul speaks of Christ's resurrection as the "first fruits" (*aparchē*) of a much larger harvest yet to come. This is an important category through which to consider the full impact of the Resurrection. When viewed against the background of the Old Testament, where the first sheaf of the harvest was brought to the temple so as to consecrate the entire harvest of grain which had not yet ripened or been harvested, so too, Christ's resurrection consecrates the entire harvest of those who also will be raised from the dead—that is, all of the elect, who are already seen as "raised with Christ" (cf. Eph. 2:4–7). Although the point is rather obvious, it is easy to overlook. The very fact that the Resurrection constitutes the "first fruits" of a much larger harvest guarantees that there will be a much larger harvest yet to come. This should give us great optimism as far as the missionary enterprise is concerned, because the great multitude before the throne who are raised with Christ is so vast they cannot be counted (cf. Rev. 7:9). The harvest will be huge.

He Must Reign

Raised with Christ

Second, the fact of the Resurrection serves as the guarantee of the future bodily resurrection of Christian believers at the end of the age. The New Testament is filled with references to the fact that Christ's own resurrection on the first Easter is the basis for the New Testament's repeated assertion that the believer *has already been* raised with Christ (cf. John 5:24; Eph. 2:4–7). Christ's bodily resurrection in the past, not only points us ahead to a future resurrection of the body, it gives life meaning now. Because of what Jesus has already done for us in conquering death and the grave, this establishes what is yet to come—that we too will be raised bodily from the dead on the last day. This is why Paul can speak of Christian believers as presently seated and raised with Christ in heavenly places. This is what we mean when we speak of the already/not yet distinction found throughout the New Testament.[1] Because we are "in Christ" and already seen as seated with him in heavenly places, we can be assured of the promise of the not yet—the resurrection of our bodies—a point we will take up when we discuss the nature of the resurrection body (vv. 35–58).

To put it yet another way, the first coming of Jesus Christ and his resurrection ensures that in the present age, every Christian believer is *already* raised with Christ. Christ's resurrection from the dead also ensures that the believer also will be raised (bodily) at the end of the age. Not only does the Resurrection establish proof of Jesus' deity—that he is God in human flesh whose death upon the cross for us and in our place accomplishes our salvation—the resurrection of Jesus Christ from the dead marks a major turning point in redemptive history. When Jesus leaves the tomb on that first Easter Sunday, this is the birthday of the new creation (cf. 2 Cor. 5:14–18). The

---

1. Richard B. Gaffin, *Resurrection and Redemption: A Study in Paul's Soteriology* (Phillipsburg: Presbyterian and Reformed Publishing Co., 1987), 60.

empty tomb is the beginning of the end, the dawn of the final era in redemptive history.

Third, in conquering death and ushering in a new and final era of redemptive history, Christians have been living in the last days from the time of Jesus and the apostles (Acts 2:17; Heb. 1:2). In the meantime, we await the end of the age when Jesus returns. This too is implied when Paul speaks of Christ's resurrection as the "first fruits" (*aparchē*). Although the term "first fruits" in 1 Corinthians 15:20ff., is commonly understood to refer to the fact that Christ's resurrection is chronologically prior to all those who will rise after him (i.e., it occurs prior to the general resurrection), Paul's use of the term "first fruits" is intended to demonstrate an organic unity between Christ and his people who have been raised with him in his own resurrection. Jesus might be the first to rise from the dead, but he is not the last. All those who are his will rise with him!

The language of "first fruits" indicates that Christ's resurrection marks the initial resurrection from a larger group to follow (i.e., the harvest). Our Lord's "resurrection is the representative beginning of the resurrection of believers."[2] This point is far from theoretical because Paul is reminding us that, if we are trusting in Christ, his victory will be ours, for we are part of that great harvest he has already secured. Barring the Lord's return while we are still in the land of the living, sickness, suffering, and death inevitably will come—but these things cannot separate us from the love of God which is in Christ (cf. Rom. 8:31–39), nor will they prevent us from participating in the great day of resurrection yet come.

The Two Adams

In verses 21–22, Paul sets out a contrast between "two Adams" as the key to understanding the big picture, so to speak, of re-

---

2. Gaffin, *Resurrection and Redemption: A Study in Paul's Soteriology*, 34.

demptive history. Paul does the same thing here he does in Romans 5:12–21. In verse 21 of 1 Corinthians 5, Paul begins to develop the "two Adams" theme for the Corinthians. "For as by a man came death, by a man has come also the resurrection of the dead."

Paul begins by reminding the Corinthians that death is the penalty for Adam's violation of the terms of the covenant of works (Gen. 2:17; 3:17–19). This curse comes to us through Adam—death came by a man (Adam), and was passed on to all of Adam's descendants. Therefore, the reversal of the consequences of the curse (death) must also come through a man—the second Adam, Jesus Christ.

Since Adam acted as the federal and biological head of all those under the covenant of works (the entire human race), Adam brought the curse down upon all those whom he represents (all of humanity). So too, the redemption of the human race, by the means of a once for all sacrifice for sin, and in the resurrection from the dead, must also come through a man. This man is the second Adam, Jesus Christ. To express this yet another way, Jesus accomplishes his redemptive work on behalf of all those whom he represents under the covenant of grace. Our redemption depends upon our Lord's incarnation ("a man") and the facts of the gospel (Christ's obedience and death), culminating in Jesus' bodily resurrection from the dead. Jesus, as the second Adam, undoes the consequences of sin brought down upon the human race by Adam. As we read in the *Westminster Shorter Catechism*, Q & A 37–38:

> Q. 37. **What benefits do believers receive from Christ at death?**
>
> A. That the souls of believers are at their death made perfect in holiness, and do immediately pass into glory; and their bodies, being still united to Christ, do rest in their graves till the resurrection.

Q 38. *What benefits do believers receive from Christ at the resurrection?*

A. At the resurrection, believers being raised up in glory, shall be openly acknowledged and acquitted in the day of judgment, and made perfect blessed in the full enjoying of God to all eternity.

This is why, in verse 22, Paul contrasts the effects of the fall (in Adam) with the work of Jesus Christ (the second Adam) in undoing the effects of the fall of the human race into sin. "For as in Adam all die, so also in Christ shall all be made alive." In this verse, Paul concisely summarizes the consequences of Adam's fall. Adam plunged the entire human race into sin and death. We will all die because of Adam's act of rebellion. Under the covenant of works, Adam represented all men and women, so the effects of Adam's act of rebellion extend to all human beings without exception (universal). Likewise, all those raised by the second Adam (Jesus) will be made alive (the elect—those redeemed by Christ). As Charles Hodge puts it, "We are in Adam because he was our head and representative, and because we partake of his nature. And we are in Christ because he is our head and representative, and because we partake of his nature through the indwelling of his Spirit."[3]

In Paul's "two Adams" scheme, Christ represents all those under the covenant of grace (the elect), but not the entire human race—those who are in Adam. This can be seen by the comparison between the effects of sin, and the effects of Christ's resurrection. Adam represents the entire human race. Jesus represents all those given him by the Father. The two Adams stand in stark contrast to one another.

---

3. Hodge, *I & II Corinthians*, 324.

He Must Reign

Everything in Its Proper Order

In verse 23, Paul now speaks of the fruitfruits of the harvest as those who "belong to Christ." "But each in his own order: Christ the first fruits, then at his coming those who belong to Christ." The harvest begins with Christ's bodily resurrection, but the harvest does not come in all at once. In fact, although the full harvest is guaranteed by the empty tomb, the full harvest does not come in until the end of the age when Jesus returns to judge the world, raise the dead, and make all things new. Because the events connected to the harvest will occur in a particular sequence, Paul lays out a brief map of the future, discussing the time between Christ's resurrection and our own—this present evil age (the inter-advental age).

The word translated "in order" is *tagmati*. It is a military term which referred to a detachment of soldiers.[4] Each "group" or detachment, participates in the harvest in its proper order. How one understands this order of events is vital in determining whether or not he is premillennial (Jesus returns and establishes his one thousand year rule on the earth) or amillennial (Jesus currently reigns over all things and returns to establish a new heaven and earth, not a millennial kingdom).

Clearly the first *tagma* (detachment) is Jesus Christ, who is the first fruits of the harvest. Although it would be unusual to speak of only one person constituting a *tagma*, in verse 22 Paul has just stated that, in his own resurrection, Jesus Christ represents all those who are raised in him (believers). The first *tagma* then is Christ's bodily resurrection and those who are raised in him, which ensures the second *tagma*, our own bodily resurrection at the end of the age. The starting point on Paul's map of new covenant redemptive history is Jesus' resurrection, the first Easter.

---

4. Wright, *The Resurrection of the Son of God*, 336.

The second group (*tagma*) is composed of "those who belong to Christ at his coming," a reference to Christ's second advent (*parousia*). Paul understands Christ's resurrection and the final harvest as two redemptive-historical bookends. On the one end (the starting point), is Christ's bodily resurrection (in which all believers are raised, and seated with Christ in the heavenlies). On the other end (the destination), we have the bodily resurrection of believers at the end of the age (the harvest). This understanding of Christ's resurrection anticipating our own resurrection is a serious blow to all forms of millennialism (pre or post). There is no mention anywhere in the New Testament of a golden age for Christianity upon the earth occurring between Christ's resurrection, the first Easter, and the general resurrection at the end of the age. Paul makes absolutely no mention of such a golden age here, where one would certainly expect to find it if Paul taught such an age would be manifest.

Then Comes the End

In verse 24, Paul speaks of the final destination on his redemptive-historical map. "Then comes the end, when he delivers the kingdom to God the Father after destroying every rule and every authority and power." The key to understanding Paul is the meaning of the adverb "then" (*eita*). Although premillennarians claim otherwise, Paul does not indicate that what follows in verses 24–26 is a third *tagma*, (i.e., a millennial reign of Jesus Christ upon the earth after he returns to judge the world, raise the dead, and make all things new). Rather, *eita* should be understood in the sense of "thereupon" and is used to indicate that those elements listed in verse 24, and following, occur at the time of the events described in the preceding verses.[5] In other words, when the dead are raised, *then* the end has come and the conditions set out in the following verses will become a real-

---

5. Barrett, *The First Epistle to the Corinthians*, 356.

He Must Reign

ity. The final event in human history is Jesus' return to earth to bring an end to human existence as we now know it.

The critical point is that, by the end (when Jesus comes back), Christ's kingdom will have conquered all of God's enemies, including the greatest of our enemies, which is death, as indicated in verses 25–26. "For he must reign until he has put all his enemies under his feet. The last enemy to be destroyed is death." The imperative in verse 25 is hard to miss. Jesus *must* reign (in heaven) until that time that his kingdom has conquered his enemies and he returns to earth to judge the world, raise the dead, and restore all things. The imagery Paul uses reminds us of Job's hope (cf. Job 19:25–27) that one day we will be raised bodily from the dead and see God with our own eyes. The fact that the last enemy to be destroyed is death, is a strong argument that Paul is referring here to our Lord's second advent and the resurrection, the final judgment, and the creation of a new heavens and earth—the final consummation of all things.

Therefore, when Jesus Christ returns, the dead are raised and death is completely destroyed because all of the consequences of the curse have been undone when Jesus bears the curse upon the cross. This becomes clear in the following verses (vv. 27–28).

> For "God has put all things in subjection under his feet." But when it says, "all things are put in subjection," it is plain that he is excepted who put all things in subjection under him. When all things are subjected to him, then the Son himself will also be subjected to him who put all things in subjection under him, that God may be all in all.

The opening words of verse 27, refer to the Father, who is said to put all things under the feet of the Son. This clearly echoes the words of Psalm 8:6. "You have given him dominion over the works of your hands; you have put all things under his feet." Jesus Christ has been given that dominion that God originally gave to Adam. Yet, in this post-resurrection context of Christ's victory over death and the reversal of the curse, Christ's dominion is much more far-reaching, and entails the same kind of universal dominion that Adam would have been given had he obeyed the covenant of works, and been confirmed in righteousness (and thereby glorified).[6] Since Adam disobeyed, Jesus must obey.

By virtue of his bodily resurrection, Jesus Christ has been given dominion over all things (except over the Father). The aorist tense, "he has put" points to a single act of subjection, but the perfect tense (*has been put under his feet*) indicates a continuing state. All things remain in subjection to Christ. One act of the Father (Christ being placed over all things), has ongoing importance. All things are (and remain) under the authority of Christ, awaiting the second coming. According to verse 28 then, the climax of human history is secured when Jesus Christ willingly subjects himself to the Father, so that God's Lordship over all creation is complete. When Jesus Christ, who has placed all things under his feet, in turn gives all things to the Father, human history has run its course and the consummation (the end of all things) is at hand.

The Big Picture

Paul's box-top image of the puzzle of redemptive history can be summarized as follows:

- The Fall of the human race brings about death, which requires someone to defeat death and remove the curse (vv. 21–22). "For as by a man (Adam) came death, by a man (Jesus) has come also the resurrection of the dead. For as in Adam all die (as a result of

---

6. Meredith G. Kline, *Kingdom Prologue*, self-published, 1993, 60ff.

the Fall when Adam acts as the representative of the human race under the covenant of works), so also in Christ shall all be made alive" (those who are represented by Christ under the covenant of grace—the elect).

- In verses 23–24, Paul adds, "But each in his own order: Christ the first fruits (Christ, and those raised in him), then at his coming those who belong to Christ (the bodily resurrection of those already raised and seated with Christ). Then comes the end (when Christ returns), when he delivers the kingdom to God the Father after destroying every rule and every authority and power" (the final consummation, the end of history).

- What occurs between Christ's resurrection (Easter) and the general resurrection at the end of the age is spelled out in verses 25–26. "For he must reign until he has put all his enemies under his feet. The last enemy to be destroyed is death' (which indeed Jesus destroys when he returns and raises the dead).

- Finally, in verses 27–28, Paul then spells out what it means for history to reach the final consummation. "For 'God has put all things in subjection under his feet.' But when it says, 'all things are put in subjection,' it is plain that he is excepted who put all things in subjection under him. When all things are subjected to him, then the Son himself will also be subjected to him who put all things in subjection under him, that God may be all in all."

The major problem for premillennial interpreters of Paul is that if Paul taught that there was a one thousand-year interval between Christ's second coming and the final judgment, then "it seems unthinkable that Paul, if he believed in such a kingdom, should pass over it without a word."[7] There is no indication whatsoever of any delay of a thousand years between Christ's second coming and the final judgment (as premillennarians teach). According to Paul, the end comes *immediately* at the time of Christ's appearing, when the dead are raised. Christ's second coming is accompanied by the "resurrection of Christians and ushers in the end, at which the main event is the handing over of the kingdom by Christ to God."[8] When Jesus returns, the consummation, the day of judgment, the general resurrection and the new creation will all come to pass. This is the final and glorious outcome of redemptive history.

Even as we eagerly await that glorious day when our Lord returns, Paul reminds us that until that day, Jesus must reign over all things. Our Lord Jesus is even now directing the affairs of people and nations so that human history will one day come to its appointed destination, the full and final salvation of God's people. Although we must wait for that day, because Jesus' resurrection is the first fruits of a great harvest, even now we are already seen as seated and raised with Christ. Because Jesus was raised bodily from the dead, so too, we shall be raised from the dead. This is the basis for all Christian hope. In the triumphant words of the Charles Wesley Easter hymn (*Christ the Lord Is Risen Today*):

> *Soar we now where Christ has led, Alleluia.*
> *Following our exalted head, Alleluia.*
> *Made like him, like him we rise, Alleluia.*
> *Ours the cross, the grave, the skies, Alleluia.*

---

7. Barrett, *The First Epistle to the Corinthians*, 356. See also Geerhardus Vos, *The Pauline Eschatology*, 236–246.

8. Barrett, *The First Epistle to the Corinthians*, 356.

31

In the Twinkling of an Eye

1 CORINTHIANS: 15:35–58

I tell you this, brothers: flesh and blood cannot inherit the kingdom of God, nor does the perishable inherit the imperishable. Behold! I tell you a mystery. We shall not all sleep, but we shall all be changed, in a moment, in the twinkling of an eye, at the last trumpet. For the trumpet will sound, and the dead will be raised imperishable, and we shall be changed. For this perishable body must put on the imperishable, and this mortal body must put on immortality. When the perishable puts on the imperishable, and the mortal puts on immortality, then shall come to pass the saying that is written: "Death is swallowed up in victory." "O death, where is your victory? O death, where is your sting?"

We have all thought about it. We talk about having eternal life, but what does that *really* mean? How will we spend eternity? What, exactly, will happen to us on that day the Lord returns to judge the world, raise the dead, and make all things new? What will our resurrection body be like? In 1 Corinthians 15:35–58, Paul tells us.

Paul concludes his discussion of Christ's resurrection and its importance for us by discussing the nature of that body in which we will be raised at the end of the age. The very idea of a bodily resurrection presented a problem for first century Greeks who believed that the body was the source of urges and passions from which people finally escape at death. Paul must correct this false assumption by making a compelling case that God will indeed raise the dead bodily.

What Kind of Body?

In this section of his Corinthian letter, Paul asks and then answers a question using a number of analogies, beginning with that of seeds and bodies. "But someone will ask, 'How are the dead raised? With what kind of body do they come?'" (v. 35). The question is either rhetorical—Paul asks the question that a hypothetical person might ask in light of his previous discussion about the resurrection of the body—or else the question actually comes from the letter sent by the Corinthians to Paul. We do not really know which of the above is the case. But the question is basic and profound. "How are the dead raised?" "What will the resurrected body be like?"

Not only would Greeks have trouble with the physical body being raised, but once the body decomposes, how can it be raised? What would such a body be like? How can God reanimate a dead and decaying corpse? There may be a bit of Greek skepticism lurking beneath the question. But as we learn in verse 36, Paul will have none of such skepticism. "You foolish person! What you sow does not come to life unless it dies." Paul even speaks of such an objection as "foolish," a reference to someone who has not truly considered God's perspective on this subject.[1]

---

1. Fee, *The First Epistle to the Corinthians*, 780.

In the Twinkling of an Eye

Once again, Paul uses irony to make a point since the Greeks considered themselves to be wise, while the cross remained foolishness to them. The reason such a question is considered to be foolish is because there are several well-known analogies which illustrate the very thing Greeks did not consider to be possible—a bodily resurrection. Paul lays out several of these analogies in his response.

Two Analogies: Flesh and Seeds

The Corinthians were very familiar with the process of planting and harvesting—their very lives depended upon it. Those who sowed seed, buried that seed in the process of planting. When the seed was buried, its present existence as a seed was destroyed. Jesus speaks of the sown seed as dying. "Truly, truly, I say to you, unless a grain of wheat falls into the earth and dies, it remains alone; but if it dies, it bears much fruit" (John 12:24). New life (the plant which comes forth from the seed) cannot come about unless and until the seed dies (germinates). Why, then, should people be surprised by the thought of the human body being raised in a similar manner? As Paul asks in verse 37, "And what you sow is not the body that is to be, but a bare kernel, perhaps of wheat or of some other grain." A seed is not very spectacular. The seed (whether it be wheat, flax, or anything else) is small (in comparison to what it produces), and for all intents and purposes looks to be dead before it is planted.

When the seed is "sowed" (buried), it becomes a living plant, which flowers and then produces more seed. While there is identity between the two (the wheat seed produces a stalk of wheat, not a head of corn!), there is also a marked difference between the glory of what is sown (buried) and what comes forth from the ground. The one (the seed) pales in contrast to the other (the plant). In verse 38, Paul adds yet another consideration. "But God gives it a body as he has chosen, and to each kind of seed its own body." Paul envisions God as sovereign over this process. God gives everything (even seeds and plants) their form and purpose, and therefore their meaning. God gives us seeds, and he determines what these seeds will become upon germination. Obviously, Paul is laying the groundwork for a point he will make later on.

In verse 39, Paul moves from seeds and plants to the flesh of humans and animals. "For not all flesh is the same, but there is one kind for humans, another for animals, another for birds, and another for fish." Obviously, not all kinds of flesh are the same. Animals have one kind of flesh, birds have another, and fish yet another. The same is true of human flesh—it is not the same as that of animals.

Another Analogy: Heavenly Bodies

In verse 40, Paul draws yet another contrast, this time between heavenly and earthly bodies. "There are heavenly bodies and earthly bodies, but the glory of the heavenly is of one kind, and the glory of the earthly is of another." Although we use the term "heavenly bodies" in reference to stars, that is probably not Paul's point, since he specifically refers to stars and planets in the next verse. The contrast the apostle sets up is between earthly *bodies* (not the earth) and heavenly *bodies* (not stars). Paul is arguing that earthly beings have earthly bodies which are appropriate to their earthly existence, while heavenly beings have heavenly bodies appropriate to their heavenly existence. The splendor of each is of a different order because earthly and heavenly bodies are different.

But in verse 41, the apostle does contrast the splendor between the moon (as a planet) and the stars. "There is one glory of the sun, and another glory of the moon, and another glory of the stars; for star differs from star in glory." The moon and the stars each manifest a unique kind of splendor, specifically connected to their form and function.

In the Twinkling of an Eye

Paul's point in listing these diverse elements (plants, animals, earthly and heavenly bodies, the moon and stars—along with the human body) is that God creates all things and then gives each of them a uniqueness (and therefore a particular splendor) appropriate to its divinely-given purpose. This sets the stage for the conclusion Paul reaches in verse 42. "So is it with the resurrection of the dead. What is sown is perishable; what is raised is imperishable."

It is against the backdrop of the fact of different kinds of bodies with different degrees of splendor that we should understand what Paul says here—"so it will be with the resurrection of the dead." The human body is sown (buried) as perishable (corruptible). This perishable condition (death) is the consequence of human sin. The body which is perishable will be raised imperishable—that is, a wonderful transformation will take place. This transformation is the very heart of the doctrine of the resurrection.

The Same, Yet Different

Again, we find distinction between identity and differentiation. Although gloriously transformed, the body which is raised is still a human body (and just as in the case of our Lord), our own body. But it is raised with a new glory so that it is now incorruptible and, therefore, no longer subject to decay, as it had been before. This would have been an important point to make with Greeks, who felt the decay of the body at death was the reason why a bodily resurrection was thought impossible, and why the focus of Greek thinking about death focused upon the soul, especially in the sense that death liberates the incorruptible soul from a corruptible body. Paul acknowledges the point that people die because of the corruptibility of human flesh. It is the present body which is subject to decay. But the Christian hope is that this corruptible body will be raised with a new splendor and will be utterly transformed so that it will become incorruptible. The hope of the afterlife is not disembodied existence, but the resurrection of our bodies. This was difficult for ancient Greeks to grasp, just as it is for those among us who speak of heaven in terms of "liberation" from our bodies and who think of eternal existence in images of spiritual bodies floating on clouds. If we are in Christ, we will be raised bodily and live eternally in resurrected bodies. In verse 43, Paul continues to chip away at Greek resistance to a bodily resurrection. "It is sown in dishonor; it is raised in glory. It is sown in weakness; it is raised in power." Our body is sown (buried) in dishonor because of human sin. The word "dishonor" (*atimia*) often refers to the loss of citizenship and those rights that go with it. A corpse has no rights![2] Furthermore, the Jews regarded the dead body as unclean (Num. 19:11). In a world which knows not refrigeration nor mortuary science, a dead body immediately decomposes, smells, harbors disease, and is hardly something to be honored. This is why Paul says that our present bodies have been sown in weakness—a weakness which is manifest through the limitations of bodily existence, sickness, and by decay at death.

But it is important to notice the precise nature of the contrast Paul sets out—that same dishonored and weak body will be raised in such a way that its glory will far surpass the corruption of present human existence. Just as the seed produces a plant of much greater glory than the seed, so too, the same will be true of the resurrection body. Just as our current bodies are weak and corrupt, the resurrection body will know no such weaknesses or limitations, because that body will be incorruptible and no longer subject to decay, because the consequences of sin have been overturned. As Paul puts it in verse 44, "It is sown a natural body; it is raised a spiritual body. If there is a natural body, there is also a spiritual body."

---

2. Morris, *1 Corinthians*, 222.

In the Twinkling of an Eye

Natural and Spiritual Bodies

The natural body (*pyschikon sōma*) is part of the natural world. Such a body is not appropriate for the glories of the age to come. When the natural body is buried at death, it will be raised as a spiritual body (a *pneumatikos sōma*), a body, which, while material (in identification with the body that was sown), is transformed so as to be a body suited to the glories of the age to come. A spiritual body does not mean an "immaterial" body, or a foreign body, but our own resurrected body which now bears the likeness of Christ's resurrected body (v. 49). Paul's contrast then is between that body which is appropriate to earthly existence (corruptible) and a body which is appropriate to a heavenly existence (incorruptible).

Having already mentioned in verses 21–22 of this chapter that in Adam all die, while in Christ all those who are his will be made alive, Paul returns to the account of the creation of Adam from Genesis 2:7 to support the analogy he has just made in verse 44—believers will be raised with a spiritual body which is incorruptible, exactly like that of Jesus Christ in his resurrection. Throughout this section (vv. 45–49), Paul's Adam-Christ analogy is the basis for understanding creation, fall, and redemption (resurrection). The contrast centers on the difference between being "sown" in corruption (Adam) and being "raised incorruptible" (in Christ).

In verse 45, Paul writes, "Thus it is written, 'The first man Adam became a living being'; the last Adam became a life-giving spirit." Loosely paraphrasing from Genesis 2:7, Paul inserts "first" before "man," and "Adam" after "man." Paul's point is that man was created as a "living being," composed of a body and a soul (*psyche*). This was not only true for Adam, it is true for all of his descendants. What is characteristic of Adam is characteristic of the entire human race. Ours is an existence thoroughly appropriate for earthly life. But because of human sin, corruption is the characteristic of this present evil age. At present, we are not *pneumatikos* (spiritual), even though we are already indwelt by God's Spirit. It will take the resurrection of our corruptible bodies for such transformation to the *pneumatikos sōma* (spiritual body) to take place.

Paul adds to the Genesis quotation his own assertion that Jesus Christ is likewise the head of another category of people (all those raised "in Christ"). Notice that Paul speaks of the "last Adam," not the "second" Adam, to indicate the contrast between the two key figures in redemptive history, Adam and Jesus Christ. Just as the characteristics of Adam are typical of his descendants (corruption), so too, Jesus Christ also stands at the head of a new category (the last), which has been redeemed and restored via regeneration and resurrection (to be raised incorruptible). Because Jesus is the last Adam, all of his glorious characteristics are "stamped" upon all those who are his.[3]

This is true because Christ is said to be a "life-giving" spirit. There is a long-standing debate about what Paul means by this statement as well much discussion devoted to identifying that moment when Jesus became such a life-giving spirit; through the incarnation, the resurrection and ascension, or even the second advent.[4] But this debate (the trees) misses Paul's main point (the forest), which is really quite simple. Jesus is not only the pattern of the redeemed (the archetype), he is also the source of that transforming power which raises us from corruption to incorruption. The dead are raised "in Christ" because he alone has the power to do so.

---

3. Morris, *1 Corinthians*, 223.

4. Much of this debate is summarized in Thiselton, *The First Epistle to the Corinthians*, 1283–1285.

In the Twinkling of an Eye

The Two Men: Adam and Christ

In verse 46, Paul reminds us that there is a divine order to things. "But it is not the spiritual that is first but the natural, and then the spiritual." Redemptive history gives us the key to understand the way in which these things will occur. In the creation account just referred to by Paul, the natural order of things is manifest in the creation of Adam. Only after the coming of Jesus Christ and his triumphant resurrection from the dead does the spiritual (*pneumatikos*) become the order of things (i.e., in the new creation). As men and women who descend from Adam, we enter natural life first. It is only after Christ has accomplished his redemptive work in the resurrection that men and women can enter into the spiritual existence in resurrected bodies, which is not fully realized until the bodily resurrection at the end of the age.

Paul may be refuting a notion widely held by Jews, and which appeared in the writings of the philosopher Philo, to the effect that God created a heavenly man first and only later created a natural, or earthly, man. No, the opposite is the case. The natural precedes the heavenly. Paul also may be correcting an over-realized eschatology held among the Corinthians (preterism), which erroneously assumed that Christians have already entered into the fullness of the *pneumatikos* when they were converted. Since Christians are presently indwelt by the Holy Spirit, Christians have provisionally entered that state. But the *pneumatikos* is not fully realized until the resurrection at the end of the age when our bodies are raised after the pattern of our Lord's body (cf. Eph. 1:13–14). Therefore, even though we have already been raised with Christ and are seated with him in the heavenlies, the bodily resurrection is "not yet."

In this, the contrast between Christ and Adam could not be greater. "The first man was from the earth, a man of dust; the second man is from heaven" (v. 47). Paul continues to explain the *pneumatikos* in relation to the creation account. The first man is Adam, who was created from the dust of the earth. Paul affirms both the historicity of the Genesis account as well as the biological unity of the race. But the second man (Jesus Christ) stands in contrast to the first man. Jesus Christ represents the heavenly order (i.e., that of the age to come). Jesus represents a different category of life (heavenly), yet which must be understood in the sense of transformed earthly existence. Though Jesus took to himself a true human nature (and therefore fully identified himself with Adam's fallen race so as to redeem us from the guilt and power of sin), Jesus' origin is heavenly (through the power of the Holy Spirit), in contrast to Adam, who is of the dust.

We need not read more into Paul's language here (no, he's not really addressing the nature of the incarnation) than to realize that Paul was contrasting Adam's earthly origin, with that of our Lord, whose origins are heavenly. In the next verse (48), Paul points out that through our union with Christ, believers now share in both kinds of existence. "As was the man of dust, so also are those who are of the dust, and as is the man of heaven, so also are those who are of heaven." Paul sees Adam and Christ as the heads of two distinct types of existence. Adam stands at the head of the human race as fallen (and therefore corruptible), while Christ is the head of the redeemed (incorruptible). According to Paul, Adam is the pattern for all of his descendants. Adam, and all of his descendants, are of the earth. In Adam, we all die (v. 22). As the last Adam, Jesus Christ is head of a different and heavenly order.

Much of the way this is phrased has to do with Paul's polemic against the Greek notion which sees the soul/spirit as immortal, and the body as a hindrance to truly spiritual existence. It is self-evident that our earthly bodies are corrupt and that they decay at death, although the soul lives on (which is much

In the Twinkling of an Eye

more difficult to prove than the fact that bodies decay). Paul's point is that all those in Christ are not only connected to Adam and therefore possess an earthly existence, but they are also identified with Christ and possess a heavenly existence (which, as Paul has already pointed out, entails a spiritual and incorruptible existence).

The Resurrection Body

This means that we shall be like Jesus Christ in the resurrection. We will be raised from the dead with the same kind of resurrection body that Jesus now has. As Paul puts it in Philippians 3:21—"[Jesus] will transform our lowly body to be like his glorious body, by the power that enables him even to subject all things to himself," a point made plain in verse 49 of 1 Corinthians 15. "Just as we have borne the image of the man of dust, we shall also bear the image of the man of heaven." Since we are "in Adam," we bear the likeness of our first father. Our normal state is earthly, and our existence is appropriate to life on earth. Even as we now bear the likeness of Adam (corruptible), so too, one day we will bear the likeness of the second Adam (Jesus) as a consequence of the resurrection at the end of the age.

This remarkable chapter now comes to its climax. Gordon Fee calls it a magnificent crescendo when Paul makes it clear that all those in Christ, yet who are still corruptible ("flesh and blood"), will be raised from the dead.[5] In an instant, we will all be changed on the great day of resurrection! Our bodies will no longer be subject to death and decay, as they are now. In the resurrection of Jesus Christ, we too triumph over death and the grave! This is the basis for Christian hope. The grave will not have the final word. When the last trumpet sounds, the dead will be raised!

---

5. Fee, *The First Epistle to the Corinthians*, 797.

In verse 50, Paul summarizes much of what has gone before. "I tell you this, brothers: flesh and blood cannot inherit the kingdom of God, nor does the perishable inherit the imperishable." Paul makes a solemn declaration—"I declare"—to ensure that his reader/hearer does not miss the significance of what follows. For Paul, flesh and blood is yet another way of speaking of the present existence of all those in Adam. The fact that our bodies are flesh and blood, reminds us of our weakness and the fact of our subjection to death and decay. The fact that we cannot inherit the heavenly kingdom in our present state of existence clearly indicates that our present bodies must be transformed, in order to enter into the glories of the age to come. Our present perishable flesh (sinful and corrupt) must become imperishable (redeemed and incorruptible). And it will when our bodies are raised.

As spelled out by Paul in verses 51–52, this transformation occurs at the second advent of Jesus Christ. "Behold! I tell you a mystery. We shall not all sleep, but we shall all be changed, in a moment, in the twinkling of an eye, at the last trumpet. For the trumpet will sound, and the dead will be raised imperishable, and we shall be changed." Once again, Paul affirms the importance of hearing (understanding) what follows—"behold." Paul reveals to the Corinthians (or reminds them, as the case may be) the timing and nature of the great mystery. When the last trumpet sounds, the dead are raised (cf. 1 Thess. 4:16). The word "sleep" is a metaphorical reference to death, since those "sown" will be raised when our Lord returns.

The critical point is that all those in Christ will be changed from a perishable and corruptible existence to an imperishable and incorruptible existence when the Lord returns. Notice the stress upon continuity between our present and future existence. Change implies not an entirely new existence, but a transformed existence. The problem facing the Corinthians is the exact opposite of the problem Paul faced in Thessalonica

In the Twinkling of an Eye

(cf. 1 Thess. 4:13ff.). In that church, the problem was the fear that those who died before the *parousia* would miss out on the resurrection. Paul informs the Thessalonians that the dead will rise first. With the Corinthians, the issue is one of process. How will flesh and blood, which is corruptible, inherit that which is incorruptible? How can flesh and blood be transformed?

The Final Victory!

Paul's answer is direct. We shall be changed when we are raised from the dead at the end of the age. This change will be instantaneous—in a flash, in the twinkling of an eye. Furthermore, this will occur at the last trumpet (not at death, as preterists erroneously teach), which is clearly associated with the end of the age (cf. Matt. 24:31; 1 Thess. 4:16). When our Lord Jesus returns, we will be instantly changed and raised imperishable! Our present existence must be changed as a matter of necessity, since our present nature is not suited for the age to come. Paul makes this point in verse 53. "For this perishable body must put on the imperishable, and this mortal body must put on immortality."

The corruption of human nature due to sin (including death and decay), must give way to that which is imperishable (life and immortality). As we are presently clothed with the likeness of the earthly man, in that day we must be clothed in the likeness of Jesus Christ. The resurrection body will not be subject to death nor decay. As Paul indicates in verse 54, we will have the same kind of body our Lord had after his resurrection (our bodies, now raised and transformed). "When the perishable puts on the imperishable, and the mortal puts on immortality, then shall come to pass the saying that is written: 'Death is swallowed up in victory.'" As one unknown wag once put it, "The best news the world ever had comes from a graveyard!"

First Corinthians

For Paul, this not only fulfills biblical expectations—he quotes from Isaiah 25:8—this is the great climax of redemptive history. Our greatest fear has been conquered. Our greatest enemy—death—has been defeated! So great is this victory, Paul can mock death, singing of the glorious triumph yet to come in the following verse. "O death, where is your victory? O death, where is your sting?" (v. 55). Paul's words also contain a loud echo from Hosea 13:14—"Shall I ransom them from the power of Sheol? Shall I redeem them from Death? O Death, where are your plagues? O Sheol, where is your sting? Compassion is hidden from my eyes." Death has been totally defeated by Jesus Christ. The sting of death is now gone.

Even as he finishes up with his words of triumph, in verse 56 Paul returns to the reason why death came about in the first place—human sin. "The sting of death is sin, and the power of sin is the law." As Paul puts it in Romans 6:23, the wages of sin is death. Here, he tells the Corinthians the reason that we die is because in Adam we are all sinners—as he said in verse 22, "In Adam we all die." Ironically, it is the law, which is holy, righteous, and good, and which instead of giving us life (because we are sinful—cf Gal. 3:21), the law actually exposes that sin which lies within, and therefore condemns us by inflicting the curse upon all of us for our infractions of God's commands, which is death (cf. Rom. 3:20).

Paul does not leave the Corinthians under the word of condemnation. "But thanks be to God, who gives us the victory through our Lord Jesus Christ" (v. 57). As if he were not clear enough, Paul reiterates one more time that our victory over death is not ours. It is a victory which has been won for us by Jesus Christ through his shed blood for us which turns aside God's anger toward us, and in his triumphant resurrection! This is not something we earned, but something we have been given.

In the Twinkling of an Eye

This leads Paul to one final word of exhortation in verse 58, "Therefore, my beloved brothers, be steadfast, immovable, always abounding in the work of the Lord, knowing that in the Lord your labor is not in vain." In the light of what has just been said, Paul exhorts the Corinthians to consider that because Jesus Christ has given us such a glorious victory, they are to stand firm and not be moved. "The saints are not satisfied with that measure that at any time they have attained, but are still pressing, that they may be more dutiful, more fruitful to Christ."[6] The Corinthians are not to be double-minded. Despite the present circumstances and the uncertainty they are facing as a congregation, the Corinthians must continue their labors because the final outcome has been secured through Christ's resurrection.

The same holds true for us. Jesus Christ's resurrection not only ensures our final victory in the end, his resurrection gives meaning and purpose to everything we do here and now. There is no reason to give up in despair and "eat and drink" as people without hope. The labors of God's people are never in vain. No matter what difficulties and trials we are called to endure in this life, we know how the great redemptive drama will end. Every tear will be wiped from our eyes, there will be no more pain or tears (Rev. 21:4), we will receive our glorious inheritance in Christ (Eph. 1:11–18), and we will finally see God with our own eyes (cf. Job 19:26–27). This is the basis for Christian hope. The degree to which we learn to keep this glorious final outcome before our eyes, the greater our strength to persevere during times of trouble. The more we fix our faith on the final outcome of history, the greater our ability to live lives of gratitude before our gracious God.

Death (when body and soul are torn apart because of human sin) is not the end. For on that great Day, when Jesus

---

6. Owen, *Communion with the Triune God*, 270.

Christ comes back, the dead in Christ will be raised, and we shall all be changed. We will be immediately transformed from lowly to heavenly bodies, from corruptible flesh to incorruptible bodies like Jesus had in his resurrection. And so "in a flash," in the twinkling of an eye, we shall all be raised. What a glorious hope we have!

Maranatha! Come quickly, Lord Jesus!

32

Be Watchful

1 CORINTHIANS: 16:1–24

Be watchful, stand firm in the faith, act like men, be strong. Let all that you do be done in love.

In the last chapter of 1 Corinthians, it were as if we are reading someone else's mail. We read of people we know little about, and who we will never meet until we see them in glory. We read of critical events and important travel plans that have no impact upon us today, yet which were vital to the Christians in Corinth struggling against the spirit of the age. We read of Paul's marching orders to this church and then wonder why subsequent events necessitated at least one more letter being sent to this church from Paul—a second Corinthian letter. Yet, these people and their struggles mattered to Christ, just as Christ cares about us and our struggles today.

As Paul wraps up this epistle, we learn a number of things. We find Paul's personal comments about those in the Corinthian church who have earned the apostle's respect and who should serve as examples to the Corinthians. We read of several exhortations which Paul extends to members of this church who are struggling to leave behind pagan ways of thinking and doing. We also learn of Paul's personal desires and future travel.

plans, and we see the apostle bristle a bit in defending his flock. Although this letter is addressed to a particular congregation (Corinth), we learn much about the early church and the expectations which the apostle had for this congregation which he helped to found. Yet, what Paul says to the Corinthians, he says to us as well.

As we come to the end of our study of this remarkable letter and look back at the ground we have covered, it is apparent, I hope, how important this letter is for those of us living in the midst of a pagan culture at the beginning of the 21st century. There is, perhaps, no letter in the New Testament which speaks as directly to the issues we currently face as Christians as this one. The religious and cultural issues facing the Corinthians are very similar to those with which we must deal in our own age.

Paul has made his response to the report from the members of Chloe's household (1:11) about the factions plaguing the church, and the unwillingness of this church to discipline erring members, as well as responding to the questions put to him in writing by the Corinthians (7:1) about marriage, the sacraments, gifts of the spirit, the proper manner of worship, speaking in tongues, and the resurrection. Paul now concludes his letter with a number of specific instructions about collections for the poor, a discussion of his travels, before Paul proceeds to offer personal greetings to the Corinthians from the brothers and sisters in the church in Ephesus.

The Collection

In verse 1 of chapter 16, Paul writes about the matter of collections (offerings). "Now concerning the collection for the saints: as I directed the churches of Galatia, so you also are to do." The grammar of this verse tells us that Paul is introducing a new topic after concluding his discussion of the resurrection (chapter 15), specifically the taking of a collection. This is one

Be Watchful

of several instances in Paul's various letters mentioning a collection being taken among the Gentile churches for the poor of Jerusalem (2 Cor. 8–9; Rom. 15:25–32). As recounted in the Book of Acts, this collection was one of the reasons for Paul to undertake yet a third missionary journey.

This particular collection was very important to Paul since he was not only concerned about the well-being of his own people (the Jews), but relief from Gentiles would demonstrate that Christian charity was not tied to race or ethnicity. While Paul speaks of this offering as being "for the saints," the reference to Jerusalem in v. 3, makes it clear that this offering is for the poor in Jerusalem (i.e., Jewish Christians). Unlike the Jews, who taxed synagogue members a half-shekel annually and then sent the money to Jerusalem to support the temple (based upon their understanding of Lev. 23:15–21), Paul intends this to be a "free-will" offering based upon charity (as the motive) and prosperity (the basis for the size of the offering). Paul's instructions here are the reason why Christian churches collect "free-will" offerings and do not "tax" congregations.

The reason why this collection from the Gentile churches is so important is that Jewish Christians in Jerusalem were suffering greatly at the hands of the Sanhedrin (the Jewish ruling body). Having become followers of Jesus, Jewish Christians were considered apostates from Judaism, and were openly persecuted. Jewish Christians were no longer entitled to benevolence and gifts distributed by the Sanhedrin and the synagogues, and there are several references to a severe famine in the Jerusalem area (Acts 11:28–30) at the time. Under such circumstances, things were very difficult for the church in Jerusalem. Paul is very concerned about his Jewish brethren in the Jerusalem church.

An offering from Gentile churches would do a great deal to heal any rift which still existed between Jewish and Gentile Christians, especially since there had been such an important debate (recounted in Acts 15:1–35) about the mission to the Gentiles and the Gentile's obedience to the Law of Moses. A successful offering from the Gentile churches scattered throughout the Eastern Mediterranean region would demonstrate solidarity between the Gentile churches and the Jerusalem church, and it would do much to unify Jews and Gentiles. It would also lend great credence to the Gentile mission among the leaders of the Jerusalem church who were understandably reluctant to send missionaries to the Gentiles when the Gentiles did not understand their culture, and when their own people (the Jews) were so openly hostile to them because of the Jerusalem church's mission to the pagan Gentiles.

Instructions from Paul

In verse 2, Paul instructs the Corinthians how such an offering is to be taken. "On the first day of every week, each of you is to put something aside and store it up, as he may prosper, so that there will be no collecting when I come." Paul makes several points in this verse which are important but easily overlooked. For one thing, it is abundantly clear that the church met on Sunday for worship (the first day of the week). The reason for the change from worship on the Jewish Sabbath to the first day of the week (the Lord's Day) has to do with the fact that Jesus rose from the dead on the first day of the week, the sign of the new creation, which universally became the day of Christian worship. Calvin notes that "the Lord's Day was chosen in preference to all the others, because the resurrection of our Lord put an end to the shadows of the Law. Therefore that day is a reminder to us of our Christian freedom."[1]

---

1. Calvin, *The First Epistle of Paul to the Corinthians*, 350. For more background on the topic, see Michael Horton's outstanding book on worship: *A Better Way* (Grand Rapids: Baker Books, 2002), or R. Scott Clark's equally fine book: *Recovering the Reformed Confession* (Phillipsburg: P & R Publishing, 2008), 227–342.

Be Watchful

Paul also instructs "each" of the church members to set aside a specific sum of money based upon income. While Christians are to give freely as they are able—there is no specific amount of money mentioned (i.e., "a tithe")—all the Corinthians are to give something, in accordance with whatever measure each one has prospered. The application for us is simply that all Christians are to give according to the measure in which God has blessed us. We know from writings of the church fathers (i.e., Justin, *Apology* 1.67.6), that offerings were collected during the Lord's Day worship service, which reflects the practice of the Christian churches since that time. This is also why many churches take an offering during the worship service, because giving our gifts to Christ's church is itself an act of worship.

Furthermore, Paul does not want any last minute offering collected immediately before his visit. Collecting offerings from God's people for the poor (and then later for the administration of the church) are to be part of the church's weekly worship. Everything we have and then freely give in return, is to be consecrated to the Lord. We are to give because it benefits others, and we are to give because it is good for us to do so. When we give, we are reminded that all we have comes to us from the hand of God. As the people of God, we are called to support the work of God through our tithes and offerings—whether that be word and sacrament (the ordinary means of grace), diaconal mercy (benevolence to those in need), missions and evangelism, or institutions (seminaries, colleges, and universities). God loves a cheerful giver (cf. 2 Cor. 9:6–15).

In verse 3, we also see a practice from the early church which has carried over in modern times in some of the churches (i.e., the Canadian Reformed Church)—a letter verifying membership. "And when I arrive, I will send those whom you accredit by letter to carry your gift to Jerusalem." Letters of commendation were very common in the ancient world, and Paul will send them with those who physically carry the offering to Jerusalem. This letter verifies that the messengers are from Paul and also explains the purpose of the offering. Churches today will give such letters to their members who travel (or who go on vacation), so that they can then present themselves to the consistory or session of elders of the church they visit, so as to be admitted to the Lord's Supper. This is not a bad practice.

Having been approved by the church, the messengers from the Corinthian church would then go on to Jerusalem with the offering. Not only does this establish a direct connection between this largely Gentile church in Corinth, and the first Christian church in Jerusalem, it also frees Paul to continue his missionary duties without entangling himself with finances (and any potential trouble that goes with it). Regardless, Paul will do what is necessary. "If it seems advisable that I should go also, they will accompany me" (v. 4). Should it prove to be advisable for Paul himself to return to Jerusalem from Ephesus, then he will accompany those chosen by the Corinthians when they transport the offering.

Paul's Travel Plans

In verses 5–7, Paul takes the occasion to let his friends in Corinth know about his upcoming travel plans. The apostle informs the congregation that he might need to spend the winter in Corinth, depending upon how things work out in Ephesus. "I will visit you after passing through Macedonia, for I intend to pass through Macedonia, and perhaps I will stay with you or even spend the winter, so that you may help me on my journey, wherever I go. For I do not want to see you now just in passing. I hope to spend some time with you, if the Lord permits." Paul has already hinted at a return visit to Corinth (4:19—"But I will come to you soon, if the Lord wills"), now he is much more definite about a future visit. After he travels through Macedonia

Be Watchful

(the region to the north of Corinth), visiting the churches there, he hopes to end up in Corinth and spend the winter. Rain and cold weather greatly disrupted travel in the first century world, even with the excellent Roman system of roads.

While Paul is not certain of his plans, Corinth would not only be a good place to spend the winter, it would enable him to stay for a longer period of time—something which is quite important to him. This would give the Corinthians the chance to help Paul to prepare to be ready to go wherever the Lord sends him next. Paul will not only need supplies, but also means of travel (ship, draft animal, wagon, etc.). No doubt, the Corinthians will be able to help him with these arrangements.

The fact that Paul again states in verse 7 that he wants to make an extended stay, indicates how serious he is about making this visit, and yet, Paul is fully aware that the Lord may intervene and send him elsewhere. In the meantime, we can see in verses 8–9 that Paul's immediate plans are settled. "But I will stay in Ephesus until Pentecost, for a wide door for effective work has opened to me, and there are many adversaries." While there is much for Paul to do if and when he gets to Corinth, the fact of the matter is his current labors are not yet finished. Therefore, he will stay on in Ephesus until Pentecost (the Jewish feast), because the Lord has opened the door there for an effective work—the perfect tense indicates that the door remains open, even though, Paul still faces a great deal of opposition to his work throughout the city as recounted in Acts 19, when the merchants of the city of Ephesus rioted, because the converts to Christianity were no longer buying pagan trinkets.

Help Is on the Way!

In verse 10, Paul discusses the possibility of his young pastor friend Timothy coming to Corinth before Paul can arrange his own visit. "When Timothy comes, see that you put him at ease among you, for he is doing the work of the Lord, as I am." Paul had already mentioned in this letter the possibility that he might send Timothy to Corinth because of the current crisis the Corinthian church is now facing (cf. 4:17—"That is why I sent you Timothy, my beloved and faithful child in the Lord, to remind you of my ways in Christ, as I teach them everywhere in every church."). Paul instructs the Corinthians to take care of Timothy should he arrive in their city. Paul's comment that the Corinthians are to make sure that they set Timothy at ease, may refer to the fact that Timothy was young and may have been a bit timid.

Whatever the case, as we read in verse 11, Timothy will come to Corinth with Paul's full blessing. As a minister of the gospel, Timothy is carrying on the Lord's work, just as Paul is. "So let no one despise him. Help him on his way in peace, that he may return to me, for I am expecting him with the brothers." Given the unfortunate divisions and factions within the Corinthian church, there is the possibility that some might reject Timothy as a duly appointed representative from Paul—wanting Paul to come immediately instead of sending Timothy first. There is even the possibility that since Timothy was considered by some among the Corinthians to be "on Paul's side," Timothy might be refused permission to minister in Corinth. So, Paul instructs the Corinthians to make certain this is not the case. And then, after Timothy finishes his work in Corinth, Paul anticipates that Timothy will be joining him along with some unnamed brothers.

In verse 12, Paul speaks about a future visit to Corinth from Apollos, who had already spent some time in the city among the believers there. "Now concerning our brother Apollos, I strongly urged him to visit you with the other brothers, but it was not at all his will to come now. He will come when he has opportunity." No doubt that the Corinthians held Apollos in high esteem and in their letter to Paul they may have pled for Apollos' return to minister to them. Paul had likewise strongly urged Apollos to go to Corinth with some unnamed brothers, but at the time of this writing, all that Apollos agreed to do was to consider going at a later time. Since Paul speaks of Apollos quite affectionately, this would diffuse any concerns in the church that Paul did not think highly of Apollos, or that Paul had not done everything in his power to make sure that Apollos came to help out.

Final Exhortations

As Paul begins to wrap up this letter, in verse 13, the apostle makes a series of brief exhortations to the Corinthians. The first of these exhortations is for the Corinthians to "be watchful, stand firm in the faith, act like men, be strong." The verb is in the present imperative, indicating a command (*grēgoreite*). The word means to be on the alert and not sleep. The word is often used in connection to the second advent of our Lord (cf. Matthew 24:42ff.; 25:13). This is probably the meaning here, especially in light of the previous chapter (and the discussion of the resurrection of our bodies occurring at our Lord's return).

Paul also exhorts the Corinthians to stand firm in the faith, something which the Corinthians were struggling to do, especially in the face of so many challenges, some of which were self-inflicted. The Corinthians are to act as men, that is, they are to demonstrate courage as well as resolve in the face of the serious difficulties facing this congregation. They must remember that the strength they need comes from God, who will freely give them everything they need.

This is not all Paul commands of them. "Let all that you do be done in love" (v. 14). It is significant that the command to do everything in love, follows the command to behave as men. It is not only necessary to watch and stand firm in the face of trouble, but it is important to watch and stand firm in the right way. Our motivation to do these things should be that love we are to have for our brethren, since all Christians have been baptized into the one body of Jesus Christ, a single body with many different members. This is why all that we do—even when it involves some sort of spiritual combat, and even though Paul uses military metaphors and strong language—is to be done in love. No one is to act in their own interests, even while standing firm and acting like men! We must do all these things in love, including defending the faith and disciplining erring members. Admittedly this is difficult to do in an age where people are hypersensitive about any criticism or disagreement (and often see it as a personal insult), or in an age such as ours, when people are so litigious.

Considering all that the Corinthians have been through as a congregation, Paul gives them examples to follow. The first of these is that of Stephanas and his household—people whom Paul himself had baptized. As we read in verses 15–16, "Now I urge you, brothers—you know that the household of Stephanas were the first converts in Achaia, and that they have devoted themselves to the service of the saints—be subject to such as these, and to every fellow worker and laborer." Stephanas and his household are devoted servants of Christ, and the Corinthians are to submit to such people, because they are good examples to them, and because these people are devoted in their service to the Corinthians.

In verses 17–18, Paul can say of others, "I rejoice at the coming of Stephanas and Fortunatus and Achaicus, because they have made up for your absence, for they refreshed my spirit as well as yours. Give recognition to such men." Paul is glad to have such men as co-laborers with him, because they had unique gifts and abilities (along with the maturity) which the Corinthians so desperately lacked. Not only were such men an encouragement to Paul, refreshing his own tired and worn-out spirit, but the Corinthian congregation needs to recognize their gifts and acknowledge their service. They already have very capable men in their midst.

Final Greetings

In verses 19–24, Paul sends his final greetings. Remember, these are people whom he knows well and for whom he is very concerned. "The churches of Asia send you greetings. Aquila and Prisca, together with the church in their house, send you hearty greetings in the Lord." In Paul's day, Asia is Asia Minor (modern Turkey/northern Syria), and Paul sends greeting from the churches of this region (including the region of Galatia and the cities near Ephesus). Aquilla and Pricilla (a husband and wife) were widely known throughout the churches. We know from Acts 18:1–3 that they moved from Rome to Corinth after the edict of Claudius in which all the Jews were expelled from the city. They were allowing Christians to meet in their home just as they had done in Rome (Rom. 16:3–5).

Although some have recently argued that this comment establishes that house churches are to be the norm, this is simply a matter of expediency. This couple owned a home (probably a villa) with sufficient room to hold meetings (a large covered patio). It was not like there were plenty of churches/synagogues in town available for rent. There were many public spaces in which meetings could be held, but the art (much of it sexualized) and architecture of the guild halls and public buildings was dominated by pagan themes and images, hardly a proper venue for Christians to conduct public worship.

There are other greetings for Paul to extend as well. "All the brothers send you greetings. Greet one another with a holy kiss." The unnamed brothers are in Ephesus with Paul as he writes this letter. "I, Paul, write this greeting with my own hand." Unlike the Book of Romans, which Paul dictated to a professional scribe (Tertius), Paul penned this letter to the Corinthians himself. It is written in his own hand.

In verse 22, we come to what at first glance is a rather surprising comment from Paul. Paul pronounces a curse upon all those who do not love the Lord Jesus. "If anyone has no love for the Lord, let him be accursed. Our Lord, come!" The solemn curse is followed by an apostolic blessing. Given the thorny issues with which Paul has had to address throughout this letter, when he pronounces the word of curse, Paul is probably referring to those in the church who name the name of Christ, but who divide the church and agitate God's people, or else he is referring to those outside who persecute the church, or even perhaps to both.

The curse is immediately followed by the Aramaic expression, *Maranatha*, which means, "Come, O Lord!" Since Greeks would not have used this language, the expression must have come from the Palestinian church, an indication that this was an early and common Christian benediction. It was already widely used throughout the churches, along with words like "Amen" and "Hallelujah." From the very beginning, Christians have longed for our Lord Jesus to return.

As is his custom, in verse 23 Paul closes with a benediction for his readers/hearers and offers a heartfelt personal expression of his love to those in the Corinthian congregation. "The grace of the Lord Jesus be with you. My love be with you all in Christ Jesus. Amen." With that, Paul's letter to the Corinthians is concluded.

If we are to learn anything from our study of 1 Corinthians, it is this: We are not only individual followers of Jesus—people who personally trust in Jesus' death to save us from our sins, and who know that Jesus' perfect righteousness covers our unrighteousness—we are also members together of Christ's church. To be Christ's disciple through faith is, at the same time, to be

Be Watchful

a member of Christ's body. When we come to faith in Jesus, we are added to Christ's church. Although we are justified as individuals, we are not sanctified in isolation, nor are we to live our Christian lives apart from Christ's church.

Remember, Paul's Corinthian letter was not written to individuals, but "to the church of God that is in Corinth, to those sanctified in Christ Jesus, called to be saints together with all those who in every place call upon the name of our Lord Jesus Christ, both their Lord and ours." To be a Christian is to be conscious of our duties and obligations to each other and to Christ's church. There is a gospel to believe, to proclaim, and to defend. But there is also conduct appropriate to our membership in Christ's church. That proper conduct, therefore, is what this letter addresses.

Let us do as Paul exhorts us to do. "Be watchful, stand firm in the faith, act like men, be strong. Let all that you do be done in love."

AUTHOR

KIM RIDDLEBARGER (Ph.D. Fuller Theological Seminary) is senior pastor of Christ Reformed Church in Anaheim, California (URCNA), co-host of the popular radio-internet broadcast, White Horse Inn, and author of *A Case for Amillennialism* and *The Man of Sin*. He is a regular contributor to *Modern Reformation* and *Tabletalk* magazines, and has also served as visiting professor of systematic theology at Westminster Seminary California.

SERIES EDITOR

JON D. PAYNE (M.Th. New College, University of Edinburgh; D.Min., Reformed Theological Seminary) has served as pastor of Grace Presbyterian Church (PCA) in Douglasville, Georgia since 2003. Dr. Payne is a Visiting Lecturer in Practical Theology at RTS Atlanta and the author of *In the Splendor of Holiness* and *John Owen on the Lord's Supper*.